FOLK ENGINEERING

FOLK ENGINEERING

PLANNING SOUTHERN REGIONALISM

STEPHEN J. RAMOS

The University of North Carolina Press
CHAPEL HILL

© 2025 Stephen J. Ramos
All rights reserved
Manufactured in the United States of America

Designed by Lindsay Starr
Set in Miller and Futura Now Text
by codeMantra

Cover art courtesy Howard Washington Odum Papers, 1908–1990s, Wilson Special Collections Library, UNC–Chapel Hill.

Frontispiece: "Acele" acetate rayon factory in Waynesboro, Virginia. Howard Washington Odum Papers, Wilson Special Collections Library, UNC–Chapel Hill.

Library of Congress Cataloging-in-Publication Data
Names: Ramos, Stephen J., author.
Title: Folk engineering : planning Southern regionalism / Stephen J. Ramos.
Description: Chapel Hill : The University of North Carolina Press, 2025. | Includes bibliographical references and index.
Identifiers: LCCN 2025015460 | ISBN 9781469690100 (cloth ; alk. paper) | ISBN 9781469690117 (paperback ; alk. paper) | ISBN 9781469690124 (epub) | ISBN 9781469690131 (pdf)
Subjects: LCSH: Odum, Howard Washington, 1884–1954. | University of North Carolina (1793–1962). Institute for Research in Social Science—History. | Regional planning—Southern States—History—20th century. | Regionalism—Southern States—History—20th century. | BISAC: SOCIAL SCIENCE / Ethnic Studies / American / General | ARCHITECTURE / History / General
Classification: LCC HT392.5.S65 R36 2025 | DDC 307.1/20975—dc23/eng/20250512
LC record available at https://lccn.loc.gov/2025015460

For product safety concerns under the European Union's General Product Safety Regulation (EU GPSR), please contact gpsr@mare-nostrum.co.uk or write to the University of North Carolina Press and Mare Nostrum Group B.V., Mauritskade 21D, 1091 GC Amsterdam, The Netherlands.

FOR JANE AND EMILIO RAMOS

CONTENTS

IX   LIST OF ILLUSTRATIONS

XI   ACKNOWLEDGMENTS

1   Introduction: Folk Engineering the Southern Region

31   CHAPTER 1. Round Table on Regionalism: Planners and Poets

47   CHAPTER 2. A Regular, Orthodox, Almost Professional Southerner: Institutions, Foundations, and Networks

72   CHAPTER 3. Telesis and the Sociocracy: Social Sciences in the Natural World

97   CHAPTER 4. Race and Place: As American as the Cotton Plantation

127   CHAPTER 5. Regionalism: A Living, Breathing, Pulsating Riot

157   CHAPTER 6. Planning Apocrypha: The Case for Regional-National Social Planning

183   Conclusion: Stateless Southern Planning Doctrine

195   NOTES

237   BIBLIOGRAPHY

269   INDEX

ILLUSTRATIONS

ii	"Acele" acetate rayon factory in Waynesboro, Virginia
xiv–xv	Gully control, DeWitt County, Tennessee
21	Gully control, Roane County, Tennessee
21	Gully repair, Roane County, Tennessee
30	Aerial photo of dam and industry
46	Howard Odum in front of his cabin
53	Psychology Conference Group, Clark University
57	Howard W. Odum lecturing at the IRSS Regionalism Lab
86	*Nature and the Folk at Work*
87	Filming folk
89	Odum's data portraiture of automobiles per 1,000 inhabitants in six major regions in the United States, 1929
89	Odum's data portraiture of retail automotive sales, 1929
90	Map of canals and improved waterways with depths at low water for six major regions in the United States, 1929
90	Map of "Nation's Wealth of Streams of Water, 1929"
98	Howard Odum with Guy Johnson
109	Odum in an Atlanta bookshop promoting *Rainbow Round My Shoulder*, 1928
128	Rupert Vance
148	Odum's state-bloc proposal for the six major regions in the United States
149	"The Six Major Regions Basic to the Southern Regional Study"
156	"Regional Planning and Development" meeting, Chapel Hill, 1950

160 Banker Donald Brown reviews soil conservation poster by fifth graders

161 Fifth graders report on soil conservation

163 Southern gullies, Lumpkin, Stewart County, Georgia, 1936

182 Southern gullies, Lafayette, Mississippi, 1938

ACKNOWLEDGMENTS

Folk Engineering began with a conversation in Cambridge, Massachusetts. The Doctor of Design alumni at the Harvard Graduate School of Design were celebrating thirty years of our program, and Peter G. Rowe, one of my doctoral mentors, asked how I was enjoying my position down south at the University of Georgia. We also discussed possible topics for my next research project, and based on my new location, he suggested I ought to look into the work of Howard Odum. The last name was familiar because the ecology school at my new university was named after Eugene P. Odum. Before I arrived, however, the Departments of Ecology and Design had recently gone through an institutional separation (how do you separate from ecology?). "*Howard* Odum," Peter clarified. "The father at the University of North Carolina."

I'm not from the South, but my maternal grandfather was. His family was from Mississippi and Tennessee. He lived through the Depression and like many, he joined the military. He married a woman from Maine, and his family insistently referred to her as "that *northern* woman." Or so I'm told. One of their daughters, my mother, married a Lebanese man from Venezuela, my father. My wife is Catalana. These are stories of movement and new homes without the luxury of nostalgia. The notion of any place-based identity is difficult for me to connect with. None of my family stories would fit any regional-spatial index of homogeneity. Nevertheless, as fate would have it, my family and I moved south. The land of my grandfather, and he and I never really got along. My kids know it as home; they go to school here. I decided to take Peter up on his suggestion.

In September 1940, Eugene P. Odum accepted an instructor position in biology at the University of Georgia. Like his brother, Howard T. Odum, Eugene had completed his PhD in zoology, but during the 1940s each grew impatient with the limited scope of the natural sciences. They collaborated on the development of an earth-spanning research of ecosystems, and in 1953 they coauthored the canonical *Fundamentals of Ecology*. Elder brother Eugene, who received most of the praise for the book, would come to be known as the "father of modern ecology."[1] Odum's concept of ecology was grounded in an "understanding of the environment as a system of interlocking biotic communities," which he credited (in part) to the influence of his father, University of North Carolina sociologist Howard W. Odum, who repeatedly reminded his sons "never to lose sight of the big picture."[2] With brother Howard T. at the University of Florida, the Odums were a kind of Southern state-school blue-blood family, and their legacy is still influential on ecological research and policy throughout the US Southeast. The legacy also underscores the complex relationship between nature and society in the historic institutional production of the South that spans the twentieth century. In the first half of that century, particularly during the period historian Richard Hofstadter identifies as "the age of reform," Howard W. Odum and colleagues attempted to bend a holistic, interconnected social science into what they called "Southern regionalism."

After doing some preliminary research on Howard W. Odum, I spoke with my neighbor Stephen Berry, a member of the university history department, which happens to the be among the best in the country and among the very best in Southern history. We got breakfast biscuits at Mama's Boy, and he offered to introduce me to his history colleague James C. Cobb. The three of us eventually met over beer, and my research project began to take on a personality. There are many people to thank for their support throughout this project, but I'm particularly grateful to Peter, Steve, and Jim for their encouragement in helping me to get things off the ground.

I would like to thank the patient, generous, and insightful readers who offered to review drafts of the book, including Joshua Barkan, Harris Feinsod, Mark Reinberger, and (again) Peter Rowe. I'd also like to thank Melissa Vaughn, Timothy Mennel, Diana Graizbord, Elizabeth Crowder, Mary Carley Caviness, Judy Long, Daniel Perez, John Martin Taylor, Mikel Herrington, and Megan Morgan for their editorial support and advice. I particularly want to thank Lucas Church, Lindsay Starr, and Thomas Bedenbaugh of the University of North Carolina Press for their help and support throughout this project.

I thank Nicholas Allen, Winnie Smith, and staff at the Willson Center of the Arts and Humanities, along with Vice-Provost Marisa Anne Pagnattaro and the interlibrary loan staff for their support at the University of Georgia. I thank the Johns Hopkins Tidewater Initiative as well. I'm also grateful for the diligent, kind, supportive help from the staff at the Louis Round Wilson Special Collections Library at the University of North Carolina at Chapel Hill, particularly Jason Tomberlin and Lyric Grimes. Thanks to Betty Jean Craige, John Schelhas, and a special thanks to Vic Vance.

I thank the great international planning history community, including Carola Hein, John and Maggie Gold, Gabriel Schwake, Richard Hu, Wesley Aelbrecht, Nuran Zeren Gulersoy, Ian Morley, Florian Urban, Li Hou, Stephen Ward, Brent Ryan, Robert Fishman, Kristen Larsen, Ellen Shoshkes, Emily Talen, Eugenie Birch, Dirk Schubert, Sabine Luning, Paul van de Laar, Han Meyer, Lawrence Vale, Ellen Bassett, Leslie Sharp, Robert Wojtowicz, Javier Monclús, Carmen Díez Medina, Filippo De Pieri, Robert Freestone,

Diane Davis, Andrew Whittemore, Adrián Gorelik, Leandro Benmergui, Barbara Brown Wilson, Andre Sorensen, Domenic Vitiello, Clément Orillard, Christopher Silver, Sonia Hirt, David Goldfield, and Lui Tam. I also thank my *New Geographies* mentor, Hashim Sarkis, and colleagues Gareth Doherty, Rania Ghosn, El Hadi Jazairy, Antonio Petrov, and Neyran Turan.

Closer to home, I thank colleagues and students at the College of Environment and Design, particularly Doug Pardue, Scott Nesbit, Umit Yilmaz, and Sungkyung Lee. And I'm thankful to Nik Heynen for introducing me to the Hogg Hummock community on Sapelo Island through his work with the Cornelia Walker Bailey Program on Land and Agriculture. A shout to James Enos, Annie Simpson, Forest Kelley, Jan Derk Diekema, and all the collaborators of the Port Futures & Social Logistics platform.

Many thanks to my friend Nils Folke Anderson, a Southern artist at heart.

I'm grateful to my brother Peter for all the discussions we've had about this book. Among many other things, he came home from his first year at college possessed by William Faulkner. I knew something was up.

I thank my beloved parents, Jane and Emilio Ramos, a couple of migrants. They passed during the research and writing of this book. I dedicate it to them.

Finally, I thank my family: Núria, my life partner, and GJ and Enzo, my children. Their love, support, and patience are everything.

OVERLEAF Gully control, DeWitt County, Tennessee, 1940. Howard Washington Odum Papers, Wilson Special Collections Library, UNC–Chapel Hill.

FOLK ENGINEERING

> The region, then, is the place of what Derrida would call *différance*: the region *is not* because it always defers itself to a hypothetical future, it translates, trans-poses itself to a moment that is the coming back of an original past—the ideal of human bliss and perfection.
> —ROBERTO MARIA DAINOTTO

> There is [a] view of regionalism, which envisions it as a tool of administration, of control, and of planning. The region in this sense is a tool of social engineering. The delineation of such regions, to be effective, obviously cannot proceed without taking due account of the region as a fact and the region as a set of interrelations between facts.
> —LOUIS WIRTH

INTRODUCTION

FOLK ENGINEERING THE SOUTHERN REGION

Howard W. Odum, his Institute for Research in Social Science (IRSS) at the University of North Carolina in Chapel Hill, and the Southern regionalists are familiar to scholars of Southern history and sociology, but there remains a gap separating US regional planning history from Southern regionalism.[1] The Regional Planning Association of America (RPAA)—more renowned than the IRSS—was established in New York City in 1923, while Odum began his academic career developing Southern regionalism at the University of North Carolina's sociology department in 1920. As planning historians John Friedmann and Clyde Weaver observe, "There has never been an adequate investigation of Howard Odum's part in laying the foundation of American planning.... Odum's essential contributions have been all but passed over."[2] Friedmann, one of the most influential scholars of urban planning in the twentieth century, trained just after World War II at the University of Chicago's prestigious Program in Education and Research in Planning, which Rexford Tugwell helped establish after completing his term as governor of Puerto Rico.[3] That program is credited with moving planning education out of design and engineering and into the applied social sciences to "better fit the American brand of welfare state liberalism."[4] But Odum and colleagues at the IRSS helped develop this social science conceptualization of planning years before the war.

Lewis Mumford and the RPAA expressed mutual admiration with Odum and his Southern regionalist colleagues. Both the RPAA and the IRSS participated in the University of Virginia's Institute of Public Affairs Round Table on Regionalism in July 1931, where, with explicit regionalist and planning sympathies, Franklin D. Roosevelt, then New York's governor, announced his presidential candidacy.[5] In 1949, during a visiting professorship at the North Carolina State College of Design in Raleigh, Mumford praised Odum and the IRSS for making "Chapel Hill and the University of North Carolina . . . the home of modern regionalism in America."[6]

Mumford believed that his work with the RPAA "laid the ground for a new approach to planning," and that "Odum and his fellow regionalists at Chapel Hill belong[ed] to the same company."[7] Odum reciprocated the admiration, citing the "immeasurable" influence of the RPAA on the work of his institute.[8] He read Mumford's "Regions—to Live In" essay in the RPAA's famous 1925 *Survey Graphic* issue on regional planning, and he was inspired by its opening lines: "The hope of the city lies outside itself."[9] When the RPAA re-formed and reactivated as the Regional Development Council of America after World War II, Clarence Stein invited Odum, Rupert B. Vance, and their North Carolina colleagues to form a Southeastern chapter of the council to expand its agenda beyond New York.[10] Such overlap and mutual admiration notwithstanding, Odum, Mumford, and their respective groups advocated for regionalism from very different geographic perspectives in the 1920s and 1930s.[11]

Each was part of the post–World War I movement in the United States that brought together large-scale philanthropy and social science research to forge the "institutional structure of social research" for the interwar period.[12] The ideology that united the group of philanthropists and social science entrepreneurs was a mingling of social investigation, natural science, and engineering for the improvement and control of a rapidly changing US society.[13] Southern regionalists and the RPAA were of their time, inspired by "the hubris that took hold between the wars, the faith in big research by government, universities, and foundations that spawned high-brow committees to comment on recent social trends, national resources . . . all aimed at achieving the totalist view of American life as an objectified, quantified mechanism."[14] This richly intertwined network would ultimately form a significant recruitment base for President Franklin Roosevelt and his New Deal administration.

The South served as the regionalists' laboratory, where resource development proposals became a model for US regional planning. Such influence developed particularly through the ambitious Tennessee Valley Authority (TVA), the New Deal's trophy river basin project, and the regional development model that US agencies exported through postwar US "good neighbor" foreign policy.[15] Internationally, cultural approaches to regionalism in the first half of the twentieth century occurred in other countries experiencing parallel processes of modernization and urbanization.[16] Reflecting on the role of social sciences in the construction of Southern regionalism helps situate the movement within a broader context of cultural and territorial responses to international economic and political dynamism of the period, particularly in terms of how regional planning, in its various expressions, would become widely accepted as the appropriate response to these changes.[17]

The ideological manifestations of the discourse and practice of regional planning had enormous effects on the relationship between race and place in the United States, particularly in the South. Odum believed that regional planning served as a methodology to preserve Southern identity as what sociologist Robert Redfield termed a "folk society."[18] Though at times critical of the "extreme elements" of the Jim Crow South, Odum was a segregationist and a defender of traditionalist Southern white supremacist beliefs and territorial structures.[19] Odum drew inspiration from evolutionary natural geography and cultural geography—race *and* place—to explain the deep-rooted Southern social contract, which he naturalized along with his studies of the ecology that sustained it in a holistic analytic frame of rurality, land, and folk culture. Regionalism in the South, with its secessionist past, sketched out the cultural/territorial aspects of regional planning that later functionalist modeling avoided without geographic specificity.[20] During the interwar years, Odum's seemingly moderate New South political vision of increased regional autonomy within a federal framework struggled against the longer shadow of regionalist "Lost Cause" independence. With a Northern academic pedigree and institutional support, Odum looked for a future through regional planning with hopes of resolving these tensions. Southern regionalism helps us better understand the complex proposal of regional planning as defined for a territory of imagined cultural homogeneity, particularly during the period's high rates of national and international migration.[21]

This book refocuses the history of US regionalism and regional planning on the South, and it develops several implications for planning history from this resituated perspective. First, the Southern regionalists' insistence on regional planning to revive the agrarian economy, and the cotton sector in particular, demonstrates how their view of planning served as a politics—submerged in universalist organic framings of nature, folk, and culture, and mediated through the Southern racial contract—for future claims on regional autonomy within an overarching nation-state project. Southern regionalists made these proposals against what they perceived as encroaching Northern nationalist pressures for industrialization, urbanization, and social and racial integration: a comprehensive political-economic mandate for progress along these transitioning axes. Their planning proposals would come to inform the New Deal administration's Southern policy throughout the 1930s, though clearly from a different governing perspective at the national level.

Next, to make these planning claims, Odum and IRSS colleagues developed social sciences and a research institution to investigate and catalog regional social facts, the lingua franca of governmental power during the interwar years. This was particularly true for Odum, influenced by the academic institutionalism of one his mentors, G. Stanley Hall. Until an empowered regional governing authority could be established, Odum believed in the Southern academic institution and its sociocratic possibility as a quasi-governing regional body to establish policy through fact, and to set the pacing of cultural change accordingly.

Further, and constituent of the first two points, the Northern academic and philanthropic institutions and networks that Odum and colleagues participated in were electrified with the broader power and politics of the period. They paid for Odum's academic aspirations at the University of North Carolina and helped propel both his career and institution to the national stage. The particular story of the opportunities and tensions of IRSS participation in these networks helps us to understand how these relationships served as a blueprint for Odum's "regional-national" planning proposal, one in which the South would be nurtured through Northern funding toward planning and governing autonomy. Moreover, these North-South relationships presage the complex politics of international institutional development in the postwar period.

Southern regionalists' work also helps illuminate the tensions inherent to regionalism as nostalgic cultural practice, particularly when paired with future-oriented planning ideology.[22] In 1958, historian George Tindall reflected that Odum had "a new vision of the potentialities of regionalism," which in his conceptualization was "a grandiose concept that must be grasped whole or not at all, else it degenerates into a kind of 'sectional-local' provincialism."[23] Odum's proposals for "social planning" and "regional-national planning" were his attempts to interpolate Southern regionalist perspectives into a broader national governance frame at a scale at which federal authority and states' rights autonomy might find middle ground: a balance. Through their work, Southern regionalists provided a legibility of their land and social structure for Roosevelt's New Deal administration statecraft, which then informed nationally led regional planning projects such as the TVA and the Agricultural Adjustment Administration (AAA).[24]

Interrogating Southern regionalists' use of social science to focus on folklore and culture, the social construction of nature, and their accumulation of regional data to pathologize the South also helps elucidate the more conservative cultural motives of US regional planning during the tumultuous interwar period. Southern regionalist discourse provided an ideological template for New Deal projects' success with Southern leaders by avoiding a frontal criticism of Jim Crow institutional racism. The Southern regionalists' story contributes to the histories of planning theory and practice circulation across institutional networks, and to the inclusion of the US South as one of the regions engaged in these networks.[25] Southern regionalism also adds to more recent understandings of the fruitful engagement of planning history with adjacent intellectual social science disciplines.[26]

Finally, Southern regionalism contributes to what planning historian Leonie Sandercock refers to as "insurgent historiographies" in planning history—counternarratives to the established premise of planning heroism.[27] She clarifies that while the planning profession dates back to the late nineteenth century, planning history only emerged as an academic discipline in the past fifty years. For Sandercock, in the "official story" of that history and its modernist portraits, "the hero, Planning, has no fatal flaws. If the battles are sometimes, or even often, lost, it is not the fault of the hero but of the 'evil' world in which 'he' must operate. . . . The rise of the profession is, simply, cause for celebration rather than for critical scrutiny."[28] She circumscribes planning history to a subfield of planning practice, focusing principally on actions and outcomes.[29] But the US South in the 1920s and 1930s was still majority rural, with no apparent planning equivalent to the great urbanism of the industrial North. It was a lagging, very poor region resistant to the promise of planning's expert rational reform. Or any reform, for that matter.

Considering Southern regionalists' achievements and flaws increases our understanding of those of the broader US regional planning history. In Sandercock's framing, Southern regionalism opens planning history to the broader history of ideas, debates, people, and conflicts leading the entire country into the Depression and the New Deal. Further, if the intellectual traditions of regional planning are traced only from Europe to the

Northeastern United States, then we miss how regionalism moved through the South within the university and philanthropic networks in which Odum participated.[30] In many ways, Odum's work in the South served as a testing ground for post–World War II international development, and understanding this history contributes to recent reconceptualizations of US Southern history within the broader Global South.[31]

REGIONALISM: A GENEALOGY

Henry Estill Moore, who coauthored *American Regionalism* (1938) with Odum, conducted an exhaustive review of international regionalism, going back in history to position and support their own Southern national-regional claims. The philosophy of "variety" is a useful way of understanding the historical emergence of regionalist concepts, which I review in this section in relation to Southern regionalism. When describing what she terms "the uses of variety," literary critic Carrie Tirado Bramen underscores the tumultuous period in which the concept of variety became fused with "Americanness" amid multiple crises at the end of the nineteenth century. This period saw a shift from homogeneity and what sociologist Franklin Giddings—Odum's mentor—called the "consciousness of kind" to the heterogeneity of industrial societies. Bramen quotes philosopher George Santayana: "'Variety' is a good only if a unity can still be secured embracing that variety"; she also clarifies that within this process, balance amid change, homogeneity, and heterogeneity, variety retained as a whole helped the status quo to conceptually maintain and "negotiate the extremes of an expanding capitalist economy through a principle of moderation."[32] The historical moment of change was one of modernization, "at times full of radical potential and at other times deeply reactionary."[33]

Regionalism emerged in the second half of the nineteenth century with the consolidation of the centralized nation-state and the spatial integration of town and country through the expansion of industrial capitalism.[34] In the post–Civil War period, the United States invested in railroad and waterway circulation infrastructure to enhance interregional trade, mobility, and communication, and regionalism articulated a reaction to the centralizing social and economic trends enabled by new transportation and communication technologies.[35] This period of urbanization accelerated in the 1880s, when European immigrants arrived in US urban centers to take advantage of the industrial labor opportunities.[36] During the two decades following Reconstruction, from 1877 to 1900, the Northern Gilded Age of industrial expansion produced an uneven spatial development inscribed across the national territory between industrial metropolitan centers and peripheral rural agricultural areas.[37] US spatial patterns developed during this period in parallel to similar patterns of industrial capital development in Western Europe, where "internal peripheries emerged that served primarily as suppliers of raw material and cheap labor for core industrial regions within each nation state."[38]

One prominent line of thinking about this era of regional identities consolidating in the systems of global capital runs from Gramsci to contemporary critical geography. In Italy, Antonio Gramsci explored this geographic dynamic between labor and industry in "The Southern Question."[39] An uneven spatial pattern was reproduced at the global scale through colonial relationships of command center cores controlling the flow of capital and subordinate countries providing cheap labor and raw materials, articulated most famously in Immanuel Wallerstein's "world-systems" theory.[40] Of these exploitative politico-spatial relations, geographer Edward Soja elaborates that "regionalization and regionalism are seen as social processes hierarchically structured by the fundamental relations of production. Regions in this sense are people, classes, social formations, spatial collectivities, active and reactive parts of the geographic landscape of capitalism."[41] He concluded by emphasizing the spatial differentiation of regions as contingent relationships based on "an active consciousness and assertiveness of particular regions *vis-à-vis* other regions as territorial and social enclosures ... grounded in the geography of power."[42]

Along similar lines, economist Ann Markusen emphasizes the relational character of regions as "historically evolved, contiguous territorial societ[ies]" comprising the "physical environment, a socioeconomic, political, and cultural milieu, and a spatial structure distinct from other regions and from the other major territorial units, city and nation."[43] Her relational definition considers regions as dually created "through both (1) their mutual contrasts and distinctions and (2) their location and on the scale of spatial unit." For Markusen, "the category 'region' connotes territorial units with unique physical and cultural traits," in contrast to cities, which represent a "special form of human settlement that exhibits regularities of function and spatial structure regardless of location," and nations, which are "a special type of region which possesses political sovereignty."[44]

As a mode of intellectual inquiry, particularly in the fields of sociology and geography, regionalism responded to the perceived excessive political and economic centralization of capital-spatial restructuring.[45] Drawing inspiration from utopian socialists such as Robert Owen and Charles Fourier, Ebenezer Howard developed his Garden City proposal from 1880 to 1898 in response to Victorian London's deplorable social conditions and its excessive size, power, and influence over England.[46] Regionalism also had roots in the anarchist movements and the autonomous regional federalism and decentralist ideas of Russian Peter Kropotkin and Frenchman Jacques Élisée Reclus.[47] Born of French anarchist social theorist Pierre-Joseph Proudhoun's ideas, particularly following the short-lived 1871 Paris Commune, over the next thirty years French regionalism would encompass a spectrum of ideologies ranging from progressive to conservative, anarchist, socialist, and technocratic.[48] Jean Charles-Brun, for instance—a disciple of Proudhoun—founded the Fédération Régionaliste Française in 1901.[49] In contrast, his 1911 book *Le Régionalisme* assumed a more technical, "apolitical" policy tone for fear of precipitating state repression.[50]

By the turn of the century, the European (particularly French, German, and Scottish) regionalist tradition had inspired a variety of regional social sciences, the most influential being those of Frédéric Le Play, Patrick Geddes, and Paul Vidal de La Blache.[51] Geddes in particular was an essential nexus and channel for the crossing of European regionalist thought to the United States, not only through his own travels and contacts, but also through the networks of his US disciple Lewis Mumford and the RPAA.[52] Geddes translated Le Play's interrelated concept of *famille, travail, lieu* into "place-work-folk," and visually illustrated the concept in his valley section, or natural region, to advocate for Le Play's regional survey method. Along with the valley section, which assigned human economic activity with descending sectional altitude from mountain to sea (miner, woodman, hunter, shepherd, peasant, gardener, fisher), Geddes also organized his three terms into a nine-quadrant frame, intended to be read from the starting quadrant *place* (geography) over and across to the quadrant nine objective *folk* (anthropology).[53] Famously obtuse in his thinking and communication, Geddes believed that this diagram provided a simple Cartesian logic for approaching complex geographic and economic processes.

Although far from simple, the valley section nonetheless offered a diagrammatic simplicity and comfort that charmed a world experiencing the modernist flux of the capitalist industrial machine. Like Howard's Garden City, the section was fundamentally and unequivocally a reformist mode and method for transforming the industrial city. To accomplish such reforms, which included the monumental "task of replanning the industrial city, it was first necessary to have an in-depth knowledge of the nuances and special attributes of not only the city itself but its surrounding regions as well."[54] The river basin development proposal in Geddes's valley section would become the starting point for the next half century of regional planning around the world.[55] Geddes's work influenced the RPAA, the British Land Utilization Survey, Sir Patrick Abercrombie's Greater London Plan of 1944, and countless others, including the work of Odum and his IRSS's regionalist social science.[56]

Regionalism was part of an international literary and artistic movement that positioned geographic location and cultural identity within complex relationships to the modern modernization dialectic.[57] Regionalism was "distinctively modern," part of broader movements between 1870 and World War I to "invent traditions" by "inserting agrarian and artisanal orders into a new web of national market relations."[58] Regional identities grounded in such artistic tradition in Western Europe emerged as nineteenth-century phenomena after the French Revolution and the Napoleonic period but took on a more political nature after 1880, as regional elite interests clashed with nation-state projects.[59]

Historian Eric Storm recounts that these politico-cultural movements continued through World War II, offering examples such as the 1937 Paris World Exhibition, where the French capital presented itself as the Centre Régional; the 1929 Iberian-American Exposition in Seville, which showcased elaborate regional pavilions; and the German Volksguiste folk-regional discourse. In addition, a plethora of interwar modern architecture engaged in regionalist forms, including designs by Marcel Poète, Gaston Bardet, and Alfred Agache in France; Paul Schultze-Naumburg, Robert Mielke, and Theodor Fischer in Germany; and Leopoldo Torres Balbás, Leonardo Rucabado, and Aníbal González Álvarez in Spain.[60] Storm claims that the fascist turns of some regionalist movements in Germany were at odds with the more accepting aspect of pluralism inherent in these artistic movements, which was one of the tensions that led, of course, to war and the end of this chapter of the European regionalist era. Yet of these various movements, Storm concludes that they remained regionalist in most cases and rarely aspired toward separatist, competing nationalism. Perhaps counterintuitively, their "regional identities supplied the corresponding national identity local roots."[61]

In the United States, similar regional movements arose during the interwar years that transformed the national culture. Examples include the Vanderbilt Southern Agrarians' *I'll Take My Stand* (1930); Walter Prescott Scott's regional survey *The Great Plains* (1931); B. A. Botkin's *The Southwestern Scene* (1931); Mari Sandoz's *Old Jules* (1935); the literary undertakings of Willa Cather, William Faulkner, and James Agee; the work of artists Dorothea Lange and Thomas Hart Benton; and broader cultural and artistic movements such as the Harlem Renaissance and the Arts and Crafts movement.[62] The IRSS at the University of North Carolina produced work in this field that was among the best of the period, including Rupert

Vance's *Human Factors in Cotton Culture* (1929) and *Human Geography of the South* (1932), Guy Johnson's *John Henry* and *Folk Culture on St. Helena Island* (both published in 1930), Arthur Raper's *Preface to Peasantry* (1936), Margaret Jarman Hagood's *Mothers of the South* (1939), W. J. Cash's *The Mind of the South* (1940), and Arthur Raper and Ira De A. Reid's *Sharecroppers All* (1941).[63]

Particularly for the US South, as historian George Tindall observes, "somewhere between academic treatise and *belles lettres* fell a literature of social exploration and descriptive journalism that formed the Southern expression of the 'now innocent, now calculating, now purely rhetorical, but always significant experience in national self-discovery' that occurred in the 1930s."[64] The breadth of regional cultural production during the interwar period signified its central thematic concern across cultural media. But following that course forward, historian C. Vann Woodward notes, regionalism eventually "converges at not too remote a point with the American Way," again providing a national identity with regional roots.[65]

During these years, the IRSS and the University of Chicago were centers of place-based social research. In 1951, Vance noted, "If the University of Chicago holds out, we bid fair to learn more about this city than was ever known of any other metropolitan region. I am tempted to say the same thing of Howard W. Odum and the Southeast."[66] Regionalism was an investigative theme that connected social scientists across universities from north to south, east to west, through conferences, journals, university presses, philanthropic networks, visiting research positions, and letters. These researchers and writers were in collective search for methods and means to elevate descriptive, place-based evidence and sensibility beyond a mere analytic to an all-encompassing social theory.

There was a general interest in organic processes, from Robert E. Park's ecological patterns in Chicago to Odum's folk forms in the South: naturalized and self-corrective, deployed to ground social change in reassuring parallels with an imagined stable constancy of nature and community.[67] Nonetheless, these thinkers' attitudes toward cities varied. While Lewis Mumford and the RPAA criticized metropolitan regionalism for overemphasizing the role of cities in its definition, their own "authentic" regionalism still held that the city played an important cultural role.[68] Odum, in contrast, was essentially anti-urban, critiquing the centralizing functions of cities as part of his broader problems with technology and urbanization leading (somehow?) to totalitarianism and possibly fascism. For Southern development, Odum believed the region "need not lag, on the one hand, nor, on the other hand, follow blindly the paths of a hectic, urban, technological, transitional period of civilization."[69]

In the United States at the turn of the century, the progress imperative and its forward momentum—with ascendant modernism, modernization, and urbanization—precipitated a certain anxiety concerning the march of history. At the same time, a second, backward-looking vortex was propelled by that same motion, enticed by the security of the past. Across scientific and artistic fields, "the modernist century began with . . . nostalgic desire to construct a radically simplified world of the 'primitive.'"[70] "Ironically," Dorothy Ross observes, "illiberal historicism, designed to tame the uncertainty of history, deepened the gulf between the modern future and the American past."[71] In 1905, E. R. A. Seligman described the United States as both "the youngest and the oldest of economic societies," one that was "still in many ways a frontier society" yet also "leading the world and . . . showing other countries what stages they have to still traverse" with "confusing" results.[72]

By the time the Depression set in during the 1930s, there remained a shared ambivalence toward progress, in association with both technology and market capitalism, grounded in the concern that intellectual hope in progress may have actually been one of the causes of the country's economic downturn. This was a moment during which national and Southern crises aligned with such concerns, resulting in an ambivalent attitude toward social engineering—one that would remain consistent for Howard Odum throughout his career. In the 1920s and early 1930s, Odum emerged as the premier Southern social scientist studying the region and gained national prominence for his work. As historian Daniel Rodgers summarizes, the South in the first half of the twentieth century had a "complex and uneasy relationship with progress," one that reverberated in national concerns of the era; thus, "if Odum's accent was not quite the familiar one, that was because, for a moment in the 1930s and 1940s, that troubled reckoning with progress was not only the South's but the nation's as well."[73] Regionalist groups in the great urban centers of Chicago and New York pitted metropolitanism against an "authentic" regionalism in the 1920s, but these debates were fundamentally Northern, as urbanization was more advanced in the North than in the South.[74] The South would not be majority urban until the 1940s, and its cities were considerably smaller.[75] Southern regionalists did not seek to disaggregate great cities, as the RPAA did, but to preempt industrialization and urbanization from taking over what Odum and colleagues believed to be agrarian Southern society.[76]

Historian Richard Pells observes of the regionalists—Northern and Southern alike—that they were "social reformers, progressives, and liberals, [and] they had one thing in common: they were all radical innovators with profoundly conservative goals."[77] Regionalists deployed what Raymond Williams identifies as a "selective tradition"—literary critic Van Wyck Brooks's "usable past" to address modernization.[78] There was a concern among writers and other members of the intelligentsia that they did not exert sufficient political impact on or intellectual guidance over the rapid changes occurring in the post–World War I society. Pells notes that these individuals' "insistence that thought, action, art and science, morality and mechanization were in constant battle was not just a passing commentary.... They identified their own difficulties with the plight of culture in modern America, seeking to expand its importance as a means of strengthening their influence in the larger society."[79] If that was true for regionalists of the nation (of any accent), it was acutely so for the Southern regionalists.

FOLK ENGINEERING/ENGINEERING THE FOLK

In the wake of Northern industrial disputes between capital and labor, particularly surrounding the Pullman railroad strike in 1894, a synthesizing ideology emerged that combined admiration of scientific managerial order with a reformist attitude toward corporate excess in an attempt "to occupy a middle ground, urging cooperation between capital and labor in the interests of the greater social good."[80] While the disputes were identified as social problems of acclimation for an industrializing urban society, sociologist Harvey Zorbaugh insisted the problems were essentially political, and named the bourgeoning expertise in social planning in response to them "social politics."[81]

Led by social reformers such as Graham Taylor and Jane Addams—founders of the Chicago Common Settlement House movement and deeply intertwined with the philanthropic and activist networks of the era—the Progressive movement advocated for the "rights of the public as the third and greatest party in industrial struggles," in addition to capital and labor, and viewed the "enlightened individual as the primary agent of social change."[82] The reformists' roots were associated with Protestant social movements of the late nineteenth century, but after 1900, the Progressive ideology was secularized, shifting focus from "improving the individual's moral condition to improving the social and environmental conditions that produced the individual."[83] As reformist professionals ascended into management positions, the rationalization of managerial science crystallized into engineer Frederick Winslow Taylor's "scientific management" movement, which he articulated in his highly influential 1909 book *The Principles of Scientific Management*. Taylor believed that management could be "rationalized through the application of science" and drew parallels between the factory and society at large.[84] His work influenced, among many others, institutionalist Thorstein Veblen, who endorsed the concept of planning as a form of social engineering to improve behavior and efficiency.⁸⁵

Social engineering was a kind of industrial uplift ideology, which proposed applied methods to improve social welfare "in the hope of transforming slumdwellers and factory workers into respectable American citizens."⁸⁶ Social welfare in the early twentieth century was broadly defined as encompassing the entire "comfort and improvement, intellectual and social, of . . . employees, over and above paid wages."⁸⁷ If the Pullman strike rejected the corporate paternalism of the company town, "the alternative social-welfare models that replaced the rigid paternalist company control . . . tended to be presented as rational and benign in the more official literature."⁸⁸ The meliorative social sciences were closely tied to both social welfare and social engineering concepts and practices.

The US social sciences were taking shape during this same period, and fields such as sociology, political science, and psychology also shared an interest in "mastering social process in a manner analogous to natural science."⁸⁹ A naturalized society was a rationalized one—one that applied sciences could continually master and improve. "Variously known as 'social control' and 'social engineering,'" the trend "turned practically every discipline in the direction of the application of its precepts."⁹⁰ For sociology, this endorsement of institutionalism and "the state as a benign and rational actor" dated back to its eighteenth-century positivist founder Auguste Comte.⁹¹ Comte's deep "faith in technocracy and meritocracy" enjoined social scientists to instruct national leaders on "the power of technical reason to determine what is correct, to persuade the ignorant and the doubtful, and to forge the consensus needed for public action."⁹²

As urban planning scholar John Friedmann explains, Comte's positivism was influenced by the ideologies of Henri de Saint-Simon, his professor at the French École Polytechnique, and Saint-Simonianism's emphasis on the social importance of scientists and managers as advisers to government; Comte, according to Friedmann, viewed engineering not only as a technical field but also as a nation-building political method: "Engineering applied the knowledge of natural science to the construction of bridges, tunnels, and canals. . . . Why should not a new breed of 'social engineers' apply their knowledge to the task of reconstructing society?"⁹³ This combination of positivism and the field of engineering, broadly interpreted and applied, were later deeply influential on John Dewey's pragmatism, and on the work of influential social scientists such as Thorstein Veblen, Rexford Tugwell, and Herbert Simon, "all of whom were enthralled by the idea of 'designing society.'"⁹⁴ In the first third of the US twentieth century, this broad group of reformers "identified themselves as both the 'public' and the 'competent,'" albeit neither fully democratic nor representative of all social sectors, as New Deal backlash would prove.[95]

Political scientist James C. Scott notes that, in Europe, World War I was "the high-mark for the political influence of engineers and planners."[96] Having dedicated their coordinated efforts to winning the war, they then "imagined what they could achieve if the identical energy and planning were devoted to popular welfare rather than mass destruction."[97] A similar belief in social engineering crossed over to the United States and became one of the core ideological pillars of the New Deal administration, articulated as a revolutionary hope. But in terms of social control, it was also a *counter*revolution.[98] In 1934, economist George Soule imagined "the final disappearance of government," replaced by an ascendant corporate leadership, writing confidently that "as more and more people—both engineers and others—come to understand the inherent superiority of the engineering approach, the traditional business way of doing things is bound to lose its popularity."[99]

The South, however, privileged different social engineering concepts. In 1861, Frederick Law Olmsted had observed of the region that its lack of cities resulted in an underdeveloped sense of civics in the Northern urban sense.[100] By the turn of the century, much of the paternalist spirit of social engineering had been directed explicitly at the socialization and instruction in common manners, behavior, and conduct of the new urban immigrant workforce. Urban planning practices shared a similar focus.[101] In the South, paternalism formed the bedrock of the patrician cotton society, from mill towns to plantations.[102] The plantation was the site of its most violent expression through the forced extraction of labor, first from enslaved people and then from freed sharecroppers for the meagerest of subsistence. If Southern writers such as Ulrich Phillips and Arthur Raper vehemently disagreed on the value of its legacy (and the extent of its brutality), each confirmed that the plantation was "the seed-bed of the South's people and her culture," and that the old planter class interests continued to define Southern society in the post-Reconstruction era.[103] Those government welfare programs tolerated by the planter class played limited roles, generally informed by the Protestant charity tradition and continued into the early twentieth century by groups like the Red Cross.[104] The shared aspirations of the Southern "public," such as it was, did not resonate with those in the North. This public Odum reframed as selective, racialized, and mystified, with a paternalistic nod to the period's white populism, as the Southern "folk."

Howard Odum and the Southern regionalists critiqued the pathologies of the plantation society and its legacy in the South, but they also recognized how deeply those pathologies and social structures constituted the Southern grain, which Odum mythologized in the mores and institutions of the region's folkways. He began his career by studying Black folk music, aiming to understand the nature of the Black "soul," but the timeless folkways of the region as he conceived them were inherently white.[105] Odum made broad claims for the role of science in society but also qualified his own version of social science as "folk sociology," an odd and often awkward combination of the meliorist social sciences he had learned at Clark and Columbia Universities, infused with Progressive notions of societal behavioral prescriptions for social improvement.[106] He subdued his scientific claims with the folk qualifier, hoping that this blunted presentation would serve as a kind of tonic to make those expert prescriptions for change more palatable to a skeptical white Southern audience.[107]

Further, Odum complicated his positivist sociology with the imperative of social learning through application, described thusly by Friedmann: "Knowledge is derived from experience and validated in practice, and is therefore integrally part of action" as an "ongoing dialectical practice."[108] Odum took great conceptual liberties in his Southern social "engineering" to accommodate calls for Southern reform, tempering it with the evolutionary, generationally paced, *slow* social change of a mystic white folklore. He believed that such conceptual flexibility assisted him in managing the multiple politics of communities from the Northern academic and philanthropic networks to the reactionary white Southern audience. When Odum succeeded, as he did with his 1936 book *Southern Regions of the United States*, it seemed to be with the help of historical events aligning to help his work surge despite his own internally inconsistent narrative. When, he called on colleagues for feedback and critique after failures, these came stingingly, if often not unkindly, and were not what he wanted to hear. Odum both conjured the need regionalist social planning had for the human and natural resources of the South, and undercut these efforts in cautioning that the folk would only accept such expert recommendations in the hazy, undefined regional future of later generations.[109]

In these imagistic constructs of regional planning, however, Odum was not alone. Historian Robert Dorman notes that the "'science' of regionalism . . . was a science that was aestheticized and ethicized, a *folk science* . . . an attempted fusion of the modern with the traditional."[110] Benton MacKaye, the central regionalist philosopher of the RPAA, described the need for "the coordinated visualization of several kinds of specialists or 'engineers'" across natural and social management to comprehensively produce "'regional engineering,' or by the more usual name, 'regional planning.'"[111] Dorman suggests, however, that to "arrange the environment" in accordance with folk society would also require a "'folk engineering,'" necessitating that regional planners like MacKaye, Odum, and Lewis Mumford "[extend] their mimesis of integrative folk culture even further, beyond the philosophy of planning to the actual techniques of regional reconstruction."[112]

Odum, as the utopian regionalist booster, envisioned an economically revitalized South, with a restructured agricultural sector that would not disturb the social and racial status quo alongside a limited industrial sector that would at least keep the South apace with Northern notions of development. As the Southern folk sociologist, however, Odum feared the social change that any definition of progress might bring. How does one engineer the immutable traditions of the folk? Before the Depression, the prospects seemed no less utopian than convincing a Jim Crow Southern society to adopt a centralized national social planning program.

In his presidential address to the American Sociological Society in 1930, Howard Odum celebrated "folk sociology," stating his firm belief that it revealed the "universal societal constant in a world of historical variables."[113] For Odum, "the folk-region society is bottomed in the relative balance of man, nature, and culture."[114] Odum's societal frame for the region placed the "folkways" counter to "stateways," which he argued required balance for regional development. The third element of society, technology ("technicways"), helped develop and maintain dynamic equilibrium between the former two. The region was a work of art in which small, decentralized towns, not the large metropolises of the North, could be constituent.

Odum's folk society was an evolutionary conceptualization as "the elemental and basic cultural definitive of all societies in process," best observed in "the folk regional society, which is the smallest comprehensive unit of society."[115] In parallel, "over against the folk society" was "the universal trend toward the state society, characterized by stateways and technicways."[116] Whenever "the folk society and the state society conflict, the folkways will always predominate."[117] Odum believed that when these two societies "work in concert, change and achievement result; when they are at odds, there is tension, disorganization, conflict, and ultimately decay."[118] In the future, "the definitive, evolving society will be a reality when there is balance and equilibrium between folkways, stateways, and technicways," which "may be generally accomplished through social planning."[119] He advised that "the resources of the social and physical sciences must be brought to bear in bridging the theoretical and the practical and in conserving the folkways which help the society adapt to the new state and technicways."[120] Odum believed the stateways must be bent toward folkways with "greater emphasis on individuality, upon primary groups and processes, and upon balanced regional development as an antidote for centralization."[121]

After Odum's death, George Simpson remarked of his doctoral adviser and IRSS colleague that he "was no folklorist" and did not "suggest that the clock be turned backward" toward the Old South.[122] Instead, Simpson believed, "Odum was interested in modern society—the present." In Odum's words, "the social technicways, in the form of social planning, will accelerate development and . . . harmonize conflicting forces."[123] As a complement to city and regional planning, and in tandem with Chicago's social engineering movement, social planning deployed a public-minded managerial expertise to address social disturbance resulting from modernization and urbanization.[124] To resolve, or at least elide, the tensions between these forces—and between his own sociological and regionalist ideas—Odum had to conceptualize and present a regionally scaled "social planning . . . as a gradualistic approach without elaborating on detail."[125]

Folk engineering, applied in both the eugenically inflected planning to which Odum subscribed and the management of societal structures and natural resources, was Odum's approach to social and regional planning for the South. As a doctrine, Odum's Southern regionalism was no different from regional planning elsewhere in its reflection and reproduction of the "underlying social relations in production," and thus tended to "legitimize the existing distribution of power in society."[126] Regionalists advocated for the decentralization of power and culture in the United States, aiming to "decenter New England, and more generally, the Northeast, as the cultural arbiter of . . . taste."[127]

Southern regionalism projected a racialized notion of region that helped inform contemporary discussions of Black geographic migration during the Jim Crow era, and how the Great Migration of African Americans out of the South impacted the traditionalist foundations of regionalism in that historic process of socio-territorial change.[128] Like their Northern RPAA peers, the Southern regionalists celebrated Frederick Jackson Turner's settler-colonialist frontier imaginary, turning, with Victorian "willful innocence," their understanding of that essentialized, naturalized vitality southward into a perceived and desired parallel ruggedness of the plantation.[129] Historian Daniel Singal observes that the Southern uplift ideology of the Jim Crow era demonstrates that the broad hope and claims for societal engineering were also myths and constructs—indeed, that "there is a spiritual uplift in every sort of material construction."[130] The ambitious cultural and ecological objectives of Odum and the Southern regionalists help us better understand that historical interwar planning gap in the South between the slowly emergent role of municipal administration and public welfare in the early 1920s, and the transformation of planning into the more circumscribed economic development aspirations of the post–World War II Sunbelt.

HOWARD W. ODUM AND THE INSTITUTE FOR RESEARCH IN SOCIAL SCIENCE

Planning historian Clyde Woods observes that "in many ways the federal tradition of regional planning in the United States began in the South as an attempt to resolve the North-South schism."[131] In contrast to the urban practice of city planning, regional planning originally focused on natural resource development and extraction, which had defined the Southern society and economy for more than three centuries.[132] Regional planning proposed an evolutionary framework for transitional societies to deal with the spatially uneven development between what were perceived as backward rural communities and the more advanced urban cultural centers, a "cultural lag" that sociologist William Ogburn claims separated the South from other regions.[133]

Once these lagging communities were properly integrated into an evenly developed metropolitan structure, the thinking went, regional planning would no longer be necessary, and metropolitan planning could simply maintain this integration through the ever-aspirational discourse of "balance."[134] As liberal social reformers, regional planners—largely unburdened by an understanding of the structural spatial necessity of uneven development to capital or the essential geographic contradictions of industrial capitalism—sought an idealized, timeless future equilibrium, informed by their understanding of biophysical and cultural processes.[135] In this equilibrium, nature and humans, industry and agriculture, city and countryside, progress and history, and an endless litany of neo-Hegelian frames could all align in equal proportion.[136] For regionalists, achieving these balances required simply the necessary surveying, interpreting, and planning at the imagined regional scale.[137]

In parallel to regionalism, as a more local response to the overlap of territorial town and country, intraregional society and economy, regional planning was the practice of spatial organization to enable national economic integration through natural resource extraction and commodity value creation across unevenly developed regions. Geographer Anne Gilbert provides a heuristic of the geographic literature on regionalism, broadly categorizing it into work on region as local response to capital processes, region as focus of identification, and region as medium for social interaction.[138] She describes the literature of the second group as examining regions defined by "cultural relationships between a group and particular places ... a symbolic appropriation of a portion of space by a group, and as constituting element of its identity."[139] Culture produced identity via geography "by virtue of its observable effects on the landscape" and "the material artifacts that distinguish one society from another."[140]

Southern regionalists at the University of North Carolina were the principal contributors to this cultural field of regional research. Howard W. Odum established the University of North Carolina's School of Social Work and Department of Sociology upon arriving in Chapel Hill in 1920. In 1922, he launched the *Journal of Social Forces*, which served as the premier platform for regional reform debates into the post–World War II era. In 1924, Odum founded the Institute for Research in Social Science (IRSS), a national pioneering prototype of the social science institute, to critically survey the US South in hopes of leading its reform from within.

The 1920s marked a new moment in the development of Southern social sciences, with raised economic expectations and an increased (though still limited) acceptance of social welfare.[141] Institute researchers included Rupert B. Vance, Guy Johnson, Arthur F. Raper, Margaret Jarman Hagood, Katharine Jocher, and Thomas J. Woofter (among others), and through applied research, they believed that the social sciences, social planning, and social action could usher in a Southern cultural renaissance able to draw on its past without being shackled to it.[142] They established a trans- and interdisciplinary Southern "area studies" research program at the IRSS.[143] The region was a scale too large to design, so, for these scholars, the social sciences helped abstract, describe, and project it toward an organic, balanced territorial structure.[144] Southern regionalists conceived the scope and scale of their projects entirely through the cultural lens of the social sciences as a sociological and ideological construct.[145] The region was presented as a scale of expertise, one of such complexity that only the scientifically trained could properly survey and knowledgeably engineer it.

Historian Michael O'Brien observes that "regionalism, especially but not exclusively in its Southern variety, was—apart from Marxism—the nearest thing to a central vogue that American literature had in the 1920s and 1930s."[146] It was what North Carolina journalist William T. Polk described as "the Golden Age of the Gadflies," and its "two main species" were "the sociological-research gadfly and the literary gadfly."[147] The IRSS at the University of North Carolina was the Southern center of the former, but, as Victor Branford noted, the planner needed "the aid of the poet," and Odum had (or believed he had) a touch of the poetic as well. The IRSS's talented researchers came together under Odum's leadership in the 1920s to help articulate the broad research analytic of Southern regionalism, of which Odum and Vance were recognized as the leaders. Within this analytic, Odum conceived of regionalism as "a tool of analysis, an instrument for the effective synthesizing of the social sciences," but also for studying "the whole of society," conceived as the "folk-regional society," a gestalt "in which all factors are sought out and interpreted in their proper perspective."[148]

With time, general consensus recognized Odum's protégé Rupert Vance as the institute's major force, helping establish the University of North Carolina as "a center of regional scholarship and what is nowadays called 'policy research'" and ultimately cementing Chapel Hill within "the national academic map."[149] Educated in the tradition of the first US social scientists, Odum set his regionalism within his mystified and timeless folkways (mores, institutions), while Vance, although a sociologist, gravitated more toward human geography. The two strands would help inform, respectively, their notions of Southern social planning and national-regional planning.

More recent analysis of the Southern regionalists notes that they were promoting what today is called "sustainable development" through their proposals for a region of exhausted, depleted social and ecological geographies. Tom Rudel and Chun Fu highlight that regionalist practices and definitions, whenever possible, were based on natural features such as river basins and soil composition that, along with variation in the extent and quality of natural resources, determined uneven development.[150] Further, the closing of the US frontier meant an end to the wasteful squandering of the "limitless resource" mentality, thereby necessitating a more efficient use of resource management.[151] Regional planning would help increase this rationalization of land use and management. Southern regionalists studied "poor, natural resource dependent populations," and adhered to a "'territorial regional planning' which promoted democratically determined changes in the human and natural resources of specific regions."[152] After World War II, however, human capital proved to be far more influential on regional

TOP   Gully control, Roane County, Tennessee. "Huge gully resulting from unprotected terrace outlets. Gully banks will be slopes and banks of the gully will be seeded to Bermuda grass to prevent further damage erosion." Howard Washington Odum Papers, Wilson Special Collections Library, UNC–Chapel Hill.

BOTTOM   Gully repair, Roane County, Tennessee. "The same hillside ten years later. The building of check dams, planting of lespedeza and grass and the setting out of black locust and shortleaf pine seedlings has reclaimed the land. In another decade the owner will have a crop of merchantable timber. TVA has furnished landowners in the Tennessee Valley more than 150,000,000 seedlings for erosion control and establishment of wood-lots." Howard Washington Odum Papers, Wilson Special Collections Library, UNC–Chapel Hill.

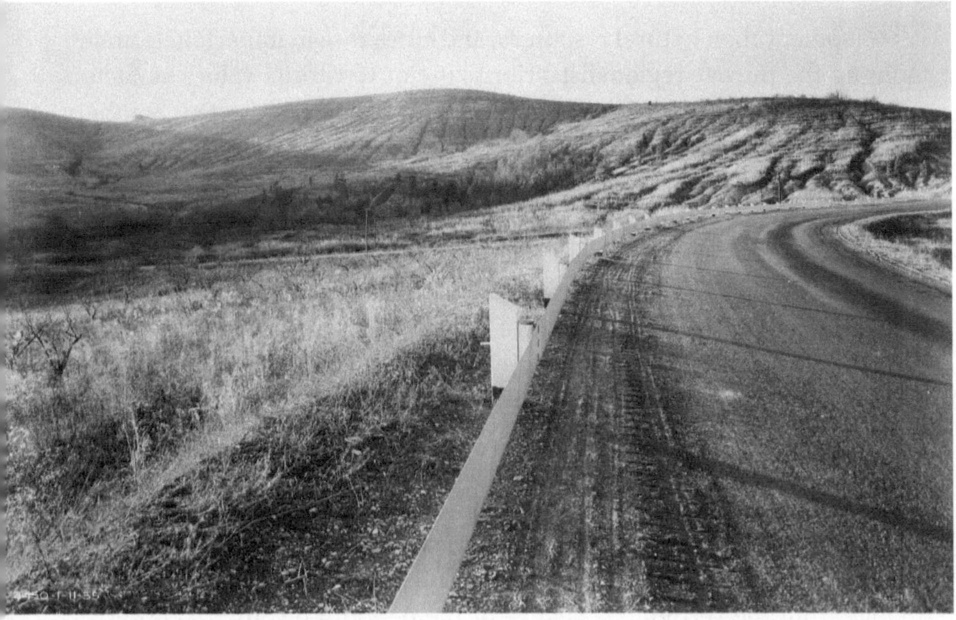

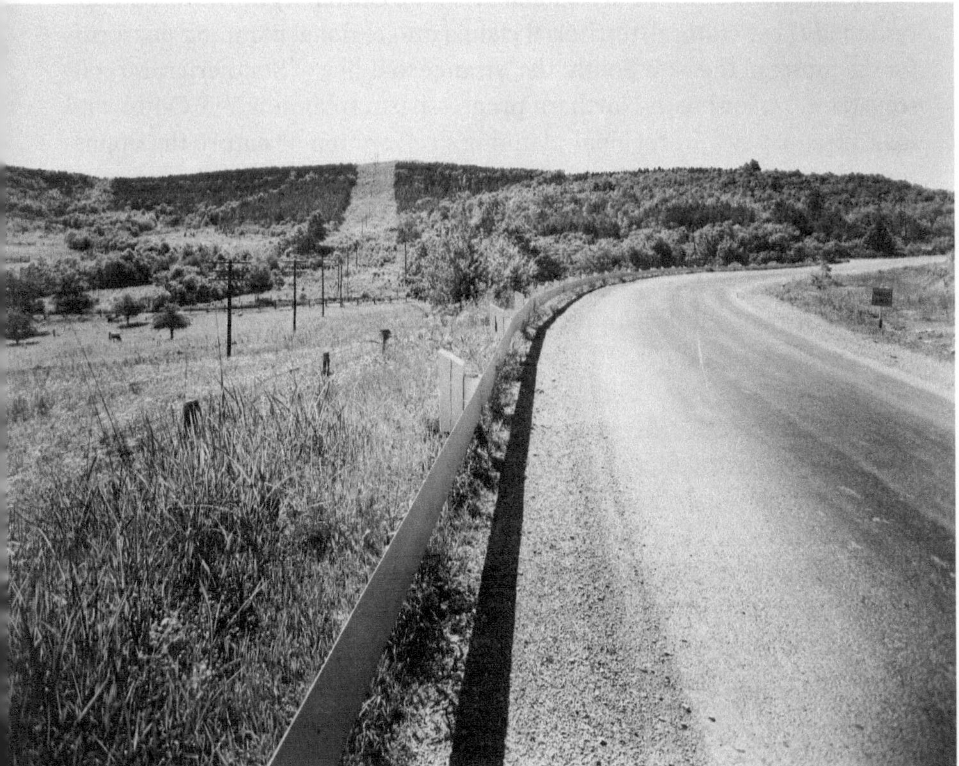

development than natural resources, and cities rose in importance, undermining the prewar regionalist prioritizing of territorial values as factors for development.[153] But from its outset, as Vance later reflected, Southern regionalism "embrace[d] policies and advocate[d] programs."[154]

Regionalists throughout the country were wary of the industrial city.[155] Some looked back to medieval European models and pre-nation-state territorial structures for inspiration, others to Indigenist imagery and essentialized notions of land connection in the United States and Latin America, still others to Southern Black and white folklore.[156] Capitalism, consumerism, and their impact on local identities in the post–World War I era provoked an artistic backlash that imagined a perceived authenticity of natures and folk cultures of peripheral pastoral areas. It was a narrative of loss and of local culture under threat from distant urban power centers. Lewis Mumford lamented in particular the loss of small-town New England life in his 1926 book *The Golden Day: A Study in American Experience and Culture*.[157] In addition to history, nature—or its construction—provided an ideological refuge from the vertiginous change of the period. Edward Soja observes, "In the context of society, nature, like spatiality, is socially produced and reproduced despite its appearance of objectivity and separation. The space of nature is thus filled with politics and ideology, with relations of production, with the possibility of being significantly transformed."[158]

Odum and the Southern regionalists at the University of North Carolina refracted these cultural/territorial claims into regional planning platforms for the future of the New South: the "strange wedding of Southern rural conservatism [region] with Northern progressivism [planning]."[159] Odum and his colleagues saw in regional planning's celebration of nature the opportunity to advance their Jeffersonian agricultural values of Southern landed culture, and to reposition that culture in a new regional-national frame.[160] Odum's organicist, conciliatory bias was also expressed in his understanding of Southern race relations, which he "subsumed . . . under the larger considerations of regional development and the adjustment to social change."[161] The strategy later influenced New Deal Southern policy.[162] As Clyde Woods notes, Odum sought to elide associations between his own "regionalism" and "questions of Southern white identity and rebellion," distancing those questions under the older concept of "sectionalism" to allow *his* regionalism to be deployed as "a tool for analysis and for multi-state planning. This methodology was a key component of the effort to build a constituency for massive federal economic intervention in the South."[163]

Odum employed an ever-widening definition of regionalism to accommodate the institutional dexterity required of increasingly disruptive Southern encounters with progress throughout the 1930s, and to jockey for funding from the Northern philanthropic community by positioning himself and the IRSS as the primary reporters of the "facts" of Southern realism to the national social science community. "Southern regionalism" was "a descriptive term for a massive factual reinventory of the South's assets" that "grew into an agenda the social reconstruction of the South, then into a scheme for national planning, and finally into a theory of social change that Odum thought was as sweeping as the general theories of Max Weber and Talcott Parsons!"[164]

While incorporating a rhetorical frame of oppositional sociogeographic phenomena (North/South, white/Black, city/country, natural sciences / social sciences, industry/agriculture, stateways/folkways, planning expertise / haphazard and uninformed development, and so on), Odum's moral judgment showed clear preferences that helped him pledge allegiance — implicitly and explicitly — to the Southern cause so that none would confuse criticism for abandonment.[165] His work contributed to the broader "go slow" philosophy for moderate Southern white liberal reform. After Odum's death, Dr. Martin Luther King Jr. observed of this philosophy in 1960, "They are never honest enough to admit that the academic and cultural lags in the Negro community are themselves the result of segregation and discrimination.... It is both rationally unsound and sociologically untenable to use the tragic effects of segregation as an argument for its continuation."[166]

Odum's IRSS colleague Rupert Vance warned against such broad definitions of regionalism, noting, "There is danger lest the concept come to mean all things to all men."[167] Lewis Mumford also cautioned against Odum and coauthor Harry Estill Moore's expansive definition, suggesting that "the all inclusiveness of region does the term to death."[168] Louis Wirth agreed, noting, "The failure to discriminate the many distinct factors that underlie the emergence and persistence of region is a serious fault of present-day scholarship and research."[169]

At the dawn of the 1930s, however, Odum's broad conceptualization of "regionalism" provided sufficient malleability for the term to accommodate conflicting, reflexive positions on planning and progress with enduring folk traditions during the national period of crisis. If Odum's attitudes did change over time on issues of folk and race, as some claim, he and his colleague Rupert Vance nevertheless consistently celebrated planning as that instrument of social science capable of bringing "the whirl of change under control, to design a set of 'social technicways' that would ... provide, somehow, the equilibrium that 'intellectualism' had destroyed."[170] During this interwar period, modernism, in undeniable "dialectic with modernization," reached the South, "but its success was not thoroughgoing."[171] For Southern regionalists, regionalism and regional planning in the South were in a similar dialectic. They were transitional agents of change, and identified as such, but as the interwar period caught up to the very reforms that the regionalists were calling for, Odum "came to voice regret and concern at the rapidity of the changes even as he became identified with progress."[172]

REGION AS FACT. REGION AS FUTURE.

Historian John L. Thomas observes that "vision . . . involves first of all a vantage point." Patrick Geddes's vantage point was his Outlook Tower in Edinburgh, nearly 100 feet off the ground, while Lewis Mumford's was "high on the piers of Brooklyn Bridge on a windy morning in 1915." And for Benton MacKaye, the vantage looked out from atop his projected Appalachian Trail as if a giant, "his head just scraping the skyline as he strode along its length from north to south."[173] Odum looked the other way, from the South to all points in the United States and back, but his vision, paradoxically, was place focused without a specific vantage. It was more diffuse, set in what were then small towns where the North Carolina coastal plain met the foothills. It was a self-conscious Southern vision, looking to the cultural field of social planning that had been paired with city planning and hoping that it might be applied to a future regional-national planning governance. An understanding in which region (South) and nation (United States) respected each other's organic culture and development needs, and through expert reading of folk traditions and natural resource inventories might find the plans—the telic supports—to achieve a shared future in due course. He saw the descriptive whole, "old and new, the folk and academic, the agrarian and the industrial, the spiteful and the generous."[174]

Odum and the Southern regionalists were transitional figures in the ushering in of urbanization and modernization to the region. In tracing their intellectual and institutional histories, I hope to de-center the New York debates and protagonism in the 1920s and 1930s to better document that national scope of regionalism and regional planning thought. Through this, a new network map emerges in which the IRSS is a node amid the national-regional thought network, including W. E. B. Du Bois's work in Atlanta, the work of the Chicago School of Sociology, the literary figures in Nashville, Carl Sauer at the University of California, Berkeley, the RPAA in New York, and, finally, the Washington brain trust and its reports.

The book is organized into chapters that move from chronological/historical logics to broader thematic discussions. I spend a great deal of time weaving the intertextual discussion of rich primary and secondary texts from and about the interwar period, drawing from the broad interdisciplinary subjects that the scholars of the IRSS researched and wrote on in their Southern area studies.

In chapter 1, the curtain opens on the University of Virginia Round Table on Regionalism in 1931. The university was the first south of Washington, DC, to be nominated to the prestigious Association of American Universities in 1904, and the state's son Woodrow Wilson was only ten years out of the US presidency in 1931. And of course, Thomas Jefferson—planner, architect, and president—had founded the institution. The University of Virginia was both national *and* Southern. Against the backdrop of the Depression, the round table was designed to bring together regionalism and regional planning groups from around the country.

Thematically, the chapter introduces national and regional planning, and the debates around the South's relationship to and participation in what was to become Roosevelt's New Deal. Roosevelt first announced his preliminary proposal for the Tennessee Valley Authority at the round table, precisely when Odum and his colleagues were studying development in the Tennessee Valley and cautioning that it would take time to study and develop its culture in preparation for the river basin project. These were the political tensions in the air, both interjurisdictional, among levels of government and autonomy, and internal, within various groups from the South pondering tradition and proposing development. Which interfered with which? A set of problems emerged from the round table discussions that challenged regional planning's promise out of descriptive literature and into a viable practice and policy that could address the scale of national crisis.

In chapter 2, I trace Odum's biography and the institutional and financial circumstances out of which his Institute for Research in Social Science emerged. Much of the chapter focuses on the early period of Odum's career, from graduate school through his early positions until the 1920s. It includes the launch of his *Social Forces* journal and the founding of the institute with the support of Northern funders whom he contacted through his graduate school networks. The nature and importance of Odum's participation in these networks as a kind of second-tier Southerner would increase and intensify, as he and many of the networks' actors eventually assumed important roles in the consultative Washington government brain trust of the 1930s. I also review Odum's relationship with his three principal education mentors—Thomas Pearce Bailey, G. Stanley Hall, and Franklin H. Giddings—and how their respective influences on him carried forward in his views on race, institution, the social sciences, and the future battles over his social science methodology. I then look at Odum as mentor, and at some of the bibliographies of researchers whom he recruited to the institute, which was perhaps the greatest achievement of his career and his most enduring legacy.

In chapter 3, I explore the intellectual history of the United States and Southern social sciences in which Odum was trained. I begin with nineteenth-century Southern social scientists such as John C. Calhoun, Thomas R. Dew, George Fitzhugh, and Henry Hughes. Theirs was a tradition of reactionary proslavery activism and antebellum defense in their observations of Southern society and economy. I review the impact of Charles Darwin's work on evolution, and its misinterpretation and nefarious instrumentalization in the social Darwinism of Herbert Spencer. I then look at William Graham Sumner's work on folkways and social mores, Lester Frank Ward's notion of telesis, and Franklin H. Giddings's concept of consciousness of kind, exploring how each deeply influenced Howard Odum's social science training and his subsequent writing.

In the 1920s, after successfully securing funding from them, Odum received stinging feedback from the influential leadership of the Social Science Research Committee. The leaders criticized Odum for his descriptive portraiture method, which they believed was not quantitatively rigorous enough. To add insult to injury, they underscored their disappointment because Odum was a former student of Giddings, who actively endorsed the importance of quantitative methods in sociology. The criticism was likely part of Odum's decision to later include exhaustive data and indexes that the IRSS research assembled for his lauded 1936 *Southern Regions of the United States*. Such maneuvering demonstrated Odum's resilience as a network operator able to change with the times, and a willingness to construct the regionalism argument with a certain plasticity according to varying academic and institutional circumstances. These methods also reflect the dynamic relationship between different sociological modes of analysis: regionalism and quantification, and documenting traditional folkways versus the use of rational planning to intervene and induce evolutionary progress. The chapter ends with a detailed documentation of Odum's communication with Carl O. Sauer, in which Sauer endorsed the Southern regionalists' work as aligned with his own human geography research interests.

In chapter 4, I interrogate Southern regionalists' conceptualization of race and place. Race was the myth on which Odum constructed his Southern regionalism and his proposal for regional planning. For Odum and colleagues, race was the scale of region. If Odum was willing to bend on method and style in crafting his regionalism for different audiences, he would not accept the issues of racial equality and integration in the South. Indeed, the very complex notions of stateways and folkways might all be understood as extensive rhetorical flourishes that advocated for a wide range of scientifically informed issues where the South might advance. But the issue of race had to be policed and measured by folkways.

Southern regionalists were celebrated as the first white social scientists to study and address the issue of race and Black folklore without truly engaging with an authentic Black perspective to explore the Southern Black experience; writer and anthropologist Zora Neal Hurston later insisted in her essay "You Don't Know Us Negroes." Yet books such as Arthur Raper's 1933 *The Tragedy of Lynching* and the 1938 *Sharecroppers All,* which he coauthored with Black sociologist Ira De Augustine Reid of Atlanta University, were seminal texts for the period, and each was approved for publication thanks in large part to Odum's influence with the University of North Carolina Press. From there, I explore Fredrick Jackson Turner's frontier theory, and how Rupert Vance and Odum each redirected its popularity to the South as a new social frontier. I also trace this influence to Benton MacKaye's Appalachian Trail proposal in the early 1920s, which I compare with the interregionalism of W. E. B. Du Bois's book *The Philadelphia Negro,* written twenty years earlier.

In chapter 5, I return to theories of regionalism in the 1930s, as both Odum and Vance oriented their conceptualizations more specifically to proposals for Southern regional planning and its administration. I closely review Vance's notion of the "regional complex," based on his work on the Southern cotton industry, with Odum's folk regionalism. Vance was clearly more comfortable and direct in naming the social, political, and economic factors and pathologies of the Southern planter society, which then led to his more clearly articulated policy recommendations for a reform-minded regional planning agenda.

After, I explore Odum's insistence on a distinction between Fredrick Jackson Turner's definition of the geographic "sections" that made up the country, advocating instead a future regionalism that, in contrast to Turner's sectional antagonism, would "put nation first." When his 1938 *American Regionalism* didn't receive the wide reception his previous book had, Odum sought opinions from social science colleagues around the country. The extensive response helps to better understand how his proposals were critically received in the late 1930s, particularly the state-bloc definitions for his six US regions. Together, the responses generally point more favorably in content and sociological rigor to Vance's work.

The chapter ends with Vanderbilt poet Donald Davidson, one of the proudly "unreconstructed" Agrarians who, interestingly, offers the most precise political critique of Odum's regionalism. The regionalists and Agrarians were Southern university groups who were supposedly ideologically at odds with one another, but Davidson's critical insight demonstrates prescience—for example, for regional-national projects such as the Tennessee Valley Authority river basin project. In many ways, Davidson's paranoia concerning the nationalist reach and ambitions of such major infrastructure projects was proved correct.[175]

In chapter 6, I focus specifically on Vance's and Odum's respective proposals for Southern regional planning, continuing with themes laid out previously that contrast more radical interventions with gradualist approaches, and the national and regional tension over the right to engage in regional planning and benefit from its practice. Odum conceived of a social planning as culture primer to ready the South for eventual leadership based on fact and expertise. He saw planning as the summation of his research in administration, welfare, psychology, sociology, and the South, and he sought to capitalize on the national popularity of planning practice and the New Deal funding opportunities for it. I closely review Odum's 1934 "Case for Regional-National Social Planning," along with its inherent tensions for planning, as a telic mechanism for progress, with ultimate deference to folkways to determine regional balance.

Rupert B. Vance's human geography was more closely aligned with French regionalism, and he spoke of Geddesian regional planning with greater precision than Odum's instrumentalization of those traditions for his more personal objectives. Vance clarified his terminology and intentions, and he advocated for concrete reforms for the Southern agricultural sector, promoting the society-land connection that resonated historically with the region. But the proposals were to remain on paper unless Southern regionalists were able to develop the institutional capacity and influence to carry them forward. In early 1938, Odum proposed a Council on Southern Regional Development to take on many of the functions he set forth in his regional administration frame, only to encounter opposition and disapproval from other competing Southern groups. Also in 1938, the Roosevelt administration's National Emergency Council (NEC) published its *Report on Economic Conditions of the South*, which incorporated Southern regionalist discourse, famously concluding that the South was the nation's "no. 1 economic problem." These were the tensions present at the 1931 University of Virginia Round Table on Regionalism among regional and national figures, along with the internal intergroup competition for the right to define and administer regional research and policy. Finally, the regional modernism that Odum and IRSS colleagues hoped for couldn't materialize without a state—local or regional—to give authority to those aspirations.

The Southern regionalists proclaimed a subjectivity and their right to plan the region's future. These concepts contrasted with the historic object-ness of their societies, and with natural resources instrumentalized toward national and international value production as a colonial economy, which regionalists believed the South was reduced to. It was a white subjectivity claim, for which they also fought to preserve and maintain the Southern racial contract for as long as the folk would admit. The complexity of Southern regionalism is not a shoulder shrug of "both-sidesism," nor is it a resigned deference to simply accepting that history as "of its time." It is an invitation to sit with that complexity and consider how its diversity of thought—from Southern defense, to Southern apology, to ravaging Southern critique—all lived within (graduated from, or were inspired by) the same institution and publications under the leadership and mentorship of Howard W. Odum. In this way, we understand more clearly how the New Deal development projects and plans that focused on the US South throughout the 1930s were often introduced or managed by Odum and his IRSS colleagues and alumni; these individuals were involved to an equal if not greater degree than the RPAA members who eventually traveled South in the participation of those projects. The book is an exploration of the meanings of region and planning, and of the geographic and cultural specificity of these topics combined discourse and practice in the US South during the interwar years.

Aerial photo of dam and industry. Howard Washington Odum Papers, Wilson Special Collections Library, UNC–Chapel Hill.

CHAPTER 1

ROUND TABLE ON REGIONALISM

PLANNERS AND POETS

On July 6, 1931, a group gathered at the University of Virginia's Institute of Public Affairs for the Round Table on Regionalism conference to discuss how a diverse amalgam of disciplines and interests might form an active movement for regionalism and regional planning throughout the nation. During the interwar period, the theme of regionalism was abuzz—nationally and internationally—in both academic discussion and the popular press.

Regional planning had emerged in the late nineteenth and early twentieth centuries as an effort to survey nature with the tools of the social sciences.[1] Among those pioneering this approach was eccentric Scotsman Patrick Geddes (1854–1932), who conducted research in Edinburgh from his Outlook Tower facility. He developed an applied regional observational science whose mantra to "survey before the plan" proposed that if a region's resources could be appropriately recorded and its patterns properly divined, such information would show planners how society should be organized and engineered around its natural functions: "The survey prepares for and points towards the Plan."[2] For Geddes, the survey comprised not only "the resources of such a natural region," but also "the human response to it, and of the resulting complexities of the cultural landscape: in all his teachings, his most persistent emphasis was on the survey method."[3] With this approach, Geddes launched a comprehensive planning methodology incorporating natural and social science survey techniques to catalog regional resources.

Geddes's research drew on nineteenth-century French geography and Romantic utopian socialism. He was an admirer of Herbert Spencer and Thomas Henry Huxley, whose study of the Thames River Basin influenced Geddes's concepts of the biological region and the valley section, the blueprints for his river basin development model.[4] A still greater influence on Geddes's valley section, however, was French forest ecologist Charles Flahault's botanical survey research on tree species distribution. According to Flahault, trees were "social species" that clustered in patterns that, if discerned, could help reveal the potential economic opportunities of the valley region.[5] Geddes sought to structure these economic opportunities into a settlement pattern that followed another natural system—the riverway—up to its source at the mountaintop. In reaction to expanding urban industrialism, Geddes looked to a region's natural resources as systems that could properly determine and instruct regional planning initiatives.[6]

Aiming to bring Geddes's methodologies across the Atlantic, Lewis Mumford, a Geddes disciple and the preeminent US spokesman for regional planning philosophy, formed the New York–based Regional Planning Association of America (RPAA) along with colleagues Clarence Stein, Benton MacKaye, Catherine Bauer, Henry Wright, and Stuart Chase in 1923.[7] In 1925, the RPAA produced a special issue of *Survey Graphic*, edited by Mumford, that is credited as the first US regional planning declaration.[8] The issue launched a tremendous subsequent outpouring of regionalist work up through World War II and beyond.

At the dawn of the new decade, despite their essentially *decentralizing* character, Mumford believed that regional and national crises could provide the opportunity to unite disparate regional projects. Shortly before the University of Virginia Round Table on Regionalism, Lewis Mumford observed in a letter to Geddes, "The Southerners, particularly the younger intellectuals, have lately become conscious of themselves as the repositories of the agricultural and regional traditions of the country." Mumford and the RPAA engineered the 1931 conference to connect with the Southern regionalists, whose "academic home was Howard Odum's sociological laboratory" at his Institute for Research in Social Science (IRSS) at the University of North

Carolina in Chapel Hill, by then considered, "in effect, a notable counterpart of Geddes's Outlook Tower in Edinburgh."[9] Writing specifically about the Agrarians, a Southern literary group based at Vanderbilt University in Nashville whose members had recently published an antebellum-style manifesto provocatively titled *I'll Take My Stand*, Mumford remarked, "[Although] they tend to be slightly reactionary, still dreaming of the past instead of shaping a more integrated future, they may prove valuable allies."[10] Mumford later noted that the conference was the last major event in which he and his RPAA colleagues would participate before their dormancy in 1933.[11]

Despite the social science emphasis of Geddes's methodologies, by "invoking the organic nature of urbanism, a complex web involving the growth of cities in relation to their environment, and human society within the built environment of the city, Geddes opened a Pandora's box."[12] Questions abounded: How to draw geographic boundaries for culture? Where do the systems begin and end? Dialectically, how *much* surveying to conduct before planning, and how to synthesize a potentially tireless engine of research — powered by the magnetic poles of nature and culture — for planning? In another letter, Mumford quoted Geddes's collaborator British sociologist Victor Branford's belief that "the town planner needs the aid of the poet."[13] Howard Odum would later paraphrase this concept: "Any adequate picture of the South must combine the poetic with the scientific."[14] The balance of each is found in the practice of regional planning: for Odum a science, for Mumford an art.[15] The Virginia round table had no shortage of either.

Robert L. Dorman asserts in *Revolt of the Provinces*, "If the 1920s had been the era of manifestos, the 1930s were an era of conferences."[16] For US regionalism and regional planning, the Virginia round table inaugurated that era. Stuart Chase opened his remarks on "The Concept of Planning" by quoting the dean of the Yale Law School on the recent popularity of planning: "Why it is getting so that one is as loath to appear on the street without a Five-Year Plan as without his trousers!" He went on to identify the culprits: October 29, 1929, and the efficient, effective success of the Russians.[17] Almost two years after that ominous date, with the national economic situation worsening, the United States was searching for planning leaders, ideas, and examples to efficiently and effectively address its collective fate.

The round table was hosted by University of Virginia rural economist Wilson Gee and Stringfellow Barr, a native Virginian who had recently begun his term as editor of the literary magazine *Virginia Quarterly Review*.[18] Throughout the week, themes the conference addressed ranged from "Historical Consideration in Regional Planning" to "Cultural Aspects of Regionalism," "Regional Planning," and "Sociological and Economic Aspects of Regionalism." The proceedings included presentations from Southern

Agrarian John Gould Fletcher, RPAA members Lewis Mumford, Benton MacKaye, Henry Wright, and Stuart Chase, and sociologists Roderick D. McKenzie of the University of Michigan and Howard W. Odum of the University of North Carolina, among many others. The inaugural remarks on "State Planning" were delivered by New York's then-governor Franklin Delano Roosevelt. Clarence Stein had traveled to Albany to personally persuade the governor to present at the Virginia gathering, but the future president already viewed the group as potentially valuable allies, and he gladly accepted.[19] Of the governor, Rexford Tugwell later observed, "He always did, and always would, think people better off in the country and would regard the cities as rather hopeless."[20] Stein reported back to the RPAA, tentatively approving of Roosevelt's commitment to regional planning: "[He is] one of us."[21]

Roosevelt's strategy was impressive. Addressing an audience of Southern academics and literary figures, he began, "I did not come here with any prepared speech this morning. I came to present to you very informally a subject that is very close to all of our hearts, a subject which I think needs and deserves much public and private discussion and needs and requires perhaps just as few formal public addresses as possible." His disarming, folksy appeal continued with an ode to the Southern university's founder, Thomas Jefferson, "the great planner of our nation; an architect of buildings, an architect of industry, and most of all, an architect of government." "It is only in the last generation, our generation," Roosevelt continued, "that we have returned to thoughts of planning for the days to come." Roosevelt proceeded to highlight the importance of the New York agriculture industry and voiced concern that cities like New York were growing too big too fast. Echoing Ebenezer Howard's famous fusing of the benefits of town and country, he suggested that the way forward for many states was rural industry, with cooperative units that would offer meaningful work to the rural young and prevent them from wanting or needing to move to the city: "We may call them factory-farmers, one simple term that will connote just that position of keeping people on the land with agriculture as what you might call their roots, way down in the ground."[22] If the audience fancied itself the repository of agricultural and regional traditions, the New York governor cosigned this presumption.

Roosevelt spoke anecdotally of his summers in Warm Springs, Georgia, clarifying his Southern bona fides, and followed with the confession that his state was implementing a regional dairy protectionism that was "of doubtful constitutionality"—states' rights braggadocio from one who would become among the nation's strongest executives of the century. He framed planning in agricultural terms of crop rotation responding to seasonal change and market competition, but his final topic, regional planning, was one he wanted to "pass over quite rapidly." Roosevelt wanted to strip the concept of any hint of government overstep, endorsing regional planning as providing the opportunity "in our own locality and community and county and our own state, to do not merely what is a good thing to do, but to do what is a common-sense thing about the generation that is coming after." He finished with a joke about a man coming "out of the middle west" who, when asked how things were in his state, replied, "Looking up." "Really?" the questioner replied, to which the man responded, "It's absolutely inevitable. Things are flat on their backs now, and they must be looking up."[23]

Roosevelt's performance could easily have been given by Will Rogers or Mark Twain. The conference welcomed the speech warmly, and afterward, future Virginia senator Harry F. Byrd prophetically celebrated Roosevelt as "our next President."[24] In 1932, in a campaign speech at Oglethorpe University in Atlanta, Roosevelt would again emphasize planning as central to his platform and proposed state planning boards with federal coordination to be established across the country.[25] His presidential campaign was masterfully launched at Charlottesville with an ode to the South, agrarianism, regional planning, and Southern regional planning.

Regionalism, in this era, was both a cultural movement and the cultural motive for regional planning "lest it relapse," Mumford warned, "into an arid technological scheme."[26] At the round table, Connecticut forestry specialist Benton MacKaye described his framework for regionalism and regional planning: "Regionalism is a philosophy of regional planning—a search for the ultimate things wanted in developing the industry and culture of a region. Culture is the use of industry. Industry is the conversion of natural resources into finished products, and culture is conversion of finished products into the ultimate need of human welfare and happiness. The objectives of industry are finite only—the delivery of food, clothing, houses, things; the objectives of culture infinite—the quest of the mysteries and melodies of creation."[27]

MacKaye, who had developed and helped implement the Appalachian Trail, may have appeared an odd choice to present on the "Cultural Aspects of Regionalism" to poets and literary figures. But regionalism fused a Romantic literary imagining of place with descriptive positivist social science, which in the US tradition had been substantially influenced by the development of the natural sciences since the publication of Darwin's *On the Origin of Species* in the mid-nineteenth century.[28] MacKaye proposed all regional planning projects as syllogisms in which regionalism provided the major premise, the regional survey the minor premise, and the regional plan the conclusion.[29] Culture and biophysical systems were fused as conditioning factors that formed the unique characters of place and people.[30] They also celebrated enduring folk cultures that, like nature, could provide a solace of stability amid the dramatic changes of the early twentieth century.

On the last day of the Round Table on Regionalism, Odum and Roderick D. MacKenzie spoke on the "Sociological and Economic Aspects of Regionalism." MacKenzie, who had trained as a human ecologist with the University of Chicago School of Sociology, gave sobering statistics on the force of population concentration in urban areas throughout the country, along with the movement of people and goods.[31] He saw the urban challenge of security as a pressing issue amid the rupture of traditional communities through the individualization processes of urbanization. MacKenzie provocatively concluded, among the communitarians and agrarians, that the pressing metropolitan security challenge of "how to organize for stability and yet mobility" would certainly not be met "by going back and sitting around the old apple tree." Great migrations were arriving from Europe in the United States, and from the US South to the North, while regionalism and regional planning represented and projected essentially static land ideals. To the round table participants, MacKenzie asserted, "We will have to mobilize on the basis of movement and fluidity."[32] MacKenzie's position was fundamentally grounded in the metropolitanism endorsed by the New York Regional Planning Association, which Mumford and his RPAA colleagues had ideologically contested.[33]

MacKenzie's was a convincing argument, addressing the importance of transportation infrastructure and the economic structures of cities over the country's commodity trade-flow geographies, which centered on command functions, goods consumption markets, and jobs in cities, toward which population flows also traveled in pursuit of opportunity. In addition to these pull factors, push factors included agricultural overproduction, mechanization, and land tenancy, which had all been rural-to-urban migration factors in the West since eighteenth-century enclosure.[34] One could perhaps disagree with MacKenzie's socially focused identification of security as the central challenge from the circumstances he described, but the sociology was grounded in rigorous, evidence-based analysis. He speculated about interregional competition and the increased similarity of regions based on industrial spatial restructuring, in essence predicting the kinds of functionalist modeling that would characterize US regional planning in the 1950s.[35]

In the presentation that followed, Howard W. Odum invited the audience out of the city and back to his South. Like Roosevelt, Odum and his colleagues at the IRSS saw an opportunity to elaborate on Southern regionalism in the regional-national showcase provided by the round table. Odum began by summarizing MacKenzie's presentation as "theoretical," to which he proposed the organic complement, the "practical," because these aspects were "so interrelated that consideration of each is naturally an inseparable part of the whole."[36] Odum then listed many possible categorical criteria for regionalism, which he believed to be the essential lens through which to study local cultures to obtain better understanding of universal patterns and truths: "Regionalism might be conceived of as a cultural specialization within geographical and cultural bounds in an age which continually demands wider contacts and stabilization activities; or it may be a way of quality in a quantity world. Or again . . ."[37]

Regionalism for Odum was evergreen, his proposed shibboleth for a Southern future that was defined, like Whitman's United States in *Leaves of Grass*, by long lists of possibilities—and an equally long list of qualifiers for what it was not. Regionalism was not the "sentimental romanticism for the local area or for the historical period" that literary new regionalism offered, which he dismissed—stung, perhaps, by similar critiques of his own work—as "little more than the infatuation of the regionalists for their land and folk."[38] Odum cited historic examples of industrial regionalism in Germany, political regionalism in France, and economic regionalism in America, as well as other possible region-defining factors encompassing physiographic, geological, ethnological, topographical, or general ecological areas: "It is all of these and more, a totality in which all past historical experience . . . is utilized in the projection of regional planning of the future."[39] Historian George Tindall later reflected on Odum's regionalism as "a grandiose concept that must be grasped whole or not at all. . . . Whatever the value of the insights into objective reality, Odum had a new vision of the potentialities of regionalism."[40]

At the round table, Odum then pivoted from this broader abstracted discussion of the possibilities of regionalism to his preferred geographic example: the South. "In the explanation of Southern society, past and present, and to venture planning for the future . . . what neither the Nation nor the South seemed to comprehend in a practical way was the simple fact that the key to the whole situation was found in the fact that it was all a normal problem of social culture, essentially an American problem, and secondarily a Southern problem."[41] True, the South had problems to face, and in due time these would be resolved, but in the meantime, the nation also needed to provide patience and understanding. The South's "extraordinary, bi-racial, and economic elements" meant that the "problem of the new equilibrium" required "strong leadership, unusual courage, skillful adaptation, powerful reserve, as well as common sense and intelligent cooperation from the rest of the Nation." Here, as with regional planning, Odum conjured the ever-aspirational "equilibrium" as that promised and resolved future objective.

After his careful analysis, Odum asserted his conclusion that "not a single one" of the "major deficiencies and limitations" facing Southern status and resources "had been borne due to other than temporary, superficial, and remedial causes."[42] It was simple. Triumphant. With some vision, assistance, and balance, the South faced a great regional future in tandem with the nation.

At the very end of Odum's address, however, as if hidden away in appendixes, he also listed some "danger currents" that, if allowed to run their course, could lead to "radical change in the form and philosophy of Southern government and civilization." He warned of dangers that only expert analysis and planning could correct and help prevent: "the whole attitude and philosophy toward education and culture, crippling institutions of higher learning, minimizing the artistic and cultural values"; "some millions of poorer farmer folk neither economically or culturally self-supportive"; "the Southern cotton market economic crisis"; "several millions of Negroes whose status[was] changing afford[ing] media both for mob action on the part of the White South, as well as the basis for economic conflict." Odum listed these critiques of Southern culture matter-of-factly, neither attempting to identify the causes of these "currents" nor explaining exactly how regionalism or planning was going to prevent them from progressively evolving. Such warnings echoed Odum's later work, which invoked the fear of latent extremism in white Southern culture and Black "race consciousness" as undercurrents that threatened regional progress.[43]

For Odum, regionalism required a focus on the future potential of the South, not the traditional sectional grievances from the past that he saw his Agrarian contemporaries as continually airing. Nevertheless, he did mention them, in his own peculiar manner and regionalist framework. If regionalism was to draw on the past to plan for the future, perhaps agency for futurecraft could come in editing and reformulating that past.[44] The contrast with other Southern regional attitudes of the round table was illustrative of Odum's position.

One such contrasting figure was John Gould Fletcher, who traveled from London to present to the Round Table on Regionalism. The son of a wealthy Arkansas family, Fletcher had achieved significant success as an Imagist poet in the European expatriate community. In 1927, he returned to the South for a lecture tour, where he met with Donald Davidson and John Crowe Ransom at Vanderbilt University. They had formed a group of writers who called themselves "the Fugitives" but were also identified as the Southern Agrarians. Their famous volume *I'll Take My Stand* was published in 1930, including contributions from twelve prominent literary figures such as Robert Penn Warren and Allen Tate.

At the round table, Fletcher reiterated the Fugitive position against both economic industrialization and the associate cultural "cosmopolitanism," arguing that culture could not flourish in what he believed to be the misguided values of industrialism. He admonished the cosmopolitanism of New York and Chicago because "one cannot make a community cosmopolitan. . . . Each community should have its own way of looking at things; a way symbolized best by Patrick Geddes in the trilogy of place, work, folk."[45] For Fletcher, cosmopolitanism (a thinly veiled reference to social integration) must rest atop a strong regional culture if it is to produce "more and better universities, more and better books, plays, poems, music, painting, sculpture, architecture." He advocated against the valuing of cultural and commercial imports, which he broadly bundled as "more and better factories . . . Broadway successes, jazz bands, and Hollywood art-products."[46]

This South was a fiction, fully realized in popular perceptions of the period for a receptive Northern reading audience that "took 'folk' forms and from them wove modernist visions."[47] Fletcher continued, "We must get back to the point where we were before the Civil War, when we could produce our own local cultures, and could make them prevail. We must do something not to mend, but to end industrialism."[48] Southern Agrarians celebrated the antebellum South and its culture, in direct defiance of industrialism and the urban value system they associated with it.[49] Fletcher's address—presaging fellow Fugitive Donald Davidson's high-profile critique of federal government expansion into the South in his 1938 book *Attack on Leviathan: Regionalism and Nationalism in the United States*—confirmed Mumford's perhaps understated description of the group as "slightly reactionary." Such rhetoric notwithstanding, John Gould Fletcher was not wrong in seeing that regionalisms sought to "educate America with a principle alien to its whole historical development."[50] He predicted that issues of power, and their irrational configuration in politics as usual, would provide regionalists, certainly those in the South, with a sobering education in the 1930s. The fissures on the Southern regionalist front were apparent.

If participants at the round table shared some appreciation for planning, Thomas Jefferson, and the promise of regional planning to safeguard and nurture regionalism, for others, particularly the Southern literati, there were unaddressed issues of interregional histories and power dynamics that would not simply vanish in the new era regionalists called for. Offering a more colorful critique of the "engineering" that Mumford and his RPAA colleagues were promoting in trying to form a unified regionalist movement was *Virginia Quarterly Review* editor Stringfellow Barr, a traditionalist who would eventually launch the classics curriculum at St. John's College in Annapolis, Maryland. He elaborated on what he saw as a Southern "crisis of tradition" and why its intellectuals preferred "drinking instead of thinking": "Once the values of the Southerner seemed destroyed, and given the fact that the North's values seemed to him unattractive or merely fatuous, he had quite simply no values at all with which to think. Moreover, a number of Constitutional Amendments, backed up with Northern bayonets, forbade him to test his thinking with the appropriate laboratory experimentation. That crippled him still further. So with nostalgia in his heart, he took to his cups."[51] For his part, Donald Davidson later remarked on how Odum would eventually have to see that issues of Southern culture and economics were fundamentally political, whether called sectional or regional.[52]

Barr's analyses were refreshingly direct and undeniably reactionary. In a room otherwise filled with the great potentialities of a kind of symphonic national democracy, Barr offered a colorful postmortem of the section's past.[53]

> It has been observed . . . that the minute a community becomes self-conscious about its own peculiar culture, the culture is already undergoing an autopsy. . . . Or, in other words, if "Virginia" as a cultural region were still alive, this group here today would not find it possible to discuss regional culture in relation to Virginia. . . . If we as a "cultural region" become engrossed in the problem of how to achieve universal values in terms of our special environment, we should soon lose interest in a crusade to preserve regional culture. Whereupon, we should find ourselves in that happy state implied by the cynical observation I have just quoted: we should not be inclined to discuss regional culture because we would have it and take it for granted.[54]

Both Fletcher and Barr identified a tension not only in the various regional perspectives participating at the Round Table on Regionalism, but also in the very notion of "Jeffersonian planning" informed by regionalism. Regional planning was itself an odd combination of regionalism as sectional nostalgic cultural practice and the (then) forward-looking Progressive Era planning ideology.[55]

Such tensions would later play out in the "programmatic fragility" of the New Deal, in which "allegiance to Jeffersonian ideals inhibited planning," and program co-optation by powerful private national and local interests abounded.[56] The limits and limitations of planning either "secured or increased" corporate monopoly power.[57] The specter of totalitarianism in Europe was often brought up to oppose the perceived threat of federal planning omnipotence, but "there was also such a thing as *too little* (government) interference, especially in the eyes of those seeking basic social and economic reconstruction."[58] The fragility of regional planning required "dynamic equilibrium," in which, for example, the national ambitions of the multistate Tennessee River Basin development could somehow respect the local folk traditions of those whom the project was displacing. Further, although the Tennessee Valley Authority was celebrated as the optimal example of regional planning, its scope, ambition, and cost were only possible with national federal support and the national development political premium.[59] The RPAA and the Southern regionalists called on territorial folk culture for some conceptual latitude to accommodate these tensions. In the South, the balance of regionalism's dynamic equilibrium also required myth.[60]

Franklin Delano Roosevelt's homage to Jeffersonian planning for the new era at the 1931 Round Table on Regionalism presaged another address, given nearly seven years after it to the day. On July 4, 1938, Roosevelt announced the findings of the National Emergency Council's (NEC's) *Report on Economic Conditions of the South*: "It is my conviction that the South presents right now the nation's No. 1 economic problem—the nation's problem, not merely the South's. For we have an economic unbalance in the nation as a whole, due to this very condition of the South."[61] Roosevelt had assembled the NEC from his administration—Clark H. Foreman, Clifford J. Durr, and Arthur Goldschmidt—to write the report based on data gathered from leading Southern social scientists, particularly Howard W. Odum and his colleagues at the IRSS at the University of North Carolina.[62] Odum's regionalism grew out of a "very realistic examination of the southern region," with "special emphasis on the problems of deficiencies and question of capacity for more abundant development."[63] His opus *Southern Regions of the United States*, published two years prior in 1936, was an atlas of comparative social, economic, and geographic indexes illustrating the brutal circumstances of Southern poverty, ecological degradation, out-migration, and wasteful resource extraction without the appropriate technology to increase efficiency and wealth accumulation. This data was clearly meant for readers to draw the same conclusion as Roosevelt had.[64]

The report marked a "watershed" in national New Deal policy in the South, as the Roosevelt administration grew bolder in entering the Southern political sphere with economic restructuring policy.[65] In November 1938, a broad coalition of Southern Black and white supporters of the New Deal met in Birmingham, Alabama, to establish the Southern Conference for Human Welfare.[66] Odum viewed this organization as direct competition, particularly since he had, in January 1938, proposed a Council on Southern Regional Development, an independent organization featuring a twelve-year program and a $2 million budget to be raised from private individuals and foundations (much like the IRSS, he already ran). This council would focus on four general themes: race relations, land tenure and farm relations, economics and labor relations, and public relations and administration—not coincidentally, the same focuses Odum researched at his Institute for Research in Social Science at the University of North Carolina, thereby positioning him as the de facto leader of his proposed council.[67] Opposition arose, both from other Southern political groups insisting on a more ideologically rooted platform and from like-minded groups on how and who best to lead such planning efforts, scuttling Odum's plans.

Odum, who was known to be part of a minority of white Southern liberals, seemed to be an unlikely opponent of the NEC and its report.[68] Yet Odum was far from happy. In private letters, he wrote, "Between the Right Honorable FD (Roosevelt), the Southern Conference for Human Welfare, and twenty other groups that are literally taking the lead to do what the Council ought to do, I think I'll presently go heat-wave hay-wire!!!"[69] Odum held many grievances: Roosevelt's assignment of the report to NEC policymakers who had gathered information from Odum's own institute's work; the formation of the Southern Conference for Human Welfare, which Odum was not a part of and viewed as competition; and, finally, Roosevelt's devastating and decisive conclusion on the Southern condition. Roosevelt's national call for Southern action "cut clean across Odum's desire to move with only deliberate speed" in regional reform.[70] Odum's optimistic vision for the South's fertile potentials in a regional future were dragged back to a contemporary national problem, stirring all the sectional ghosts he had attempted to vanquish through regional science.

Roosevelt's 1938 speech recalled W. E. B. Du Bois's famous introduction in *The Souls of Black Folk*: "How does it feel to be a problem?"[71] Odum was comfortable as a Southern sociologist problematizing region and race, but not when the New Yorker president and his NEC infringed on the regional expertise and sovereignty of Odum's academic "empire."[72] He believed that Roosevelt's speech had defined the region in "Tobacco Road" sensationalism as a "missionary territory" to be converted.[73] Senator Byrd from Virginia was loudly silent on the Roosevelt assessment of the South, while other Southern leaders protested that the region's colonial conditions, such as freight rates and tariffs imposed from the North, were to blame for its social and economic circumstances.[74]

Roosevelt's 1938 address—influenced, and at times written, by those Southern industrialists he'd conjured at the Round Table on Regionalism—problematized the South to promote New Deal Keynesian developmentalism for the region.[75] It anticipated Harry Truman's "Four Points" speech the following decade, which, at a new scale of ambition, problematized global poverty as justification for what became the development industry launched worldwide in the second half of the century.[76] The NEC's report on the South also presaged the 1951 United Nations' *Measures for the Economic Development of Underdeveloped Countries* report, which broadly assigned countries, not merely economies, as underdeveloped.[77] Planning, particularly regional planning, served as a disciplining, rationalizing practice for state administration and emerging market preparation to meet the comprehensive challenges of countrywide underdevelopment territorial conditions spanning rural and urban spheres. Amid the crisis of capitalism and the vertiginous international economic and social restructuring of the period, the various expressions of regional planning were strategies of "spatial Keynesianism," widely accepted around the world as the appropriate response to these changes.[78] But before World War II, the South, the Midwest, and the Far West of the United States served as laboratories to construct regional planning projects and ambitions nested in entrenched, decentralized regionalist cultures.

While much was made of the rivalries of Southern regionalists versus Agrarians, University of North Carolina versus Vanderbilt University, sociology versus literature, New South versus Old South, etc., in truth, the overlaps of agreement outweighed any discord.[79] Donald Davidson noted that Odum had raised no issues with their publication of *I'll Take My Stand* until he believed that Benjamin Kenrick was threatening his position as head of the Southern Regional Council in 1934, at which point Odum deployed the accusation of a perceived Agrarian reactionary attitude that stood in the South's way forward. In their correspondence, Odum invited Davidson to write up his critique of regionalism for a special issue of *Social Forces* that same year, and he gladly accepted.[80] In his acceptance letter, Davidson confided that for his first publication in a sociological journal, he would appreciate the proper guidance for any unfamiliar literature criticism perspective. But he continued, "It isn't so odd, after all, to be bursting out in a sociological way. For years I have been wondering about this polite poaching in which we have all been engaged—with the sociologists becoming literary, and the literary people becoming sociological. I am glad that it can cease to be poaching and become a frank interchange of views on a ground where we can all meet."[81]

Davidson and Odum would later engage in similar spirit during "Why the Modern South Has a Great Literature?," a talk at Mississippi State College in 1953.[82] Native son William Faulkner had won the Nobel Prize in Literature four years earlier, and Davidson asked Odum whether his concept of regionalism and Southern underdevelopment could account for Faulkner's success at the vanguard of the international literary world despite his origins in Mississippi, as opposed to Ohio or Massachusetts.[83] Odum could offer no explanation, simply adding his admiration and noting that he shared a particular insight into Faulkner's world, having taught school in rural Mississippi after graduating from Emory College.

Odum and Faulkner were among the most famous Southern intellectuals of the first part of the twentieth century: each sharing a kind of defensive, loving ambivalence for the region, each with a shared sense of urgency that Guy Johnson later described as a commitment both to folkways and to change that remained cautious for fear that progress might destroy "something precious that ought to be preserved."[84] Perhaps each might also have had a "premonition that time was short for him (them) as well as for the South."[85] Odum clearly borrowed from Faulkner's stream-of-consciousness writing (without Faulkner's literary talent) to produce his unique portraiture technique, a "poetic sociology"—another divide that Odum hoped his applied social science could bridge.[86] W. E. B. Du Bois and Zora Neale Hurston also strived for social science / literary achievement, reaching varying degrees of success.[87] But Faulkner avoided addressing any sociological issues, or regionalism in general directly, believing that they were "only coincidental to the story."[88] It's hard to imagine *Absalom, Absalom!* summarized into any kind of five-year regional plan.[89]

But these were the worlds and disciplines that Odum's Southern regionalism attempted to traverse, if not unify. Odum synthesized a broad range of literatures into sociological textbooks, and he wrote across social science and fiction. The colleagues that he recruited to his institute in Chapel Hill researched socioeconomic phenomena in the South with a clear-eyed reformist view, but with literature, Odum could take Victorian "refuge in [an] idealized vision of ahistorical innocence" to "resolve his confusion about southern history."[90] Carey McWilliams referred to this as the regionalists' "will to be naïve," an "anachronistic," "soft sentimentality unsuited to the rough social and economic climate of the 1930s," across the literature, social science, and the arts of the periods.[91] How could one operationalize the broad cultural spectrum of regionalism into the conventional parameters of planning?

When trying to apply the Geddesian logic to developing his Greater London Plan of 1944, Sir Patrick Abercrombie felt cursed with the overwhelming charge: "There was a time when it seemed only necessary to shake up into a bottle the German town extension plan, the Parisian Boulevard and Vista, and the English Garden Village, to a mechanical mixture which might be applied to every town in the country.... Pleasing dream! First shattered by Geddes as he emerged from his Outlook Tower in the frozen north to produce that nightmare of complexity, the Edinburgh Room at the great Town Planning Exhibition of 1910."[92] In this regional planning, who was dreaming and who was shattering? The Geddesian charge to survey regions through conceptual and disciplinary tools, now updated in the US interwar period to include literature, the arts, sciences, and history itself, provided a very broad frame through which to consider regional planning in many different guises.[93] For Odum and his Institute for Research in Social Science, and perhaps its legacy, regional planning became a kind of synthetic *final* social science, inheriting what Comtean positivist sociology had long believed its all-encompassing research domain of *everything* social, with an even wider field of vision.[94] And, of course, the "aid of the poet."

"Howard Odum in front of a reconstructed cabin on his farm. Late 1920s or early 1930s, judged by the 'hard straw hat' because for a while it was a 'trademark' with him." Howard Washington Odum Papers, Wilson Special Collections Library, UNC–Chapel Hill.

CHAPTER 2

A REGULAR, ORTHODOX, ALMOST PROFESSIONAL SOUTHERNER

INSTITUTIONS, FOUNDATIONS, AND NETWORKS

Southern regionalism was Southern institutionalism. Regionalism and the regional planning it would inspire emerged in distinct cultural movements across Europe and in the United States, within interregional differences at the subnational level as well. In the United States, Odum's University of North Carolina group was trained in the national intellectual traditions that saw the social sciences emerge from the Gilded Age into Progressive Era reform through the pragmatism of William James and John Dewey and the institutionalism of Thorstein Veblen.[1] Dewey believed that applying the rigor of the scientific method to the examination of society might open new avenues to study and resolve the social problems that accompanied the transitional moment of industrial modernism in the late nineteenth and early twentieth centuries. Viewing society as a great laboratory, Dewey saw social planning as "the only course which could help democracy survive in an industrial age," and institutional education as "the way to organize for social planning."[2]

In contrast to the dominant laissez-faire tradition, Veblen's evolutionary economics were considered unorthodox due to his holistic anthropological application of a social Darwinist frame of progress from "savagery" and "barbarism" toward "civilization," which was reflected in slow institutional change. For Veblen, institutional behavior provided the clearest insight concerning economic systems, and, dialectically, he reasoned that "social systems governed economic behavior."[3] Veblen celebrated technology as a central force for industrial change, particularly the field of engineering. The force of his ideas later influenced and justified public investment in building both physical infrastructure and institutions during the New Deal, and shaped the broader ideology of national planning and social engineering for comprehensive progress.[4]

Howard Odum was a network agent who actively channeled these currents southward, his impassioned belief in reformist academic institutionalism forming the core tenet of his regionalism. Odum moved not only in the top social science academic circles at the turn of the century—having earned entrée through his elite psychology and sociology doctoral studies—but also within philanthropic foundation networks looking to academia to help inform their social reforms through social science institution-building investments.[5] Odum reported on Southern conditions and, perhaps not always knowingly, extended a developmental ideology for industrial capital expansion and public Keynesian economic investment. These "new state spaces," as termed by sociologist Neil Brenner, emerged during the crises of the interwar period and were advanced as responses to such crises by state practices of regional planning. Odum participated as a second-tier actor in the Washington brain trust that informed policy for Hoover and Roosevelt. Odum's position—as regional outsider within the national inner circle, as Southerner in the belly of the very "Leviathan" of which Donald Davidson warned, as hesitant espouser of social planning and social action in cautionary deference to the slow, generational, evolution-paced change of a regionalism based in folklore—illustrates precisely the complexity and contradictions of this transitional period that regional planning was fashioned to tenuously encompass. This morass was arguably even more contorted in the South, where regionalism was even further from the progressive planning to which it was attached in the North.

Odum was a man of letters—literally. His archives at the University of North Carolina are filled with epistolary documentation of his prolific communication and orchestration of national political, academic, and philanthropic networks on all manner of subjects, ranging from international regionalism to purebred cow husbandry.[6] These communication networks guided his institutional and academic aspirations and informed his scholarship. Odum used the relationships between his Institution for Research in Social Science and Northern philanthropy groups as a model for what a regional-national planning frame could look like, where national grants would fund regional research and planning initiatives. The history of Odum's research and training, institutional affiliation, and the North-South geography and politics he traversed establishes the background for the work conducted by Odum and his colleagues in articulating regionalism and social planning throughout the 1930s.

ODUM, BAILEY, HALL, AND GIDDINGS

The history of Southern regionalism unfolded simultaneously with Howard W. Odum's life and career in the Jim Crow era, and the transitioning and recycling of historic patterns throughout the region. Odum was born in Bethlehem, Georgia, in 1884, seven years after the end of Reconstruction, which had emerged after the Civil War in response to Southern states' newly legislated Black Codes, designed to control the labor of formerly enslaved peoples and restrict their landownership. Despite President Andrew Jackson's veto, Congress sent federal troops to these states to arrest this regression to prewar governance.[7] Beginning with the Reconstruction Act of 1867, African American men gained new rights to vote in elections and to hold office in Southern legislatures and the US Congress.[8] The ratification of the Fourteenth and Fifteenth Amendments to the US Constitution during this period guaranteed equal protection to formerly enslaved people, along with the right of formerly enslaved men to vote.[9] But this historic moment was short-lived. By 1877, a national compromise awarded Republican Rutherford B. Hayes the presidency in exchange for the removal from South Carolina, Florida, and Louisiana of federal troops protecting Reconstruction gains. The withdrawal marked the beginning of the reactionary Jim Crow era, which lasted, technically, until the US Supreme Court ruling *Brown v. Board of Education* legally enforced the integration of Southern public school systems in 1954. This was also, perhaps fittingly, the year in which Odum passed away.

Odum was born into a Methodist family, and his father's family identified with the humble Southern yeoman tradition. His maternal grandfather, in contrast, had been a major in the Confederate cavalry, owned land, and accumulated wealth, only to have it all disappear by the end of the Civil War.

Odum's mother ingrained in him this history and the family's bitterness at their loss, hoping that through a genteel upbringing and education, Howard might recover the family's wealth and status. The dual Southern myths of cavalier and yeoman thus competed within Odum from a very young age.[10] He wrote of his early family life in idealized portraiture, viewing historical events and conceptualizing the South through his personal experience, and much of his work became a collage of autobiography and selective social science recounted through an aspiring literary voice. This scholarly bricolage, "whether derived from his family's experience or projected back upon it . . . is the face that Odum turned upon all manner of relations within the Southern society and upon regional-national relations."[11] To understand these projections, one must consider the life events that were formative for Odum and, to a large degree, determined the course of his intellectual career.

From Bethlehem, Odum and family moved to neighboring Oxford, Georgia, in 1897, where he studied at the Methodist Emory College. Upon graduating in 1904, Odum traveled west to Oxford, Mississippi, for graduate study in classics at the University of Mississippi. There, his "passion shifted from Sophocles to social science, from Greek literature to black song."[12] He took Thomas Pearce Bailey Jr.'s seminar, titled Psychology of the Negro Problem, which introduced him to the period's sociological and psychological understandings of social evolution and race. Bailey exerted a profound influence on Odum and sparked his intellectual interest in the social sciences. Inspired by this foundation, Odum began to document and record African American folklore, albeit without much interest in the social conditions out of which the songs and legends sprung, instead habitually describing their origins as mysterious and unknown.[13] Throughout his graduate career, however, Odum witnessed and participated in the Progressive Era's professionalization of the social sciences, grounded in the Progressive faith in their potential for transformative human improvement.[14] This professionalization ultimately resulted in "a social science bold enough to commit itself wholeheartedly to social betterment, and sufficiently established in its institutional academic setting to sustain that commitment."[15] Although Odum's interest in Southern Black folklore remained throughout his career, he nonetheless generally reserved the ameliorative potential he saw in regionalism for Southern whites.[16]

Thomas Pearce Bailey Jr., a South Carolina native, received his PhD from the University of South Carolina and subsequently studied with G. Stanley Hall as a fellow in psychology at Clark University in Massachusetts in 1892. Under Hall's mentorship, Bailey's work focused on character formation and the "psychology of character." Bailey's influences ranged from John Stuart Mill to Harvard psychologist William James, as well as his strong belief in

"Protestant Christianity, social justice, and democracy" and view of history as an evolving progressive movement.[17] After completing his fellowship, Bailey taught education at the University of California, Berkeley and the University of Chicago before arriving in Mississippi in 1903.[18]

Like many Progressive Era academics, Bailey "believed the objective presentation of facts would inspire leaders to alleviate racial tension and promote social stability," although such approaches nevertheless "required the maintenance of enlightened white supremacy."[19] In 1909, however, he was pressured to leave his position at the University of Mississippi for daring to express the slightest hint of concern regarding prevailing social and economic conditions in his studies of race issues, even if that concern was largely centered on Southern white education. Bailey adhered to the New South Creed, which endorsed education and industry to "rationalize" poor whites against irrational populism. The creed proposed that Southern renewal and the renaissance of antebellum aristocracy would be best attained through the Northern mechanisms of capitalism, industry, and educational institutions.[20] It retained Southern Victorian concerns pitting "civilization" against "barbarism," insisting that educational uplift was only possible for poor whites. Segregation was accepted and endorsed as a moral necessity, and consensus held that Black education should focus on superficial issues such as punctuality.[21]

In 1914, Bailey published *Race Orthodoxy in the South, and Other Aspects of the Negro Problem*, which was as stark a text on white supremacy ideology as the period would produce. The book included a list of expressions cited by "the Southern people" as their racial creed, with Bailey describing statements such as "blood will tell," "no social equality," "no political equality," and "only Southerners understand the negro problem" as indicating "the leadings of Providence."[22] Historian C. Vann Woodward later observed that Bailey's book expressed the racial ideology of white Southerners with "such candor and accuracy that it may serve as the best available summary."[23] Sociologist Robert E. Park, then a recent arrival at the University of Chicago, reviewed the book, noting that while Bailey appeared to take issue with the crudeness of this credo in its "present shape," he nonetheless apparently accepted its "underlying meaning" as correct. Park concluded that Bailey's book "may be said, on the whole, to be an interpretation and a justification of this 'underlying meaning.'"[24] The book's other essays included an analysis of Nicholas Worth's *The Southerner*, described by Park as a sociological novel "in the form of an autobiography, or rather an autobiography written in the form of a novel."[25]

The influences of Bailey's work on Odum's future work were manifold. Perhaps inspired by *Race Orthodoxy*, Odum often deployed his own autobiography, which he cast in a sociological light in his writings, most clearly in the 1930 *An American Epoch: Southern Portraiture in the National Picture*. This fusion of the sociological and autobiographical formed the basis for his portraiture method, which he would repeatedly be asked to defend to funding agencies and the national sociologist community.[26] Bailey's influence on Odum was also reflected in the academic attention both scholars paid to the common Southern white ideology, which they believed they needed to articulate, translate, refine, justify, critique (very slightly, mostly for its coarseness), and, ultimately, affirm. Bailey's *Race Orthodoxy* defined the contours of the racial creed system that served as the foundation for the ideology Odum imagined as "Southern folkways."

Bailey sent a copy of the book to W. E. B. Du Bois in November 1914, along with a letter asking him for his thoughts. In the space of a few short paragraphs, Bailey managed to be apologetic, patronizing, and presumptuous all at once. After calling Du Bois an idealist, Bailey continued, "And why do I fear your adverse reaction? Because you are the one colored man for whose judgement I have the most profound respect, and I fear that you will be unable to put yourself at the angle that will enable you to see the problems as a disinterested-interested student of character sees it."[27] In this last phrase in particular, one can observe signs of Hall's influence on Bailey's thinking concerning race and character. Bailey signed off by wishing Du Bois success, even though he could not feel that Du Bois "and other like-minded men of the Spirit really appreciate the underground forces working against you successfully."[28] At this point, Du Bois had already written *The Souls of Black Folk* and *The Philadelphia Negro*, cofounded the National Association for the Advancement of Colored People (NAACP), founded the Niagara Movement in opposition to Booker T. Washington's 1895 Atlanta Compromise accepting Black inferiority, and established his prolific research program at Atlanta University.[29] Needless to say, Du Bois was intimately acquainted with the forces—whether apparent or "underground"—working to oppress African Americans and Black people in the US South and worldwide.

Following Bailey's example, Odum went north to Clark University to study psychology with G. Stanley Hall for his first PhD, which he completed in 1909.[30] Hall's interest in Odum's work on Southern Black folklore arose from his belief in the psychological study of the "contemporary primitive." Odum had read Hall's 1904 book *Adolescence*, in which he warned that "modern intellectualism was destroying the possibility of unmediated experience."[31] Instead, Hall believed that "children, pre-Modern medieval knights, and contemporary primitives" were the models that needed greater study to recover pre-Modern perspectives.[32] Hall arrived at his psychological and nascent anthropological interests by way of Freud and the modern anthropology research from Papua New Guinea.[33] He introduced Odum to the work of Wilhelm Wundt, with whom Hall had studied in Leipzig, Germany, in the late 1870s. An organic psychologist, Wundt was also interested in the "child soul," what he termed the "folk soul," as an important perspective to document before children's modern corruption. In 1902, Wundt published the first volume of what would become a ten-volume megalith on the psychology of folk titled *Elemente der Völkerpsychologie*, which would later inform Odum's proposal for folk sociology.[34]

Hall was a strong personality with many international connections.[35] He invited Sigmund Freud to lecture at Clark for an international psychology conference in September 1909, which also included anthropologists Franz Boas and Alexander Chamberlain and psychologist William James. Odum attended this conference, later reflecting on the importance of the experience for him: "The group might be called an example of irreversible

Psychology Conference Group, Clark University, September 1909. *First row, left to right*: Franz Boas, E. B. Titchener, William James, William Stern, Leo Burgerstein, G. Stanley Hall, Sigmund Freud, Carl G. Jung, Adolf Meyer, H. S. Jennings. *Second row*: C. E. Seashore, Joseph Jastrow, J. McK. Cattell, E. F. Buchner, E. Katzenellenbogen, Ernest Jones, A. A. Brill, Wm. H. Burnham, A. F. Chamberlain. *Third row*: Albert Schinz, J. A. Magni, B. T. Baldwin, F. Lyman Wells, G. M. Forbes, E. A. Kirkpatrick, Sandor Ferenczi, E. C. Sanford, J. P. Porter, Sakyo Kanda, Hikoso Kakise. *Fourth row*: G. E. Dawson, S. P. Hayes, E. B. Holt, C. S. Berry, G. M. Whipple, Frank Drew, J. W. A. Young, L. N. Wilson, K. J. Karlson, H. H. Goddard, H. I. Klopp, S. C. Fuller. Howard Washington Odum Papers, Wilson Special Collections Library, UNC–Chapel Hill.

change—there will never be another such group."[36] Hall also maintained a friendship with the eccentric Scottish sociologist and regional planner Patrick Geddes, to whose influential work he also introduced Odum. Hall was a consummate institutionalist. He was the first president of the American Psychology Association and one of the founders of its *American Journal of Psychology*. As president of Clark University, he advocated for higher education institutions as social engineers and the central agents of improvement for society.[37] Hall's "vision that the modern research university, established on German principles of graduate study and underwritten by private or state wealth, should shape American society and that university-builders should see themselves as social engineers" would prove highly influential on Odum's own pursuits.[38] Indeed, Hall's "Comtean vision" for the leadership of an intellectual elite to guide social betterment deeply affected Odum and his vision for social work and applied sociology.[39]

After leaving Clark, Odum went to Columbia University in New York to pursue a second PhD in sociology with Franklin H. Giddings. Giddings, regarded as one of the "four founders" of US sociology, was the first full professor and chair of Columbia's sociology department.[40] He was an evolutionist and a positivist who believed that quantitative empiricism should provide the methodological grounding for the discipline.[41] His principal theoretical contribution was the "consciousness of kind" as an innate, collective, and associative urge and sympathy within social groups.[42] While the sociology departments at Columbia and Chicago would develop competitions of both theory and personality during the period, each incorporated Giddings's consciousness of kind as a starting point for researching new polyethnic urban immigrant communities in Northern cities of the period.[43] For Odum, the concept helped him justify the cultural contours and scale of his Southern regionalism, allowing him to argue that "the region finds its boundaries overlapping state lines or rivers and valleys in accordance with the natural and common indices basic to regional homogeneity in question."[44] The issue of precision in mapping cultural boundaries would continue to frustrate Odum throughout his career, but the notion of a homogeneity index, first introduced by Giddings in his 1901 work *Inductive Sociology*, provided both a justification and a conceptual compass for regionalist research.[45]

Odum's Southern homogeneity index was based on his research around Oxford, Mississippi, and Oxford and Covington, Georgia, all of which were small towns in rural surroundings that provided the folklore traditions and social patterns he was looking for. He later distributed letters and surveys to similarly sized small towns by mail. This tautological method confirmed and secured Odum's rather simple preconceived notions about Southern white and Black folklore. He elided research in Atlanta, where W. E. B. Du Bois had been conducting his surveys since the turn of the century, and in other urban centers that might show "inconvenient evidence ... with its black professional classes and their distinguished institutions and neighborhoods."[46] This selective rural vision later carried into the Southern regionalist projects at Odum's Institute for Research in Social Science. Historian Daniel Rodgers notes the tension inherent in this approach: "That this narrow slice of the South *was* the South represented no less partial a statement ... than the one it so quickly replaced, and it bleached out almost as many of the region's complexities and contradictions."[47] He concludes, "Odum was too good a sociologist not to know an ideal type when he helped construct one."[48] Odum's "South" was always primarily conceptual, but specifically comprised the Southeastern states of the Old Confederacy, including Kentucky and excluding Texas.[49]

Odum completed his PhD at Columbia in 1910 and published that dissertation, titled "Social and Mental Traits of the Negro," in the same year. In it, Odum sought to scientifically essentialize the African American biological and social limitations and pathologies that his Southern upbringing and academic training had ingrained in him.[50] Odum was initially unable to secure an academic position in the South following his graduation from Columbia and instead took a position with the Philadelphia Bureau of Municipal Research to conduct a survey of Black schoolchildren. Still insistent on racial biological differences, Odum explained in his report that the students showed promise despite those differences. Moreover, evidencing Odum's reluctance to address research conducted by African American scholars, his study essentially repeated the social study Du Bois had conducted during his research for *The Philadelphia Negro* fifteen years earlier, making Du Bois's work "probably the first sociological research to be replicated."[51] Such odd after-the-fact surrogacy would come to define Odum's professional relationship with Du Bois.[52]

Having completed two PhD degrees, Odum, "possessed of what was probably the finest social science education in the United States at that time," or at least what was then considered to be so, made no subsequent attempts to critically reflect on or update that education.[53] For example, he did not study in Europe, as contemporaries did.[54] Historian Allen Tullos has described the social sciences canon in which Odum was trained as "an undigested amalgam of psychological and social science theories, largely from an antiquated, organic worldview," with a "near-fatalistic and frequently racist view of the slowness of cultural change."[55] Moving forward, Odum's "peculiar blend of pre–First World War sociology" steadfastly refused influence from European academics such as "Weber, Durkheim, Pareto, Tönnies, [and] adaptations of Marx."[56] Nonetheless, although Odum may have interpreted and deployed his professional training in eclectic and sometimes confused ways, it still reflected the foundational assumptions of his elite Northern education. He took this "intellectual mélange to the South" and, at least throughout the 1920s, was able to apply it within the schema of Southern institutional politics with only a few glitches, also successfully attracting Northern philanthropic investments to fund his ambitions. Odum's arrival at the University of North Carolina in 1920 marked the beginning of his successful, prolific career there. The intervening decade of the 1910s, however, would prove bumpy.

CHAPEL HILL, *SOCIAL FORCES*, AND THE INSTITUTE FOR RESEARCH IN SOCIAL SCIENCE

In 1912, Odum returned south to accept a position at the University of Georgia (UGA) as an educational sociologist. There he met Eugene Cunningham Branson, who had just established the UGA Department of Rural Economics and Sociology that same year. Branson also helped develop the university's extension program, which included county-by-county surveys of rural economic and sociological conditions. Branson and Thomas Woofter Jr. were the leading rural sociologists of the period seeking to adapt the Wisconsin model of committed university community service and outreach to Southern universities.[57] Similar agricultural extension programs were established throughout the South prior to World War I to study issues of agricultural marketing, land tenure, and rural credit systems.[58] Odum was drawn to Branson's rural reform interest and enthusiasm, as well as his focus on local community development as the scale for effecting cumulative statewide change.[59] Two years later, in 1914, Branson moved to Chapel Hill, where he was charged with developing the University of North Carolina Department of Rural Economics and Sociology, along with a new school of social science that the university was planning. Branson would go on to study rural cooperative development and its basis in Danish folklore in Denmark in the early 1920s.[60] Upon Branson's arrival in Chapel Hill, he entreated Odum, whom he viewed as a kindred spirit, to join his North Carolina adventure. Odum would eventually do so, although he first took a detour to Atlanta.

In the early part of the twentieth century, Southern elites accepted the role of the federal government and external aid through the limited channels of social welfare and relief via groups such as the Army Corps of Engineers and the Red Cross, which did not disrupt local political or economic regimes.[61] Odum served in World War I as state director of social work for the Georgia Red Cross chapter. At the end of 1918, he accepted a

Howard W. Odum lecturing in the Regionalism Lab at the University of North Carolina at Chapel Hill in the 1930s. Howard Washington Odum Papers, Wilson Special Collections Library, UNC–Chapel Hill.

position as dean of the School of Liberal Arts for his alma mater Emory, now a university located at its new campus in Atlanta.[62] Groomed as an institutionalist since his time with Hall, Odum quickly took to the administrative tasks at Emory, but his fast-paced, ambitious plans to reform the university with new curricular ideas did not sit well with the conservative Methodist chancellor Warren A. Candler.[63] In 1920, Harry Woodburn Chase, Odum's Clark University classmate and newly appointed president of the University of North Carolina at Chapel Hill, reached out with an invitation to join the faculty there as professor of Sociology and to direct the newly formed School of Public Welfare. Odum, deeply frustrated with the ideological and administrative tensions at Emory, enthusiastically accepted.[64]

The 1920s were the decade in which North Carolina surpassed Massachusetts as the nation's leader in industrial textile production value, and the South was courting Northern industries with a cheap, plentiful nonunionized labor supply.[65] Against this background, "it seemed natural enough, in 1920, for Massachusetts-born, New England–educated Harry Woodburn

Chase to assume presidency of the University of North Carolina" and lead the university's mission to produce the workforce for the newly industrializing state.[66] In his inaugural speech, Chase posed the challenge to the university that he believed all industrial societies encountered: Would it serve "machine or man" when facing the future? Chase envisioned a middle way. The South, with "her sturdy respect of human and spiritual values," had the opportunity to transform industrial efficiency into a humane endeavor and to employ industry as "a great instrument for achieving the ideals and aspirations of democracy itself."[67] Chase's appeal to the university, and perhaps to the entire South, endorsed a new industrialism in what he referred to as the Southern tradition: efficient, democratic, humane. It was the kind of overture that Franklin Delano Roosevelt, then New York's governor, would incorporate into his address to the University of Virginia Round Table on Regionalism in the following decade, and one that Odum internalized whenever possible. Chase's was a discourse of social engineering, proposing what historian Allen Tullos has called "habits of industry" in terms he hoped were culturally meaningful in the South.

After World War I, social conditions began to change in the South thanks to the late arrival of the Progressive Era, during which "the public service concept of government became firmly established. . . . State councils of social agencies and schools of public welfare and of social work were created; the professionalization of educators, social workers, and welfare specialists gained momentum; and the first modern universities began to emerge in the region."[68] The ameliorative spirit of social improvement, with its accompanying interest in knowledge for control, imbued both the social sciences and social work of the period.[69] These social sciences, however, still lagged behind in the South. Historian Dewey Grantham notes that, with the notable exceptions of W. E. B. Du Bois at Atlanta University and Monroe N. Work at the Tuskegee Institute, there were few examples for social science in the South beyond history, psychology, and the rural economics and sociology credited to Branson, who tended not to confront traditional Southern conservative views on labor issues. Indeed, universities in the former Confederate states awarded only ten PhD degrees in the social sciences prior to 1920, nine of which were history degrees.[70]

Such challenges notwithstanding, Southern universities began to respond to the increasingly evident needs arising from this confluence of municipal reform and emerging public welfare and social work services. These arenas, like the region's burgeoning industrial sector, required workers, and economic expectations for both individuals and institutions were rising in parallel. Even the former Confederate states, like North Carolina, could not avoid these tides; in 1917, for example, the North Carolina Conference of

Social Welfare had passed legislation for a relatively progressive county-unit welfare system despite predominantly conservative public opinion.

Many of these reformist energies converged in the early 1920s at the University of North Carolina, where Chase launched a frenzied transformation that included new Departments of Commerce, Economics, Public Welfare, Sociology, Journalism, and Music, as well as the formation of a scholarly university press.[71] Between 1920 and 1924, enrollment at the University of North Carolina more than doubled (from 1,200 to 2,500), and in 1922, the university joined the University of Virginia as only the second Southern member of the prestigious Association of American Universities.[72] Chase understood that the school's New South aspirations for higher education institutional development were aligned with the state's industrialization processes. He also knew that the social sciences needed to be part of the plan, so he offered a job to his friend Howard Odum to found and lead the new sociology department and the School of Public Welfare.

Odum, a charismatic institutional reformer in the spirit of G. Stanley Hall, arrived in North Carolina like "the onslaught of a cyclone."[73] For an opportunist like Odum, with his Southern origins and elite Northern university social science credentials and network connections, the University of North Carolina was an ideal site for synchronizing his own professional ambitions with the university's aspirations to national recognition and prestige. Yet while Chase and Odum viewed the university as a leader for social change, North Carolina and the South were in less of a hurry. Chase, who already had to manage university trustee concerns regarding his reform agenda, mildly cautioned Odum to lead the School of Public Welfare with "a spirit of social mindedness," hoping for something sounding more like a minister than a Eugene V. Debs.[74] Odum immediately launched into a cascade of projects to promote the social sciences in the South.

In 1922, after helping establish the School of Public Welfare and the Department of Sociology, Odum established the *Journal of Social Forces* (shortened in 1925 simply to *Social Forces*) on the premise that "the South needs criticism and severe criticism."[75] Historian James Cobb notes that the journal was "the foremost outlet for such criticism among reform-minded southern academics and intellectuals for at least a generation, and it drew fire from conservatives, not only in North Carolina, but throughout the South."[76] The journal was to be the "primary instrument for Odum's plan of shaking open the Southern mind."[77] Following the front matter, which included editorials and articles, the journal structure also included section headings for "Teaching and Research in the Social Sciences," "Inter-State Reports from the Fields of Public Welfare and Social Work," "The Community and Neighborhood," "Church and Religion," "Inter-Racial Cooperation,"

"Government and Public Affairs," "Social Industrial Relationships," and "Library and Work Shop" for book reviews. These research areas would also become the principal interests for the Institute for Research in Social Science.

To honor his mentor, Odum invited Franklin Giddings to write the journal's inaugural article in 1922. In the inaugural editorial, Odum declared, "Social problems constitute today the basis of intellectual tension, as did science and theology in other decades.... With all that has been done and is being done, a beginning has scarcely been made, whether it be in teaching the social sciences, in making adequate studies and researches, or in interpreting the studies to the people."[78] This sermon-like tone would inflect Odum's *Social Forces* editorials throughout the 1920s, which were less "careful, scientific expositions" than "patently moralistic essays" and "sweeping admonishments to change."[79] Nevertheless, the journal quickly became a widely respected social science publication for both the region and the nation.[80]

In the ameliorative spirit of social improvement that defined much of his own social science training of the late Progressive Era, Odum made it clear that the journal would use social science to "teach the people."[81] He set out to critique Southern fundamentalisms and the self-satisfied lethargy, boastful mediocrity, and religious demagoguery that he believed social science had the power to help correct and evolve.[82] *Social Forces* served as a platform for Odum to articulate his moderate critiques, in conversation with colleagues from across the South and the nation, concerning issues of race, community, mill towns, social work, regionalism, and planning.

Under the guidance of Chase and Odum, the long-awaited social science institute, which Eugene Branson had enjoined Odum to be part of in 1914, finally moved forward in 1924 after ten years of delay. Odum, who enjoyed recognized status within the country's sociology and philanthropy networks—particularly in New York, thanks to his time as a student of Giddings at Columbia (one of the "F. G. boys," as Dorothy Ross calls them)—was the fulcrum of this culmination.[83] Regional research necessitated "extensive extra-regional resources" that Odum was extremely successful in securing.[84] The intervening decade since Branson's invitation had seen the First World War and the numerous challenges and surprises it precipitated, not least of which involved war planning. The capacity for proactive planning, grounded in a greater understanding across a multitude of fields, quickly came to be viewed as a national necessity, including by the country's top philanthropists.[85] To address the challenges of the age, economic intelligence, broadly construed, was required, and this quest prompted a surge of institutional responses across sectors, from the establishment of the Brookings Institution to the founding of the National Bureau of Economic Research.

The postwar fallout also induced existing institutions to shift or expand their focus. One such expansion was undertaken by the John D. Rockefeller Foundation, founded by the Standard Oil magnate, his son (John D. Rockefeller Jr.), and his associate Frederick Taylor Gates. The Rockefeller Foundation, which had secured its charter from the State of New York in 1913, had originally funded public health and medical research, but following the war, it launched a new initiative to "make the social sciences its chief objective." In 1922, the Laura Spelman Rockefeller Memorial—first incorporated as a general philanthropic fund in 1918 in honor of Rockefeller's late wife—was reenvisioned, its new mission being the promotion of social science research throughout the country.[86] This new mission was supported by a substantial gift from Rockefeller, who had expanded the memorial's original endowment of approximately $13 million by an additional $60 million in 1921.

Beardsley Ruml, who had completed his PhD in psychology at the University of Chicago in 1917, was appointed as director of the fund and its redirected vision in 1922. Under Ruml's leadership, the memorial distributed approximately $41 million between 1922 and 1929 to fund multidisciplinary research, with emphases on "realistic studies" of "concrete social phenomena" to enable a "united attack on social problems."[87] Institutional recipients included the University of Chicago for the study of urban community, Harvard University and Radcliffe College for economic and legal research in international relations, the University of Wisconsin for studies of rural tenancy and landownership, and the University of North Carolina for social, economic, and governmental research in the South.[88]

Ruml had been working, informally, since early 1923 with Charles Merriam—then president of the American Political Science Association and a professor at Ruml's alma mater, the University of Chicago—and a group of social scientists from various national associations to develop a better infrastructure for funding, integrating, and promoting social science research.[89] Their ambitions would be formally incorporated in December 1924 as the Social Science Research Council (SSRC). Also in 1924, Ruml came into contact with Odum through their shared network of elite academic and philanthropic connections, and they first met with University of North Carolina president Chase at a hotel in Charlotte in May of that year.[90] Impressed with Odum's enthusiasm and Chase's leadership at the university, Ruml saw promise in the idea of a regional social science research institute.[91] Soon after, Odum successfully obtained a grant from the Laura Spelman Rockefeller Memorial for $97,500 over three years to launch and fully fund the Institute for Research in Social Science (IRSS), the first of its kind, with the aim to conduct the "cooperative study of problems in the general field of social science, arising out of State and regional conditions."[92]

Grants from the memorial to the University of North Carolina would total nearly $500,000 over the next several years, which earned Odum a great deal of institutional independence for funding his projects.[93]

Raymond B. Fosdick, a collaborator at the memorial, later chronicled its guiding principles under Ruml's direction: "But most of the emphasis throughout this period was on institutional research, and the philosophy behind it, as we have seen, was based on the belief that the understanding and control of human phenomena lie in the scientific analysis and appraisal of facts. The techniques of social sciences had lagged so far behind those of the natural or laboratory sciences that concentrated efforts were necessary to break down the old classical methodology and give impetus to a new kind of realism in social research."[94] Reflecting on the fund's legacy in 1929, Chancellor Robert Hutchins of the University of Chicago observed, "The Laura Spelman Memorial, in its brief but brilliant career, did more than any other agency to promote the social sciences in the United States."[95]

Support from the Laura Spelman Rockefeller Memorial fund gave Odum a certain independence from the university and its public opinion concerns. The memorial, however, had its own stipulations. Early in its history, the Rockefeller Foundation had funded an "industrial relations" initiative that resulted in "public misunderstandings" when this initiative was revealed to be a labor organizing campaign.[96] Following these "misunderstandings," the foundation largely eschewed any "controversial" projects to avoid similar scandals, and the support Odum obtained from the memorial was to be explicitly nonpolitical.[97] The memorandum between the memorial and the IRSS specified that no money be allocated to any reform legislation initiative, to direct activity in social welfare, or to influence research findings with bias.

The Spelman Rockefeller fund was clear in its emphasis on "training social scientists in university centers and the accumulation of raw data."[98] Unfortunately, the Southern social science concerns of interest to Odum and the IRSS included issues such as mill towns and labor relations—the latter of which had been the explicit source of the very public, and very embarrassing, controversy the Rockefeller Foundation had weathered in 1914–15. Leonard Outhwaite, a memorial staff member, enjoined Odum to "be a good fellow" and pursue those research topics that were also of interest to the fund.[99] Although Northern philanthropic financial support largely freed Odum from interference from the University of North Carolina, the university also provided little in the way of financial backing. Thus, Odum's dependency on Northern funding came at the price of "diminished intellectual autonomy"—a bargain that he successfully managed to live with.[100]

Odum's network of Northern philanthropic groups included the Rockefeller agencies—the foundation and the Laura Spelman Rockefeller Memorial fund—and the SSRC, which collectively included the leadership of William Ogburn, Charles Merriam, Wesley Mitchell, Beardsley Ruml, Sydnor Walker, and Edmund Day. This powerful group of the nation's leading social scientists worked toward the standardization and professionalization of social science research through philanthropic investment in academic research and institutions. Ruml famously called Odum a "master manipulator" of the philanthropic networks, opportunistically aligning his Southern research interests with the funding opportunities made available to him.[101] In return, Northern social scientists and philanthropists viewed Odum as a kind of "Columbia man in the South," reporting to help them better understand what W. J. Cash (a student of Odum's) would later call the "Southern mind." But in letters, Odum revealed insecurities about his scholarship, the IRSS's work, and his ability to bring the social sciences to a generally intolerant Southern audience, as demanded by his financial backers.[102] His ambivalence toward participating in and benefiting from this network meant that he both deferred to his patrons' advice and reported what they wanted to hear, and that he simultaneously believed the Northern incursion to be a sort of "imperialistic exercise of intellectual authority" that he and his colleagues resented but "acknowledged out of practical necessity."[103]

IRSS AND THE FIRST FIVE YEARS: SACRED COWS

In the first five years of the IRSS, both Odum and his institute struggled on multiple fronts in their pursuit of national recognition in the social sciences and of regional influence and authority in their reform efforts.[104] The SSRC leadership, many of them also the leaders of the top national associations of social science, prided themselves in this period on objective, meticulous quantitative research, of the kind Giddings had called for, to standardize and universalize social science methodology and rigor. Odum's more Romantic interests in regional themes were not what the SSRC directors were looking for, so in exchange for funding support, he continually had to defend his research agenda. Odum mistakenly believed that general popularity and acceptance would naturally lead to increased academic credibility among funding networks.[105] These contrasting opinions came to a head during a trip to Hanover, New Hampshire, for a SSRC meeting in the fall of 1925, as I discuss at length in chapter 3.

Odum's work also faced challenges within the region, perhaps the most pressing of which was how to create public discourse with "a sufficiently 'constructive' atmosphere for socially transforming data to be fairly considered.

Considering the closemindedness of the collective Southern mind in the 1920s, this was, in itself a substantial task, one which involved Odum in both efforts of criticism and encouragement as an editorialist."[106] To study social phenomena in the South was inevitably to encounter its "sacred cows" of power. Odum and colleagues launched their reformist research boldly, but the sacred cows were not silent.[107]

Several high-profile reactions to his North Carolina research got Odum into trouble. In 1925, Odum and economist Harriet L. Herring, then working as a research assistant at the IRSS, announced their proposed study on the "social industrial problems of the Piedmont Cotton Mill areas," and Herring began to interview textile and cotton companies to gather information.[108] At a time when "sociology" and "socialism" sounded suspiciously similar to the Southern ear, word reached journalist David Clark of the *Southern Textile Bulletin* that Odum and his colleagues were out to criticize the cotton and textile industries. With the full support of the industrial leaders his *Bulletin* represented, Clark launched a wave of criticism directed at Odum beginning in January 1924. Odum had to navigate university politics to defend himself and his institute against these allegations. His timidity would continue well into the decade, as he would eventually ask Herring to tone down the critical light of her *Welfare Work in Mill Villages*, in particular asking her to sidestep child labor issues in the book.[109]

In 1925, a national furor would encapsulate the tensions between religion and science, progress and provincialism, North and South. During this period, the issue of teaching evolution was hotly debated in the South. March 1925 saw the passing of Tennessee's Butler Act, which banned the teaching of evolution in schools and, within months, prompted the famous John T. Scopes trial in the small rural town of Dayton, Tennessee. In North Carolina, David Scott Poole put forth legislation to ban the Darwinian hypothesis altogether.[110] This polemic captured the nation's attention, as did the multiple constituents who rallied around each side in the fevered press coverage. As they swarmed this quiet town in rural Tennessee, "journalists and national elites saw . . . everything that seemed backward and reactionary in Jazz Age America."[111] H. L. Mencken, a friend of Odum's, was perhaps the most recognized writer covering the Scopes story, recording sardonically, "The town, I confess, greatly surprised me. I expected to find a squalid Southern village, with darkies snoozing on the horse blocks, pigs rooting under the houses and the inhabitants full of hookworm and malaria. What I found was a country town of charm and even beauty."[112] Mencken had no qualms criticizing what he thought were backward customs and beliefs opposed to scientific teaching. But for Odum, who was also present in Dayton that July, the Scopes trial exemplified the tragic chasm of misunderstanding between

Southern white folk culture and positivist scientific thought—the bridging of which he saw as his life's mission.[113]

Compounding this charged moment, two articles appeared in *Social Forces* that irked the North Carolina religious community. Henry E. Barnes, whom Odum knew through his alumni connections to both Columbia and Clark, wrote book reviews and editorials for the journal that were often controversial.[114] In a series of comparative book reviews, Barnes called Frederick O. Norton's *The Rise of Christianity* "mild mannered scholarship," citing it as vastly inferior to F. C. Conybeare's *Myth, Magic, and Morals*. The mention of Christianity and magic in the same sentence, let alone a *comparison* between them, was considered outrageous to the religious community, but Barnes's entire article was essentially a catalog pitting what he believed to be serious religious scholarship against other pious blind-faith books.[115] The other article, from the same volume, was a more serious piece by Luther L. Bernard about progress and the psychology of religious belief.[116] The North Carolina fundamentalist community was equally incensed with both, and as angry letters arrived, Gerald Johnson joked about what he had long feared might happen: "Somebody has read the *Journal of Social Forces*."[117]

Bewildered and depressed, Odum quickly set out to appease the religious criticism by engaging with the ministers and inviting them to visit Chapel Hill to discuss their concerns. He emphasized his pious upbringing and Methodist faith, and in reference to their criticism of his Southernness, he boasted that he was "a regular, orthodox, almost professional, Southerner!"[118] Moreover, he diminished the stature and importance of *Social Forces* as merely technical in scope, with a limited readership. Historians disagree on just how influential these experiences were for Odum, but biographer Wayne Brazil believes this to be the moment when Odum ceased to endorse Southern reform with his former clarity and force, instead switching tone to what he believed was a more muted, evenhanded analysis of the region's weakness *and* potential. This unfortunate situation required Odum to backpedal on the very pressing points of Southern reform—and the reputation of his journal—that he and colleagues worked so hard to promote.[119]

Toward the end of the 1920s, Odum would, along with Rupert B. Vance—Odum's former doctoral student who then became an IRSS researcher—begin to frame the IRSS's multithemed research agenda in terms of regionalism. This shift would prompt him in the subsequent decade, in the midst of the Depression, to recommend social planning as an instrument to develop regionalism. Throughout the IRSS's early years, however, the researchers, with varying directness, were most effective in problematizing Southern conservative traditionalism. Although Odum pursued a research agenda that sought "to discredit and dismantle the old, closed intellectual order" of the South, he was nevertheless "fundamentally unclear and tentative in outlining in what ways and to what degree an open regional dialogue would assist in bringing about substantial social and economic improvements in the South."[120] The contrast between Odum's hesitance and the approaches adopted by other IRSS researchers became more pronounced in the 1930s, when Vance and Odum pursued very different tones in their prescriptions for Southern regional planning.

IRSS RECRUITS: STUDENTS OUTRUNNING THE PROFESSOR

The South was rife with sociological phenomena waiting to be properly surveyed—sharecropping, mill villages, chain gangs, paternalism, folk culture, racial segregation and violence—and the Laura Spelman Rockefeller Memorial saw in Odum's new institute the opportunity to learn about this remote area. The IRSS, although the first of its kind in the United States, was soon replicated over the next five years at Columbia University, the University of Virginia, Stanford, and the University of Texas, which further extended the academic and institutional networks in which Odum and colleagues participated.[121] For its funders, the primary goal of the IRSS was to promote the social sciences in the South and to improve research opportunities for the region's social scientists. A review of the organization's researchers and their accomplishments demonstrates its success.[122]

Institute researchers included Rupert B. Vance, Guy Johnson, Arthur F. Raper, Margaret Jarman Hagood, Katharine Jocher, Harriet Herring, and Thomas J. Woofter Jr.[123] Vance's research—a combination of human geography and cultural anthropology—focused on the Southern cotton economy and land tenancy; Johnson and Woofter were sociologists working on Black folk culture and race relations; and Raper, also a sociologist, researched sharecropping and lynching.[124] As historian Daniel J. Singal explains, these researchers shared "a determination to understand southern society by probing to a deeper level than had ever been attained before through social science."[125] Although Odum could be hesitant to cross certain lines of critique for fear of having his Southernness questioned, these four demonstrated no such concerns in their own endeavors. Vance's understanding of cotton culture and its Southern human geography led the IRSS's most rigorous work on regionalism and, later, regional planning. His efforts helped cement "Odum's vision of Chapel Hill as a center of regional scholarship and what is nowadays called 'policy research.' In both volume and quality, [Vance's] publications helped put North Carolina on the national academic map."[126]

Rupert B. Vance was born to a humble family in the small town of Plumerville, Arkansas, in 1899. Vance contracted polio at age three and was homeschooled until age ten. He witnessed his father, a staunch believer in the New South's bootstraps work ethos, work tirelessly as a smaller farmer and a shopkeeper, only to lose his farm early in the Depression. It was an education in high skepticism concerning the New South Creed.[127] Vance was a prodigious reader of Darwin, Marx, and Freud, and in 1921, he earned a master's degree in economics under Augustus Dyer at Vanderbilt University. Yet Vance remained dissatisfied with economic market explanations of the cotton industry's failures, having personally lived through the pain of watching his father's frustration. Dyer had also introduced Vance to the burgeoning field of sociology, which he decided might hold greater explanatory power for understanding Southern cotton culture. Vance applied to the nation's leading doctoral programs at the University of Chicago and Columbia University, but he had also become a loyal reader of Odum's *Social Forces* journal, inspired by this platform that appeared to provide the intellectual freedom to study the South "objectively," free from convention and moralism."[128] He chose the University of North Carolina to study sociology with Odum beginning in 1926 and completed his PhD in 1928, after which he joined the IRSS as a researcher.[129]

In 1929, Vance published his dissertation as the book *Human Factors in Cotton Culture*, in which he explored what he called the Southern "cotton culture complex." He referenced the concept of "natural region" that he had learned from the French School of human geography, in which natural features and systems—soils, climate, and terrain—formatively influence regional culture and character. Nonetheless, Vance cautioned against geographic determinism, arguing that the "cotton complex" comprised irrational choices and cultural influences that, although "intangible," were indeed a "very real thing."[130] As he would later write, "History, not geography, made the Solid South."[131]

Singal underscores that Vance evinced no trace of Odum's internal conflict between reverence for the South and the urge to reform it: by the late 1920s, "Victorian optimism had given way to dogged empirical realism . . . producing an image of the South that belonged unmistakably to the twentieth century."[132] I address Vance's work in greater depth in the regionalism chapter, with particular focus on his second book, *Human Geography of the South*, but it must be underscored from the outset that if Odum was the most famous of the Southern regionalists, Vance "[set] the standard for other sociologists of his generation in the South to focus on the region's manifold dilemmas" by identifying specific causality and the conflicting interests that formed it.[133] Although Vance would ultimately be less enthusiastic than Odum about the promise of regional planning, this skepticism was precisely because the intellectual and conceptual latitude it required in the South was not something he would afford.

For race studies, Odum recruited Guy B. Johnson and Thomas Woofter Jr. to the University of North Carolina. Johnson was originally from Texas, and after undergraduate studies at Baylor University, he traveled north to the University of Chicago to complete his master's research in sociology with Robert E. Park and Ellsworth Farris. His research focused specifically on the Ku Klux Klan, which caught Odum's attention. Johnson published an article on the topic in *Social Forces*, after which Odum successfully recruited him to the University of North Carolina for his doctoral work beginning in 1924. When British anthropologist Bronislaw Malinowski visited Chapel Hill in 1926, Johnson served as his host and guide. This experience would influence Johnson's research on Black communities, particularly the importance of folk culture in providing the psychological foundation for systems of meaning.[134]

Upon Johnson's arrival at the University of North Carolina, Odum had asked him to coauthor two books that continued his work on Black folk songs in Mississippi, but Johnson's rigorous training in Chicago made him question whether this project was "true sociology."[135] Despite these misgivings, Johnson ended up working with Odum, focusing on "innate musical ability" in Black schoolchildren and university students.[136] Johnson also researched the John Henry folk story, at the recommendation of American man of letters H. L. Mencken, to determine whether it was based on a historic figure and how the folk song structure and references uniquely portrayed the character. In contrast to the work of Odum and other white researchers on Black folklore, Johnson's examination did not merely identify character flaws and degeneracy in the lyrics, but instead depicted a more complex, nuanced understanding of the song. It was good training for his next project.

In 1927, Odum applied to the SSRC for a research grant to study the Black Gullah culture on St. Helena Island off the coast of South Carolina. In 1930, Johnson published *Folk Culture on St. Helena Island, South Carolina*, which proved controversial both for its claim that the island's folk songs bore a striking resemblance to early white spiritual songs, thus contesting the African-purism narrative of the island's culture, and for its root contestation of the Victorian premise that white culture (civilized) and Black culture (uncivilized) shared much in common throughout their 400 years of engagement.[137] This debate would continue throughout the twentieth century. Johnson's 1934 essay "Does the South Owe the Negro a New Deal?" was not only an impassioned plea for equality but almost an open call for integration.[138] By the 1940s, however, Johnson had returned to the interracial-cooperation stance, which held that reforming entrenched white Southern folklore required racial gradualism, as opposed to immediate integration, so that these slower achievements could have a cumulative effect.[139]

In 1927, Thomas J. Woofter Jr., arrived at the University of North Carolina as a new member of the sociology department. Woofter was from Athens, Georgia, and his early work on Black education reform had inspired the research Odum had conducted before arriving in North Carolina.[140] Woofter was also an antilynching activist and educator who was active in the Southern interracial-cooperation movement.[141] Woofter had worked as a statistician in the American Expeditionary Force for his military service, after which he completed his doctoral studies on Black migration at Columbia University. After working with the Atlanta Commission on Interracial Cooperation, in which Odum also participated, he accepted a position at the University of North Carolina, also funded by the Laura Spelman Rockefeller Memorial.[142] Woofter published a report for President Herbert Hoover's Colored Advisory Commission on African Americans in the US economy that was criticized by W. E. B. Du Bois for a lack of emphasis on racial discrimination factors. He also wrote "The Status of Racial and Ethnic Groups" for Hoover's President's Research Committee on Social Trends, on which Odum served.[143] Woofter would go on to work with the Tennessee Valley Authority in 1933, with Odum's recommendation. The shortcomings of their research notwithstanding, it is noteworthy that Vance, Johnson, and Woofter were, at the height of their careers, willing to extend their modern analysis of Southern social phenomena without Odum's concern for temperance in the name of essential Old Southern fidelity.

Perhaps the most visionary of the IRSS's researchers was Arthur F. Raper, born in 1899 in Davidson County, North Carolina. The son of a successful tobacco planter, Raper attended the University of North Carolina as an undergraduate. For graduate work, he went to study sociology at Vanderbilt University, where he wrote his master's thesis on "Negro Dependency in the Southern Community," but he returned to North Carolina in 1925 to do his doctoral work with Odum.[144] In 1926, however, Raper received an invitation from Will A. Alexander, head of the Commission on Interracial Cooperation in Atlanta, to conduct sociological research in the rural environments of Georgia, which he accepted.

Opinions vary on the Commission on Interracial Cooperation's work in the South. Its activism generally did not address Southern racism head-on, but hundreds of local committees advocated against lynching. Perhaps similar to Odum's position on racial issues (he would finally accept an invitation to serve on the commission in 1927), membership on the committee was enough to mark one as a white Southern liberal of the period but, in contrast with a member of the NAACP, one still sufficiently circumspect that Southern whites might at least listen to the organization's campaigns.[145] The commission also helped channel financial support from the Rosenwald Fund in Chicago, and later the New Deal, to help finance scholarships for Black students and funding for historically Black education institutions. Based on his experiences with commission work in Georgia, Raper published *The Tragedy of Lynching* in 1933, which immediately became the authoritative text on the subject. He used a quasi-journalistic tone based on numerous interviews and lynching case studies. Rather than editorialize, Raper relied on the brutal detail in what he hoped would be enough to get through to readers. For many, it was.[146]

In 1934, on the advice of University of North Carolina Press editor William Couch, Raper revisited and updated his doctoral work, which he published in 1936 as *Preface to Peasantry*. He examined the Black rural-to-urban migration patterns in 1920s Georgia from around the state to Atlanta, tracing them to the breakdown of the plantation system. Breaking with regionalist nostalgia for the pre-Modern medieval age, Raper compared sharecropping and worker insecurity to serfdom, only acknowledging that the system of serfdom at least had the security of sustainable crop-rotation practices, as opposed to the frontier wastefulness of Southern monocropping and erosion. Rather than espousing any pretense of sharecropping as a ladder for future landownership and success, Raper viewed it as simply a preliminary introduction to the peasantry that he saw gathering in poverty in Atlanta as the shattered results of a brutal system. Raper followed this in 1938 with *Sharecroppers All*, which he coauthored with Black sociologist Ira De Augustine Reid of Atlanta University. It was an unapologetic, precise critique of the Southern racial system across the rural-urban divide. As they had expected, Raper and Reid faced heavy criticism and backlash for their direct language and analysis. Despite loud criticism of Raper's work from Donald Davidson, Odum and Couch relented, and it was published through the University of North Carolina Press.[147]

As Singal notes, "For the new leaders of the region's intellectual life just prior to the Second World War, the New South Creed had been consciously and vehemently repudiated."[148] This demolition was not the result of Odum's own work, but that of the people he recruited, the grants he wrote, the networks he plied, the work he endorsed, and the institute he built at the University of North Carolina in the interwar years. Yet "if he wasn't ready to go as far as his students and identify the plantation system as the culprit, he was at least prepared to dispense with the myth that the South was the land of continuous harmony."[149]

GETTING AT FACTS

Odum and his colleagues came together in the Institute for Research in Social Science, funded by Northern philanthropy, and set out to establish a reformist regional social science that could take aim at a Southern society resistant to change. From his birthplace in Georgia, Odum went west to Mississippi, where Thomas Pearce Bailey redirected him north once more to the social sciences of Clark and Columbia Universities. Odum's Methodist upbringing was secularized into his social sciences and became a kind of crusade, only for him later to encounter ambivalence concerning the very progress and social engineering doctrines he had embraced. In 1924, in one of his editorial notes for *Social Forces*, he quoted his mentor Franklin Giddings at length to promote the social sciences as "practical" and even "moral," words Odum believed were more appropriate for a Southern audience suspicious of intellectuals and experts: "Science is nothing more nor less than getting at facts, and trying to understand them. . . . Helping us to face facts . . . facing facts that the social sciences are making known to us . . . should enable us to diminish human misery and to live more wisely than the human race has lived before."[150] His was the promise of Southern social engineering in the guise of local common sense. He endorsed social sciences through the popular language of the folk, consoling readers — either straight-facedly in confidence or slyly in strategy — that his was a nonacademic form of applied research. Despite the work of the IRSS colleagues he had recruited, this same contradiction and confusion would continue in his work on regionalism and regional social planning.

> Savoir pour prévoir, afin de pouvoir.
> —AUGUSTE COMTE

CHAPTER 3

TELESIS AND THE SOCIOCRACY

SOCIAL SCIENCES IN THE NATURAL WORLD

Introducing *An American Epoch*, one of his most famous books, Howard Odum wrote in 1930, "It will be at once apparent that the reading of all of the book is essential to the full understanding of any parts of it, or to the comprehension of the whole American epoch of which it attempts partial portraiture."[1] Portraiture provided an overarching comfort of stability through generational change—the maintenance of a status quo for the region and for the country as each confronted deep crises. In this book, Odum gave a semifictional account of his family's four generations during the antebellum, Civil War, Reconstruction, and Jim Crow eras through the "Southern-national and national-southern figures they were."[2] Odum wrote the book while traveling extensively throughout the South in the late 1920s, and the portraiture technique allowed him to catalog "regional facts" to be "set forth as a sort of artistic realism."[3]

In his introductory note, Odum explained the work as "rooted in realities of the period," representing an "effort toward critical analysis based on sympathetic understanding of the facts rather than either hypocritical attack or unseemly praise." After the criticism levied at his Institute for Research in Social Science (IRSS) by regional interests, and the methodological criticism of his research by members of the Social Science Research Council (SSRC) for what they considered as the lack of objective, factual analysis in the Giddings tradition, Odum's introductory note to *An American Epoch* announced not only his purpose in its writing, but also what he believed to be the sociological contribution of a work of fiction. For Odum and his interpretation of the South, "It is as if a new romantic realism were needed to portray the old backgrounds and the new trends and processes."[4] Romanticism itself, however, was not new to the Southern social sciences.

Odum further clarified his commitment to this all-encompassing portraiture method in his presidential address to the American Sociological Society that same year, refashioning portraiture into the Wundt-inspired "folk sociology" as a declaration of a new subfield that aligned with the growing interest in regional trends and subnational cultures.[5] Folk was the region, and the region must be understood through its folk—specifically, its white folk. Odum's portraitures were syntheses, like those of his textbooks, that often joined multiple, even contradictory, social science positions into wide-reaching, self-serving claims that incorporated any perspective necessary—objective analysis? sympathetic understanding?—to legitimize reform or deflect criticism in the name of either science or empathy. This approach would continue throughout the 1930s. It was perhaps the generational difference that distinguished Odum's work from the more clear-eyed, critical, hard-boiled understanding of the social sciences of Rupert B. Vance, Arthur Raper, and Odum's other colleagues at the IRSS.[6]

By the time Odum and Harry Estill Moore, who earned his doctorate in sociology at the University of North Carolina in 1937, published *American Regionalism* in 1938, Odum was explicitly deploying his claims about portraiture both to describe what was now a conceptualization of regionalism, and to plead for sympathy if the authors could not supply or defend the exact geographic contours of their proposed regions.[7] As Odum and Moore explained in their book, "These regions, flexible and susceptible to adjustment, may then constitute the basis for uniform study and planning for the vivid portraiture of the nation both for scientific and practical purposes and for creating popular interests and for giving a satisfying sympathetic understanding of the nation's dilemmas and progress."[8] Such an argument was not the most confident and convincing—or perhaps even convinced—case for adding an entirely new level of government to the entire United

States public sector. Odum sought to disaggregate regionalism into what he called the "fundamental distinction between the formal regionalism measured through technical processes at the top and the social or folk regionalism characterized and conditioned by social processes at the bottom."[9] His distinctions, however, essentially aligned with the folkways and stateways claims that he repeated from his mentors. For regional planning, these distinctions seemed to point in different directions, particularly at the height of government social engineering ideology of the period.

Beginning with Odum's participation on Herbert Hoover's President's Research Committee on Social Trends, this chapter then reviews the history of the US and Southern social sciences in which Odum was trained. In the 1920s, the influential leadership of the SSRC heavily critiqued Odum's portraiture method, which humiliated him and diminished his work. However, just as the Great War had placed the coda on Progressive Era meliorism and sparked the rapid rise of objective social science methods, the Great Depression ushered in a general suspicion that such methods were *overly* objective. It was an affinity with Carl O. Sauer's human geography that helped restore confidence in the IRSS's work.

THE PRESIDENT'S RESEARCH COMMITTEE ON SOCIAL TRENDS

In the summer of 1929, six months after his election, President Herbert Hoover appointed the President's Research Committee on Social Trends. Hoover, "the great engineer," gained early success as a mining engineer and, later, fame as "the great humanitarian" in World War I for his work with the US Food Administration coordinating missions to feed European allies. After the war, as secretary of commerce under Presidents Harding and Coolidge from 1921 to 1928, Hoover was a celebrated "wonder boy" for activating and expanding the relatively new department. He convened more than 3,000 conferences to promote standardization and efficiency in industry and government, and this precedent of expert consultancy for efficiency and "waste" reduction continued into his presidency.[10] Hoover believed that "the country was in need of more action in the social field," so he charged the President's Research Committee on Social Trends to provide him with a "complete, impartial examination of the facts," hoping that its report would "serve to help all of us to see where social stresses are occurring and where major efforts should be undertaken to deal with them constructively."[11] Sociologist L. L. Bernard believed that "social facts" were as fundamental as the laws of astronomy or physics and that all social organizations required them in order to engineer social behavior.[12] The research committee was to provide social facts for social action.

The committee and its research were privately funded by the Rockefeller Foundation and administered through the SSRC in New York City. Wesley C. Mitchell of Columbia University chaired the group, with Charles Merriam of the University of Chicago (and one of the cofounders of the SSRC) as vice-chair. William Ogburn, also of the University of Chicago, was the director of research, and Howard Odum was the assistant director of research. Other members included Shelby M. Harrison of the Russell Sage Foundation and Alice Hamilton of the Harvard Medical School.[13] Mitchell, who was then also the director of research for the National Bureau of Economic Research, endorsed the committee as "a venture by the President to apply the procedure of social technology to social problems."[14] The unwelcome arrival of the Depression in the fall of 1929 delayed the publication of the committee's final report, Recent Social Trends, until after the 1932 election.

Recent Social Trends was an objectivist's fact catalog. The influence of British mathematician Karl Pearson and his book The Grammar of Science on the committee's social scientists was clear. Pearson believed in both describing and measuring social phenomena, and the essence of US Progressive Era meliorative scientific practice was grounded in data collection.[15] Nonetheless, there were internal disagreements among committee members, with Ogburn believing that the report should convey "facts and facts alone," unaccompanied by opinions about those facts, to inform the Hoover administration's decision-making. Merriam and Mitchell did not view the data as ready to inform planning decisions, but rather as only the grounds for laying "plans for making plans."[16] The final 1,500-page report, and its "vast, dense, and often obscure contents," received mixed reviews.[17] Psychologist John Dewey praised the report as a prudent statement of facts, while economist Adolf A. Berle Jr. worried that perhaps "the desire for objectivity has been carried entirely too far."[18] Historian Charles A. Beard speculated that the report marked the end of "simplistic empiricism" in which data produces inevitable, self-evident outcomes "akin to physics or mathematics."[19] Rupert B. Vance, an IRSS researcher, later noted that the report "took little notice of regional characteristics," yet its pages were "full of data which invited a regional interpretation."[20] To address the scale and gravity of the nation's economic and social challenges, the report, much like Hoover's administration, was overstudied and ineffectual.

Nevertheless, Odum's participation on the President's Research Committee on Social Trends was important to him for several reasons. He viewed it as an opportunity to practice the principles of applied social science that he had long called for to "harmonize the forces of science with the forces of the social process."[21] Odum's chapter on public welfare in Recent Social Trends linked his earlier work to an expanded government agenda for social action.[22] His appointment also boosted his confidence as a social scientist, particularly after several humiliating encounters at the SSRC summer meetings in Hanover, New Hampshire, where his methods and scholarship had been slighted.[23] Moreover, this appointment elevated Odum's national status as a social scientist: He was nominated president of the American Sociological Society in 1930, and in 1934, his national colleagues ranked his University of North Carolina sociology department among the country's most prestigious.[24] The committee was engaged with national social trends and data, which Odum recognized as the first time that his research moved beyond the boundaries of Southern social phenomena, and this work provided the comparative frame for his subsequent regional-national proposals.[25] Finally, Odum had recently published *Man's Quest for Social Guidance* (1927) as a treatise on the application of the social sciences for collective progress, and his role on the committee gave him the opportunity to advise the president on such matters at the highest executive level.[26]

Riding high, in 1930, Odum was invited to direct the social science exhibit for the upcoming Century of Progress International Exposition in Chicago. The exposition would celebrate the city's first centennial since its founding by decree of the 1833 Treaty of Chicago, which formalized the removal of the Indigenous Ojibwe, Odawa, and Potawatomi nations. In 1893, the World's Columbian Exposition—often known as the Chicago World's Fair—designed by Daniel Burnham, Frederick Law Olmsted, John Root, and Charles B. Atwood had been a resounding success, with many visitors promenading through the Beaux-Arts grounds and taking in the wonders of technological uplift.[27] Forty years later, promoters announced that the 1933 exposition would again celebrate "scientific idealism" and "the service of science to society and the benefit of humanity brought about by this scientific and industrial development."[28]

The exhibits for the 1933 exposition stressed the importance of the natural sciences and engineering in the advancement of industrial capital and the state. The social sciences had to be shoehorned in, and for Odum, the fit was not entirely comfortable. His response to the exposition's industrial emphasis conveyed his ambivalence, noting that along with progress, industrial applications of science also created "social 'problems,' which in turn gave rise to the need for social engineering" from social scientists.[29] For Odum, there could be "no sound static society; nor . . . social progress without the continual multiplication of social problems."[30]

Odum's call for social engineering reflected the trend in the US interwar years of viewing engineering as the inspiration for the new social administrator, "as a technique . . . now available to the economist, to other social scientists," and to business owners.[31] Odum would later use the term "technicways" for this social engineering, which he viewed as the behavioral acclimation to scientific progress through technology. The convergence of scientific research, technocratic reform, and economic managerialism jointly, albeit tenuously, supported social utility and scholarly objectivity. The meliorative spirit of the prewar social sciences transitioned into social engineering's discourse for technocratic institutional progress.[32]

His caution notwithstanding, Odum heavily anticipated the 1933 exposition, envisioning a grand theme-park entertainment spectacle to communicate and celebrate the applied achievements and possibilities of the social sciences in service to the broader community. In a preparatory memo, he observed, "The Exposition presents both an opportunity and obligation for the Social Sciences to demonstrate for the first time the progress of Social Science and Social Research and their application to human interest and human welfare."[33] Although the fair did include a recreation of a Mayan temple called the "Temple of Science," this was not exactly what Odum envisioned. Like many of his social science peers, he was concerned that the discipline was being represented as lesser in comparison with the natural sciences and engineering, but he was unable to raise money to fund his ambitions for a social science pavilion. The social science entertainment project, which would have been costly even in normal circumstances, was untenable amid the Depression. Odum accepted the defeat of his social science dream exhibition, and he resigned from his post in December 1931. The directorship for the social science exhibition passed on to anthropologist Fay-Cooper Cole of the University of Chicago, who staged it more humbly on the north side of the Electrical Building, far from the Temple of Science.[34]

This anecdote illustrates Odum's concern over the prestige and status of the social sciences compared with those of the natural sciences. Odum already held second-tier status among colleagues such as Ogburn, Mitchell, and Merriam, who viewed him as lacking in critical thinking or substance to convincingly communicate the social engineering rhetoric of the period. Although he shared a common sociological mentor with his objectivist social science colleagues in Giddings, Odum was nonetheless out of step with them. He brought social engineering rhetoric to his work in the South, but it was qualified, tempered by an insistence on folk society and folk sociology to pump the brakes against the modern industrial claims of progressive engineering. Although Odum was "a somewhat sloppy thinker and writer who rarely revised his material," historian John Jordan concludes that his "use of the social engineering paradigm illustrates how accessible the notion had become to reformers."[35] Odum enjoyed the prestige he had gained in the early 1930s, but he remained conflicted.

Odum's ambivalence regarding social engineering for progress toward a more perfectible future society was aligned in many ways with the foundational themes that he'd learned from prewar US social sciences. Odum's approach to the social sciences conflated "descriptive study with objective study," thus aligning his "methodological orientation more . . . with Progressive-era sociology than the quantitative techniques observed by contemporary objectivists."[36] His approaches were characterized as having "liberal values, practical bent, shallow historical vision, and technocratic confidence . . . modeled on the natural rather than the historical sciences and imbedded in the classical ideology of liberal individualism," while also providing a historical imaginary to embrace "history and biography and the relations of the two within society."[37] Odum and his colleagues reviewed and synthesized a broad sampling of social science and produced various textbooks to promote it, in the 1920s and later in his career.[38]

The extent to which Odum contributed to sociological theory, however, is debatable.[39] During his career, he drew heavily if opportunistically from his educational mentors in sociology and psychology. Odum biographer Wayne Brazil points out that "he took the premises of thought from established scholars without trying to synthesize them into coherent theory. Seemingly untroubled by great logical inconsistency, he appeared to be buffeted by contradictions and tensions between ideas and assumptions derived from an incredible number of writers."[40] Colleague Guy Johnson would later more critically describe Odum's understanding of early sociology as a "sort of hodge podge, not systematized."[41]

Odum's organic societal conceptualization tensely joined two traditions—"folkways" and "stateways"—among the many dualities he believed social scientists needed to both balance and bridge.[42] Odum opportunistically deployed social sciences that identified all constituent "parts" of society and aspired to comprehend their interrelationships in forming an organic "whole."[43] Only from that whole could a path forward toward progress be determined and recommended: from many Souths, *one* South. As he moved away from a reformist stance in the 1920s, Odum's social science in the new decade "operated increasingly as a softening, diluting, even opposing force upon his reform-minded public personality."[44] The organic themes of nature, social change, progress, and society, and the authority of the applied social sciences to unite and fix them, were the core issues of these social sciences at the time when Thomas Bailey first introduced them to Odum in Mississippi.

A RENEWED SOUTHERN SOCIAL SCIENCE

Eighteenth-century Enlightenment philosophers believed in a cosmopolitan universalism and a continuity of human traits across time and geographies that emphasized the role of particular interests, rather than cultural essences, in determining sectional identities.[45] Romantic nationalist social theory flipped the Enlightenment, stressing geographical groupings as the source of unique cultural essence. With Romanticism, "mechanistic theories of society were transmuted into organic analogies. Society was not a machine, from which one could subtract or add cogs at one's leisure, but a living thing which might die if the gardener was too cavalier."[46] Folk mysticism displaced Enlightenment rationalism, and classicism was supplanted by an interest in the early medieval period. In the late eighteenth century, German philosopher Johann Gottfried Herder celebrated nationalist German philology and folk songs in protest against the trend of intellectuals valorizing and imitating the French. Above all, he believed individuals to be "part of a whole," and he held that their "individuality [was] defined and expressed through . . . membership in the group."[47]

Without European historical statues to remind citizens of their glorious shared past and group identity, the new United States turned to nature to define and understand itself. American exceptionalism was a core belief for the new nation, affirmed through religious piety and the natural sciences celebrating the bounty of a timeless country with boundless resources.[48] But the South—that "'great exception' in American history"—had an uncomfortable relationship with the "national ideology" of American exceptionalism and "its political implementation."[49] Prior to the Civil War, a divergent system of political theory, political economy, and sociology arose in the South in defense of the proslavery society—and in opposition to American exceptionalism. Writers such as secessionist John C. Calhoun and economist Thomas R. Dew bent European political philosophy to justify and accommodate the white Southern agrarian interests and cultural norms.[50]

In the 1850s, Southerners George Fitzhugh and Henry Hughes introduced the word "sociology" to the United States.[51] Fitzhugh wrote *Sociology for the South; or, The Failure of Free Society*, which directly refuted American exceptionalism, stating that "slavery had always existed in human society supported by God and nature." He celebrated the institution of slavery, referenced precedents for it in world history, and asserted his belief that the United States should be no exception, but instead embrace "the new world of railroads, banks, and cities, enclosed in autarkic provincial units, led by a landed aristocracy and organized around a graded system of dependent labor."[52] Fitzhugh valued democratic values less than social order, for which he saw Christianity and slavery—with the South as his model—as the institutions required to maintain "discipline and order."[53] Henry Hughes's *Treatise on Sociology, Theoretical and Practical* defended the slave system as "morally and civilly good."[54] This brand of Southern social science continued after the Confederacy and its proslavery vision were politically and morally defeated, and its nefarious message continued to fuel Southern populism well past the war.[55]

The publication in the 1850s of Herbert Spencer's *Social Statics* (1851) and Charles Darwin's *On the Origin of Species* (1859) marked a revolution in the natural sciences' understanding of evolution, natural selection, and heredity.[56] In the ensuing decades, Spencer's and Darwin's work influenced the social sciences and a broad variety of research seeking to justify claims of racial difference, superiority, and inferiority. Spencerian social sciences believed in natural law as an organizing principle for society. Karl Marx and Friedrich Engels admired Darwin's work, but they resisted its societal implications, believing that he had simply transposed the "bourgeoise economic theory of competition" to nature.[57]

However, the more common assumption about Darwin's work went in the other direction: the belief that Spencer's (mis)interpretation of Darwin's work, summed up in his catchy phrase "survival of the fittest," could be loosely applied to society in the conservative claim that "*fittest* inevitably connoted *best*" and that "struggle and survival" could be linked to "a doctrine of progress."[58] This was the foundation of social Darwinism, which interpreted Darwin's work through what adherents believed to be its social significance.[59] Francis Galton came up with the term "eugenics" in the 1880s, claiming that it was a "science of improving stock."[60] Yet historian Robert C. Bannister points out that, in fact, "early Darwinians were not social Darwinists; many social Darwinists (such as Spencer) were not Darwinians."[61] Darwin shirked responsibility for the interpretation or misinterpretation of his work, but psychologist Howard Gruber asserts that Darwin would have agreed with the later eugenicist notion that "survival of human species must be, in the years to come, a struggle to develop social forms that enhance cooperation and rational, long-term planning for collective ends."[62] Geddes, and later Odum, agreed.[63]

Despite the influence of the European Romantics and the emerging evolutionary sciences on the US South—early newspapers cited inspiration from Herder and other Romantics—Michael O'Brien has cautioned against a linear reading of the intellectual grafting of European Romantic theory onto the South.[64] Rather, it was more in the creation of "the South" as such, upon the defeat of the Confederacy after the Civil War, that Southern states began to recognize themselves in Herder's definition of nation: a culturally unified group removed from the formal ruling institutions and practices of state.[65] It was a South "fully realized" in national popular culture, propagated in literature, music, art, and, later, movies that took "'folk' forms and from them wove modernist visions."[66] The New South Creed attempted to reconcile these positions by combining Southern mythos—"the inarticulate stepchild of Romanticism"—with an aspirational institution-building project throughout the interwar years and World War II.[67]

In the United States, the postbellum period brought upheaval, which Mumford has described as the breakdown of the medieval synthesis of Christian and Aristotelian philosophy that backed the societal authority of divine law.[68] The past and present had grown apart, tradition was disrupted, and the authority of religion was shaken by scientific discoveries. The exit of divine authority meant that the US social sciences had to design a secular civic social order in its place, which required a plasticity of nature and history as conceptual materials for the new construct. Realism addressed this confusion with a call for a new empiricism to provide "the facts of society."[69] Through the empirical sciences, "social scientists hoped to discover fundamental laws at work alike in nature and history."[70]

William Graham Sumner, appointed to Yale University in 1872, initially proposed a Comtean positivist sociology based on the laws of history as they determined progress for society.[71] He was conservative in his outlook, and the 1877 railroad strikes caused him concern for the pace of change the country was experiencing. Ultimately, Sumner "became one of the few members of his generation to doubt ideas of progress."[72] From a Tönnies-like preoccupation with the accelerated transformation of the country into one of relationships based on contracts, Sumner adopted a strong laissez-faire stance against social progress ideology, concluding that libertarian, individualist natural and economic market forces were the best way to preserve an independent citizenry and the fixed course of societal evolution.[73] Although widely repudiated today as a repugnant, racist rationalization for white supremacy, in the late nineteenth and early twentieth centuries in the United States, social Darwinism was woven into "the virtues that Spencer and Sumner preached—personal providence, family loyalty and family responsibility, hard work, careful management, and proud self-sufficiency," which were broadly accepted as white "middle class virtues."[74]

In opposition to Sumner, Lester Frank Ward developed an entire sociological framework around the notion of self-improvement and scientific progress inspired by the natural sciences. Ward's training was in law, then in botany and paleontology, and he worked as a geologist and paleontologist for the US Geological Survey from 1882 through 1905. Only later, in 1906 at age sixty-five, did he accept the position of chair of sociology at Brown University, which he held for the last seven years of his life.

An "extreme organicist," Ward introduced botanical terms to the new social science.[75] He separated sociology into pure and applied categories, believing that the latter was the application of natural sciences as an artificial means of intervening in the spontaneous laws of nature. Ward proposed "planned social change and the purposeful application of human intelligence in accelerating social evolution."[76] He further divided these processes into the categories of "genesis" and "telesis," with genesis initiating what he termed the "spontaneous development" of nature and social structures along Spencerian lines. Telesis, for which Ward was better known, was a definitively anti-laissez-faire Spencerian sociology advocating concerted, intentional effort for the human "conscious improvement of society."[77]

Ward proposed the concept of collective telesis as a practice to connect the social science concern for progress to the forces of natural law. Sociologist E. Franklin Frazier noted that Ward "rejected the theories of Galton concerning superior races and superior classes."[78] James Quayle Dealey summarized Wardian telesis in Odum's 1927 edited volume *American Masters of Social Science*: "Telesis implies that the social ends to be attained are well known and that the ways and means whereby the ends may be attained have been scientifically ascertained. . . . The next step is that social forces move towards the ends desired, guided by the 'directive agent,' the intellect, following the ways and means determined in advance. *Telesis*, therefore, is not merely purpose, it is purpose combined with the scientific knowledge of how to accomplish one's purpose."[79]

Ward and Sumner fundamentally disagreed throughout the 1880s. Ward "was calling not simply for intelligent action in dealing with human problems but for social engineering."[80] For him, this possibility of social intervention for improvement opened sociology to the arrival of the reformist Progressive period, if only for limited liberal change against other countervailing natural forces of evolution. In true technocratic form, politics would give way to order through rationality, and progress would occur through learning, intervening, and controlling (in a limited way) natural law.[81] Ward believed that a proactive human telic component could have an impact in catalyzing evolutionary processes—a kind of hacking of history—to accelerate the otherwise slow-moving, multigenerational pace of selection and adaptation.

Ward's series of dualities also included what he called "social statics" and "social dynamics." Rather than the survival of the species, Ward believed in the survival of social structures, or the "struggle for structure." He wrote a glowing review of Thorstein Veblen's *The Theory of the Leisure Class* in support of his understanding of institutional evolution.[82] What Ward called "synthesis" (a clear Hegelian reference) included the parallel processes of social statics, or the social equilibrium and order to build and stabilize society, and social dynamics, or changes in social structure, in pursuit of progress.[83] Discussing Sumner and Ward in the *American Journal of Sociology*, Harry Elmer Barnes wrote, "Control of dynamic forces of nature and society through the adjustment of means (evolution) to ends (intervention) is what Ward designates as 'telesis.'"[84]

Further, Ward believed that the state was the highest, most important human institution guiding social progress. In an evolution of the state, he proposed three stages: autocracy, aristocracy, and, finally, democracy, which also needs to phase through democratic physiocracy and plutocracy to attain the idealized "sociocracy."[85] Following Plato and Comte, Ward believed that "perfect government could only come when society and government were controlled and directed by sociologists."[86] Dorothy Ross similarly observed, "Government may directly improve the condition of society in a conscious telic manner if the legislators will only become social scientists. There can be no scientific government, no important development of the ameliorative function of government until the legislators have gained a knowledge of the nature and means of controlling the social forces in the same way that the applied scientist discovers the physical laws of nature and applies this knowledge in controlling them and adapting them to his needs."[87]

In the sociocracy, the rational study of order and progress would replace politics as means for enlightened social governance, and equal opportunities for all races and classes would lead to equal achievement.[88] Of course, Ward assumed the benevolence of these social science legislators in possession of the knowledge of social forces in guiding society toward improvement rather than corruption—a decidedly idyllic vision during the country's rampant corruption throughout the Gilded Age.[89] The sociocracy model inspired Odum's institutional aspirations and, later, his recommendations for regional development, governmental policy, and proposal for a United States planning agency.[90]

Ward served as the first president of the American Sociological Society (later the American Sociological Association [ASA]) in 1906, a position Odum would later hold in 1930. Franklin H. Giddings, Odum's mentor, recognized Ward's contribution to sociology, but in 1924, he declaimed against Ward's social engineering, stating, "The telic process in human society does not supersede the genetic process."[91] For Odum and his discovery of social planning as a potential practice grounded in social sciences, collective telesis accommodated natural laws, their social application of the period, and limited social intervention through planning to move society toward progress in the qualified Southern reform platform that he and colleagues would devise.

In the 1890s, the University of Chicago and Columbia University were the first US universities to establish chairs in sociology—for Albion Small and Franklin H. Giddings, respectively. During this period of great immigration to Northern cities and the concurrent rise of Jim Crow in the South, the rising popularity of evolutionary biology and racial anthropology gave legitimacy to racist and nativist sentiments and policies, and influenced both sociology and the functionalist psychology of William James and John Dewey.[92] Giddings was a leading voice among social scientists for such sentiments.[93] Like Sumner, Giddings was deeply influenced by Spencer's sociology and its positivist evolutionary frame comprising physical and social forces as "normative natural law."[94]

Planning scholar Clyde Woods describes Giddings as a leading figure in the "plantation social science movement" for his social Darwinist position and his emphasis on racial association and empathy.[95] In 1896, Giddings published *Principles of Sociology*, in which he proposed his concept of "consciousness of kind" as an explanatory psychological frame for associative empathy and sympathy among social groups, and a defense of "racial exclusiveness."[96] According to Giddings, the "conscious perception of likeness" could draw groups together or keep them apart through "racial hatred and class prejudice," which associations, he concluded, must be driven by natural law. Pioneering sociologist W. E. B. Du Bois, unimpressed with what he saw as the unscientific methods of Spencer and his disciples, saw Giddings's "consciousness of kind" as typifying the "gross and troublesome" abstractions of the period.[97] Du Bois's innovative empirical research at Atlanta University responded directly to this early period of US sociology, which he described as "work always wearisome, often aimless, without well-settled principles and guiding lines, and subject ever to the pertinent criticism: what, after all, has been accomplished?"[98]

Like the early psychologists, Giddings was a behavioralist, and his work would greatly influence not only Odum but most of the post–World War I social scientists and their reformist objectives. Odum quoted Giddings often: "When all is said, history is human behavior."[99] Giddings viewed behavior through the lens of its "similarities with engineering practice and turned an immense bitterness engendered by the war into a fervent pursuit of scientific sociology." While social engineering involved 'an acceptance of scientific principles as the basis for practice, and a following of technical methods in applying them,'" Giddings believed that these engineering "benefits remained untapped."[100] He saw "consciousness of kind" as how "social values and institutions . . . carried on processes of social selection."[101] Through this view, Giddings forged a kind of synthesis between Sumner and Ward. These various positions converged in general agreement to coalesce around the new discipline of sociology at the first meeting of the American Sociological Society, held in Ward's new home city of Providence, Rhode Island, in 1906.[102]

That same year, Sumner published his book *Folkways: A Study of Sociological Importance of Usages, Manners, Customs, Mores, and Morals*, an anthropological turn to the cultural origins of society. In it, he added to his previous deference to natural and market selection the "psychic construction" of folkways and rationalizing mores. In this new frame, folkways are inherited, predominantly determinant, and fatalistic, aligned with the mysterious processes of natural selection. According to Sumner, "humanity is driven by the four basic instincts: hunger, love, vanity, and fear," an assertion based on which he constructed a naturalistic view of folkways as a reflection of "trial and error" through which "one method of satisfying demand becomes customary for all or a significant part of the society."[103] His incorporation, through what he viewed as a scientific process, of the concept of mores allowed the "statesman and the social philosopher" the potential to conjure great energies to influence both folkways and the natural processes shaping them.

Sumner chose to contrast the Anglo-Saxon "folk," with its connotation of "unconscious ways," with the Latin "mores" as an amalgam of the intentional "customs and morality" guiding societies.[104] Inspired by Karl Pearson's emphasis on quantitative data gathering, Sumner asserted that "mores have the authority of facts."[105] In the South, Sumner wrote that after the Civil War, "legislators and reformers" proposed new laws to reconstitute race relations, but this legislation could exercise no influence on the mores of the Southern society.[106] His assumption became the basis for Odum's fatalist belief, passed down from his mentors, that "folkways" will always prevail in society and that "stateways" cannot impose or change them.[107] Despite such views, Sumner was still recognized and welcome among the founding "Big Four" of US sociology, who found a "professional compromise" possible due to the "hint of scientific control" in his approaches, even if his ideas represented "only a momentary lull in an otherwise heavy sea of evolutionary determinism."[108]

This compromise conceptually wedded Ward's telesis and Giddings's consciousness of kind to Sumner's mores, albeit from different positions regarding progress, in service of a foundational sociological scientific discipline. If progress could not be the theme around which the discipline could cohere, at least purposeful scientific intervention could engage with what were understood as spontaneous, wasteful processes of Spencerian natural selection. Sumner's hope for "the emergence of a scientific outlook, however narrowly defined, revealed that he was unable to resist entirely the appeal of the modernization model."[109] Historian Richard Bannister has helpfully summarized the importance of Sumner's influence on Odum's work: "Folkways effectively proposed a radical relativism coupled with the hope that a scientific outlook would replace the forces that produced it. By placing science within the mores, Sumner attempted to resolve the dilemma without totally accepting either relativism or modernization."[110]

This convergence, however, was short-lived. The violence and destruction of the Great War shook the early sociological melioristic faith in human rationality and progressive social development; in the ensuing years, "in a world of human behavior determined by largely non-rational factors, the chief function of social sciences became the description of social facts and forces rather than the uncertain social enterprise of influencing societal development."[111] Giddings's advocacy for quantitative methodology consolidated the discipline after the war, with many of his disciples developing "objectivist" tendencies. The interwar period also saw the channeling of prewar developmentalism into the technocratic social engineering project.[112] Amid these changes, Odum and the IRSS were navigating the credibility and scientific rigor of their "Southern project" with their partner institutions.

BIG DATA: THE OBJECTIVIST REBUKE

Odum established the Institute for the Research of Social Science with a grant from the Laura Spelman Rockefeller Memorial fund.[113] The IRSS was

Nature and the Folk at Work. Folk crafts and living at home. Photo by Bayard Wootten. Howard Washington Odum Papers, Wilson Special Collections Library, UNC–Chapel Hill.

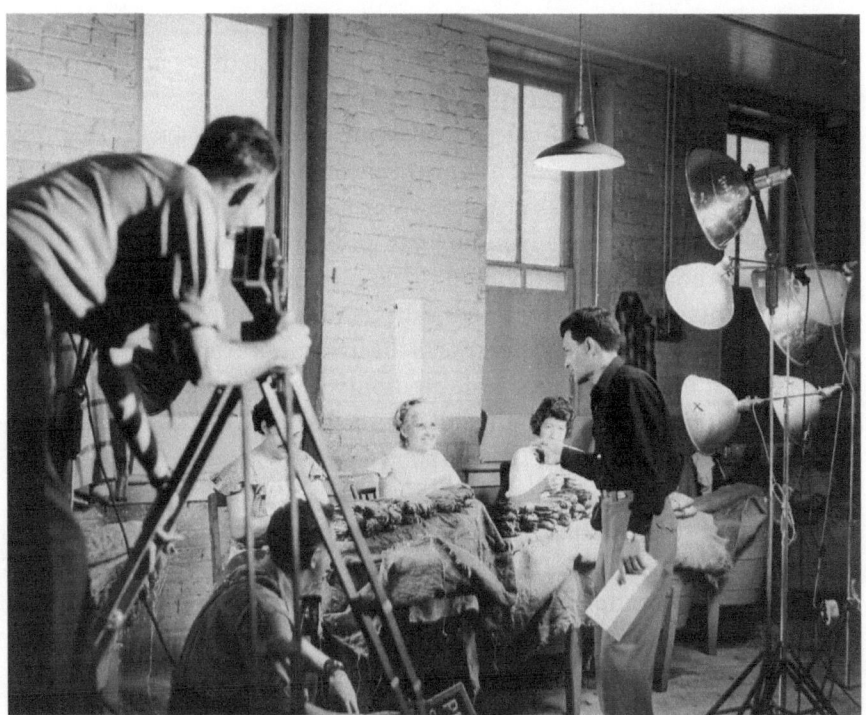

Filming folk, Southern Education Film Production Service, Athens, Georgia. Howard Washington Odum Papers, Wilson Special Collections Library, UNC–Chapel Hill.

a leader in the consolidation of a social science complex, funded through national philanthropy, to produce research to inform policy for the technical, scientific improvement of society. The IRSS also sought to promote the social sciences in the South—which meant promoting its research on the South to the social sciences. In Odum's view, the national leadership of these social sciences comprised the SSRC, the Rockefeller funding agencies, and his national social science colleagues (particularly from the University of Chicago and his alma mater, Columbia) at the tops of their respective fields, all of whom played prominent roles in managing these funds, and hence in leading and guiding the direction of the social sciences.[114] These "objectivists" sought to examine the "root problems" of social ills through standardized research methods calling for quantifiable, statistically based social sciences to match the certainty and authority of the natural sciences. Particularly in the period of "complacency and relative tranquility" prior to the crises of the Depression, Odum saw these scholars as a Northern hegemonic bloc in the social sciences whose "objectivism thrived in an environment of acute professional self-interest."[115] This hegemony's deployment of the "banner of science enhanced a façade of social disinterestedness and increased researchers' credibility as agents of the status quo."[116]

In contrast to this dominant emphasis on quantitative science, Odum's studies of Black folk songs, his literary aspirations in the "Left-Wing" Gordon trilogy, and his portraiture style were hardly likely to impress these elites. The years between 1924 and 1930 proved difficult for the work of establishing the IRSS, its work, and its reputation within the region, with Odum and his colleagues routinely skirmishing with the regional textile industry and clergy for what they saw as the institute's overcritical positions. Odum's quest to establish academic credibility for his work and that of the IRSS with the primarily Northern objectivists would prove equally challenging during this period. In *An Introduction to Social Research* (1929), Odum and colleague Katharine Jocher praised statistical methodology as "the consummation of the scientific ideal," providing "a precision . . . which can be secured by no other . . . common to all and upon which all must depend."[117] This effusive celebration of quantitative methods would prove descriptive more of how Odum hoped his work would be received by his Northern peers than of his own honest commitment to objectivist methods.[118]

In preparation for the SSRC meeting at Hanover, New Hampshire, in the summer of 1925, Charles Merriam invited Odum to chair the policy committee to help set the agenda for research and funding initiatives. Odum's proposed topics appeared to the committee "like emanations from the discredited earlier history of sociology": "probable change in social structure in America," "social-religious-moral attitudes of the great mass of people," and "the social-industrial structure."[119] He was removed from the committee, a rebuke that would stay with him for the rest of his career.

But rather than fully committing to objectivist agenda, which would have required far more clearly defined methods that were completely at odds with his own, Odum decided instead to clothe his work in the scientific terms of "folk portraiture." In a speech given in 1930, Odum (then president of the ASA) presented the technique as "folk sociology," of which he believed his book of the same year, *An American Epoch: Southern Portraiture in the National Picture*, was the foremost example.[120] The sweeping descriptive tone of this work, which was an attempt at balancing what he considered the positive and negative characteristics of the South, along with the personification of those characteristics in thinly drawn characters, shared a great deal with his previous oeuvre, only now the term "portraiture" was declared in its title as a new, self-described "radical" technique.[121] Odum described this method as a first step in research from which more critical studies would proceed, offering a "way of evaluating" research to present "regional

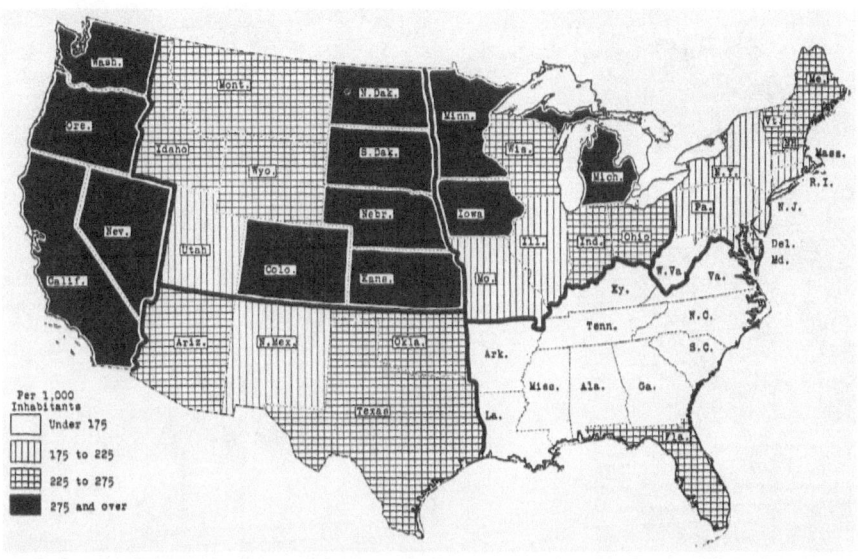

STATE	Total Automotive Group (000 Omitted)	Per Cent of U.S. Total	Gasoline Filling Stations (000 Omitted)	Per Cent of U.S. Total	STATE	Total Automotive Group (000 Omitted)	Per Cent of U.S. Total	Gasoline Filling Stations (000 Omitted)	Per Cent of U.S. Total
Southeast......	*1,167,626*	*12.1*	*236,520*	*13.2*	*Middle States*..	*2,975,258*	*31.0*	*601,006*	*33.5*
Virginia.........	118,669	1.2	23,610	1.3	Ohio............	608,910	6.3	132,796	7.4
North Carolina...	136,980	1.4	36,522	2.0	Indiana.........	274,300	2.9	51,214	2.9
South Carolina...	62,318	.7	13,907	.7	Illinois..........	620,733	6.5	110,482	6.2
Georgia.........	126,535	1.3	23,926	1.3	Michigan........	506,672	5.3	109,068	6.1
Florida..........	111,811	1.2	30,887	1.7	Wisconsin.......	249,884	2.6	48,961	2.7
Kentucky........	107,721	1.1	16,548	.9	Minnesota.......	214,067	2.2	46,720	2.6
Tennessee.......	128,857	1.3	18,984	1.1	Iowa............	224,813	2.3	48,341	2.7
Alabama........	103,838	1.1	18,424	1.0	Missouri.........	275,258	2.9	53,419	2.9
Mississippi......	89,856	.9	17,115	1.0					
Arkansas........	89,244	.9	17,992	1.0	*Northwest*......	*759,170*	*7.9*	*150,416*	*8.4*
Louisiana........	91,790	1.0	18,597	1.0	North Dakota....	62,089	.6	10,766	.6
					South Dakota....	68,502	.7	14,848	.8
Southwest......	*789,248*	*8.2*	*161,436*	*9.0*	Nebraska........	138,692	1.4	29,413	1.6
Oklahoma.......	215,924	2.3	51,407	2.9	Kansas..........	199,955	2.1	44,344	2.5
Texas...........	494,865	5.1	97,031	5.4	Montana........	61,155	.6	10,113	.6
New Mexico.....	28,968	.3	4,812	.3	Idaho...........	43,336	.5	6,268	.4
Arizona.........	49,490	.5	8,185	.4	Wyoming........	26,905	.3	4,242	.2
					Colorado........	112,032	1.2	21,763	1.2
Northeast......	*2,808,638*	*29.2*	*445,484*	*24.8*	Utah............	46,502	.5	8,654	.5
Maine...........	65,380	.7	6,987	.4					
New Hampshire..	40,152	.4	5,418	.3	*Far West*.......	*1,057,076*	*11.0*	*186,931*	*10.4*
Vermont.........	36,638	.4	4,388	.2	Nevada.........	12,884	.1	1,350	.1
Massachusetts...	344,135	3.6	52,319	2.9	Washington.....	168,328	1.8	28,267	1.6
Rhode Island....	53,547	.6	8,796	.5	Oregon..........	105,767	1.1	16,957	.9
Connecticut.....	145,897	1.5	26,387	1.5	California.......	770,095	8.0	140,356	7.8
New York.......	965,835	10.0	142,791	8.0					
New Jersey......	325,147	3.4	54,549	3.0	United States....	9,610,882*	100.0	1,793,149*	100.0
Delaware........	20,695	.2	4,254	.2					
Pennsylvania....	629,958	6.5	102,570	5.7					
Maryland........	97,480	1.0	17,903	1.0					
West Virginia....	83,768	.9	19,117	1.1					

*Includes District of Columbia.

TOP   Odum's data portraiture of automobiles per 1,000 inhabitants in six major regions in the United States in 1929. *Southern Regions*, 26. Howard Washington Odum Papers, Wilson Special Collections Library, UNC–Chapel Hill.

BOTTOM   Odum data portraiture of retail automotive sales, 1929. *Southern Regions*, 26. Howard Washington Odum Papers, Wilson Special Collections Library, UNC–Chapel Hill.

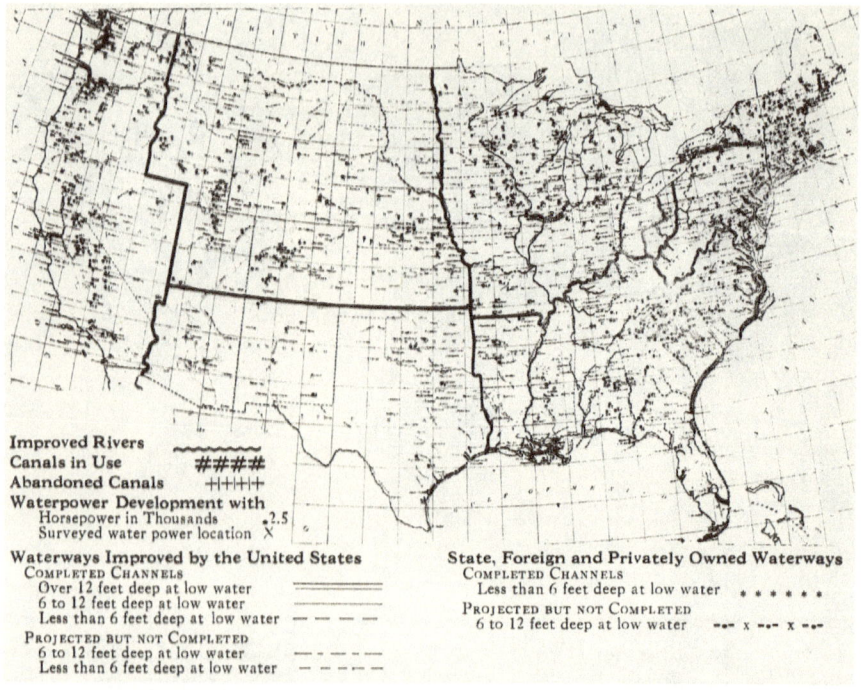

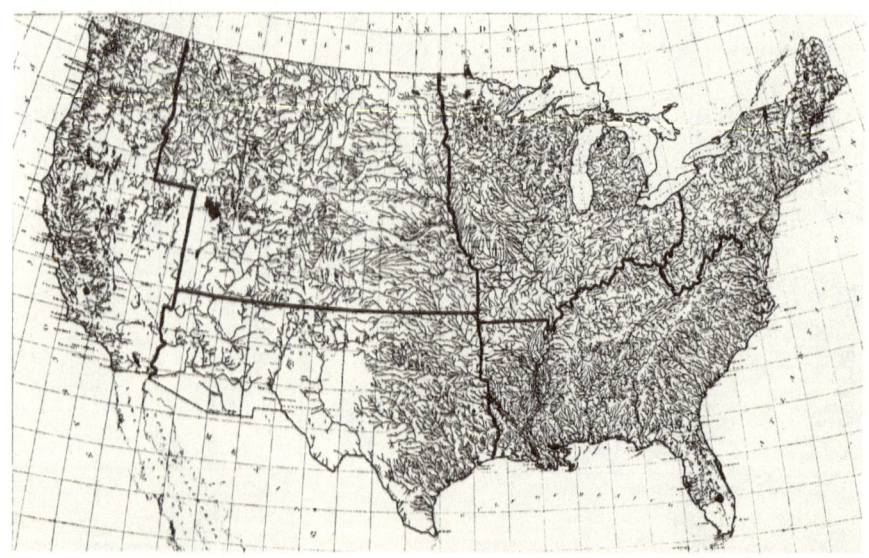

TOP Map of canals and improved waterways with depths at low water for six major regions in the US, 1929. *Southern Regions*, 294. Howard Washington Odum Papers, Wilson Special Collections Library, UNC–Chapel Hill.

BOTTOM Map of "Nation's Wealth of Streams of Water, 1929." *Southern Regions*, 294). Howard Washington Odum Papers, Wilson Special Collections Library, UNC–Chapel Hill.

facts" with an artistic sensibility—essentially, an aesthetic realism.[122] But the promised critical work never really materialized, and whether called "regionalism," "science," or "folk studies," portraiture remained Odum's core academic mode throughout his career.

Historian Daniel Singal notes that for many Southern authors and academics during the transitional period of the 1920s, "the hallmark of their writing was a thoroughgoing ambivalence" in which they distanced themselves rhetorically from "what they were in fact saying."[123] Portraiture was Odum's technique for this rhetoric, "a depiction of southern society that laid bare the pathology and many of its causes without analyzing or identifying it by name," thereby staying safely in description without venturing into analysis.[124] The approach was grounded in the organicism that Odum had learned from early sociology and the belief that society was a whole that could only fully be comprehended as such.

Odum incorporated regional description as "word painting," and in his regionalist work in the 1930s, he added "data as photography" to these descriptions.[125] Edward Soja, in his reading of Borges's "El Aleph," identifies the fundamental dilemma for cultural and physical geographic description: The linguistic despair resides in the fact that geographies are "stubbornly simultaneous," while language "dictates a linear flow of sentential statements bound by the most spatial of earthly constraints, the impossibility of two objects occupying the same precise place (on the page)."[126] This dilemma was clear in Odum's work and further exacerbated by his inability to resolve the fundamental tension between his dual aspirations for Southern development and reform and his admiration for the South's traditional power structure. In the evolutionary frame, progress and folklore were like accelerator and brake pedals that he depressed simultaneously, identifying the condition of stasis with loud noise as balance.

A fundamental aspect of Odum's portraiture technique involved universalizing the Southern experience by using types—often from his own family—to portray Southern social classes and perspectives.[127] In *An American Epoch*, Odum deployed two characters embodying the Southern white folk inheritance: Uncle John, the common yeoman (on Odum's paternal side), and the Old Major, the cavalry "aristocrat" (on Odum's maternal side). Conspicuously omitting any mention of their status as slaveholders, Odum praised this folk combination as "the backbone of the Old South," the essence of dignified Southern white folk culture, above the irrationality of populism and the demagoguery of Southern politicians and thus "the model behind a new, more capable South."[128] *An American Epoch* recounts "four generations of Southern Americans" as a regional tale to better understand American life through "the study of regional situations and folk society . . .

a sweeping American development reminiscent of *universal culture*."¹²⁹ In this description, Odum joins the celebrated Romantic folktale to an Enlightenment universalist spirit. The whole—the *universe*—limitless and yet conveyed in temporal and spatial terms—constituted through folklore at the family, regional, and national scales. Many Souths, *one* South; many folks, many regions, *one* universe.

Such universalizing rhetoric helped Odum set a course that avoided the excessive Lost Cause nostalgia of Southern sectionalism, from which he wanted to distance himself, while maintaining a certain distance through abstraction so as not to appear overly critical of that nostalgia.¹³⁰ Historian Michael Milligan refers to this tension as Odum "making scientifically universal the peculiar case of Southern backwardness."¹³¹ Odum, "rather than directing blame for regional deficiencies at specific individuals and ruling class interests ... cited vast societal forces, unrealized capacities and adjustments, and earlier stages of development."¹³² This approach echoed Ogburn's notion of "cultural lag," allowing Odum to present Southern pathologies as evolutionary conditions of development. Thus, Odum's "sociology of universal causation ... had the effect of distancing social phenomena from society's actors."¹³³ In *An American Epoch*, Odum affirmed that the regional challenge of 1930 for the South was "essentially that of any modern society challenged to find its way forward through effective adaptation to new difficulties, new problems, and new environments."¹³⁴ It was an issue that science and time could resolve through the slow pace of the telic technicways in intervening and improving these adaptations.

Moreover, in this period, the Chapel Hill group was not the only group to be considering approaches beyond exclusively "objective" methods relying on quantitative data. Despite the reprimands Odum and his IRSS colleagues received from some of the social science and philanthropy community of the SSRC, they were to receive support and praise elsewhere.

PERILOUSLY FAR DOWN IN THE SUBSOIL

In 1930, Herbert Blumer, a young sociologist at the University of Chicago, wrote a severely critical review of *An American Epoch* in the *American Journal of Sociology*. He faulted the work for lacking scientific method, which stung all the more because it was published during Odum's tenure as president of the ASA. It would turn out, however, that Odum's paranoia aimed at his colleagues in the University of Chicago sociology department was exaggerated. Columbia's sociology program, where Ogburn had trained, was a far more ardent proponent of objectivity and statistics than the University of Chicago, where Ogburn landed in 1927. Moreover, Robert Park, Ernest

Burgess, and their school of human ecology at the University of Chicago shared considerable commonalities with the empirical descriptive methods employed at the IRSS.[135] By the mid-1930s, even Blumer was criticizing excessive objectivism in the social sciences.[136]

Human geographer Carl O. Sauer was also an ally and kindred spirit of Odum. Sauer studied geography at the University of Chicago and graduated in 1915, just five years after Odum completed his sociology PhD. Deeply engaged in debates around standardizing methods in the social sciences, Sauer was critical of any normative or overly theoretical position. He argued for empirical research as a field to test theories grounded in history and geography, or, as he termed it, a "cultural geographic" approach.[137] Sauer's famous 1925 book *The Morphology of Landscape* laid his claim for morphology as a geographic interpretive method aligned with the German geography of the period. Sauer spent most of his professional career at the University of California, Berkeley, so when Odum was planning his 1935 summer residency at the University of California, Los Angeles, he wrote to Sauer about the possibility of visiting him.

Sauer's response helps to position Odum's work within the national academic community of the period, as well as to clarify, more eloquently than Odum himself could, the IRSS's contributions through its exploratory, experimental regionalist approach in addressing the South's cultural landscape via its history and geography. I quote Sauer's response extensively to highlight the men's relationship of admiration and aligned objectives:

> I have watched for years with growing interest the publications emanating from your institute, as records of what is to my mind the most interesting experiment in social science in America. The Germans have a word for it—"*Volksbodenforschung*"—though it bears the taint of unfortunate national ambition. But the heavy German word does, I think, apply very well to what you have been doing-folk-soil-study. . . . Therefore, however much you may grope and wander you are doing something which in the end will be methodically helpful to all of us. Of course you are also fortunate in the field that belongs to you. The South certainly has a quality of culture, vividness of problem, and historical personality that makes it an enviable ground for the social scientist. Personally I have long thought that the country's most interesting and most dramatic human problems, both past and present, were in the South.
>
> I like the way you have insisted that you were dealing with the reality of the South, that life was and would be different in its problems in your part of the country than from others, that it was your

job to examine the personality of the South, and that you are going about this business of understanding by whatever means would get results. I think you have been right in not being too formal in your procedure; we are inclined to be a bit professorial in the social sciences, and you have not been particularly worried [about] appearing academic on all occasions. I like the method, the objective, and the spirit with which your group has been at work. I wouldn't swap it, personally, for all the social science theory or statistics in the country, because you are documenting an important part of the American scene and, being concerned about how a distinctive part of the American people has lived in its distinctive land, you proceed properly, as you have done to a consideration of how that people on its land may become a balanced integrant of the national economy.[138]

In later correspondence, Sauer responded to Odum's concerns regarding Rockefeller research funding thus: "I have thought for years that your group has been traveling right down the main track of social science research and that you have been doing invaluable pioneering work for the rest of us. . . . I do think we are methodically still in almost embryonic form. If I may hazard a very broad generalization, it is that we social scientists take the so-called theoretical studies too seriously and still hold in contempt the descriptive studies."[139] Sauer went on to underscore the importance of both historically based research and comparative research as ways to move beyond what he termed the technique of the abstracted "logical dialectic" he saw in economics.

Sauer understood the dramatic circumstances of Southeastern ecology as an emergency that required immediate attention, so he celebrated Odum and the IRSS as if they were emergency triage whose exploratory methods suited the exceptional Southern crisis of soil depletion and economic waste. He particularly praised IRSS researcher Rupert B. Vance's work on the region, referring to it as Vance's "South-at-the-cross-roads thesis":

You are perilously far down in the subsoil right now, and I should say that most of the [Southern] country that I saw literally faces extinction of its economic structure in about one generation. We can muddle along out in this part of the world and still make quite a few mistakes, but there is a good deal of the South where the penalties likely to be incurred are pretty staggering. Hence, especially, I wish more power to your little band of investigators who do not dodge the responsibility of becoming prophets crying in the wilderness.[140]

Sauer praised the IRSS for its long-term regional engagement and commitment in its work, underscoring his belief in geography and history as essential components for inductive research, for which methods should necessarily accommodate the means to best discover and describe the particularly regional relationships between land and people. By this point, Sauer had established his Mexican folklore research, also based in cultural landscapes—his of the Southwest and Mexico's Indigenous cultures—out of Berkeley.[141] He was more confident than Odum, able to endorse descriptive, historical, qualitative research full-throatedly within the objectivist faction. Odum, always the opportunist, asked Sauer whether he could report his praise to the Rockefeller Foundation as an academic endorsement, which request Sauer obliged. Even more important than the pathos of this exchange, however, is how Sauer's letters speak to the IRSS's contribution to the social sciences through its multidisciplinary, exploratory, regionalist approach. Although dismissed by some as antiquated or eclectic, Sauer demonstrated that this approach was influential well beyond the borders of the South.

Sauer's work in Mexico was followed by University of Chicago anthropologist Robert Redfield's research and his work *Tepoztlán, a Mexican Village*. Redfield then cowrote *Chan Kom: A Maya Village* with Mexican anthropologist Alfonso Villa Rojas. Redfield proposed an evolutionary development continuum, with Indigenous territorial folk culture changing through migration patterns toward larger, more disorganized urban settings. In these settings, urban acculturation replaces Indigenous folk and territorial cultural heritage.[142] Redfield spoke of the folk society as one that is territorially rooted, and for which land is an essential unifying factor for identity and social cohesion.[143] Carrie Tirado Bramen has called this an act of ventriloquy, where "a modern urban outsider ... projects onto the native a pristine, authentic space immune to historical changes shaping their own lives."[144] This device was used by regionalists and the "local color" literature of the 1920s and 1930s in the service of regional identification.

Sauer's praise of Odum and the IRSS privileged their exploration of the South's natural resources and the ecological dangers they faced. In particular, he mentioned the work of Vance, whose *Human Geography of the South* was an exhaustive review of Southern ecological resources and challenges. Vance concluded that, finally, history made the solid South, not geography, noting the largely endemic challenges of misguided Southern political decisions, shortsighted resource extraction, and speculative Northern greed. Sauer's praise excused Odum's methodological social science shortcomings, and perhaps those of the IRSS, due to his certainty that the cultural and ecological importance of the territory, and its critical state, validated any regional attempt to discern how Southern society needed to adjust to better steward the territory on which its culture depended. This legacy of environmental concern for the region is among those celebrated by Odum and IRSS researchers.[145]

The attempt to use territorial nature and biophysical systems to justify and naturalize Southern social contracts via the reading of the soil itself was a more complicated matter, yet one with which Sauer also agreed. He told Odum, "We geographers and anthropologists have been talking about the concept of culture and the fact that culture is a spatial manifestation, but your group is about the only one that has done anything about it in terms of *our* white man's civilization."[146] Nevertheless, as Robert Dorman notes, the regionalist movement of Odum, Sauer, Lewis Mumford, and colleagues was not "limited to the anxieties and aspirations of these few visionary artists and intellectuals," because their work "took on the most basic and most broadly held of regional-national myths: the myths of mobility, the myth of white supremacy, and the myth of the frontier."[147] These were the myths of the period, naturalized and reified in the period's social sciences to preserve and protect the status quo. C. Wright Mills, after a review of more than thirty social science textbooks of the era (including Odum's *Man's Quest*), noted that even the reform-minded texts lacked the true will to reform that status quo—a tradition that Odum's conflicted work actively carried on.[148]

CHAPTER 4

RACE AND PLACE

AS AMERICAN AS THE COTTON PLANTATION

Howard W. Odum was a man of broad-ranging research interests, but his "first and most persistent interest" concerned race relations and the lives and folk traditions of Black people in the American South.[1] In their posthumous edited volume of Odum's published writing, his colleagues at the Institute for Research in Social Science (IRSS) appraised his work on these issues as the core focus that defined the trajectory of his research, which expanded over the years from the study of Black folk songs "to the folk society and folk sociology, from race relations and the southern region to regionalism and regional-national planning, from folkways to technicways and stateways, from social values to social action" to project the course of Southern history.[2] For Odum, race was the myth on which he sought to build Southern regionalism—and, by extension, his proposals for regional planning.

Howard Odum with Guy Johnson. Howard Washington Odum Papers, Wilson Special Collections Library, UNC–Chapel Hill.

In his treaty on modernism and modernization, philosopher Marshall Berman writes, "In relatively backward countries, where the process of modernization has not yet come into its own, modernism, where it develops, takes on a fantastical character, because it is forced to nourish itself not on social reality but on fantasies, mirages, dreams."[3] Such fantasy mythmaking offers a schema that, "by projecting a people's deepest dreams and fears onto a series of external characters and events . . . can become an organizing framework for the society's shared emotions, providing its members with their most fundamental sense of unity and purpose."[4] Psychologist Jerome Bruner notes that myth occupies the space between fantasy and reality, a "balance that must be maintained, for if it descends into pure fantasy, it can become 'fanatical and obsessive and begins to serve as a substitute for reality.'"[5]

Myth in the South was nothing new. Historian Daniel Singal dates the role of Southern myth to the seventeenth century, when Virginia tobacco planters sent letters to England to ward off accusations of "frontier crudeness."[6] From their rural society, they claimed an aristocratic culture that rivaled London itself, yet they proved incapable even of building the frontier villages that were quickly developing in the North. By the nineteenth century, mythmaking in the South was "far more serious business."[7] Particularly during the post-Reconstruction Jim Crow era, Southern myth was not lacking in fanatics, many of whom clung to the cavalier myth of the aristocratic Southern white gentleman, a man capable of taming the landscape and bringing order to what he viewed as an otherwise chaotic, savage world.

Singal views the period between the late nineteenth and mid-twentieth centuries as transitional, marking a shift in the South from Victorian to modern thought, arguing that Odum and his colleagues are essential in understanding this gradual change. Moreover, although modernism made inroads into the South in this period, historian Michael O'Brien has argued that "its success was not thoroughgoing."[8] The "progressive evolutionism" of turn-of-the-century social sciences, with their faith in those sciences to improve society, was met in the New South with the countervailing force of traditionalism.[9] All regionalists called for balance, but in the South, this balance between progressive and traditional culture and ways of thinking was the one the white elite needed to maintain. The contradiction between these two epistemological approaches is glaring: If the claims of modernity were based on progressive evolutionary assumptions about culture and thought, how best to balance them with Victorian and even earlier modes of traditionalism? How could a balance be struck between Old South and New South? Like William Faulker, Odum believed that the South needed time for its white society to "go slow" in evolving toward the modern egalitarian cultural demands often viewed as imposed from the North.[10] Against his training in the ameliorative organic social sciences of the early twentieth century, Odum struggled "to articulate a kind of planning at cross-purposes to time."[11]

James Baldwin, writing in 1956—twenty-five years after the Virginia round table—countered this pleasant "go slow" mythology with acerbic skepticism. In response to Faulkner's assertion that "emotional" white Southerners would move gradually away from segregation if left on their own time, Baldwin pointed out, "The question left begging is what, in their history to date, affords any evidence that they have any desire, or capacity to do this. And it is, I suppose, impertinent to ask just what Negroes are supposed to do while the South works out what, in Faulkner's rhetoric, becomes something very closely resembling a high and noble tragedy."[12] Citing *Brown v. Board of Education* attorney (and later Supreme Court justice) Thurgood Marshall, Baldwin observed, "They don't mean go slow, they mean don't go."[13]

Assumptions like Faulkner's, however, were not specific to the South. Historian Charles M. Payne demonstrates their endemic nature, remarking that with the 1896 *Plessy v. Ferguson* Supreme Court ruling, the "whole United States is Southern!"[14] The *Plessy* decision's language misrepresented the Southern segregated racial system not as structural, involving "power, privilege, or exploitation—something the law might do something about," but as a set of interpersonal feelings and choices of "'separation,' 'customs,' a normalized 'way of life,' and 'social equality.'"[15] Southern white leaders adopted this language, turning blind eyes to the "political disenfranchisement, racial terrorism, and personal degradation" of Black people in the South. They chose instead to celebrate "a system that worked for everyone's benefit," allowing each group to "develop in its highest potential, at its own pace, in its own way, maintaining its distinctive cultural values."[16] This conceptualization was, in essence, evolutionary, conveying a forward-looking optimism in the midst of what writers later termed the "nadir" of the Southern Jim Crow era of white brutality and lynching.[17]

The more famous shorthand identifier for *Plessy* was "separate but equal," a phrase that had been employed by leaders of the moderate New South movement since the 1880s—mostly "when northern audiences were involved."[18] This ideology, too, was a glaring contradiction: If equal, why separate? If separate, why equal? The New South, headed by Henry Grady, was a group of "merchants, industrialists, and planters" who worked with Northern capital and came to wield a "disproportionate influence on southern economic and political interests."[19] The "separate but equal" ideology mollified Northern white reformers with the guarantee that "the 'best elements' of the South had the Negro Question well in hand," and this reassurance "formed the basis for the national reunion of whites."[20]

Historian David Brion Davis has claimed that the Confederacy won the Civil War ideologically, and that a national reconciliation of North and South was only possible if grounded in basic agreement that repudiated Reconstruction as a "disastrous mistake," promoted the wide-ranging white acceptance of "Negro inferiority" and white supremacy in the South, and minimalized the historic interpretation of slavery as an "unfortunate but benign" institution.[21] By the 1920s, "separate but equal" had become the "preferred language of the white South," and by midcentury it was "deeply embedded in the national thinking about race."[22] Reviewing the racial policy, political institutions, and industrial philosophy established in post-Reconstruction America after 1877, historian C. Vann Woodward confirmed in 1961, "There has been no break with the founding fathers of the New South."[23]

The *Plessy* ruling's wide acceptance also found its way north in regional planning. At his farm at Mount Olive, New Jersey, outside New York City, Regional Planning Association of America (RPAA) founder Charles Whitaker spoke of an encounter in 1921 with racialized Italian immigrants shopping at a local market (and thus encroaching on his pastoral refuge), reporting that he and friends had looked "askance at them" and kept their distance.[24] Reflecting this distaste, in their famous neighborhood-unit model proposal—and in its realized prototype in Radburn, New Jersey—Clarence Stein and his fellow RPAA members saw racial segregation as necessary for the project's prospects for success.[25] In 1929, when the RPAA reached out to W. E. B. Du Bois for his support of the Radburn project, Du Bois reminded its members, "If a proposition of this sort is carried through and persons of Negro descent are refused any chance for residence ... then the result of your effort is not merely negative, it is a positive drawing of race and color lines, which is going in the *future* to have tremendous affect [*sic*] upon American civilization."[26] In defense of their rejection of integration, association members merely cited concerns over property values and the "problems" that integration would bring.[27] Lewis Mumford and his RPAA colleagues were drawn to an imagined folk rurality at the outer edge of the metropolis, where the group hoped to find refuge from the teeming, immigrant-rich New York of the 1920s. Yet this imaginary was an act of ventriloquy, the RPAA's projected indigenous connection to region itself a construct for exurban-suburban land development.[28]

The Chicago School also endorsed racial/ethnic segregation for the urban neighborhood and playground infrastructure in their human-ecology models.[29] Robert E. Park, an urban sociologist whose work contributed to the study of behavioralist social control for social planning, arrived at the University of Chicago in 1914, after working with Booker T. Washington for ten years at the Tuskegee Institute in Alabama.[30] In his presidential address to the American Sociological Society in 1925, titled "The Urban Community as a Spatial Pattern and a Moral Order," he emphasized "the importance of location, position, and mobility as indexes for measuring, describing, and eventually explaining, social phenomena."[31] He then underscored the importance of expertise in the observation and analysis of spatial phenomena "because social relations are so frequently and so inevitably correlated with spatial relations; because physical distances, so frequently are, or seem to be, the indexes of social distances."[32] For Park and his Chicago colleagues, urban planning was the social engineering needed to consider these subtleties when curating, projecting, and controlling metropolitan space.[33]

In 1936, following his retirement from the University of Chicago, Park moved to the South, where he taught at the private, historically Black liberal arts college Fisk University in Nashville, Tennessee. Park and Odum maintained a relationship in letters throughout their careers, but what was observed of Park with relation to race could also be said of Odum: "While Park's theorizing went through change, sort of catching up with events in the world, it should be made clear that he was no militant in the cause of racial equality. 'For all his concern with race relations, it is striking that the achievement of social and economic equality never emerges as a dominant goal in Park's thought.'"[34]

Odum continually called for equilibrium and balance to bring together societal "parts" into an organic whole. But what did equilibrium mean in the South? Odum came of age at the dawn of the twentieth century, when social reform movements in the South were achieving modest gains for African Americans even as reactionary responses simultaneously undermined their transformative potential and "foreclosed certain possibilities and promises."[35] The "paradoxical nature" of the Southern reforms of the period are summarized by historian Natalie J. Ring:

> At the turn of the century, the highest stage of white supremacy coincided with a wave of southern reform. Anti-Black violence and lynching reached its highest level during this period and was marked by a ferocity not seen since the immediate post–Civil War years. Throughout the South, white lawmakers codified the social separation of Black from white people and continued to observe this practice by custom even where no law existed. The system, known as Jim Crow, led to segregated and inferior education, divided sections on streetcars and trains, the exclusion of Blacks from most public venues (e.g., libraries, restaurants, pools, and parks), and the development of a racial etiquette that dictated Black subservience to whites. In an attempt to disenfranchise Black men, white politicians amended state constitutions and passed an array of laws that implemented literacy tests, poll taxes, and residency requirements. Without suffrage rights, Blacks had virtually no political power. This widely entrenched southern system of racial subordination led historian Rayford W. Logan to identify this moment in history as the "nadir" of African American life. The paradoxical nature of southern reform, and the choices made by Black and white middle-class crusaders, cannot be understood without acknowledging the deep roots of white supremacy in the Jim Crow South.[36]

Odum's equilibrium was difficult for him to navigate or maintain through his chosen approaches. Through his collaboration with Will Alexander and the Commission on Interracial Cooperation, Odum and the IRSS helped fund a study on Southern lynching; Odum also supported the University of North Carolina Press's publication of IRSS colleague Arthur F. Raper's 1933 book *The Tragedy of Lynching* and defended its publication.[37] The impact of this work was immediate: "Perhaps no other social science book written about the South during this decade received as much serious attention from southerners, and perhaps none has had a greater impact on changing southern behavior."[38] In his own writing, however, Odum demurred regarding direct condemnation, instead invoking generational Southern white folkways to explain white racial violence to the (presumably Northern) "outside observer." At best, his endorsement of age-old hegemonic white folkways in other contexts confused explanation with apology.[39] In deference to Southern whites, Odum opposed federal antilynching legislation and even aligned lynching with folkways, explaining, "The folkways are so strong that the enforcement of law by local or State forces would mean literally civil war in the community. . . . Progress is being made but it is in proportion as the folkways are being changed by education, publicity, civic appeal, and courageous leadership."[40] Of course, this "civil war in the community," as Raper observed, was exactly the tragedy.[41]

In his attempts to promote a conciliatory, cooperative modernization process, Odum "vacillated between the conservative Darwinist view that progress would come gradually and naturally and the vision of progress through rational planning."[42] Historian Richard H. King calls this theoretical "fuzziness in the sociological priority given to 'folkways' over 'stateways,' customs over law," the "classic dilemma of Southern moderates."[43] It certainly posed a dilemma for Odum, who tolerated limited Southern industrial development but idealized and sought to promote a renewed agricultural sector espousing the Southern agrarian values celebrated in the classics—Virgil, Horace—he had read during his youth in rural Georgia.[44] This organicism, however, was challenged in situations placing regional development at odds with traditional white Southern culture. In response to such challenges, Odum employed William Sumner's social Darwinist formulations to assure white Southern readers of his fidelity to the racial contract, noting (with coauthor and IRSS researcher Guy B. Johnson) that *Plessy* equality would not threaten their main concerns against miscegenation and intermarriage: "The old question of social equality is not necessarily involved. . . . The races can go the whole way of political and civic equality without endangering their integrity."[45]

Convinced that no social proposal in the South that frontally addressed Jim Crow could have succeeded, Odum incorporated an "Aesopian tactic" into his position on racial equivocation in hopes that his "tortured formulations" of "legal-sociological double-talk" could offer "something for everyone."[46] Ultimately, however, his solutions for Southern racial problems were "educational, institutional, and inadequate."[47] As King summarizes, Odum essentially held that "in all areas but race, the 'rational' should triumph over the historical; the folk was a potential force for change not stasis."[48] Odum's regionalism work opened the era for more ambitious federal economic development during the New Deal.[49] In social planning, at least, stateways were to be celebrated—but not at the price of the Southern racial regime.

On race, Southern regionalists asked for "every reform short of outright social equality."[50] Johnson, Raper, Rupert B. Vance, and Odum may have differed in how directly they spoke of Southern racism, but they came together in the belief that economic development was the best policy for Southern change—a rising tide raises all boats. In *Southern Regions of the United States* (1936), Odum wrote, "The next step in race relations should be to take the inequalities out of the bi-racial system." While noting that this would require "certain new conventionalities and codes of behavior on the part of both races," he added, "These things are not impossible to attain."[51] This reformist call was nonetheless undermined by an acute awareness of the "facts of Southern political life."[52] While Odum's work espoused some forms of liberal racial reform, "his diffuse prose style, his tendency to include a wide range of opinions, and perhaps more concretely his own political vulnerability as an institutional head—all combined to soften the thrust of his antiracist arguments."[53] Historian John M. Jordan offers a more pointed critique: "Odum's influence on racial liberalism was, if not terribly vigorous, at least an attempt to stir things up."[54] Odum helped to publish social scientist colleagues' widely respected work on racial issues in *Social Forces*, but his own organicist social science "subsumed race relations matters under the larger considerations of regional development and adjustment to social change."[55]

BLACK FOLK, BLACK ULYSSES

Odum's regionalism was "integrally conservative," grounded in what he saw as the country's threatened mosaic of geographic and racialized folklore.[56] Odum believed that "the folk-regional society is bottomed in the relative balance of man, nature, and culture," and through his early study of Black folk songs he claimed a kind of surrogate insight into "the heart and soul of a race."[57] In his framing, Black folklore took place in the South and hence belonged to the South, but it was not yet fully Southern.[58] To Rockefeller and other Northern philanthropists, Odum underscored the need for Southerners to research their own cultural conditions, yet he saw no contradiction in a white man studying what he distinguished as Black folklore in the South. Odum was celebrated as among the first white Southerners to make a modern contribution to Black folk culture research, albeit more than a decade after W. E. B. Du Bois's pioneering work and under far more problematic eugenic assumptions.[59] Odum would later be "compelled to retreat from his writings of earlier decades even though they were published after Du Bois's [Philadelphia] study," as environmental conceptions of racial social construction challenged outdated biological claims of superiority and inferiority.[60]

In the objectivist debates with the Social Science Research Council (SSRC) in the mid-1920s, Odum's justification for his Black folk song research was that if a "Southern institute could collect research on the Negro—the regional issue most prone to emotional excess and social imperatives—in an objective fashion, then this 'must convince anyone' that IRSS scholars were practicing the 'scientific method.'"[61] Through this "social scientific fieldwork," some have argued, Odum hoped to "uncover the truth about black life in the South that could be used to maintain racial order and ensure regional progress."[62] Lynn Moss Sanders attributes the gradual, transformative "liberalizing of Odum's view on race" to his study of Black folklore, claiming that "the folklore changed the folklorist."[63] For Odum, it was simply too much to ask Southern whites to change "overnight the powerful folkways of long generations."[64] The defensive Sumnerian folkways were mystified as omnipotent against Southern racial reform. This tension formed the core of his regional racial gradualism apology.[65]

Guy B. Johnson noted that during Odum's life, "many dramatic changes took place along the color line," that border identified by W. E. B. Du Bois in 1903 as the new century's central problem, and which had recently been reaffirmed by the 1896 *Plessy* decision. According to Gerald W. Johnson, these "dramatic" changes occurred in attitudes and norms throughout the country, and particularly in the South.[66] James Baldwin took a less sanguine view of such changes, asserting the line as "a fearful and delicate problem, which compromises, when it does not corrupt, all the American efforts to build a better world."[67] US planning practices and proposals were codified during the 1920s following the dictates of this color line.[68] Odum never openly crossed or abandoned the line. Among his colleagues this was not unusual; most of the leading sociologists writing on race before World War II did not criticize Jim Crow (Du Bois being among the obvious exceptions).[69] As a liberal Southern institutionalist committed to both progressive reform for regional development and the cultural preservation of regional white supremacy, Odum's themes of history and change with regard to race were at once the most celebrated and the most fraught in his work.

Swedish sociologist and economist Gunnar Myrdal, in his massive 1944 work *An American Dilemma: The Negro Problem and Modern Democracy* (funded by the Carnegie Corporation), noted that Du Bois's empirical work in the 1890s sounded "more modern" than most white academic writing produced in the ensuing decades. Myrdal's *American Dilemma* incorporated the collaboration of many social scientists of the period, including Rupert B. Vance, but Du Bois noted the oddity of assigning the project to a white foreigner. It was a landmark study, but for Du Bois, it also marked the point at which race study became definitively a white academic topic.[70]

Myrdal concluded that maintenance of a solid South white political bloc was based fundamentally on "the Negro, the slavery institution, and the conflict with the North and the strain since then."[71] A unified regional whole was extended and enforced through the power of this bloc to impose its values and norms on the majority, in concert with the "cultural solidarity necessary to the specifications" of the South.[72] The white South believed itself to be under Northern colonial rule from the Civil War through the first third of the twentieth century, and in response it fashioned a politics to maintain and advance the interests of planter elites while protecting "their distinctive racial civilization."[73] This bloc alliance had kept reform movements at bay since the late 1890s.[74] Baldwin, writing just over a decade after Myrdal, synthesized the bloc's position, and the country's dilemma, more succinctly: "The North, in winning the war, left the South only one means of asserting its identity and that means was the Negro."[75]

From Odum's 1910 dissertation "Social and Mental Traits of the Negro," a Spencerian description of Black socialization in society as a reflection of biological inferiority, to the 1954 article "Agenda for Integration," published shortly after the *Brown v. Board of Education* Supreme Court decision and before Odum's death, the issue of race and race relations in his work—and that of all the Southern regionalists—is of central importance in assessing how these scholars conceptualized the idea of *region*, its society, and their proposals for regional planning as a mechanism through which experts could measure and try to mediate social change.

After the firestorms of criticism his work drew in the 1920s, ranging from *Southern Textile Bulletin* editor David Clark to the SSRC in New Hampshire, Odum decided to emphasize the IRSS's work on race and folk studies, which made up almost 50 percent of its research output over the next five years.[76] Odum had accumulated extensive material from his Black folk song research, and there was the pressing need to publish "accessible, uncontroversial" work "in a hurry" to establish the institute's credentials and authority. He saw an opportunity in the rising popularity of blues music and believed that the IRSS's focus on race studies would also benefit from the New Negro movement that emerged during the Harlem Renaissance.[77] Odum's work is cited in Alain Locke's famous 1925 book *The New Negro* in the appendix listing work studying Black folk culture, and Odum wrote the foreword to Locke's 1928 book *A Decade of Negro Self-Expression*. Odum praised (in his way) this collection of Black writing and artistry as exhibiting "the promise of balance and poise in an over-enthusiastic and charged atmosphere. A new tolerance, charity, and patience. A mellowed bitterness . . . well tempered by the twin forces of opportunity and obligation."[78]

Despite this apparent mutuality, the study of Black life—often conducted by white academics like Odum—was largely disconnected from its realities. Zora Neale Hurston, a writer and anthropologist who had studied folk anthropology with Franz Boas at Columbia, pointedly titled her famous essay "You Don't Know Us Negroes." Of the period, Michael E. Staub writes, "While the 1920s and 1930s witnessed intensive investigations into and fascination with the folkways of black Americans, few who recorded black speech were themselves black." But as Hurston's biographer Robert Hemenway comments, 'white collectors, no matter how earnest, liberal, kind, sympathetic, and well meaning, were always—by definition of race—outsiders looking in.'"[79]

In her fieldwork experience studying Black folklore, Hurston reflected that authenticity was difficult to encounter due to the remoteness or shyness of members of Black communities when speaking with outsiders, particularly white outsiders. Instead, she wrote, "we smile and tell him or her something that satisfies the white person because, knowing so little about us, he doesn't know what he's missing."[80] There is an oft-told anecdote that Odum and Paul Green, upon learning of a group of Black prisoners singing while performing forced labor in Chapel Hill, ran to the site with their notebooks to jot down the lyrics. Almost unbeknownst to them, the song lyrics quickly turned to observations of these academics: "White man settin' on the big rock wall / Easy and cool, don't work at all / White man settin' on the wall all day long / Wastin' his time, wastin' his time."[81] This protest song highlights defiance and points out the absurdity of the very sort of documentation encounters on which Odum wanted to capitalize.

Odum saw his descriptive race and folk studies as an uncontroversial way forward for both the IRSS and Black Americans. Writing to Guy B. Johnson, who had been recruited to the University of North Carolina because of his work on the Ku Klux Klan, Odum pitched the idea of collecting volumes of Black folk songs that he and Johnson would coedit: "I think if we just went in for studying race relations, which is your main interest I know, nobody's going to pay much attention and we might get in a lot of trouble because things are so conservative. But practically everybody, no matter how narrowminded he is will say, 'Oh the Negro is a natural musician, he's a great singer,' and even conservative people can appreciate black music, so here we've got this chance, so let's do this."[82] These volumes would become *The Negro and His Songs* (1925) and *Negro Workaday Songs* (1927). Hurston was unimpressed with both, writing to Langston Hughes that Odum and Johnson's work made her "almost sick," her one consolation being that "they never do it right and so there is still a chance for us."[83]

After the song books, Odum began work in 1927 on what he called the Black Ulysses trilogy, a series of novels centering on the fictionalized life experiences of a Black laborer named John Wesley "Left-Wing" Gordon, whom he interviewed for the books *Rainbow Round My Shoulder* (1928), *Wings on My Feet* (1929), and *Cold Blue Moon* (1931). Their central character is a journeyman, "a primitive man in the modern world," traveling all over the South and telling tales that Odum hoped would illustrate the true Black "folk-soul" even to those "narrowminded" people he had derided to Johnson.[84] The Ulysses metaphor returned Odum to his interests at the University of Mississippi and allowed him finally to synthesize his beloved classics with Black folklore. Given the networks in which he participated and the audiences he was addressing, Odum carefully framed his Black Ulysses as a type: a blending of what he believed to be high and low culture. For this trilogy, he invented a fictional character based on his conversations with a real person, and then wrote about Black experience based on stories he had manipulated Gordon into telling by offering him money and liquor.[85] As historian Daniel Singal suggests, "Left-Wing's embellished accounts of hustling his way through thirty-six states and World War I instantly seized Odum's imagination."[86]

By this point, Odum was no longer arguing, as he had in his very early work, for biological racial difference; rather, in the Boasian sense, he was portraying the adventures and environments navigated by a Black Ulysses to entertain his readers. Singal believes that through these fictional enterprises, Odum sought to critique the Southern planter elites through depicting their brutal treatment of the main character. Yet Odum's veiled critiques of white Southern culture and semihumanization of Black characters were hardly revolutionary, even at the time, nor were they designed to be. With his Black Ulysses, Odum merged literature with sociology to generate a folk sociology, capable at once of capturing complexity and conveying what he viewed as the cultural essence of the region and its people. He deployed his main character as an avatar of the Jim Crow South, an antihero entertainer celebrated within the confines of fiction or song—the two comfortable dimensions that would mollify a white audience—who could serve as the essential cornerstone of Southern regional identity. In this approach, Odum's

Howard Odum in an Atlanta bookshop promoting *Rainbow Round My Shoulder*, 1928. Howard Washington Odum Papers, Wilson Special Collections Library, UNC–Chapel Hill.

calculation was correct: The trilogy was widely successful and sold more copies than any of his other works.[87]

AFRICAN AMERICA

Odum frequently used oppositional conceptual framing as a rhetorical strategy for his organicism-rooted approach: North/South, white/Black, city/country, natural sciences / social sciences, industry/agriculture, stateways/folkways, theoretical/applied, planning expertise / knowledge of the "common man," and so on.[88] As well as reflecting his belief in the bridging, synthesizing task of the organic social sciences, these binaries were power alignments where Northern power over the South paralleled that of white over Black, city over country, and industry over agriculture. At the turn of the century, even during the Great Northern Migration of the period, African Americans were still generally identified with the South in the national imaginary.[89]

Aligning the South with African Americans in this way mirrored similar regionalist cultural alignments with indigenism in the Midwest and

Southwest. Regionalists fused folklore and indigenism to evoke an "earth-loving" communitarianism in their diverse "resettlement" projects across the country.[90] But these cultural claims for regionalist identities necessarily fed off the marginalized peoples of those regions. The city represented a modern site for change, so the regionalists pushed modernity to the periphery, celebrating folklore in nonurbanized landscapes where they could promote "cultural reforestation" unthreatened by the density of and proximity to either new communities, or those marginalized communities whose increasing numbers and presence were challenging white social norms.[91] Regionalisms were conceived by those with the power to shape their definitions as desired.

Lewis Mumford cited Van Wyck Brooks as an inspiration for his fellow regionalists in deploying a "usable past" for their "rediscovery of America"—what Raymond Williams called the "selective tradition"—in their endeavors as "scouts and prospectors in a new enterprise."[92] There was at once a call for a new pioneering approach to culture and landscape that was also capable of reconnecting with the "indigenous" (but hardly Indigenous) America that regionalists believed had been lost amid consumerism and standardization. Particularly during the 1920s, Mumford took up a mission that art historian Alan Trachtenberg calls the "historian as artist"—a scholar in search of aesthetic regional qualities and in the construction of history toward those ends. Mumford's work during this period is neither completely invented nor imagined but instead creative, making it difficult to disentangle his attempted historical "discoveries" from "literary inventions."[93] As with European regionalist traditions, exemplified particularly in the German *Volksgeist* discourse in the late nineteenth century, these regional folklore customs were artistic creations that simultaneously retreated to locality from urban modernity yet were broadly international in expression.[94]

Odum's literary work, particularly the Black Ulysses trilogy described above, crossed directly into the creative/aesthetic realm to create a character/caricature of a Southern African American in the United States during the 1920s.[95] To his Northern benefactors, Odum justified the sociological contribution of this technique as a work of "artistic realism," which he would continue in the more explicitly historic mode of *An American Epoch*. Odum's mentor Franklin Giddings had proposed that Black people were "plastic, yielding easily to environing influences," thus giving "hope that [they] will acquire a measure of reason."[96] Thus, in his reinforcement of alignment between African Americans and the South, Odum proposed Wardian social engineering for the development of region, culture, and people—particularly through educational institutions and under the supervision of (white) expertise—to overcome the cultural lag that stigmatized the South throughout the period.

Odum's "artistic realism," which produced what have been described by Trachtenburg as "not uncomplicated discourses in a conventional mode of historical narrative," reflected an evolutionary construct that converted this broad group clustering into "objects of development."[97] This engineered organicism was both timeless and temporally conditioned, historicist and yet selectively ahistorical, material and fiction. Amid interregional migration trends and "outside" calls for economic and racial reform, Odum naturalized the South in what he believed was the timeless, self-evident, and legitimizing stasis of nature and folk. He fused the solid Southern racial history with his spatial definition of regional contours, such that regionalism was a Southern racial construct, and race was a Southern regionalist construct. For Odum and colleagues, race was the scale of region.

At a moment when regional economies were becoming increasingly integrated into national and international economies, and political nation-state claims increased to consolidate these markets, late nineteenth- and early twentieth-century regionalism represented attempts to preserve those cultural orders threatened by new spatial divisions of labor.[98] Thus, regionalism, "like pluralism . . . responded to the conflicting trends of homogenization and differentiation, by which regional consolidation produced spatial hierarchies."[99] Odum and his colleagues proposed a forward-looking regionalism as a middle ground for these oppositional ideas, an equilibrium between the threat of the national urban-industrial elimination of cultural uniqueness among regions and the historic grievances of sectional division.[100] For the South in particular, Odum sought to incorporate the region into the national fabric on its own terms by uniting the two currents of racialization and regionalization—another duality that Odum, either willfully ignoring or pleasantly unaware of the contradictions these two positions could involve, hoped to bridge through his organic social science. While his selective historicism paid homage to an imagined authority of tradition, Odum's organicism provided an idealized "ahistorical innocence" as a refuge in which he could elide the tensions of Southern history and of his own construction of regionalism. The fusion of place and race was central to that construction.[101]

RACE, PLACE, AND CULTURE

How do people, place, and culture cocreate one another? When European regionalists of the late nineteenth century looked to the medieval period for pre-modern, pre-nation-state inspiration, they often "connected people and culture using place as grid or matrix only."[102] With no medieval period to draw from as a cultural ideal, regionalism in the United States was further challenged to invent essentialized people, culture, and place. In the Victorian mindset, the stages of development from savagery to civilization defined communities in three successive types: of blood (kinship), of territory (place), and of purpose, from which the nation could then form.[103] Given American unwillingness to recognize Indigenous contributions to "civilization" in the United States, the national preoccupation was that "the national territory seemed to antedate either the appearance of the people as a nation or the existence of any cultural characteristics commonly possessed by each and all."[104] Poet Robert Frost wrote in "The Gift Outright," "The land was ours before we were the land's. / She was our land . . . before we were her people."[105]

In the latter part of the nineteenth century, the belief developed that the people of the United States must construct their own concept of culture and link it to place, thereby developing that necessary bond between people and place.[106] By the end of the nineteenth century, anthropological debates ascended to influence broader social thought around these issues. The work of Franz Boas and Daniel Brinton emphasized environmental determinism—the anthropological importance of location—as a central part of the complex construction of character, in contrast to the biological explanations that had dominated academic discourse since Darwin's *On the Origin of Species*. Those among the American school of polygenesis proposed locus in quo to conceptualize place as an explanatory factor for evolutionary unevenness and variation.[107]

Historian Frederick Jackson Turner presented his work "The Significance of the Frontier in American History" at the 1893 World's Columbian Exposition as a new direction for anthropology that would align the field with contemporary ameliorative and speculative thought. He proclaimed, "The true point of view in the history of this nation is not the Atlantic Coast, it is the Great West."[108] Turner advocated for new study of the relationship of place and culture with a refocused historical understanding of Indigenous American cultures and landscapes—the "frontier"—as the site where European settlers, stripped of their cultural pasts, uniquely transformed Indigenous culture into a distinctly American one. Beginning with a study of his home state of Wisconsin, Turner then offered additional conceptual elasticity for the frontier idea, creating in it a "moving line of the frontier of Euro-American settlement . . . the [new] matrix against which patterns of culture and processes of cultural change might be located."[109]

This "moving line" of Turner's frontier could also be applied to the US Atlantic coast during the British colonial period or the Allegheny Mountains in the nineteenth century as a context of encounter that produced the nation's exceptionalism across sections. As Turner put it, "The frontier masters the colonist. It finds him a European. . . . Little by little he transforms the wilderness, but the outcome is not the Old Europe . . . [but] a new product that is American."[110] Turner's frontier theory became widely popular almost immediately and was used to celebrate the national character as an overarching formula of the country's essence that both united its various geographic experiences and distinguished these same regions from one another—at times competitively.

After World War I, Turner's study of United States uniqueness was appropriated, on the one hand, by the wave of "100 percent American" Anglo-Saxon white celebrations of the 1920s. On the other hand, it was appropriated by the regionalists, whose increasingly popular sentiments looked to folk cultures as the defining element of place and pluralism.[111] Artists and intellectuals pursued interests in Indigenous cultures, viewing European American and African American "folk" cultures as antidotes to the widely perceived sense of loss of identity amid increased commercial and consumer influences. The Freudian turn transformed Indigenous and Black cultures—so commonly disregarded, demeaned, and marginalized in the Victorian age—into celebrated, mythologized cultures that lived more naturally, closer to the land and free from the temptations of the consumer society so reviled by regionalists. B. A. Botkin believed folk culture to be "the traditional forces of custom, belief, locality, and speech which within a region constitute the peculiar disposition and expressiveness of a people considered as a composite of racial and geographic influence and a component of national culture."[112] Within this new (or renewed) frame, Turner, the frontier, and the pioneer, which had been waning symbols during the forward-looking Progressive period, found new relevance in the postwar period. The frontier pioneers were also celebrated for living "closest to the soil and its influences," removed from the "standardizing," ever-growing urban-industrial lifestyle.[113]

A postfrontier Turnerian, forestry-trained planner Benton MacKaye looked to Aldo Leopold's romance of the wilderness as a resource from which to draw "certain social values," akin to the pioneers.[114] Regionalists proposed a historical continuum on which periods of change were met with responses of folk culture to produce the appropriate evolutionary balance of the modern and the traditional in stages: the frontier stage, the rural-pastoral stage, and, finally, folk-regional societies, with greater differentiation in the facets of modernization.[115] In this phase, folk culture could be expressed either in the political strains of sectionalism or in the art of regionalism. In the ultimate vanquishing of folk culture by modernization processes, the folk becomes mere fetishized artifacts or is forgotten completely.[116] Lewis Mumford critiqued the pioneers' unsettled, wasteful use of land on the frontier while simultaneously aligning the frontier era with an "older America, the America of the Eastern wilderness and the Western frontier; a heritage we ignore at our peril."[117] It was an evolutionary, defeatist, fatalistic vision that tracked perfectly along the lines of Old South / New South identity crises of the period.

Breaking with the New South orthodoxy that shunned its frontier past as uncivilized, Odum claimed Turner's idea for the South as a "sort of specialized America with a continuing frontier fringe, either in physical settlement or cultural expansion." As Odum expounded, "The South has always been a frontier ... rich in struggle and conflict, romance and adventuring, victory and tragedy."[118] Through the evolutionary cultural processes posited by the frontier, Odum traced his argument from plantation to section, from section to civilization: "In this society, which began with the culture of the American Indian and continued the extension of the frontier, and, in the last part of the nineteenth century, the development of cities and industries and great individual fortunes, together with a phenomenal increase in science, education, and art, may well be found an excellent field for the understanding of human society."[119]

Along similar lines, IRSS scholar Rupert B. Vance used the Turner proposal, with Geddesian influence, to formulate his "concept of the region." If environment did influence culture rather than merely providing a matrix or background, then one must catalog the environmental resources and ecological relationships at the base of a society to develop a regional analysis from the ground up.[120] By consulting agricultural atlases of the period, Vance first established what he termed the "physical factors" of a region to determine how their differences could influence the cultural variance of regions. His work reflected his influences:

> Le Pays' famous formula is also regional: place conditions work, work conditions the family organization, and the family is the social unit which makes up society. This formula of place-work-folk has received its most brilliant American demonstration in Turner's account of the evolution of frontier society in accordance with the conditions of the wilderness. . . . The regions change as the state of agriculture and industry advances. . . . In the uses that man, in the effort to clothe, feed, house, and defend himself, makes of the map furnished by nature, Jean Brunhes finds the scope of human geography.[121]

Both Vance and Odum focused on Southern frontier qualities to celebrate the small yeoman farmer, whose character emerged from the folk "saving virtues" of family, community kinship, and spontaneous association and cooperation formed as survival tactics, idealized for conditions under which "culture and place melded." The two scholars constructed a rugged folk adaptation to the environment in an idealized past, in contrast to the contemporary commercial standardization of culture against which regionalists railed.[122] This translation of the frontier to the Southern yeoman was also a rhetorical strategy to align the South with Turner's vision and to subtly re-center Southern historical focus on their own North Carolina Piedmont region, where plantation hegemony had never taken hold to the degree that it had in the Cotton Belt.[123] Southern regionalists differed, if not in their opinions, certainly in their responses to the plantation mythos that had been established in the post-Reconstruction period. According to Vance, the power, influence ("the shadow of slavery"), and persistence of the plantation pattern over the sixty years after the Civil War offered "no cause for congratulations."[124] Such critiques notwithstanding, both Odum and Vance recognized the plantation society as retaining many of the frontier qualities that Turner celebrated.[125]

The plantation mythos was a Southern analog of Turner's frontier, celebrated as a civilizing institute for taming and domesticating both inhospitable landscapes and perceived cultural barbarism.[126] This mythos combined the Southern white cavalier's mission of imposing control and order on chaotic conditions with the yeoman's capacity to work with and live connected to the earth. In the post-Reconstruction era, this mythos became the celebration of the "agricultural ladder" and its dubious claim for the opportunities the plantation system provided through Black sharecropping and tenancy—what many called the "second slavery."[127] Moreover, the plantation offered alluring ways to conceptualize modern agricultural renewal in appropriately nostalgic ways: "With its concentration of labor under skilled management, its overseers, foremen, blacksmiths, carpenters, hostlers, cooks, nurses, plowhands and hoehands, the plantation, Ulrich B. Phillips contended, resembled nothing so much as the factory system applied to agriculture."[128] The Southern Agrarians at Vanderbilt University used idealized plantation nostalgia to counter what they saw as the regional threat to their "agricultural social order" posed by Northern industrialist interests.[129]

While Odum often criticized the dehumanizing practices of slavery and the plantation, the traditionalist in him also romanticized the plantation aristocracy, living in classical-inspired houses "filled with reflections of glory and grandeur, vivid, beautiful, and distinctive."[130] He found inspiration in the antebellum plantation style of the Washington White House as a maximal expression of "southern portraiture in the national picture... symbolic of all the South had contributed to the Nation."[131] Odum's portraiture technique reaffirmed the Southern regionalist plantation landscape just before he entered his regional-national planning phase.

Vance's father had never been able to climb any agricultural ladder promised to him, so Vance's critique of the plantation was more pointed. He may have embraced the frontier and the yeoman, but he was clear in pathologizing the landscape of Southern peoples, places, and cultures, as well as their mutual constitutions. To him, the plantation was not a civilizing institution but a nodal site of the nefarious cotton cultural complex network. Vance's unsparing critiques of the plantation system, the ever-repeated downward cycles of irrational choices that defined the Southern cotton culture, bore no trace of Odum's perennial attempt to ensure that Southern stories always had some "bright side."[132] Essentially, Vance saw the brutality against a place and a people, the frontier mindset that could simply move westward if land or social problems arose in settlement, as a lack of civics.

Thus, Turner's frontier theory could be selectively projected onto the Southern geography to celebrate the emergence of both the yeoman and a romanticized culture of land connection and cooperation. According to Vance, Southern society fused the frontier's rugged primitivism with its self-conception of aristocracy: "the popular paradox that the South is at once the most crude and the most courtly, the most promising, and the most provincial, the most backward area in the United States."[133] He contrasted the frontier and the plantation in Odum-like duality: a subsistence landscape versus a domesticated one, in which the frontier offered an escape from the near all-encompassing plantation geography. Vance deployed Turner's concept of European civilization as transformed through native crudeness to forge a distinct national character and refracted it southward, seeing the tension of frontier and plantation creating the Southern essence.[134]

But the frontier could also be traced forward to the entrenched geographic, economic, and social practices of the plantation during and after the Civil War. Arthur F. Raper's *The Tragedy of Lynching* (1933) documented brutality that he traced directly to the plantation system and the "belated frontier" stage, in evolutionary development terms, of a society without social cohesion—a society in which the dehumanization of slavery, and its legacy in Jim Crow, were inevitably turned destructively inward, most violently against African Americans in this "nadir" of history, but also in the societal inability to sustain itself beyond the interests of the planter elite.[135] In 1941, Raper followed with *Sharecroppers All*, coauthored with Black sociologist Ira De Augustine Reid of Atlanta University, which focused on the collapse of the land tenancy system but saw no hope in the coming of Southern industrialism. As Singal argues, the title of their book highlighted that "the culture of dependency generated by the plantation was just as conspicuous in southern cities . . . and even in the way the South related to the rest of the country"; thus "sharecroppers" referred, more broadly, "to the whole population of the South as it was shackled by the defective culture arising from the 'feudalistic' plantation regime."[136] Further, Raper and Reid identified the plantation as an extreme version of corporate labor and resource-extractive practices common throughout the country, boldly asserting, "Lynching, homicide, kidnapping, and unemployment are the product of no deep dark mystery. . . . They are as American as the cotton plantation."[137]

Clyde Woods observes that in much of the South, the planter bloc served as the surrogate state, particularly before increased federal funding arrived through the New Deal. Throughout post-Reconstruction until the 1930s, the South continued its dependency on the elite planter class to provide privately for the necessary infrastructure to enable commodity circulation.[138] Such reliance was by design, since, "like ranches and mines, plantations evolved as total institutions, with distinct regional, state, electoral, administrative, and judicial practices."[139] Daniel Singal summarizes the spatial and societal impacts of this total institution, whose "needs determined the South's pattern of settlement, its principal transportation routes, and the location, size, and vitality of its cities, all while sapping life from any other institution that threatened to compete for power. In short, the plantation flourished at the expense of the development of the rest of southern society."[140] This historical path dependency has been traced by historian Peter A. Coclanis throughout what he terms the "long twentieth century," dating from the 1860s up to the approximate present in the South, where the "'past mattered' a lot."[141] Echoing Singal's assertions, Coclanis concludes that "the fateful decision—or more accurately, set of individual decisions—to organize the southern economy around slave plantations, the earliest manifestations of which decisions arose in the late seventeenth century, set much of the tone for the region's economy for centuries thereafter. . . . The legacy has plagued the region over much of the long twentieth century."[142]

Southern regionalist critiques may have problematized the plantation complex, but their arguments remained locked within the evolutionary historical frame that undergirded the social sciences of the period. Many regionalists engaged in often devastating critique of the Old South and its institutions. But apart from Du Bois, most US social scientists of the period were both unwilling and unable to address African American historical claims for "the redistribution of political and economic power."[143] The spatial, economic, environmental, and cultural regimes that supported the plantation complex were deeply engrained in the Southern territory—what Allen Tullos refers to as the "terrortory"—despite the high costs of maintaining the regime.[144] High cotton prices during the first two decades of the twentieth century, attaining peak prices in 1927, artificially extended the regime's justification until the limits posed by topsoil erosion, boll weevils, the Great Depression, and World War II decisively intervened.

From his work on Black folklore and songs, through Black Ulysses's heroism and deviance (either environmentally precipitated or biologically programmed), through the stasis and social fixity he laminated via portraiture, and finally into regionalism and regional planning, Odum projected Southern white development onto the Southern Black community, measured by his celebration of how far it had come since the times of slavery. Regionalists romanticized the spirit of Turner's frontier after it closed, and they celebrated Indigenous culture after taking more than 1.5 billion acres of land through Native American displacement and the atrocities of "Indian Removal." Many of the Southern regionalists celebrated the plantation and its society even amid African Americans' Great Migration to the North. White nostalgia for the socioeconomic, political, and cultural systems of nineteenth-century America formed the core of regionalism. The following section explores the racialization and environmental possibilities across geographies that moved away from a traditionalist, territorial frame to reify people, culture, and place.

PLURALISM AND INTERREGIONALISM

In the last decades of the nineteenth century and well into the twentieth, African American migration, along with significant white migration, offered an escape from the deleterious practices of the "cotton complex" and the plantation system that Odum and his colleagues both described and often romanticized. The rural Southerners who formed the backbone of folklore and regionalism were largely moving to Southern cities and the industrial North, and westward in pursuit of economic opportunities beyond the traps of tenancy and sharecropping.[145] From 1870 to 1970, a combination of push-pull factors led to an estimated 6.3 million African Americans emigrating from the South.[146] These rates accelerated in the early twentieth century, with Odum estimating African American out-migration numbers at 448,678 in 1900, 872,233 in 1920, and 1,840,758 in 1930—together making up approximately half of the period's total.[147] In 1903, Du Bois commented that this great out-migration to Northern cities was "the most significant economic change" among African Americans "in the last ten or twenty years."[148]

Arthur M. Schlesinger Sr. described the late nineteenth century's "rise of the city" as a conscious response to Turner's frontier thesis. Vance eventually turned from examinations of the plantation to a focus on the urban South, in which the city had the potential to better equalize conditions and opportunities across regions.[149]

The turn-of-the-century concern over a modernity of "sameness" and standardization was met with several conceptualizations of variety, each searching for an overarching national vessel of "diversity within unity" that could encompass the dramatic changes of the period. The visions of pluralism and regionalism "took that which was considered divisive and made it a necessary ingredient for the twentieth-century nation."[150] If regionalism attempted to contest New England and New York as sole cultural tastemakers and representatives in a Northeast urban corridor of hegemonic modernity, pluralism sought to de-center European immigration and whiteness as the exclusive, unified subject of American character. Carrie Tirado Bramen notes that "regionalism did for geography what the hyphen did for ethnicity: it linked a subculture with national identity."[151] Accompanying this national need to reconceptualize variety to absorb difference was the move, over time, in the social sciences from "race-ism" to "place-ism," shifting from an understanding of the environmental context for society as providing only conditioning for biological character formation to a more robust belief in environmental determinism.[152] Along these multiple axes, the work of W. E. B. Du Bois and Benton MacKaye's Appalachian Trail help both to illustrate and complicate these successive tendential explanatory framings.

W. E. B. Du Bois was born in New England, in Great Barrington, Massachusetts, in 1868, and from birth he uniquely confounded essentialist understandings of place and race in the second half of the nineteenth century.[153] Educated in both the South and North—receiving his undergraduate degree from the historically Black Fisk University in Nashville and becoming the first African American to receive his master's and doctoral degrees from Harvard University—Du Bois famously described the African American experience of "double consciousness," shaped by America's history of racial oppression and violence, and the acute awareness of being both Black and of the United States.[154] Before entering the Harvard PhD program, Du Bois spent two years in Berlin, where he engaged with the premier German School social theorists of the period, training in history, economics, and sociology.[155]

In 1895, Du Bois accepted an instructor position at the University of Pennsylvania to conduct research on "the Negro problem" in Philadelphia for the Wharton School. The city had experienced violent race riots in the 1830s and 1840s that had forced out many African American immigrants arriving from the South, but a new wave of migration in the 1850s, and particularly after the Civil War, had increased the Black population of Philadelphia to 45,000 among a total of 1,046,964 in 1890. This was the second-largest African American population among the ten largest US cities of the period. Du Bois published *The Philadelphia Negro* in 1899 as the first study of an urban Black community, centered on the city's Seventh Ward district, which was home to 42 percent of the city's African American population.[156]

Du Bois's study incorporated innovative empirical methods and his insistence on a critical perspective, in sharp contrast to the pretense of objectivity common in the social sciences of the period. Both aspects of his analysis were pioneering contributions to the field of sociology. Further, Du Bois presented the nuance of Black class structures and mobility in his work, acknowledging the long shadow of slavery over urban migration and employment opportunity. He also crossed the color line to understand the structural systems of oppression in the United States and internationally, and how they impacted both Black and white communities.[157] The "problem of the color line" was one that impacted *all*. Following the publication of *The Philadelphia Negro*, Du Bois gained recognition "as the first number-crunching, surveying, interviewing, participant-observing and field-working sociologist in America, a pioneer in the multimethod approach."[158]

Du Bois was interested in the urban-industrial environment of Philadelphia as a potential place where more equal opportunities across his concept of the "races" could occur, and where opportunity for the African American community could further develop to its full potential.[159] His Philadelphia, however, was not an overly reified place but a networked one. While writing *The Philadelphia Negro*, Du Bois traveled to Farmville, Virginia, to study its rural Black community using the same multimethod research approaches he was pioneering in the Seventh Ward.[160] He approached "cities and regions as physical and social environments inhabited by interdependent agglomerations of races, each of them stamped by distinctive physiological, psychological and social characteristics derived from their biological and historical heritage, and each carrying within it a race-based genius."[161] According to sociologist Aldon D. Morris, "Du Bois believed that to understand American race relations the sociologist had to focus on both North and South and rural and urban communities because together they reflected an unbroken chain of social processes operative in both milieus. The approach was to remain a distinguishing feature of Du Bois's sociology."[162]

For Du Bois, "movement across space" was essential and broadly conceived, not only within his urban studies but also encompassing the movement from South to North, rural to urban, household to work, at multiple scales with multiple directionalities.[163] These were the politics of space that

Du Bois highlighted to provide contextual specificity of race and class without disaggregating the continuum of Black experiences along these cycles of settlement, migration, and resettlement.[164] Regions were discernible in his work, but his sociological interest focused on the Black interregional experience, where his committed empiricism and ethnographic work led him from the Seventh Ward in Philadelphia back to the South's urban and rural spheres.[165] Du Bois, through his tracking of Black interregional migratory patterns between Philadelphia's Seventh Ward back and the rural Dougherty County, Georgia, showed a far more nuanced understanding of North/South, rural/urban networks, and interdependencies of the Black experience—divides he traversed profoundly aware of their significance. In *The Souls of Black Folk*, as he left his rural Tennessee teaching experience in a Black community, his thoughts of that community captivated him as he "rides to Nashville in the Jim Crow car" of the train.[166]

In contrast, three decades later, Odum was still insisting on a regional identity and scale that generally followed the geographic contours of the rural Confederacy. With regard to race and interregional relations, Odum published Edward A. Ross's article "Sectionalism and Its Avoidance" in *Social Forces* in 1924, which optimistically suggested that African American out-migration to the North meant that more Northerners were "able to get the southern white man's point of view on the race question."[167] This understanding was prescient, of course, as expressed in Charles M. Payne's 2004 statement that the "whole United States is Southern," as well as similar sentiments by John Egerton and many others.[168] But in Ross's frame (endorsed by Odum), it is the "white man's burden" of the "race question," rather than Du Bois's belief in the future potential of African Americans buoyed by more abundant economic opportunities, that is the primary explanation that interregionalism offered to the white South. This white myopia is reflected in Du Bois's 1942 candid response to Odum's solicitation of his thoughts on Odum's regionalism proposal: "Your regional interpretation of human action must be modified . . . especially calling attention to so powerful a force as cultural antagonism, cultural lag and group segregation . . . I want to emphasize this element . . . in a series of state-wide studies of increasing intensity to fix by as accurate a measurement as possible the place of the Negro in modern culture."[169]

Perhaps the most famous interregional North-South proposal, Benton MacKaye's Appalachian Trail mirrored fellow Massachusettsan Du Bois's interregional racial migration patterns across the North-South, rural-urban fields. At the invitation of editor Charles Harris Whitaker, MacKaye first published his proposal for a "projected mountain footway" linking Maine to Georgia in the *Journal of the American Institute of Architects* in October

1921.[170] From his New England town of Shirley Center, Massachusetts—a place he called an "indigenous community"—MacKaye and his trail proposal followed Patrick Geddes's inspiration of a public realm for civic engagement with territory, across geography, regardless of whether the various trail sections be "state lands, Federal, or . . . 'Park' or 'Forest.'"[171] MacKaye was a forester and a conservationist who articulated most clearly the spatial contours of regionalism for the RPAA in New York, describing the trail as a "folkland" wilderness, a "backbone openway."[172]

The Appalachian Trail linked "neutral zones" that each community could plan and maintain along the networked north–south mountain corridor. Extending beyond the limited scope of the city planner, MacKaye envisioned that the regional planner would serve as the "composite mind" to administer and coordinate the multidisciplinary tasks of engineers, economists, and landscape designers.[173] He imagined a pre-Columbian "primeval" relationship of nature and society to be discerned and recovered, inspired by his Shirley village as the essential community spatial unit along the trail. MacKaye's vision of the regional planner was a figure who "helps nature recover and hold the middle ground and primeval territory by first surveying and then securing havens from commercial and industrial expansion."[174] The trail, too, is an evolutionary frame within which, over time, a "genuine cosmopolitan environment" can be achieved, where the "true urban" will be salvaged through the "village grown up," with the associated institutions (town hall, schoolhouse, country store) "expanded and intensified."[175]

The trail was proposed as a cordon to limit "pseudometropolitan" urban expansion westward from East Coast cities—essentially, to be a barrier to the "metropolitan invasion" into the frontier. Over time, it would also establish healthier "open ways." Using water flow metaphors, MacKaye viewed his trail as helping to "dike" that expansion through "levees," to limit its possibilities into more circumscribed areas, thereby allowing and encouraging a broader matrix of natural replenishment. MacKaye employed the Geddesian valley section to use the water movement along that slope as indicators for how planning should address the various ecological needs along the mountain crest lines and down to the coast. "Townless highways" would both communicate and protect the village settlements along the valley section. "Here is the backbone of Appalachian America," MacKaye affirmed. He continued. . . . "This Trail is in the making, and in many sections it is made, from Mt. Katahdin, Maine, down to Cohutta Mountain, Georgia."[176]

Although the trail's expansive interregional scope stretched across the traditional North/South divide, MacKaye still privileged his own New England perspective as the model for other regions to follow along the networked corridor. His near mile-by-mile analysis of the trail's movement from Maine through the Massachusetts Berkshires grows fuzzier once it extends beyond the bounds of his state. For planning subsequent ranges of the trail southward, MacKaye proposed his New England spatial precision as the model: "The main strategy is already laid down for coping with the metropolitan flood throughout New England—the main 'levees' are indicated."[177] Having established the New England prototype upon arrival at the Green Mountain Berkshire Range, the regional planner has arrived at the "backbone levee of the whole Atlantic border from Canada to Georgia."[178] As with Odum and his regional-national planning proposal, even in their overtures to broader inter- and multiregionalist concepts of national impact and reframing, regionalists made their own geographic position the prioritized starting points for those proposals.

Following the publication of MacKaye's 1921 article, Whitaker introduced him to several colleagues, thus forming a group whom he would encourage a few years later to form the RPAA. MacKaye's environmental vision for regional planning influenced the group's members to drop the terms "housing" and "garden cities" from their planned association title, with an eye toward the broader territorial aspirations established by the Appalachian Trail.[179] The trail was among the most important built legacies of United States regionalism. Despite the spatiocultural and racist-essentialist claims of the regionalists, American spaces, from the legacy of the Underground Railroad to the tragedy of the Dust Bowl to the trains and roads heading north and west out of the South, portrayed a country in flux. Du Bois and MacKaye saw this more clearly than their colleagues.

THE ACIDS OF MODERNITY

One of Odum's final publications, his 1954 "Agenda for Integration," was organized into a series of "assumptions" in which he stated that the "concept and practice of regionalism offer the most effective *areal* approach to interstate, interregional, and national problems of discrimination against and segregation of" African Americans.[180] While this statement is qualified as an assumption—hence as a logical exercise rather than a passionate belief—it does *seem* to be an endorsement of integration, coming after half a century of avoiding frontal critique of Jim Crow. "Only through such regionalism," Odum obfuscated, "basic to cultural relativity and as the tool for research and administration, can we approximate the unity and integration of diverse regions in the changing structure of American culture as part of the structure of world regionalism and world unity."[181]

Odum frequently responded more forcefully to Northern critiques of Southern race relations than to these relations themselves.[182] Odum did criticize

Southern racism, noting, "There is no escape from the verdict that the South is probably the only major regional culture in the world" to view Black "segregation and exploitation . . . as a part of virtue in preserving Western civilization."[183] But he quickly pivoted, asserting that the extremity of Southern white reaction to outside integration pressure was "often matched by the extremity of the attack."[184] He lamented that the New Deal had exerted "considerable pressures on the South," essentializing it "as an example of backwardness and badness, followed by efforts to remake its culture overnight."[185] After the fifteenth *series* of assumptions seeking to explain why the nation needed to understand Southern culture, Odum proposed "next steps" to slowly, gradually integrate states, regions, and world nations.[186] In this grand scheme of world integration, the *Brown* decision and the civil rights discussion were decidedly marginalized, presented at the end as a minor point. Odum's Whitmanesque cataloging of his concepts, particularly regionalism, opened their meanings so broadly as to allow—indeed, invite—almost anything or anyone in. This mercurial, unedited approach allowed him to describe his way out of political position or obligation—and thus to effectively, strategically avoid conflict.

Odum had planned to expand the article into a book, but the presentation of additional qualified assumptions would likely not have revealed anything new. In the 1940s and in the post–World War II years, as reforms caught up to those that regionalists had been calling for, Odum "came to voice regret and concern at the rapidity of the changes even as he became identified with progress."[187] Addressing this ambiguity less than ten years later, Baldwin offered a representative response: "Do I really *want* to be integrated into a burning house?"[188]

Although respectful of his work with Odum on regionalism and regional planning in the 1930s, Odum's IRSS colleague Rupert B. Vance had begun in later decades to move away from his regionalism research to issues of demography. In this later work, he seemed to calibrate regionalist claims to regional planning practice needs and delimit the all-encompassing, open-ended regionalist signifiers from earlier eras. In 1954—the same year Odum's "Agenda for Integration" appeared—Vance published an edited volume on *The Urban South* that focused on Southern urbanization as an "index of social change."[189] Explicitly escaping the agrarian bias of Southern regionalism and its exceptionalist claims, Vance's book profiled a post–World War II South that was becoming "more like the nation," converging as differentiation was "diminishing."[190] He conceded, however, that regionalism must still be connected to the practice of regional planning, noting that a disconnect would be "fatal to both disciplines."[191]

If regionalism was meant to explain the distinction of Southern underdevelopment—blamed partially on a deficit of cities—the transdisciplinary *Urban South* saw interregional affinity in increased urban trends. Vance believed in urbanization as a locus for social change and progress.[192] Political scientist V. O. Key agreed, observing, "The growth of cities contains the seeds to political change in the South."[193] While Vance and Key were aware of the new challenges that urbanization would bring, they were warily optimistic, in contrast to Odum's warnings about the threat of "revolutionary" change brought by racial integration via "mass urbanization."[194] Economist William H. Nicholls framed the schism of Southern rural traditionalism and urban-industrial progress as an ethical choice: "I *prefer* that the South seek further material progress" through greater industrial-urban development, "even at the costs of abandoning traditional values."[195]

Regionalism and pluralism in the early twentieth century addressed standardizing forms of modernity and cultural "Americanization" with an insistence that "incorporation did not necessarily mean assimilation."[196] In the reaffirmation of their imagined "indigenous America," its constitutive parts and peoples forming the "residual resistance," regionalists saw a way forward in "unity through differentiation."[197] Addressing the "centrifugal diversity" of immigration and movement and the "continental immensity" of America's unique geographic experiences and subcultures, they proposed a framework that sought to contain the breadth and complexity of modernity, modernization, tradition, and history to "fill the void of wilderness and modernity together."[198] Folk traditions—of First Nations peoples, of immigrant folk cultures, of pioneer agrarian republican communities—were interpreted and redirected as "organic to both people and place," "symbiotic and indigenous to a specific regional environment."[199]

African American folk culture was evoked similarly, offering inspiration for the writers and artists of the Harlem Renaissance and, for different reasons, for Howard W. Odum in the US South. American regionalism developed "unevenly," both nationally and locally, defined with the cultural authority and institutional backing to deploy regionalisms in pursuit of their cultural objective.[200] As Richard Pells points out, these figures defined multiple US crises in these cultural terms because, as social scientists, writers, and artists, culture was the realm of their expertise, and thus a realm they could control.[201]

Southern Agrarians believed in the aristocratic antebellum plantation as a civilizing institution, but Donald Davidson, one of its spokesmen, understood that Turner's frontier was "a bit of a sectional rationalization."[202] Artistry and rationalization were allowed and even required when facing the modern nihilism that would reduce all values to exchange value.[203] Walter Lippmann articulated the regionalist dilemma in 1930, lamenting, "[The] acids of modernity are so powerful that they do not tolerate the crystallization of ideas which will serve as a new orthodoxy into which men can retreat."[204] In response, Marshall Berman would later warn that in the face of regionalist claims of folk purity, "we must scrutinize the aims and interests of those who would protect their people from modernism for their own good."[205]

There is a chronological and contextual qualifier that must be allowed for throughout these considerations of race, place, and culture. Du Bois wrote *The Philadelphia Negro* in 1899 and *The Souls of Black Folk* in 1903, emphasizing Black movement across places (and regions) as various environmental spheres of conditioning, from rural to urban, that would impact Black achievement and cultural development. MacKaye's Appalachian Trail proposal arrived twenty years later, following the devastating impacts of World War I, embodying the Theodore Roosevelt spirit of an environmental civic pride seeking to inspire a new kind of nationalism that was not war based. The US Army Corps of Engineers returned from the war as water management heroes, providing a reference for MacKaye to strategically use water management metaphors to proscribe "indigenous territorial practices" and cultural management through flows analogies. Despite its national and nationalist ambitions, however, as an Atlantic coast proposal, MacKaye's trail privileged his New England transversal analysis as prototypical for the other regions as the trail wended southward.

Odum's work on race precedes his use of the term "regionalism." There are varying perspectives on whether and how he transformed his thinking on biological racialism to environmental conditioning, with some claiming that he began to change his opinion while in contact with Boas during his PhD at Columbia. Others view the shift as more gradual, with Odum demanding more empirical evidence of environment as explanation for the development of racial conditioning, in contrast to his foundational Spencerian education in racial biology.[206] While writing his books on Black folk songs with Johnson, Odum applied to the Rockefeller Foundation in 1926 for a grant to fund a "comparative study of physical characteristics, including measurement of cephalic indices and other physical traits" of both African American and white children, seeking through this phrenological investigation "to determine what if any is the effect of the Negro community upon the morals, achievements, failures, etc. of the white boys of the community." Of this gradual movement toward environmental rather than biological racial definitions, historian Michael O'Brien concludes, "All one can say is that Odum had begun to doubt segregation, but not very much."[207]

CHAPTER 5

Regionalism quickened a generation of social scientists with its vision of the "problem South," a region with obvious deficiencies but with potentialities that demanded constructive study and planning.
—GEORGE TINDALL

[Regionalism] is a season's halt of the American caravan, a temporary encampment of an advancing society, eternally on the move toward some unified goal of progress.
—C. VANN WOODWARD

Some of the clearest and most enlightened expressions of the regional political philosophy are those that have issued from Professor Howard Odum and his colleagues at Chapel Hill, N.C.
—LEWIS MUMFORD

REGIONALISM

A LIVING, BREATHING, PULSATING RIOT

Howard Odum published *Southern Regions of the United States* in 1936: a sprawling 600-plus pages of portraiture text combined with comparative maps illustrating national and regional geographic features, as well as socioeconomic indexes produced by his colleagues at the Institute for Research in Social Science (IRSS). It was his most famous academic book and was enthusiastically received.[1] In the regional-national frame, however, Odum believed that the regional focus needed a broader perspective, so "he set about extending his analysis on regionalism to the whole nation."[2] To do this, he teamed up with Harry Estill Moore, who had recently completed his 1937 dissertation at the University of North Carolina, titled "Theories of Regionalism," and accepted a position at the University of Texas at Austin. Odum and Moore's coauthored *American Regionalism: A Cultural-Historical Approach to National Integration* (1938) was another large tome

Rupert B. Vance. Courtesy of the Vance family.

structured in three parts: the first written by Odum on the history and rise of US geographic regions based on geographic and cultural features, the second part by Moore on political theory and the history of regionalism, and the third section by Odum, focusing on a survey of his six national regions, with thoughts on how regional planning could address these various areas woven throughout.[3]

When published, *American Regionalism* received less attention and a more lukewarm critical reception than *Southern Regions*, leaving Odum wondering about the importance of the work and its contribution to the social sciences. Impatient for feedback, he took initiative and published an article in *Social Forces* in 1942 titled "A Sociological Approach to the Study and Practice of American Regionalism: A Factorial Syllabus." He ordered reprints of the essay and sent them to respected colleagues around the country asking for their thoughts. Odum introduced the letters accompanying these reprints in a fairly standard way, with some personalized preamble to colleagues with whom he had friendships.

Over fifteen years after the Hanover objectivist rebuke, Odum's letter to Du Bois opened with a defense: "I have the impression that in the past most of my sociological friends have thought that regionalism was getting out of the field of sociology into the borderline of public administration, political science, and geography. It is my own conviction, however, that in our search for something to make sociology more realistic and rigorously scientific, enabling us to make systematizations and real theory from empirical studies, regionalism offers first-rate area and tools."[4] Odum then asked for answers to three questions concerning his regionalism proposal: "Is it sociology? What [are your] special criticisms of definitions, premises, assumptions, [and] postulates; [and, last,] in particular, I would appreciate your giving close scrutiny to the problem of delineation of regions, districts, states, subregions, etc."[5] The responses he received throughout the summer of 1942 were overwhelming, and he would later remark, "I have never had any series of letters or critiques so important."[6]

Responses were generally supportive of Odum's work and its ambition but skeptical that it was sociology in any strict delineation of the social science. From the University of Minnesota, F. Stuart Chapin, who had served as the American Sociological Society president in 1935, wrote, "I would think of your various assumptions and statements as a systemic effort to face some sort of a large problem in the field of philosophy of history or in the field of social philosophy, but not in the field of sociology if sociology is to be considered scientific. The concepts are too large and too vague."[7] Read Bain, editor of the *American Sociological Review* from Miami University, thought similarly: "No, it is not sociology, but that is nothing against it. . . . To ask if regionalism is sociology is like asking if the evolutionary hypothesis is zoology.... The concept [of regionalism] itself, however greatly transcends any specific science nor can the composite specialized studies of regions constitute a separate and distinctive science: Regionalism *uses* science(s) but *it is not a* science, and by the very nature of the concept, can never be."[8]

Others commented on Odum's conflict-free frame for regionalism and social change.[9] In his response, W. E. B. Du Bois briefly suggested that Odum's concept "must be modified in some cases but especially calling attention to so powerful a force as cultural antagonism, cultural lag and group segregation."[10] These were notions that Odum would repeatedly account for organically as *universal* challenges to be resolved through time, scientific expertise, and properly enlightened Southern leadership. Maurice Davie and C. Arnold Anderson also responded that regions as cultural areas are not fixed, and that that their geographies may shrink or expand over time due to cultural dynamism.[11] Odum's former student Rupert B. Vance was the most direct in his criticism. In a private memorandum he wrote in 1938 shortly after reading *American Regionalism*, he called the work "hastily done" and lacking in positionality or "point of view": "I believe I must be wanting a more hardboiled view of social change. Conflict we will always have with us. How does Regionalism take it out of the realm of hard knocks and place it in the realm of discussion and reasonable 'due process' of policymaking? And what about class conflict? Is the resolution of regional views an alternative to an increase of such conflict?"[12]

Odum's questions and the epistolary responses identify the mood of the social sciences in the late 1930s and early 1940s that received his regionalism proposals, and they also offer insightful critiques of his wide-reaching claims for the concept. Vance's understanding of regionalism through human geography serves as a counterpoint to Odum's approach that helps illuminate the generational and political differences between the two colleagues at the IRSS. A second significant conference on regionalism was held just before midcentury, at a point when regional planning was breaking away from the territorial cultural identification of regionalism and toward a more abstract, functionalist approach to planning governance and management. This conference helps to situate Odum's anxiety about his colleagues' acceptance of his regionalism concept—and perhaps about the limited time remaining for him, his social sciences, and his South.[13]

REGIONALISM IN AMERICA

On April 14–15, 1949, nearly two decades after the University of Virginia round table, a conference on American regionalism was held at the

University of Wisconsin–Madison, sponsored by the university's Committee on the Study of American Civilization and funded (as the round table had been) by the Rockefeller Foundation. The intervening decades had seen enough regional research completed that participants were less interested in investigating what regionalism was than in learning how its study had been used over the past two decades. They recognized from the outset a multiplicity of disciplinary definitions and methods for regions, but also understood how the very "nature of a 'region' varies with the needs, purposes, and standards of those using the concept."[14] Unlike the Virginia round table, however, no artists or poets participated in the conference, although regional painting, art, and architecture were discussed. There were also no aspiring presidential candidates in attendance this time. Academics spoke, with a strong showing from the regionalist state universities of Wisconsin, Chicago, North Carolina, and Texas, along with several government agency representatives from the Tennessee Valley Authority (TVA) and the Missouri Valley Great Plains Council.

Regionalism had become solidly institutional and established following the experience of massive New Deal investments in regional development, agencies, and the geographic-scaled river basin infrastructure projects that regional planning had called for thirty-five years earlier.[15] Papers at the conference reviewed the histories of regionalism and sectionalism dating back to the eighteenth century, with the work of Frederick Jackson Turner, the local figure from nearby Portage, Wisconsin, conjured frequently.[16] Given its regionalist development tradition and statewide outreach program, the University of Wisconsin was an appropriate location to host the conference. Wisconsin had also been Odum's reference at the University for North Carolina for state university commitment to community development through applied scholarship and outreach.[17]

The two-day discussion was similar to the assessment of many once au courant social science topics on the downswing of their cyclical lives, in which researchers are either beginning to gauge them historically or to clarify the footnotes of their key contributions—in Vance's words, "praising and burying."[18] Odum coordinated with host Merrill Jensen in preparation, but in the end, he decided to skip the conference and sent his paper for the edited collection to be published afterward, and Vance presented on behalf of the IRSS. Louis Wirth provided commentary on the "limitations of regionalism," only to have Odum's paper conclude the anthology with "the promise of regionalism." As with most criticism of his work, Odum recognized Wirth's points, noted they were important, and then countered that such assessments were generally a misunderstanding of what he was really trying to say about regionalism—not deflecting these criticisms, but embracing them, wrapping his own expansive organicist position around them, and doubling down on his convictions.[19] Wirth's commentary on regionalism's claims as a comprehensive social science, along with the general regional/sectional content throughout the conference's panels, was a testament to how Southern regionalist philosophy had ascended to the level of national academic discussion.[20]

Vance presented on "The Regional Concept as a Tool for Social Research." In his naturalistic analogy he pointed out that in the social analysis of regional society, the "social scientist today has come to realize the dilemma faced by the biologist yesterday. The biologist found that the only still specimen was a dead specimen . . . but when he wanted to determine the function, the physiognomy, he had on his hands for analysis 'a living, breathing, pulsating riot.'"[21] Society was both a "process of social change" and a "product in the development of social order."[22] Structure was not only "the product of ongoing processes"; structure "itself becomes a process as it goes over into function."[23]

These were only some of the challenges that regions and their analysis posed. Vance defined a region as an interrelated and balanced group of "composite major areas which in America is a group of states corresponding both to historic section and to a cultural area," understanding that the processes of decentralization and concentration, international and national federation, and regional blocs and federations were "all studies of changing structure and function."[24] The parallel Vance drew between the challenges encountered by the natural and the social sciences when observing social phenomena echoed the calls for method and legitimacy from the sociological organicism of the early century. But a riotous nature and society writhing and shape-shifting out of microscopic analysis sounded very different from Odum's calm, constant folk-regional society "bottomed in the relative balance of man, nature, and culture."[25]

SOUTHERN GESTALT

Southern regionalists at the University of North Carolina established a trans- and interdisciplinary Southern "area studies" research program at the IRSS.[26] Odum and Moore described regionalism as an "organic unity not only for its natural landscape, but in that cultural evolution in which the age-long quartette [sic] of elements are at work—namely, the land, the people, culturally conditioned through time and spatial relationships."[27] Toward the end of the 1930s, in summarizing Odum's decade of work on regionalism, Odum and Moore settled on regionalism as a comprehensive "cultural Gestalt" capable of balancing "all constituent factors of culture in the making."[28] Vance warned against such a broad definition, noting, "There is danger lest the concept come to mean all things to all men."²⁹ Lewis Mumford also cautioned against Odum and Moore's expansive definition, suggesting that "the all-inclusiveness of region does the term to death."³⁰ Chicago sociologist Louis Wirth agreed, observing, "The failure to discriminate the many distinct factors that underlie the emergence and persistence of region is a serious fault of present-day scholarship and research."³¹ At the dawn of the 1930s, however, Odum's broad conceptualization of regionalism provided sufficient malleability to accommodate conflicting reflexive positions on planning and progress with enduring folk traditions during the national period of crisis.

In contrast to Progressive Era planners and their European social science colleagues, US sociologists tended toward a smaller community bias.³² Social researchers at the University of Chicago conceptualized the city as a mosaic of multiple semiautonomous ethnic neighborhood villages.³³ Particularly in the interwar period, sociologists "identified with [a world that] was of an earlier time; a world of face-to-face relations, group cohesion, and consensus; a tight, custom-bound community that had yet to be ravaged by the disorganizing forces of industrialism and urbanism."³⁴ Sociologist Ferdinand Tönnies's 1887 book *Gemeinschaft und gesellschaft* (*Community and Society*), in which he described the maturation process from a community of personal bonds to a society of contracts, preoccupied social researchers across the urban, metropolitan, and, later, regional geographies.³⁵

When reflecting on the South's relationship with the rest of the United States, Southern intellectuals perceived the region's plantation society as a "colonial economy" for Northern industrial interests.³⁶ Rupert Vance described the Southern perspective on this relationship as one born from, "the colonial system under which it was founded, the frontier zone into which it expanded, the plantation system to which it passed, and the cotton system with its tenancy which prevailed after abolition."³⁷ Vance believed that the South remained beholden to the North into the New South era, beyond simply the cotton staple, due to its deficient human and technological development. He lamented, "The South has often sold out its undeveloped resources—pine forests, Kentucky coal, Birmingham iron, Arkansas bauxite, Texas petroleum—to outside interests at rock bottom prices, all for lack of credit to finance development."³⁸ Odum agreed, affirming that the South had been "essentially colonial in its economy," with the same "general status of an agricultural country engaged in trade with industrial counties."³⁹

The solid South was a white political bloc and regional construct based on the confluence of racism and the interests of the planter elite and the nascent twentieth-century industrial sector, which arose amid broader national and international shifts in capital-spatial development and the nested governing institutions that administered these processes.[40] But a shared acute sentiment of animosity toward the North for the Civil War victory, the perceived imposition of Reconstruction, Northern tariffs on Southern goods and their rail transport, and Northern criticism of Southern racial society's brutality and injustice was never far from the surface, even for the liberal social scientists at the University of North Carolina. The conceptual insistence of Odum and Vance on a forward-looking Southern regionalism as part of an organic national effort, leaving behind Frederick J. Turner's "section" term and its associated historical grievances, can be read in part as their recognition that such sectional sentiments were still very much alive in the South, and perhaps even in themselves.

The conceptual move from section to region was complex, and Odum could not elide the country's North/South history entirely. He knew the debt he owed to Northern philanthropy, particularly Beardsley Ruml and the Rockefeller funds invested in his work to launch the IRSS as an expressly Southern research center to promote the social sciences in the region. Odum celebrated this funding relationship as a kind of blueprint for his proposal for regional-national planning. He believed that his own experience with the IRSS could be replicated at the national level with federal money for the South to develop autonomously along the lines of its own priorities.[41] During the 1920s, the IRSS's success was based on significant research of Southern social phenomena, including the rural cotton economy, mill villages, prison reform, folk songs, and income levels, but the institute had not yet addressed the region as a whole. Yet the criticism Odum received from the Social Science Research Council (SSRC) and elite social science circles for his Southern portraiture cut deeply. It was as if the methodological quantitative-qualitative schism had taken on the character of historical geographical antagonism. Odum's personal experiences of opportunity and insecurity collided with his academic work.[42]

In 1927, after Ruml rejected one of his funding applications, Odum accepted some of the responsibility for his part in his dispute with his funders and engaged in a reappraisal of IRSS work. Based on this reflection, across the next decade Odum "reconstructed his empire on the basis of regional research."[43] He encouraged Rupert Vance to write a human geography of the South, and he spent his sabbatical year (1928–29) traveling throughout the region in preparation for his 1930 book *An American Epoch*. Odum's regionalism was inspired by this programmatic readjustment seeking to align IRSS research topics with the broader growing national interest in regionalism.

Odum received this posthumous assessment from colleagues: "In retrospect, regionalism represents the high point of Odum's achievement and influence. He had now become a public figure" who brought "a sense of history—a realization of time and place" to the national social sciences.[44] Regionalism became the IRSS's brand, an a priori Southern position around which researchers structured their work.[45] Their research questions ranged from authentic inquiry to simply reverse engineering a foregone affirmation of the region.[46] With its multiple approaches—description and prescription, analysis and catalog—Vance and Odum's work on regionalism through social science is essential for understanding the scholars' proposals for social action in social and regional planning for the South.

SOUTHERN PERSPECTIVES ON REGIONALISM

Throughout the 1930s, "the deep south was probably as underdeveloped economically as the Italian Mezzogiorno or Spanish Andalusia."[47] Upon his arrival at the University of North Carolina in 1920, Howard Odum "had no sociological theory of regionalism; he just wanted to study sociology in the South."[48] But his training in prewar sociology and psychology—particularly the Sumnerian folkways and Wilhelm Wundt's *Elemente der Völkerpsychologie*—soon combined with his Southern patriotism and his interests in public welfare and reform engineering to inspire his gradual formulation of regionalism across the rest of his career. Odum subscribed to Paul Kellogg's *Survey Graphic* for its sociological and political commentary, and he read the famous 1925 regional planning issue closely. He was particularly interested in Mumford's "Regions—to Live In" and its proposal of regionalism as the underlying philosophy that informed regional planning practice.[49] Odum reached out to Mumford with admiration and cited significant portions of "Regions" in his 1927 book *Man's Quest for Social Guidance*. Mumford later remarked that Odum was "probably the first—and possibly only—sociologist to recognize the importance of the *Survey Graphic* issue on regional planning."[50] Odum's review of the sociological survey method cited Kellogg's journal title and its definition of the survey technique as "an application of the statistical method to a study of the social problems of a community defined within certain geographic limits."[51] In both content and method, the May 1925 *Survey Graphic* issue inspired Odum.

In turn, *Survey Graphic* drew on its own inspirations. Charles Whitaker's publication of Benton MacKaye's Appalachian Trail proposal in the *Journal of the American Institute of Architects* in 1921 presaged the publication of Mumford and colleagues' Regional Planning Association of America (RPAA) platform in Kellogg's social science journal in 1925—a choice itself perhaps inspired by Patrick Geddes's work with sociologist Victor Branford. The publication of the RPAA principles and policies then caught Howard Odum's attention.[52] Geddes's Outlook Tower work, which Odum already knew of through Stanley Hall, influenced Odum's regional vision for the IRSS.[53] The connection between Mumford and Odum established through the *Survey Graphic* issue marked a moment at which regional planning in the United States branched out from an architectural project to one of the social sciences.[54] The concept of regionalism provided an encompassing conceptual frame for the IRSS's work on Southern race relations, mill towns, social work, and community, as showcased in *Social Forces*. Regionalism would also provide the theoretical foundation for the IRSS's work on social and regional planning.

Odum introduced his conceptualization of region and folk in his 1930 presidential address to the American Sociological Society (which would later become the American Sociological Association), titled "Folk and Regional Conflict as a Field of Sociological Study."[55] For the IRSS, Odum insisted on a regional-national frame that "envisioned the nation first, making the total national culture the final arbiter," consciously avoiding tones of past sectional grievance, but still conceived of the IRSS's regionalist research agenda as principally Southern and institutional.[56] Odum and Rupert B. Vance engaged with regionalism and its utility throughout the 1930s and would reflect on those proposals and their sociological value for the rest of their careers. Their divergent notions of planning were each inextricably linked to those of region. Both scholars noted the difficulty of reducing or limiting their understanding of regionalism to an exact definition. Vance lamented that "the attempt to apply the method of regional interpretation to that historical entity known as the American South bristles with difficulty."[57] However, "a large part of their difficulty stemmed from a shared belief that the concept of region was too rich in interpretive meaning and social function to be confined by a single standardized definition."[58] This open-ended approach also positioned regionalist research as the IRSS's long-term speculative agenda for continued empirical research conducted by its interdisciplinary team.

RUPERT B. VANCE AND THE REGIONAL COMPLEX

Odum may have set the regionalist agenda beginning with his 1930 presidential address, but his research colleague Rupert B. Vance was the first scholar at the IRSS to propose an explicit regionalism in his 1929 book *Human Factors in Cotton Culture* and 1929 *Social Forces* article "The Concept of the Region," the latter of which was republished in 1932 as the introduction to his *Human Geography of the South*. Vance introduced regionalism as a layered concept in which the "forces of geography, ecology, human biology, economics, and cultural and folk sociology" converged.[59] He began by quoting an interview in which Herbert Spencer shared his thoughts on the great natural wealth that United States settlers enjoyed that produced "abundantly with small cost of culture."[60] Vance then celebrated Frederick J. Turner and his frontier theory as a starting point for his regional conception, whereby white settlers' adoption of Native American "forest folkways created the frontier," thus making the American Indian "in a large sense ... [responsible for] the cultural unity of early America; and for a long time, the frontier, North and South, was essentially the same."[61]

Vance continued by examining the country's environmental riches through an exhaustive review of geological and biophysical systems (what he termed the "physiographic"), leading to his proposed "natural life areas," or biotic regions comprising "an assemblage of species and ecological characteristics differing from those found in adjacent areas."[62] Vance drew inspiration from the French regional geography tradition, particularly Paul Vidal de La Blache's notion of the natural region, for both defining and organizing territorial structure: "The very way in which the sediments have been deposited and the way in which the movements of the earth's crust have taken place implies a certain regularity of behavior."[63] According to this conceptualization, the core of the Earth upwardly and outwardly influenced, if not fully determined, region. Vance finished the naturalist section by defining the five regions of rainfall in the United States as described by *National Geographic* magazine. His sources for his expansive study included a wide range of farmer's almanacs and encyclopedias, which would also serve as the quantitative source for regional data collection for Odum's IRSS publications.[64]

Vance then pivoted to the cultural factors that form a region. He sketched out French sociologist Frédéric Le Play's organicist conclusion that in region, "place conditions work, work [conditions] the family organization, and family is the social unit that makes up society," transplanting it to the United States through Turner's account of the "evolution of the frontier in accordance with the conditions of the wilderness."[65] Vance looked to the field of geography, particularly human geography, for its scientific method in the "classification of region by human use," instrumentalizing all natural systems to their economic raison d'être for human consumption and trade. Citing French geographer Jean Brunhes, Vance wrote that "the uses that man, in the effort to clothe, feed, house, and defend himself [make] of the map furnished by nature the scope of human geography."[66] Thus, human activities become "permanently recorded on the soil and comprise the cultural landscape."[67]

Hence, while "physiographic" and biotic aspects were formative for the natural region, it is ultimately human stewardship and intervention that modify the natural region toward human use, which then defines the cultural region. The map makes the culture, and the culture then remakes the map. Vance's position underscoring human agency in the construction of regionalism was, in truth, more closely and definitively aligned with the work of the RPAA and the French tradition than with Odum's.[68] Vance concluded his essay by highlighting the work of Michigan's Land Economic Survey and Guy B. Johnson's study of St. Helena Island off the South Carolina coast, which Vance believed would illustrate "the suitability of a small natural area, homogenous in its physical and ethnic features, to interpretation as a cultural unit." He also cited F. Stuart Chapin's 1927 University of Minnesota regional survey of the Wheat Belt, and, finally, the work of the North Carolina IRSS, which sought "to give to all its southern studies a definite regional slant based on background studies of rural areas."[69]

In his "The Concept of the Region," Vance also noted the impact of infrastructure on geographic development patterns, citing "two great economic complexes" that would "force regionalism on the attention of the state": hydroelectricity and the railroad.[70] In prescient anticipation of the TVA and hydroelectric development throughout the South, he proclaimed, "Giant Power is a Region Builder."[71] While the railroad was already well along in this restructuring process, Vance reaffirmed it as an interregional agent that enabled geographic resource extraction by linking marginal "natural crop and natural resource provinces" to metropolitan centers. Grounded in these two spheres, Vance pointed to the work of Patrick Geddes and Victor Branford on "city planning and regional surveys of the hinterlands" to develop natural areas, calling these efforts "nothing short of social reconstruction."[72]

Vance's proposal for regional analysis broadly laid out the physical and cultural components, conceptually ordered their relationships, and pointed to examples of research and business practices that he saw as references for advances in the field. He concluded that in the United States, "with cooperative effort between the students of physical backgrounds and the students of culture the new direction given research may in time be expected to produce results equal to the best work of the French School."[73] It is perhaps unusual that he chose to conclude his regional thoughts on this nationalistic note, but there is no mistaking his claim that the French School was the past, and US exploration—with clear reference to Turner's frontier—was the future.

Vance would return to the problem of definition in his *Human Geography of the South*. In that book, he cited Benton MacKaye's round table syllogism (with regionalism the major premise, regional survey the minor premise, and the plan as result), observing that although there was no lack of regional plans and surveys, there remained no clear definition of regionalism, the provision of which he hoped would establish "aims, ends, goals, the definition of the situation in terms of relation of area to area, of industry to industry, of regional process to regional process"—both a "regional housekeeping and a theory of regionalism."[74] Instead of this unified conceptualization, Vance suggested that three philosophies of regionalism, endorsed by three different groups, were in competition for "mastery in the South": promoters of industrialism, promoters of agrarianism, and the Southern regionalists, whom he termed "a certain small sprinkling of liberals, technicians, and university scholars."[75] Vance called the first group the "Chamber of Commerce Movement," which he characterized as a short-sighted, neo-mercantilist, competitive industrialist movement in the South working to court Northern industrial investment by promoting the region's natural resources and cheap labor—efforts he viewed as part of his North-South "colonial economy" frame. Vance criticized the lack of coherence in this movement, seeing balkanized efforts even in railroad and power development as isolated and self-interested, leading thus far only to "overdevelopment and industrial demoralization."[76]

On the other side were the Southern Agrarians housed at Vanderbilt, of whom he said, "By virtue of mass sheer inertia ... [they] remain the strongest group in the South."[77] In their book *I'll Take My Stand* (1930), Vance saw the last gasps of the neo-Confederate position, "just as the post-war bourbons, the Confederate brigadiers, and the Moss-backs were being abandoned by southern liberals."[78] He noted that the Agrarians were a literary movement seeking broader cultural retreat into regressive isolationism and Old South romance—a stance pitting agrarianism *against* industrialization that both he (and they) knew was "unreconstructed" and defeatist. But if Vance saw the "Chamber of Commerce Movement" as the most likely to succeed in its short-term economic appeal, he recognized the Agrarians as the easier cultural path for the region, noting that "nostalgia for the old South" was "an effective sentiment around which to rally a genuine movement" that could "prove of more avail than the formulae of technicians and the undifferentiated aspirations of southern liberals."[79]

Rejecting these positions, Vance then endorsed an "eclectic" strategy for Southern regional policy espoused by what he termed the "Southern liberal" group. These Southern regionalists he described as "few, scattered, [and] non-aggressive," adding, "Some have arisen from the universities, others have sprung from the more cultured industrialists, some inheritors of the old traditions. . . . They range from technicians and engineers to journalists, scholars and artists."[80] Perhaps in jest, Vance agreed that this group had spent significant time in argument and discussion (which is odd given Odum's conflict-averse temperament), but he affirmed, "The one thing on which they can unite is regional planning, for fundamental to all they strive is the social mastery of regional resources and processes."[81]

Vance's work foreshadowed Odum's regional agenda, but it was presented through a compendium of comprehensive disciplines and methods working toward an operative definition of regionalism, rather than the mystified, ever-present specter of regionalism that appeared in Odum's writing. Vance's regionalism was activated through planning, including "orderly industrial development and agricultural reform," technical expertise without sacrificing "a place for the artist and the theorist," and the conservation of "certain regional values."[82] Vance concluded that Southern regionalism would see the "task of regionalism as a whole, but will attack it piecemeal and by projects, that the whole may come to pass."[83] As Odum would also emphasize, Vance insisted that regionalism would "so far abandon sectionalism" that national and Southern development would be equally endorsed and mutually constitutive, "worthy" of each other.[84]

After describing encouraging regional initiatives in Southern agricultural reorganization, including economic development for "marginal highlanders," flood control, beautification projects, and nascent urbanization trends, Vance finished *Human Geography* on the issue of folk: "It would be a pleasant thing to believe the South is to achieve regionalism as a folk movement."[85] He saw a folk renaissance as promising, should an authentic practice of regionalism and regional planning help to catalyze it, but he noted, "Nowhere is there a . . . genuine folk movement" similar to those observed in Denmark and Ireland "being duplicated in Dixie."[86] Reflecting the influence of Russian anarchist and geographer Peter Kropotkin, Vance's folk movement, inspired through authentic regional planning, would necessitate the education of the peasantry into a regional rural proletariat.[87]

Vance cited Danish and Irish examples of public institutional education that had helped develop peasants into a labor class in those countries, but he found no parallel for such programs in the South, where he saw "inevitable race dualism" as an obstacle. Turning to mystification—hardly his typical approach—in his consideration of racial reform, he claimed that it was "difficult to know how [Black people were] regarded by Southern leaders."[88] In his articulation of class and racial preoccupations in the South, Vance foreclosed any validity to Northern reformist critiques by dismissing them as "rabble rousers" searching only for cheap, artificial political gain. Despite such obstacles, he remained hopeful: "There exists enough of public spirit, love of native place and native folk in the nation and the region to rally men of intelligence around the banner of regionalism if its program rang true."[89] The clear political connotations of Vance's work, however, were never articulated in Odum's scholarship, nor did Odum appear to harbor the same influences or opinions.

Vance concluded *Human Geography*, after more than 500 pages cataloging the natural and cultural features of the South, with a succinct and active social research and practice agenda: "Here is nature and there stands the folk. Behind the folk stands a tragic history. What we need to know is that, in spite of its tragic history, the mold in which the South is to be fashioned is only now being laid."[90] Echoing this language, Louis Wirth would later warn that regionalism "could become a futile effort to squeeze life into a rigid mold" and a "vain gesture to retard integration of life on a wider more inclusive scale."[91]

Yet Vance conceptualized an active, future-oriented regionalism, articulated through regional surveys and (more importantly) regional planning for the development of Southern environmental resources and culture, or the social practices through which society administers and leverages natural resources for its organic, integral, comprehensive, long-term improvement. Once developed, a compelling theory of regionalism, operationalized through regional planning, would have the potential to inspire his desired folk renaissance. This renaissance would include class consciousness through training and education, offer a Southern liberal solution (then still ill-defined) to race dualism, and foster economic development through technical and cultural expertise to the aspirational "rebirth" of the folk. Vance's project reaffirmed his belief in human agency to intervene in nature and reconstruct it. For Vance, region may have begun "as a great complex of physical forces," but it "ends by being so reshaped by the human groups which occupy it that it emerges as a cultural product."[92] The same could be said of its folk renaissance. His mentor Howard Odum, however, saw things differently.

HOWARD ODUM AND THE FOLK REGION

For Odum, regionalism represented the "natural outgrowth of the whole direction of his work," including his journal *Social Forces*, the IRSS and its research agenda, and even his studies of Black American folklore.[93] His service on Herbert Hoover's President's Research Committee on Social Trends, "which sought to inventory the social resources and trends of the nation," also inflected his approach, although his extensive catalogings of the Southern regions would include far "greater detail."[94] For Odum, regionalism was a "grandiose concept that must be grasped whole or not all."[95] Ironically, despite a lifetime of writing both toward and about this notion, not even he seemed able to grasp the concept—or all that he sought in it—in its entirety.

Although focused almost exclusively on the South, "Odum's regionalism was rooted in what he perceived to be the two universals, folk culture and science."[96]

Odum merged these universals in an agenda that proposed research and action across the divide described by eminent sociologist Lester Frank Ward. Like Ward, Odum believed as a sociologist, "certain social theories implied certain appropriate social action."[97] Thus, his regionalism aspired to be both an analytic tool for survey inquiry and a field of action, "the method whereby human intelligence could be used most effectively in the solution of social problems."[98] Regional planning, or social planning in the Southern region, was the logical synthesis of these arenas. But Odum's commitment to the notion of "folkways over stateways," inherited from William Sumner through Franklin H. Giddings, confused the timing of when *calls* for social action would indeed *become* social action. His work would often explore "the difference, a matter of kind and of speed of social change," but he would never truly resolve that "focus of his thought."[99]

This regional framing of the folk society was first presented in Odum's presidential address to the American Sociological Society in 1930, in which he explored the terms "folk" and "region" at length before fusing them in an overarching call for "folk sociology."[100] As he explained, he viewed region not as "an entirely separate concept but an extension and attribute to the 'folk,'" in contrast to the "technological region."[101] Odum would later note that his regionalism was the "basic toolkit for folk sociology to counter super-state technological forces at odds with the natural course of the folkways."[102] This address in 1930 was his first full articulation of folk sociology, but he had been promising a fleshed-out concept to his benefactors since the mid-1920s, despite being primarily occupied in that period with coediting two books of Black folk songs with Guy Johnson and authoring his Black Ulysses trilogy of novels, as well as two sociology textbooks, *Man's Quest for Social Guidance* (1927) and *An Introduction to Social Research* (1929, coauthored with IRSS colleague Katharine Jocher). The textbooks tended to be bracketed as long, selective methodological and literature reviews of sociology, completed before Odum launched in earnest into the Southern focus of *An American Epoch* (1930) and his regionalist work. Nonetheless, *An Introduction to Social Research*, published in the same year Vance published "The Concept of the Region," helps illuminate Odum's formulation of regionalism across the next decade and is worth considering at length.

In *An Introduction to Social Research*, Odum and Jocher broadly reviewed social science across disciplines, topics, and methods, including the "anthropological," "politico-juridic," [and] "economic," before landing on the more overarching, expansive, Comtean "sociological." These chapters were followed by two chapters on the survey method and the case study to analyze specific geographical areas. Odum and Jocher noted that social surveys conducted by both social workers and social scientists pathologized social deviance and abnormality through contrast with "normal" social practice. They reviewed early examples of social surveys, including the work of Charles Booth and William Booth in London and Jacob Riis's *How the Other Half Lives* in New York City.[103] These early works, the authors concluded, were "more impressionistic pictures rather than statistical studies, but [they] succeeded in attracting wide interest."[104] The "muckraking" period of survey research between 1900 and 1920 Odum and Jocher dismissed, but they argued that the survey had then returned as a legitimate scientific method and "a standardized *first step* for carrying on a scientific study of a wide variety of types of studies of social phenomena."[105]

With an eye toward justifying their own research program, Odum and Jocher cited Odum's mentor Franklin Giddings extensively throughout *An Introduction to Social Research*, arguing, "A community survey may take for its field a village, a city, a county, a state, a region or section, or a nation."[106] They contrasted the survey with the case study, clarifying that the two could be conducted "as companion methods" to provide a complete temporal spectrum. "The survey method," through quantitative data, "may be said to deal with the present and possibly the future . . . to give a cross section picture."[107] In contrast, the case study "digs up origins and seeks out historical development, for it is here that the roots of attitudes are embedded," and "it is these qualitative data which furnish the source and background of the quantitative."[108] In *An Introduction to Social Research*, Odum, in conjunction with Jocher, provided a combined survey-and-case-study methodology that would later guide the IRSS's Southern studies (perhaps most clearly demonstrated in Odum's *Southern Regions of the United States*, published seven years later).

The textbook's final chapter, titled "Types of Procedure: Social Analysis and Social Denominator," introduced the notion of "folk background studies." In contrast to unsuccessful folk background work, which they believed lacked analysis, Odum and Jocher advocated for the anthropological study of peoples they described as "primitive and backwards" to demonstrate the "need and practicability of scientific analysis."[109] Aligning the promise of folk background studies with the possibilities of the regional approach, they asserted that each provided "historical backgrounds" and a "systemic knowledge of the cultural *background* on which the social drama is played in any given society, before the more general concept and hypotheses of social theory can be adequately applied or tested in their application to that society."[110]

The authors then returned to the theme of "social prepotency"—described in a previous chapter on "biological" research approaches—to review what they viewed as the potential in eugenics research to improve on the folk, once properly studied, through methods such as prohibiting reproduction by "inferiors" and encouraging that of "superiors." These tactics would counter what they saw as the worrisome trend of "inferior" overpopulation and degradation. Having fully accepted the white supremacist replacement argument, Odum and Jocher promoted folk study as a means for gathering information to help "correct" this supposed imbalance:

> The fact remains that analyses are needed which will direct social science toward the measurement of that prepotency which will enable society to reproduce itself in each succeeding generation with more and more of the "normal," "strong," and "good," and less and less of the "abnormal," "weak," and "bad," utilizing, of course, scientific analyses of these terms themselves. In the search for such analyses this hypothesis is that the study of folk background and the measurement of "folk values" will constitute an important stage from which may come discovery of both fact and method.[111]

In the ethnographic work in folk background studies initiated in anthropology, Odum and Jocher saw promise for all the social sciences. This hearty endorsement of eugenics in 1929 clearly refutes claims that Odum was already doubting the biological argument for race and instead seeking a Boasian environmental approach while writing his dissertation at Columbia.[112] Although the IRSS would later produce survey research that, for example, employed empirical regional work to reject the fiction of African Americans' natural proclivity to crime and violence, Odum's formative biological racial claims—however circumstantially conflictive—were at the core of his concepts of both folk and region, as he clarified in his presidential address to the American Sociological Society in 1930.[113]

In that address, Odum distinguished his proposal for a sociological understanding of regions. Citing Ward's address to the same institution twenty-five years earlier, he noted that the broad regional and folk definitions from European traditions and elsewhere were not "false . . . but not enough."[114] Odum's concept of folk was not simply the Sumnerian definition of past or primitive societies (although it encompassed that notion), but one that could be applied in 1930s New York to illustrate how cultural development and change must be understood through the filtered folk processes of slow acceptance over time, rather than through a faster-paced technological imperative or state imposition.[115] Folk society, for Odum, was a "phenomenon of society and not of the state."[116] Citing Giddings, Odum emphasized that, just as his aspirational equilibrium between folk society and the state was the "definitive trait of normal society," the folk society—the "normal transitional, extra-organizational [individual], and non-technological social process"—was the "definitive, comparative society itself."[117] Folk forces as Odum conceived them were natural and elemental, constituent of social evolution.[118] This position—that "social evolution itself is regional"—would be one that Odum would maintain throughout the ensuing decade.[119]

Odum concluded his address by once again endorsing social prepotency as a study of "comparative anatomy and biological sciences," "in character with a functional sociology which is telic not merely in the sense of general social guidance, but as underlying that, a functional science which conditioned both society and sociology through the nature and extent of its findings."[120] In his social evolutionary frame for region and folk, such an analogy to eugenic intervention served as a telic catalyst both for accelerating toward a "modern transitional society and providing scientific facts and interpretation for its development."[121] Given Odum's extensive discussion of social prepotency in *An Introduction to Social Research* the year before, however, there can be no mistaking the ultimate goal as anything other than racial and social engineering.

In 1945, Odum described his evolutionary conceptualization of society as follows:

> The folk society is the elemental and basic cultural definitive of all societies in process. These characteristic folkways may be best observed in the folk regional society, which is the smallest comprehensive unit of society. Over against the folk society has been the universal trend toward the state society, characterized by stateways and technicways. Whenever the folk society and the state society conflict, in the long run the folkways will always predominate. When the two societies work in concert, change and achievement result; when they are at odds, there is tension, disorganization, conflict, and ultimately decay. The definitive, evolving society will be a reality when there is balance and equilibrium between folkways, stateways, and technicways. All of this may be generally accomplished through social planning. The resources of the social and physical sciences must be brought to bear in bridging the theoretical and the practical and in conserving the folkways which help the society adapt to the new state and technicways.[122]

TURNER'S SECTIONS AND ODUM'S REGIONS

Delineating Howard Odum's seemingly endless definitions over the course of his career of what regionalism was and was not emphasizes the challenge of trying to fix the "pulsating riot" of regional analysis. As the director of research at the IRSS and under pressure from the University of North Carolina to attract grant funds, Odum found his conceptual needs for regionalism complicated by the equally present need to navigate both academic and philanthropic politics—a concern to which groups like the RPAA and even other researchers at the IRSS were not subject.[123] Odum was an indefatigable administrator, but he was also territorial and firmly believed that regionalism, particularly in the South, was his research domain. His (explicit and implicit) insistence on his position as regionalism's academic thought leader also colored his social science work on the subject.

While Vance's regionalism noted and organized the multiple attributes of a region through a human geography in which—in general alignment with European and RPAA approaches—human agency through planning could help society curate natural resources toward its social and economic benefit, Odum's regionalism was far more complicated. His organic fusion of folk sociology with multiple regional traditions across disciplines seemed to leash it perennially backward to his complex understandings of the Old and New Souths. In one of his many lists, Odum summarized his regionalism thus: decentralization is inherent in regionalism; dispersion of resources caused by decentralization would create better balance in the area, thereby allowing it to be considered as a totality; regionalism is organic, and region, time, space, and people are to be considered together; and, finally, regionalism is emphatically different from the concept of "sectionalism" put forth by Frederick Jackson Turner.[124]

Odum's history of engaging with Turner's concepts was a long one. In 1922, Turner published an article in the *Yale Review* titled "Sections and Nation," in which he concluded that "the section either conceives of itself as an aggrieved and oppressed minority, suffering from the injustice of the other sections of the nations, or it thinks of its own culture, its economic policies, and well-being as best for all the nation."[125] In "so large and diversified a nation," Turner believed, sectionalism could only become an increasingly greater challenge to a united country. Sectionalism was not his frontier theory privileging the West as defining the true national character, but an entirely more pessimistic, divisive view of the future as destined either for national unity or for sectional divide. Turner's vision foreclosed a future of autonomous culture and governance in which nation and section could coexist in a harmony of multiple citizen allegiances. Applied to the South,

Turner's sectionalism rang of the Confederate past—diametric to Odum's brand of progressive, future-oriented regionalism.[126]

In rebuttal to Turner, Odum invited Edward A. Ross to write "Sectionalism and Its Avoidance" in 1924 for publication in the still-new *Social Forces* journal. In this essay, Ross essentially argued that cultural issues would be negotiated across both nation and section deliberately over time, without Turner's predicted doom.[127] Nor would Odum's engagement with Turner's sectionalism stop there. A decade later, Odum wrote his own *Social Forces* article titled "Regionalism vs. Sectionalism," in which he defined regionalism as a balance of regions all "envisioning nation first."[128] Odum respected Turner, so rather than reject his definition of sections outright, he proposed an evolutionary frame in which sections would develop into regions moving forward: "The promise and prospect of the nation in the future is ... to be found in the substitution of a realistic and comprehensive regionalism for the older historic sectionalism."[129] This evolution of section to region, and his vision for a forward-looking US nation of regions, would consistently appear as one of Odum's defining traits for regionalism as "the opposite of its most common interpretation, namely, localism, sectionalism, or provincialism."[130]

Odum deftly deployed this conceptual contrast to dismiss the Vanderbilt Southern Agrarians' romanticized yearning for an antebellum past as sectionalist, much as Vance had. He also employed the distinction in his smear campaign against Benjamin B. Kendrick, whom he saw as a competitor for his leadership position of the Southern Regional Committee of the SSRC in 1934. Odum denounced Kendrick as an Agrarian and a sectionalist (which he clearly was not). However, he was unsuccessful, and Kendrick was assigned to lead the group. Odum, who had helped found the Southern Regional Committee, would not take this defeat quietly. As Donald Davidson noted in a letter to fellow Vanderbilt Agrarian John Donald Wade, the Agrarians' manifesto *I'll Take My Stand* had come out four years earlier, seemingly without any protest from Odum. It was only in 1934, when Kendrick gained control of the committee—essentially infringing on Odum's perceived territory—that all invective hell broke loose, with Odum unleashing multiple memoranda to the committee members.[131] Although Davidson appears to have been unaware of the *Social Forces* articles rebutting sectionalism, this anecdote helps illustrate that leadership around issues of Southern study could involve significant national funding and policy influence and attempts to manipulate that influence. Odum's sometimes petty uses of "sectionalism" as invective were not above the institutional politics of the period, which, in their way, were also regionalist—power struggles to define, describe, and plan for the region.

REGIONS AND STATES

In *Southern Regions of the United States*, published in 1936, Odum endorsed the concept of regionalism within US geography somewhat precisely, if not at all concisely. At nearly 700 pages, including 329 maps, 177 graphs, and 95 tables assembled by the IRSS research team, *Southern Regions* represented the "big data" of its era. Essentially "anything and everything that Odum's staff could quantify" was included in the massive volume.[132] To explain this extensive data, Odum deployed his Southern portraiture style of narrative prose, providing tireless definitions of and exhaustive interpretive possibilities for soil, precipitation, water bodies, cultures(!), and countless other indexes before neatly categorizing the country into six distinct regions demarcated by tidy clusters of states: the Middle States, the Northeast, the Southeast, the Far West, the Northwest, and the South.[133]

For each region, the book provided an inventory of the cultural, material, and environmental data. Unfortunately, "as they were the only figures readily available, statistics from states formed the basis" for these inventories, leading to some bizarre presentation decisions.[134] Maryland was left out

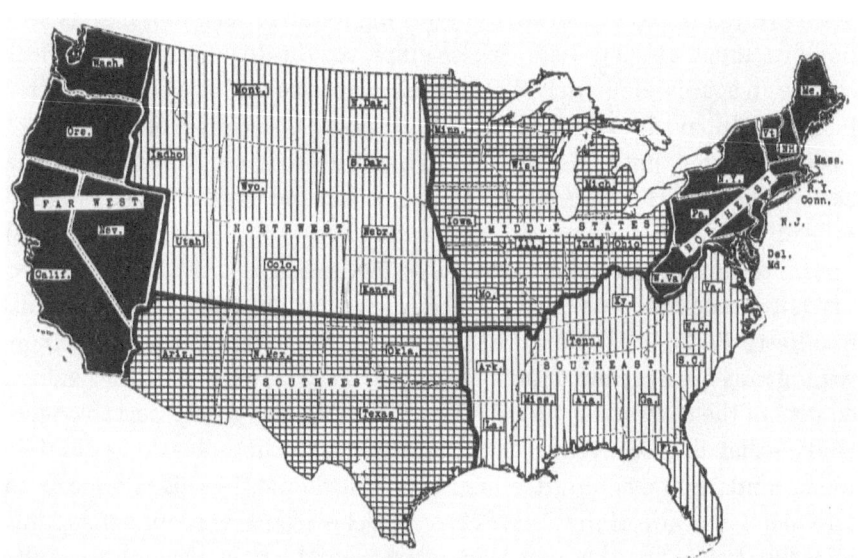

Odum's state-bloc proposal for the major regions in the United States. "The Six Major Regions Basic to the Southern Regional Study. The sixfold regional division of the nation by states, utilized in statistical analysis of the southern regional study, states lines being essential for the use of census material." *Southern Regions*, 9. Howard Washington Odum Papers, Wilson Special Collections Library, UNC–Chapel Hill.

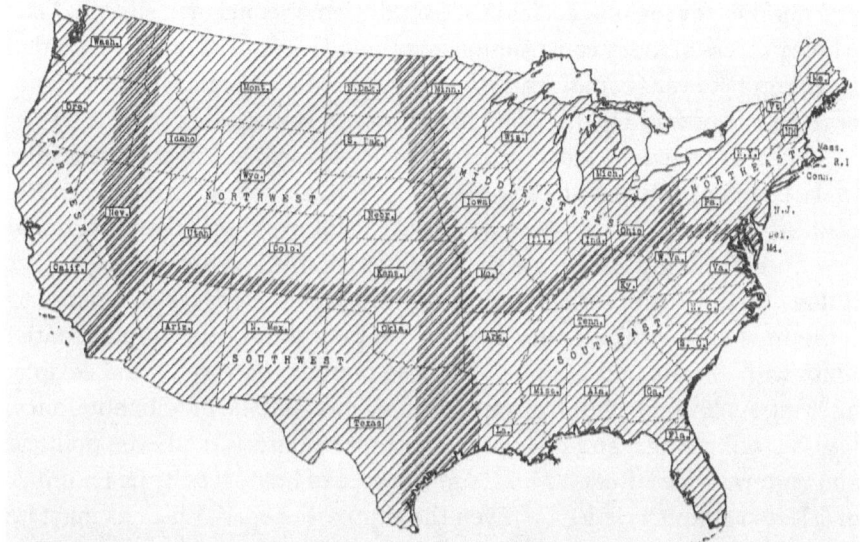

"The Six Major Regions Basic to the Southern Regional Study": "The same general sixfold division *if state lines could be ignored*. Thus the eastern bounds of the proposed shelter forest belt would mark the western bounds of the Middle States and the Southeast, properly including parts of North Dakota, South Dakota, Nebraska, Kansas in the Middle States, and parts of Oklahoma and Texas in the Southeast. So too, parts of Ohio and Virginia would be included in the Northeast while the lower parts of Missouri and West Virginia would fall within the Southeast, as would a part of Indiana and Illinois. This of course is only approximate for illustrative purposes." *Southern Regions*, 9. Howard Washington Odum Papers, Wilson Special Collections Library, UNC–Chapel Hill.

of the Southeast grouping because of certain indexes that it shared with Florida, but Florida was included because of the need for regional contiguousness. Unsurprisingly, most border states posed these kinds of challenges for Odum and his regional definitions: West Virginia, demonstrating data for possible affiliation with both the Northeast and Southeast, was made part of the North, whereas Kentucky, with a similar mix, was assigned to the South.[135]

Guy Johnson, perhaps in deference to his boss at the IRSS, assured readers in his review of *Southern Regions* that the book's groupings and "statistics had to be 'weighted' by complicated mathematical operations familiar only to statisticians to balance" the sheer quantity of data.[136] In other words, Odum's sociology of region was best left to—perhaps only interpretable by—the experts. Not everyone agreed. Vance noted that the Florida decision was "embarrassing," and in regard to Odum's self-serving data definitions and analysis for regions, sociologist Svend Riemer concluded sharply, "The whole process of index construction and that of composite indices is guided by attempts to verify empirically the existence of such regions[,] as a theory of regionalism was decided upon in advance of statistical procedure."[137]

Odum provided the most complete review of regionalism two years later, in the chapter "Implications and Meanings of Regionalism" in *American Regionalism* (1938). In that work, he offered a cultural rather than functional description: "Regionalism is envisioned for what it is rather than for what it does."[138] But the criteria defining regions were not always coherent and sometimes even contradictory. Regions were continuous geographic spatial units with "limits and bounds."[139] These bounds, however, were flexible, blurring such limits with the imprecision characteristic of "climatic zones, rainfall, soil change, and diversity of natural resources," and even political and cultural zones. Regions had "some degree of homogeneity in a number of selected characteristics. . . . Even the simplest of spatial regions must be characterized by some limiting quality or qualities."[140]

These homogenous features would in some way give the region "structure, functions and form." Through this criterion, Odum opened up notions of land use, accessibility, transportation, and power, as well as the resources for them to be functionally available. But, recognizing the disaggregating possibility of the functional criterion to generate "as many regions as there are purposes or functions available," Odum also required that a region have "a relative, composite homogeneity of the largest number of factors for the largest number of purposes in view . . . for a practical, workable unit susceptible of both definition and utilization."[141] The most important overarching factor, he stressed, was that as broadly as region could be defined, it still must have a "reasonable limit as parts of a whole . . . *a constituent unit in an aggregate whole or totality*" (his italics).[142] Quoting Lewis Mumford, Odum dismissed metropolitan regionalism as city centered, uninterested in being part of a "larger whole"—a "false cosmopolitanism."[143] Finally, Odum affirmed that regions must have "organic unity" in geography and culture, proclaiming "regionalism as a cultural Gestalt, in which are balanced all the constituent factors of culture in the making."[144] The very development and evolution of culture was thus also made a function of region.

Historian Michael O'Brien has noted the circularity of Odum's process of assigning regions. Beginning with the core poverty statistics of the Bible Belt in the Southeast, Odum saw per capita incomes steadily rise moving outward. He cut contours accordingly, with Confederate historic unity and definition as a key influence, but neither history nor emotional affinity was, in theory, part of the performative "quantitativeness" of the method.[145] Moreover, the data for these two massive books was collected in a highly unusual period for the country, during the Great Depression and on the heels of the boll-weevil cotton crisis, which had peaked in the South in the 1920s but continued into the following decade. In response both to this crisis and numerous other factors, this era saw high migration rates throughout the country, particularly moving northward and westward from the Southeast. Sociologist Floyd N. House, whom Odum and Jocher cited frequently in their *An Introduction to Social Research*, acknowledged such flux: "Regions are determined by cultural and commercial facts and are *not* necessarily fixed; they may, and in cases do, expand or shrink."[146] In contrast, O'Brien describes Odum's approach as trying "to nail firm boundaries on a fluid social reality. His Southeast would have to be static, or else it would have to disappear."[147] Social science, as Odum was continually reminded, was not a study of fixed objects but—as once described by Vance—unruly, living, moving subject matter.

When Odum asked colleagues for feedback on *American Regionalism* in 1942, George T. Renner of Columbia Teaching College, also a senior economist for the National Resources Committee, was perhaps the most pointed in reference to what he termed Odum's "regionalism versus state-blocism" definitions.[148] Renner had given *Southern Regions* a glowing review, but he shared his criticism of *American Regionalism* privately by letter. Odum had justified and defended the resource-limited convenience of the state-based technique because "there was no practical way of making statistical surveys" for regions.[149] Renner replied,

> You're right; the trouble with regionalism is—regionalism. When you add the argument that, after studying our social phenomenon with considerable accuracy, we should abandon the results of our study and for practical reasons compromise on groups-of-states, aren't you really up against a situation like this: We have pies; but we want cakes; so let's get cakes by re-combing our pies? I'm vastly interested in regionalism, but I for one, don't readily accept the premise that a re-grouping of our pies will yield the pragmatic equivalent of cakes, and I don't believe anyone will ever find the alchemist formula for effecting such transmutation. Moreover, that isn't the kind of scientific approach to social data which Giddings taught me years ago.[150]

The letter must have shaken Odum, particularly the last point, which subtly suggested that his work was essentially disrespecting the teaching of their shared mentor. Odum's reply was by turns terse and familiar, and he was characteristically unable to resist inserting a defense. After excusing his hurry—"off for Seattle . . . working hard on our beloved regionalism!!"—he continued by using a different analogy, in high-brow Odumesque:

> You have raised some very fine questions, and I think we can discuss them profitably. One analogy would be this: Just as human society has its biological and natural backgrounds in physical conditioning, just as sociology, therefore, must understand the natural and organic bases; but sociology is not a natural science in the same sense that biology or physics is; so, sociology being the science which studies society on the associational level, including the organizational, processive, etc., so the group-of-states, societal-multiple-purpose region, no matter how ruthless it is in violating natural regions, is still the only one that we can use for measuring planning or for sociological purposes. . . . In other words, you are absolutely right also [sic] so am I.[151]

The following year, IRSS economist Margaret Jarman Hagood published an article in *Social Forces* that "tested" Odum's groups-of-states regions definitions using "index values representing [the] composite of agriculture and population characteristics developed for the states," and a "correlation analysis" designed to explain Odum's regional grouping by "showing the similarity of each state to its neighbor."[152] In his review, Vance concluded, "It is fortunate that the regionalist has this rigorous technique at his command if for no other reason than to demonstrate that regions are not to be determined on the basis of whim and personal predilection."[153] Perhaps. It was certainly fortunate that Odum had Hagood and Vance at his IRSS to methodologically resolve and promote what convenience and expediency had required.

This cycle was reminiscent of Odum's objectivist debates with the SSRC in the 1920s. Odum had reached out to philanthropy groups advised by leading social scientists, making broad claims of regional analysis and promotion of the social sciences in the South only to be reprimanded for his organicist methods. Despite the self-doubt this experience provoked, he doubled down on his portraiture technique, using his platform as president of the American Sociological Society in 1930 to reaffirm it as folk sociology—not as a method that needed reorientation, but as the future of the field. Later in the decade, he solicited the opinions of friends and colleagues about his books on regionalism (which, at least for *Southern Regions*, he amply received), hoping they would provide the personal and professional validation he sought. In response to their critiques of his "bloc-of-states" compromise for regional definition, Odum admitted (privately) that the definitions needed work, noting of this correspondence that he had "never had any series of letters of critique so important."[154] Nevertheless, he would then have his IRSS colleagues reaffirm that his "clusters of states" *were* in fact the most objective, quantitative way to define US regions. Odum's methods were self-serving, as were his defenses of those methods—an oddly isolationist Southern approach to his regionalism, which he so often justified as needing to serve the "nation first."

Its flaws notwithstanding, Odum's work on regionalism in the 1930s received wide recognition for its social science contribution to the broader national interwar movement. "The mass of statistics," regionalist literature review, and synthesis assembled in both *Southern Regions* and *American Regionalism* were "overwhelming and impressive."[155] The institute's regionalist research strayed into a two-sided exceptionalism: one describing exhausted, depleted social and ecological structures and processes, and one providing near-limitless growth possibilities if its wasteful ways, inherited from plantation neglect, could only be harnessed toward the postfrontier. In the postfrontier—the "social frontier"—"potentialities" could be nurtured and developed through planning to lead the South out of its sectional past and into regional-national participation and even prominence. Across multiple fields of inquiry, "all those maps and charts were to provide cannon fodder for informed discussions about the South for decades."[156]

SOUTHERN LEVIATHAN

Southern regionalism was both descriptive and proscriptive, with an action plan that, had even its muted, often equivocating points been implemented, would have "wrought a minor social revolution."[157] Reminiscent of Lewis Mumford's recognition that his regional planning would only be possible if private property were abolished, Odum saw Southern political leadership as the principal challenge for regionalism's implementation, his assertion that "modification of the political culture of the region . . . lies at the base of any planning approach" conveniently sidestepping the issue of how to implement his "applied sociology."[158] Inspired by Odum's *Southern Regions*, W. J. Cash lamented in *The Mind of the South* (1941), "I don't know how to get information into white leadership. I just know to keep trying."[159] Odum and his fellow regionalists would later be called out by many as "apolitical technicians," and historian John M. Jordan noted pointedly that Odum's "antitheoretical theory begat apolitical politics."[160] But the first to raise this issue, and perhaps the clearest, was Donald Davidson of the Vanderbilt Agrarians.

Davidson was a racist of the Old Southern brand; open, unapologetic, and alarmist. He was a literary critic, not a social scientist, and despite his otherwise reactionary stance, he provided shrewd commentary on Odum and the regionalists' use of science as a pretense for apoliticism. Writing in 1934, Davidson seemed open to Odum's section/region distinction, but he qualified it with the observation that "sectionalism is the political approach, and regionalism is the economic and cultural approach to an identical set of facts."[161] Nevertheless, he cautioned, Odum must anticipate the political "risks of regionalism."[162] In particular, Davidson foresaw political difficulties arising from the recently launched TVA, for which Odum and colleagues had conducted some preliminary fact-finding in 1931: "When the thing really gets underway and begins to show results, does Odum think that its conduct will be utterly Utopian and will go uncriticized, merely because it is 'regional' rather than 'sectional'?" He described the challenge awaiting Odum: "[He is ill prepared to deal with] the howl that will go up from Grand Rapids when cheap but pretty furniture, made in the homes and 'small industries' of the Tennessee Valley, begins to cut into the profits of the mass production furniture trust. They will then go to Congress, or to some appropriate bureau, and raise the devil they can with Odum's regionalism."[163]

In his early role, Odum, too, had been concerned about the role of a national investment authority, outside any local or regional jurisdiction, in the Tennessee Valley. Yet after 1933, when the TVA became a fait accompli, Odum became an enthusiast, framing the authority as a helpful reference point for regional-national planning.[164] To do otherwise risked misinterpretation of his concerns as sectional grievances, thereby endangering his national connections, network of relationships, and future funding opportunities—concerns that had no bearing on Davidson.

This dilemma was one about which Odum himself had theorized. If the regional-national frame represented a future in which the county's regions were to serve "nation first," in belabored contrast to the pessimism of Turner's self-serving sections, how then to articulate a politics of disagreement—or, for that matter, of any sort? Demonstrating political savvy, the TVA leaders had promoted the project as power generation for the promotion of industry and political enfranchisement in the rural South, but had also appeased Southern agricultural interests by underscoring nitrate capture in dam infrastructure to produce much-needed fertilizer to address the region's enormous soil erosion challenges.[165] Odum found such flexibility difficult. For Odum, and many others of the regionalist movement, persuasion through clearly presented "social facts" would necessarily justify social actions based on those facts. This logic formed the rationale of his sociology education and the basis for his imagined sociocracy. Even the Southern folk, demonstrably "irrational" in other ways, would come around in time: "The people are, contrary to some opinions, open and eager to hear truth."[166]

Although Odum shared some of Davidson's concerns about a federal "Leviathan" and its impositions, he also believed that social planning policies and objectives could succeed if planners made the people (folk?) participants through "extraordinary effort in adult education, carrying to the people the power of both fact and thinking."[167] This had been John Dewey's position when he coined the phrase "social planning," but in the 1930s, this abstract core of social engineering ideology collided with the social realities of a Southern folk who did not trust experts, often did not buy books or magazines, and were generally suspicious of academic types like Odum. Put otherwise, the murky and mysterious organic social sciences from which the Sumnerian folkways, mores, and institutions of the South were supposed to have emerged provided no map for a politics of change, while the Wardian telic route required trust in authority and expertise to articulate change — trust that Odum's fictional folk may have proffered but that true Southern populism did not share. Historian Michael Milligan concludes that "Odum ultimately deferred to an older naturalistic definition of region with the assistance of a conservative strain of ecology and geography, a decision that made efforts at regional planning more difficult to envision and execute."[168]

Vance understood that Southern white folkways would present obstacles to social planning, whereas Odum's genteel approach necessitated a belief that his "audience could be both rational and participatory," since acknowledging that facts and education would not suffice "as the bond of social order" would require him "to confront the raw mechanisms of power to implement radical restructuring of the national economy."[169] Odum's concept of technicways attempted to resolve this conceptual dilemma for social planning.

"Regional Planning and Development." A meeting on the need for a program on education, research, and service in regional planning, Chapel Hill, North Carolina, November 18–19, 1950. Sponsored jointly by the Department of City and Regional Planning and the Institute for Research in Social Science. *Left to right, seated:* John M. Gaus, professor of government at Harvard University; Gordon Gray, president of the University of North Carolina System; George F. Grant, general manager of the Tennessee Valley Authority; Robert B. House, chancellor of the University of North Carolina at Chapel Hill. *Standing:* Maj. Gen. John S. Bragson, Office of the Chief of Engineers, Department of the Army; Carl Feiss, chief of the Urban Redevelopment Division and Home Finance Agency; Howard W. Odum; John J. O'Neill, assistant chief, Field Services, Bureau of the Budget; W. Whatley Pierson, dean of the Graduate School, University of North Carolina at Chapel Hill. Howard Washington Odum Papers, Wilson Special Collections Library, UNC–Chapel Hill.

CHAPTER 6

> The "engineering of human consent," to use a happy phrase of George Soule, is essential to social planning in a democracy.
> —HAROLD L. ICKES, US SECRETARY OF THE INTERIOR, 1933–46

> It may well be, however, that the societal technicways, in the form of social planning, will be the answer to accelerate development and to harmonize conflicting forces.
> —HOWARD W. ODUM

PLANNING APOCRYPHA

THE CASE FOR REGIONAL-NATIONAL SOCIAL PLANNING

Herbert Hoover's President's Research Committee on Social Trends finally released its report in 1933, in which members called for a "national advisory council" to study broad issues of the "social, economic, and governmental order," meaning not simply "economic planning" or "governmental planning," but the "comprehensive review of all the social factors involved in the formulation of national policy."[1] In July 1933, based on the recommendation of Secretary of the Interior Harold L. Ickes, President Franklin Delano Roosevelt established the National Planning Board (NPB) as part of the Public Works Administration and named Frederic A. Delano as chairman; former President's Research Committee members Wesley C. Mitchell and Charles Merriam were also invited to serve.[2] Delano was among the most knowledgeable regional practitioners in the country at that point. Born in

Hong Kong and raised in New York's Hudson Valley, he built a career as a railroad magnate in Chicago. As a member in that city's Merchants Club, he recommended Daniel H. Burnham—who had overseen the architecture of the 1893 World's Columbian Exposition—to Charles Dyer Norton to lead a metropolitan planning initiative in Chicago, which would result in the formation of the Chicago Plan Commission in 1909. Twenty-five years later, Delano chaired the 1927 Regional Survey of New York and Its Environs, which was among the country's most extensive data-based planning projects up to that point.[3]

The NPB went through several name changes, and in 1935, as the National Resources Committee (NRC), published *Regional Factors in National Planning and Development*. This comprehensive study was coordinated by John M. Gaus of the University of Wisconsin–Madison, who chaired the NRC's Technical Committee on Regional Planning. It collected eight related reports from various contributors, including regional sociologists Thomas Woofter, an Odum protégé, and Roderick D. McKenzie of the University of Michigan. One report addressed metropolitan planning, but the study's focus broadly established regionalism as a cultural imperative and regional planning as both its science and implementational mechanism, an approach that was directly consonant with the work of the Southern regionalists and of the Regional Planning Association of America (RPAA).[4]

Regional Factors frequently referenced Odum's conceptualizations of regional planning, in its ideal form, as "the development of natural resources within the context of historically defined cultural areas."[5] The committee affirmed the cultural meaning of regional planning as a process "to devise a cultural pattern which will fit a large areal unit," and a process in which "the qualities inherent in the area not only dictate in large part the features of that plan but also its territorial extent."[6] The circularity of this definition echoed the inherent unresolved issues of territory-based cultural proposals: If culture and territory were mutually constitutive, which features should define the operable scale of what they termed cultural "areal units"?[7]

The report returned to the Geddesian proposal of comprehensive river basin development already afoot in projects in the Tennessee Valley, the Columbia River in Washington, and the Colorado River between Nevada and Arizona, but the NRC also recognized that these physical boundaries could be as artificial as state-bloc regional jurisdiction in defining the scale of culture. It was a de facto compromise in deference to the parameters of federal constitutional power based on state jurisdictional governance and to the precedent of interstate, interregional, river-based development already established in the work of the US Army Corps of Engineers, as well as the projects mentioned above.[8]

Nevertheless, the influence of Odum and the RPAA on the study demonstrated the level to which their research agendas had come to influence New Deal policy. In both its content and its synthesis-review method—which Odum had helped to curate in the President's Research Committee on Social Trends report —the NRC report "marked a crucial turning point" cementing American regional planning as an established method for comprehensive river basin development.[9] Southern regionalist interests in soil erosion, flooding, resource conservation, and rural electrification, all of which had been discussed at length over the years in Odum's journal *Social Forces*, were interests central to the New Deal planning strategies. Gradually, however, regionalist advocacy for the "preservation of rural folkways and ecological settlement" was yielding to metropolitan growth and encroachment.[10] Benton MacKaye's proposed metropolitan dike was untenable, and the ambitious "new exploration" had to draw within constitutional strictures, meaning that "nationally sponsored regional planning was reproducing the functional system of which it was a part."[11]

Planning proposals falling short of their ideals in their implementation was hardly new. Recent history offered examples including the reduction of Ebenezer Howard's vision for collectively minded garden cities to a private development blueprint for new towns, and the limitation of RPAA's broad ideals for regionalism to the data-based metropolitan vision of the Regional Plan Association (RPA).[12] Clyde Weaver notes that when modern social sciences and critical thought first appeared, "utopian socialists, positivists, anarchists, regionalists, [and] liberal reformers analyzed the changing society, fomented revolution, and worked among industrial poor. Regional planning in its original form was one of their offspring."[13] Odum and his colleagues at the Institute for Research in Social Science (IRSS) in Chapel Hill all shared some version of these inspirations. Perhaps the difference with Odum was that he consistently justified his sociology, his regionalism, and, by extension, his planning proposals as grounded in applied methods to be tested through popular acceptance.[14]

When the NRC lacked clarity on whether culture defined region or region defined culture, it sided with the potentially artificial geographic contours of river basins. Odum went the other way, erring for state-bloc data and membership in the Confederacy to define, describe, and justify historically based regional culture. Speaking in terms of territory and function—as crystallized by John Friedmann and Clyde Weaver in 1979—the NRC chose a regional functionalist definition over Odum's territorial-regional concept. At some point, politics required a dissection of turn-of-the century social science organicism, and that functional turn defined the path of regional planning in the post–World War II era.[15]

For Odum, the Deweyian notion of social planning was the logical Wardian telic response to social conditions once they had been properly

Williamston Public School, Williamston, South Carolina. Donald Brown, president of the Carolina National Bank and the South Carolina Bankers Association, examines soil conservation poster made by fifth-grade students. Soil conservation course explained by Miss Fannie Copeland, teacher, and fifth-grade student Betty Copeland. Photo by Gordon Webb, 1946. Howard Washington Odum Papers, Wilson Special Collections Library, UNC–Chapel Hill.

inventoried and analyzed: In Geddesian terms, survey before plan. What others were calling regional planning, Odum conceived of as social planning, forming a crucial aspect of his Southern regionalism and his aspirational regional-national pluralistic frame. Such planning was the natural (and naturalized) summation of his research interests in administration, welfare, psychology, sociology, and the South, oriented toward the national popularity of planning practice and the New Deal funding opportunities for it. As historian Harvey Kantor put it, "Because he had done so much work on public welfare, because he saw the urban areas continuing to grow at the expense of the adjacent rural areas, and because he wanted so deeply for the South to take again a leading role in national development, Odum came to accept social planning quite easily."[16]

Broadly, Odum conceived of social planning as a scientific practice and public mechanism to maintain cultural balance for a "transitional society,"

Williamston Public School, Williamston, South Carolina. Fifth-grade students Mickey Kelley and Virginia Watkins report on soil conservation. Photo by Gordon Webb, 1946. Howard Washington Odum Papers, Wilson Special Collections Library, UNC–Chapel Hill.

specifically the South. Writing in 1953, Odum described the transitional society as "essentially an ideal type concept of process" in which "the polar dichotomies such as folk and state, early and late, simple and complex ... provide a framework ... for achieving balance and equilibrium essential to order and adjustment values in survival processes."[17] Harking back to his earlier studies, he continued, "The bio-social concept posits integration as the 'primordial requirement for survival' but in which successful living depends on progressive development in both directions in proper balance."[18] As reflected in these passages, even near the end of his career, Odum's evolutionary frame demanded balance obtained through his signature cavalier mash-up of a half century of social science. But the transitional, temporal aspect of Odum's "balanced" social planning gained acceptance in regional planning as a conceptualization of a phase for transitional rural-to-urban migration, which, in time, would stabilize into an equilibrium of metropolitan planning.[19]

In any case, as with his future-oriented regionalism, Odum's proposals were fundamentally speculative. The obvious internal contradictions would hopefully work themselves out as social scientists directed all of their efforts into survey methods for making a "plan for planning."[20] For the NPB's final report of the same name in 1934, the social scientists gathered facts in the spirit of the social trends report produced for Hoover's President's Research Committee (although without Odum's participation). For Odum, the "plan for planning" strategy provided an imagined apolitical, conflict-free future where ideas and ideologies coexisted peacefully and rationally, far from the South and the nation of the 1930s.

THE CASE FOR REGIONAL-NATIONAL SOCIAL PLANNING

Odum's experience working with peers on the President's Research Committee expanded his research interests beyond the Southern sphere, opening his ideas toward what would become his foundational notion of region serving "nation first," in contrast to sectional isolationist atavism.[21] In addition to providing the opportunity for national perspective, the committee served as a consultative brain trust dress rehearsal for what would become the New Deal national planning initiatives. Just as his travels through the South had helped him write *An American Epoch* in 1930, Odum had also been on sabbatical travel in 1934, slowly crossing the country and visiting national historic sites on his way to California. He was perhaps still stung by the personality dispute with Benjamin Kendrick and his leadership of the Southern Regional Committee of the Social Science Research Council (SSRC), which, in Odum's mind, had dusted up the regional/sectional disagreement due to what he perceived as Kendrick's allegiance to the Southern Agrarians.

Lumpkin, Stewart County, Georgia, April 5, 1936. The Stewart County gullies "noted for their enormous size and depth. The total area covers more than 100,000 acres. Gullies are from 50 to 200 feet in depth. At the head of the gullies, swallowing up good rich farm land, highways and farm building. This process has been going on more than 100 years." Howard Washington Odum Papers, Wilson Special Collections Library, UNC–Chapel Hill.

This long trip, during which he had plenty of time to ruminate, formed the context for his address to the joint meeting of the Pacific Sociological Society and the Institute of Public Affairs at the University of California, Los Angeles on July 26, 1934, titled "The Case for Regional-National Social Planning."[22]

In this address, Odum introduced his familiar list of premises and assumptions to qualify the scope of his presentation, which would be only a brief commentary on such an enormous subject as social planning. Social planning was to be more comprehensive and balanced, "in contradistinction to a mere social plan or to a planned economic order constituted as a single project in which inheres the sovereign power to execute."²³ Moreover, social planning would include the full capacity of social engineering to build "not only new structures for the nation but to carry in the meantime the traffic of all the institutions in a transitional society and within these institutions to permit of orientation, spontaneity, flexibility."²⁴

Yet, in contrast to these expansive administrative ambitions and responsibilities, the size of the country and its cultural diversity required a decentralized regional approach for any "successful permanent social planning program or procedure."²⁵ Odum warned of mismanaged planning precipitating chaos, fascism, revolution, "highbrowism," and similar catastrophes. In addition, according to Odum, "the experts and the specialists" speaking of "mere jargon" or "utopian idealism which will amount to little"—among whom he clearly did not include himself—were viewed as untrustworthy or out of touch by the general public.²⁶

Having rhetorically preempted criticism of his own ideas, Odum introduced social planning on a hopeful note as "an extension and transubstantiation of the first great American experiment in social planning, namely, the Constitution of the United States."²⁷ Despite his California audience, he centered his Southern vision, claiming that social planning would be "just as American or un-American as the genius, ability, and motivation of its social scientists and leaders direct in their heroic efforts to conserve for the nation as much as possible of the Jeffersonian democracy of the simple rural culture to which will be added the building of a still greater democracy for the vast, complex, urban, and industrial America of the future."²⁸

After a brief summary of his six regions—Northeast, Southeast, Northwest, Southwest, Middle States, and Far West, on which he would elaborate in far more detail two years later in *Southern Regions*—Odum turned the remainder of his address to his singular obsession: the South. Odum expounded on the multiple subregions in the Southeast and drew distinctions between "the two Souths."²⁹ The delicate balance of his "regional-national" frame inevitably included Southeast favoritism, tipping the scales whenever he discussed his proposed programs in any detail. The South, Odum asserted, was a region lacking "universities of the first rank," without which as sources of "support and leadership" it would be a steep, perhaps impossible task to achieve "social adequacy" and "build up . . . institutions in any reasonably short time without outside help."³⁰ In other words, Odum claimed, it was "not possible for the South to so master its situation as to transvaluate its deficiency into adequacy without a great deal of outside cooperative assistance in men and money and technics, from federal aid, from business enterprise, from endowed agencies," including the Carnegie Corporation, Rosenwald Fund, Rockefeller groups, and Peabody funds.³¹

Social planning and regionalism, for Odum, were speculative prospects that might not achieve their full potential in the immediate future but were certainly worthy of—even demanded—social science research and dedication. In his address, he considered the "current crises and future perspective" of social planning:

> While actualities of the past cannot be ignored, it is quite clear also that fundamental issues are at stake and that the task is of extraordinary proportions. Conflict and struggle will abound. It is further understood quite clearly that the people are not ready for social planning, that the facts and specifications are not yet available, and that the administrative problems seem well-nigh insurmountable. It is therefore fairly clear that not much may be expected in the immediate future in the way of comprehensive and definite action and programs. These considerations, however, although handicaps which may challenge to fear and caution on the part of public administrators and practical politicians, in no way justify the failure of social scientists to turn the full force of their thought and technique to the exploration of optimum possibilities of social planning as a reference for future economy, to pioneer to the fullest extent possible in further research and experimentation, and to make every possible contribution to actual planning programs. It is their business to lead and not to follow; to provide the facts and the foundations upon which public administrators may build the new social structure.[32]

The spirit that Odum's regionalism and social planning sparked in the South and beyond was contagious, not just in the academic world, but as a way forward to be "set in the framework of American democracy."[33] To plan for a region was to conjure and define its future, which, through such actions, might inspire an autonomy wherein Southern experts, preferably social scientists, would run the regional institutions that could own and govern that future. By tracing back his Southern rationalization of social planning, we see how it came to inspire national New Deal policies for the South—at times despite Odum's own objectives.

A TALE OF TWO SOCIAL PLANNING MODES: TELESIS AND FOLKWAYS

But what of the folkways? Odum, like most of the organic sociologists who were generally silent on Marxism except to discredit it, was "committed to the 'folk' without desiring their direct participation in the development of the South."[34] Historian Richard King has noted that Odum conveniently elided issues of class structure in his analysis by employing "the more all-inclusive term 'folk'" rather than "labeling the yeoman as a 'middle class' farmer."[35] Odum's "regionalism was for the people, not by the people."[36] This divide was conceptually manifested in his ambiguity and "fence-sitting" on the social role of planning.[37] Odum continually "groped toward planning," a practice he distinguished from the overreach of "total economic planning," or "unrealistic all-inclusive 'isms' and plans so often offered as substitutes for fundamental processes and extensions of the American order."[38] But these abstractions were also part of national conceptions of social *and* regional planning. Benton MacKaye's regional planning, for instance, offered little more human agency than the abstraction of diking metropolitan culture to prevent its "Spengler winter" from influencing a perceived pure "indigenous America."[39] The abstractions of the 1920s were fired in the kiln of the 1930s and its need for effective, responsive regional policy.

Prior to the crucible of the Depression, however, Odum had yet to fully conceptualize his folkways-driven regional-national frame. Pausing from preaching the folk imperative, he instead found himself drawn to the appeal of Wardian, expert-informed social planning.[40] In the 1920s, New York governor Alfred E. Smith's progressive endorsement of purposeful future growth, or "material planning," and Lester Frank Ward's belief in telesis represented for Odum not only a "key mental and social achievement," but obvious sources for the "whole modern field of social planning."[41] The telic approach represented "the highest manifestation of social control," through which a group of specialists could "carefully study [a] situation, comprehend the aims it desires to accomplish, study scientifically the best methods for attainment of these, and then concentrate social energy to the task set before it."[42] Social planning was thus how to face the "social frontier," which had emerged as the new sociological boundary since the closing of the Western frontier had brought to an end the fantasy of simply leaving problems behind and moving farther westward.[43]

Odum's first conceptualization of social planning came seven years before his Los Angeles speech, in his 1927 textbook *Man's Quest for Social Guidance: The Study of Social Problems*.[44] Odum dedicated a chapter of the book to social planning, calling it "a modern concept . . . much larger than the popular ideas commonly limited to town planning or city planning."[45] He credited Ward's "technical teleology" as an introductory source for this chapter, likening it to "an architect's plan" that, "together with the builder's work" of social planning, was "very closely related to the subject of social progress."[46] Frustrated by the old "laissez-faire" and "the slow, wasteful, natural evolutionary processes of society" reflected in orthodox Darwinism, Odum found in telesis a catalytic element within an evolutionary frame to accelerate and make more efficient these processes, which otherwise moved at such a slow, multigenerational pace.[47]

Social planning was the Wardian mechanism for contemplating and addressing the telic progress of the organic "whole field of social life and structure," including physical factors, population factors, "social reorganization, and experimental efforts towards social direction."[48] As examples of such efforts, Odum offered various cursory references to issues of land planning and zoning, as well as more detailed discussions of certain projects, such as the RPA's famous 1927 New York and Its Environs Plan (and the extensive studies necessary to produce it). He also lauded the Wisconsin Better Cities Contest, conducted by the Wisconsin State Conference of Social Work in 1924–25, underscoring his admiration for the Wisconsin university outreach model and his understanding of social planning as including social work, with which he was also engaged at the University of North Carolina. In a section on the suburbs, Odum briefly touched on Ebenezer Howard's Garden City movement, noting that it had run "the usual gamut of theory, experiment, failure, and success" in its quest to provide "wholesome surroundings for those who must live near cities," and to protest excessive centralization in the city planning of the era.[49]

Odum followed the suburbs section with one on regional planning. He began with characteristically broad strokes: "These physical backgrounds and objectives of social planning are so inclusive and interrelated that each unit ought to be studied and planned in connection with the whole. This larger concept, including nation, state, city, country, village, suburbs, and their interrelationships, has come to be known as regional planning." While Odum's later formulation of regional planning was oriented toward operationalizing his concept of Southern regionalism, in 1927, he took a more expansive—and somewhat more inchoate—view. Although *Social Forces* had published articles on city planning since the journal's inception in 1925, Rupert B. Vance's foundational essay "The Concept of the Region" would not appear until the end of 1929. Thus, in *Man's Quest*, Odum discussed regional planning before he or the IRSS members had consciously established their articulation and endorsement of the multifaceted regionalist project. In this chapter, Odum extensively quoted Lewis Mumford's "Regions—to Live In" article, published in a special 1925 issue of *Survey Graphic*, summarizing it as "the provocative place of regional planning ideal in the whole task of social planning."[50] But Mumford never mentioned the phrase "social planning" in that article, only observing how regional development cut across "our current political and social problems."[51] The last section of the chapter concerned "regional sociology," noting the work of Radhakamal Mukerjee and his "scientific classification of types and regions."[52]

The chapter was, Odum admitted, a "hurried review" of social planning, although he would return to the Wardian "joint efforts of the physical sciences and the social sciences" that must "take into consideration the whole problem of social values and social guidance" as an inspiration in the years to follow.[53] This sweeping Comtean conceptualization, inherited via Odum's doctoral education, positioned sociology as the last of the sciences. As such, it therefore could and must address all those sciences that came before—now to include planning—at the slow, steady pace of meliorative data gathering. Expansive and organic, the chapter—published near the fourth decade of the new century—absorbed the already broad field of planning into an even larger frame that contemplated nearly all the sciences. This wide-ranging, voracious approach would characterize much of Odum's work in the decades to follow.

The seven years between *Man's Quest* and Odum's address to the Pacific Sociological Society and the Institute of Public Affairs at the University of California, Los Angeles, outlining his regional-national frame would temper this grander approach to social planning. Moreover, Odum's intensifying regional focus was shared by other leading social scientists. In 1934, the same year as Odum's Los Angeles speech, sociologist Ernest W. Burgess gave his presidential address to the American Sociological Society, titled "Social Planning and the Mores." The following year, he included it in the published conference proceedings coedited with Herbert Blumer of the University of Chicago, which they titled *Human Side of Social Planning*.[54]

Burgess introduced the volume as "devoted to certain neglected aspects of social planning which merit more attention than they have received, especially from sociologists, in whose field they largely fall."[55] He highlighted the number of sociologists "called into service in Washington and elsewhere," listing out the Roosevelt administration's major boards, bureaus, and administrations that hired them, and he noted that these positions were "directly or indirectly" concerned with the "success or failure of the New Deal."[56] Despite his "natural gratification" with the elevation of sociologists to such posts in the "alphabetocracy at Washington," a concerned Burgess posed two questions: "Are sociologists in governmental service engaged upon research that is distinctly sociological? Are sociologists making full measure of contributions to the solution of the depression and of recovery" from a "distinctively sociological point of view?"[57] Burgess ruminated on these matters before presenting his own answer: No.

What, then, constituted a "distinctively sociological" approach to social problems? Sociology, Burgess argued, had a singular capacity to consider issues that had been "overlooked and neglected" by peer disciplines, particularly economics and political science.⁵⁸ Addressing the same Sumnerian themes of folkways and mores that Odum frequently cited, Burgess characterized these phenomena as "motivated by sentiment rather than by interest," examples of "non-logical human action" that countered the rational-choice theories espoused by political science and traditional economics. However, he did acknowledge that Vilfredo Pareto's work on economics also explored and sought to account for these irrational human behaviors.⁵⁹ For sociology, folkways and mores signified a deterministic cultural environment of mysterious origins from which emerged a moral order: societal mores, institutions, and law.⁶⁰

Folkways, according to Burgess, "can be modified, but only to a limited extent, by the purposeful efforts of men."⁶¹ Mores are customs, "changing gradually, only under the impact of changed conditions of life," that can only "evolve along lines already present in folkways and mores."⁶² Burgess presented the same folkways imperative often repeated by Odum: "Social programs of private or public bodies that run counter to the mores are foredoomed to partial or complete failure, while those that follow within their boundaries have promise of success."⁶³ In contrast to scholars' recent participation in public affairs, Burgess noted that, traditionally, sociology's interest in examining the nonrational and deviant conditions and behaviors through sociological survey methods was perhaps "the reason why the sociologist has not been called into consultation by practical men of affairs."⁶⁴ But at the height of the 1930s, planning, by any definition, was the central currency of these "practical men of affairs."

Burgess then re-centered the sociologist's role: "But what if, in the last analysis, the success or failure of any given policy and program will turn upon the so-called intangibles and imponderables in the situation?"⁶⁵ Reiterating popular claims regarding the universality of mores such as individualism, democracy, and humanitarianism in America, he suggested that any social planning that ran counter to these would fail, as would any policy taken from Europe or elsewhere beyond a US context. Under the humanitarian ideal, he noted that *temporary* relief programs would be broadly supported to confront crisis, but any such *permanent* program, particularly one focused on collective rather than individual welfare, would fail.

As an example, Burgess cited the social science field offices in the Tennessee Valley, where the massive Tennessee Valley Authority (TVA) project was being implemented, claiming they would provide the ideal setting to test how stateways would be received by the "mountaineers, individualists of the pioneer type."⁶⁶ He elaborated,

The project assumes that by a *tour de force* the industrial revolution which elsewhere in the United States required two or three generations will here be telescoped into four or five years and in that time mountaineers with their intense individualistic traditions and attitudes will become completely adjusted to the power age and modern technology.... It is only too apparent that if the customs, attitudes and reactions of the people are not as fully studied and taken into account as the geographic and economic situation, the Tennessee Valley project is likely to be a partial, if not complete, failure.[67]

Arguing along the same lines as Odum often would, Burgess claimed that for change to be evolutionary and not revolutionary (the institutional preference as well as his own), the "weight of anthropological and historical evidence" supported Sumnerian positions that mores change gradually and irrationally in response to societal change—and only over the *long durée*.[68] Burgess dismissed the Socratic possibility of education to accelerate the transformation of attitudes in younger generations concerning politics or technology, noting that New Deal Secretary of the Interior Harold Ickes "naively" encouraged the "engineering of human consent" through education as "essential to social planning in a democracy."[69] In contrast, Burgess encouraged New Deal programs be worked out "experimentally, pragmatically, and democratically" to secure not only a "more desirable economy, but also a more desirable human living."[70] Such an approach was a "surer but slower way [that] programs of social planning may obtain a more than temporary public sanction."[71] Although Thorstein Veblen's name appeared nowhere in Burgess's essay, his pragmatic institutionalism provided a tonic for Sumnerian folkways in defining the organic solution that Burgess hailed as the slower but safer policy for social planning. Social sciences, history, sociology, history, economics, and political science must all be dedicated to a specifically American "democratic solution to our economic and human problems."[72]

Burgess's review of Sumnerian social planning tracked closely with the Southern regionalists' concern about the dangers of imposing administrative policy—stateways—on society to promote social change without considering the folk mores. This concern only heightened as the New Deal and the 1933 National Industrial Recovery Act (NIRA) launched the National Recovery Administration (NRA) and the Public Works Administration (PWA). Burgess's 1934 warnings were prescient—or at least moving at the speed of government—and the NIRA would be declared unconstitutional in May 1935. As historian Richard H. Pells points out, social scientists of the era centered their own societal concerns and themselves as the experts to address them, and in this case, such positioning seemed accurate.[73]

The balance of the telic with the folk was Odum's objective, but in the 1930s, Wardian telic social planning advocacy, absent any mention of the folk, sounded rather uncomfortably aligned with the popular perception of a New Deal Washington brain trust of experts, the product of the "growing aggregation of professors" in the capital.[74] Irrespective of whether a populist, conspiratorial perception of this "brain trust" as elitist and antidemocratic was founded, Burgess noted that the study of precisely such irrationalities of sentiment, feelings, and emotions formed the distinctive core of sociological study, arguing that these sensibilities must be understood in concert with expert-informed social planning and policy. Odum knew this, and it was precisely the Southern distrust of expertise to which he deferred when concluding that the promise of authentic planning, social or regional, could only be implemented in the South when it was ready to shed its sectional past and become a region—in other words, once its folk were ready to listen to the experts. Through his social planning gradualism, Odum attempted to resolve the tension between stateways and folkways with his proposal for technicways.

SOCIAL PLANNING AS TECHNICWAYS

Odum's technicways had deep roots in the history of planning. Patrick Geddes had focused particularly on technology as part of his valley-section plan. Geddes was, in turn, inspired by Frédéric Le Play's concepts of folk society and natural region, as well as the work of Peter Kropotkin and the new technological age he had described in *Fields, Factories and Workshops* (1899). In *Cities in Evolution* (1915), Geddes deployed the terms "paleotechnics," "neotechnics," "geotechnics," and "mesotechnics," which had been in general use among academic circles since the turn of the century.[75] Geddes explained that from the "rougher hunting and warlike civilization" Paleolithic Age, with its use of "rough stone implements," slowly evolved the Neolithic Age, whose "folk were of gentler, agricultural type," using "skillfully chipped or polished" tools of "more varied types of materials, and for finer skills."[76] Geddes's review of tools as both technology and techne for their implementation was then transferred to new suffixes: the paleo*technic* and neo*technic*. As he explained, by "simply substituting -*technic* for -*lithic*, we may distinguish earlier and ruder elements of the Industrial Age as Paleotechnic, the newer and still often incipient elements disengaging themselves from these as Neotechnic."[77]

Geddes's protégé Lewis Mumford explored these historic technological processes in *Technics and Civilization*—published in 1934, the same year as Odum's and Burgess's pivotal speeches—and further in *The Culture of Cities* (1938). Noting the shifts from the industrial coal society through petroleum to "new kinetic sources of power," Mumford observed, "All these improvements indicate a revolutionary change . . . from the inorganic to the organic, from the destructive to the conservative utilization of land and energy that marks the transition from the paleotechnic to the neotechnic period, and will further mark the change from a purely mechanical ideology and the method to a biotechnic one."[78] These optimistic visions conjured a planned future moving toward (or reverting back to) a balanced organic society, which Odum and Mumford each idealized in premodern societies and towns.

The Odum of the 1930s had grown more suspicious about the role of technology since 1927, but he nevertheless understood the need to insert and accommodate it into his folkways/stateways frame, inherited from William G. Sumner via Franklin Giddings, to understand how society responded to technological change. Such investigation was concerned not with "what science and technology are doing to society, but what the processes are, through which tremendous transformations are being wrought."[79] These historical, transitional processes were the technicways that would slowly replace the folkway mores in the "modern civilized world."[80] Odum's technicways, telic in nature, could, through social planning, modify "human behavior and institutions [so] as to outmode the earlier rate of societal evolution."[81]

"In folk society," Odum believed, "the principal factor in social change is the slow growth of folkways. . . . The transitional technicways are the habits and customs that develop as adjustments to the innovations of science and technology. (They are *not* the scientific techniques themselves.)"[82] Odum would later develop the concept more fully in his *Understanding Society* (1947), but in his "An Agrarian Country" chapter of *Southern Regions* (1936), he raised the call to balance material and social technicways: "The complaint is frankly against the dominance of technology and bigness over human welfare and social evolution . . . a complaint against material technic ways of speeding up evolution helter-skelter and the lack of social technic ways to better direct those forces. It is a search for some type of balanced economy which is also primarily a 'culture' which will serve as a medium for the continuing sweep of science and technology which in turn can be made to serve mankind rather than to exploit it."[83]

In his review of Philip Boardman's biography of Geddes in *Social Forces*, Odum connected his own concept of technicways to a comprehensive approach to planning, advocating for an "understanding of the essential elements of modern civilization in terms of the state, of industry, of urbanism, of organization, technology, and the resulting rise of modern technicways" as "basic to the understanding of what planning means and what sort of planning may be assumed for modern contemporary society."[84] In his ode to Geddes, Odum wrote essentially an evaluation of his own work, a kind of projected auto-obituary into which he inserted his own ideas as direct interpretations of Geddes. But Odum's technicways proposal was different from the Geddesian approach to technology.[85] As with his proposal projecting the evolution from section to region, in Odum's view, folkways would transition into technicways as society developed. But, as Burgess and colleagues also believed, such transition would occur only at the pace that folkways allowed.

Late in his career, IRSS researcher Rupert B. Vance returned to Odum's technicways to clarify what he saw as their general misinterpretation in the sociological field. In contrast to perceptions of Odum's work as an over-romanticized vision of simpler folk societies, Vance believed that Odum's concepts were best understood as a "consideration of how technology is assimilated into [the] normative order of society."[86] Vance reviewed the sociological literature since the turn of the century, which had largely prioritized technological change as a motor for history to such an extent that Thomas Veblen had famously observed, in an inversion of the common aphorism, "Invention has become the mother of necessity."[87] In this process, multiple techniques (techne) were consistently introduced into the folkways and mores, but around only those with enduring impact would arise the technicways, which were the behaviors that would help society adjust to the new techniques. While the mores of the folkways would continue for a time in parallel to the new technicways, they would eventually be displaced. The completion of this process, across an evolutionary, transitional period, would occur when the technicways were affirmed in the practices of stateways, guided by new laws that recognized their new importance and could "incorporate, regularize and integrate technicways in the normative social order and sanctions."[88]

This whole conceptualization, of course, remained contingent on the overarching insistence that, if in conflict, the folkways would and should supersede the stateways. But should these changes align in balance, "material progress would be cumulative, the moral order would remain static, being possessed only of better ways to attain traditional goals as before."[89] This belabored distinction was important, for it accommodated a key dualism: on the one hand, the regional boosterism that Odum and the Southern regionalists saw in opportunities for federal investments in economic development that they knew to be crucial for the rehabilitation of the South's agricultural sector, and, on the other hand, a moral order that, in the South, was defined and policed through Jim Crow.

Writing in 1945, Odum and his coauthor Katharine Jocher positioned regionalism and social planning as constituting multiple bridges and balances across these transitional divides, from the conceptual, to the disciplinary, the geopolitical, the historical, and the cultural: "The resources of the social and physical sciences must be brought to bear in bridging the theoretical and the practical and in conserving the folkways which help the society adapt to the new state and technicways."[90] Both the social scientist and the social planner were tasked not merely with studying all of these processes and factors through survey methods, but also considering "right" and "wrong" in analyzing the transition from techniques to technicways based on "means and ends" and working to balance these elements. As Odum and Jocher emphasized, "When the two societies [of folk and state] work in concert, change and achievement result; when they are at odds, there is tension, disorganization, conflict, and ultimately decay. The definitive, evolving society will be a reality when there is balance and equilibrium between folkways, stateways, and technicways. All of this may be generally accomplished through social planning."[91]

Writing in the midcentury, in his last major work on social planning's role in change, Odum tenuously committed to his telic technicways as encompassing path, process, and mechanism toward achieving balance: "It may well be . . . that the societal technicways, in the form of social planning, will be the answer to accelerate development and to harmonize conflicting forces."[92] In 1934, Odum had claimed that it was "understood quite clearly that the people [were] not ready for social planning," yet in the ensuing decades, his technicways contorted in his own attempts to bridge and balance South with nation and to "engineer consent"—albeit slowly, dialectically, and perhaps primarily rhetorically—among his imagined Southern folk.

FRANK ACCEPTANCE OF THE UTOPIAN APPROACH TO REGIONAL PLANNING

In contrast to the grand if often nebulous ideas of his mentor, Rupert B. Vance's vision of both the promise and challenges of regional planning in the South was clearer and more materially grounded. Just as the last chapter underscored the distinctions between these two scholars' conceptualizations of regionalism, a comparative analysis of their positions on regional planning as the science of regionalism helps to further illuminate their distinct perspectives.

Through his concept of technicways, Odum attempted to align his understanding of regional folk culture in transitional society in the face of advancing technology with that of institutional and social change. Like many of Odum's ideas, technicways were functionally fuzzy, allowing for applied and interpretive flexibility in explaining the evolutionary processes of folk society under modernizing influences. His proposal for social planning in the 1930s required a technicways explanation to justify such stateways interventions that might otherwise be at odds with the wisdom of the folk. Odum hoped that his technicways concept might become a key aspect of his intellectual brand, much as folkways had for Sumner or "cultural lag" had for his Southern colleague William Ogburn.[93] It might also help him predict and explain how Southern mountaineers would receive the TVA: "Social planning conforms to the technicways specifications insofar as it is contrariwise to the old folkways of individualism, is subversive of the *laissez faire* traditions, and arises from known needs and technological changes."[94]

Rupert B. Vance's human geography was more closely aligned with French regionalism and spoke of Geddesian regional planning with greater clarity and precision than Odum's instrumentalization of those traditions for his more personal objectives. In the final chapter of Vance's *Human Geography of the South* (1932), titled "Reconstructing the Region: Regionalism and Regional Planning," he clarified his terminology and intentions for both regionalism and regional planning in refreshing detail. As noted in the last chapter, Vance's regionalism, in contrast to "geographic determinism," asserted the human capacity to reshape the earth and its environments into a "cultural product."[95] Based on the history of abusive Southern extractive practices of various forms of "mining," he proposed that a more sustainable "cropping" approach would be a more "constructive exploitation" of regional resources.[96] Grounded in these observations, he laid out his objectives for regional planning: "One of the highest forms of regional planning consists of the transference of resources from the mining to the cropping economy accompanied by the orderly conservation of stored resources where this is not possible."[97]

Regional planning, for Vance, was the art of "making things happen rather than waiting for them to happen."[98] He cited Geddes and Branford's "frank acceptance of the Utopian approach" to regional planning as an explication of their "survey before plan" approach. Vance explained this utopian approach as "the survey of the region-as-is is followed by a blue print of the region as it can be reconstructed."[99] He concluded, "Regional planning may then be defined for our purposes as an attempt at coordination of all regional changes and readjustments toward a desirable goal. The goal is determined after a consideration of both natural and cultural forces."[100]

The science of regional planning may have leaned "heavily on the engineering arts and techniques," but its policy arm was "part and parcel of the political process," and Vance viewed social planning as "the policy making function which determines the roles of science."[101] Nevertheless, he also believed the two needed to work together in survey *and* in plan: "The regional survey is a matter of science, cartographic, geographic, descriptive, statistical. The regional plan is a matter of applied science, technology, and engineering. Both carry out policies rather than determine them."[102] Invoking political critiques of and the regional obstacles to those processes, Vance concluded, "Unfortunately political leadership notoriously lags far behind technical and scientific leadership. While engineering science is an achievement, political science remains a figure of speech."[103] Thus, the "formulation of regionalism as a social policy" had "not yet come into existence."[104] Moreover, in the South, he stated, "if either social or regional planning [can] be regarded as a form of economic rehabilitation, it can easily be shown that the South as much as any region stands in need of such a program."[105]

Despite this pessimism, Vance's proposals for regional reconstruction generally focused on the reorganization and rehabilitation of the Southern agriculture sector, particularly in terms of the "rationalization of the cotton system" as "the primary gigantic task." He understood this as principally an economic restructuring challenge rather than one limited to the traditional regionalism and regional planning previously outlined.[106] Vance insisted, however, that these efforts should not be a "get-well-quick recovery program" designed merely to return the South to pre-Depression conditions, but rather must address and alter "the region's excessive devotion to cotton, its land tenure system, its outmoded credit system, and . . . the peculiar economic status assigned the lowest-level tenant farmers."[107] He noted that the federal Civil Works Administration (CWA) and the Federal Emergency Relief Administration (FERA) focused principally on urban unemployment, stranded populations in abandoned one-industry towns, and rural rehabilitation.[108] As Vance pointed out, federal crop subsidies through the Agricultural Adjustment Act (AAA) favored planters, including those in the South: "The monetary manipulations plus the AAA have in a short time, it must be admitted, worked wonders with gross farm incomes of the nation. The gross farm income of the United States in 1933 increased $1,240,000,000 over 1932, a gain, if one includes benefit and rental payments, of 24 per cent."[109]

The sharecropper and tenancy crises, meanwhile, went unaddressed, as did the core challenge of cotton exports. Vance recognized a divisive race policy as central to the status quo that maintained the landless masses in crisis: "The need for drastic remedies has been masked by the politicians' catchword that American farmers will never drift into conditions of European peasantry. Any self-respecting peasant proprietor in France would view with loathing the condition of a Mississippi cotton cropper. If the South has allowed the fear of the Negro to block its consideration of tenure reform, it has seriously overestimated the importance of the Negro farmer numerically as competitors. The fear of according the Negro a higher economic status has operated to prevent consideration of the plight of over a million white tenants and their families."[110] Vance's position was hardly integrationist outright, nor even an equation of Black and white tenant farmers and sharecroppers as sharing mutual interests and social plights. The flaw he criticized was numerical, not structural racism itself. Yet, in his own way, he offered a reform-minded critique of the Southern social and racial contracts.[111]

Both Vance and Odum proposed policies that might help boost cotton exports, along with regional policies that might reduce interregional cotton competition, particularly between the Southeast and the emerging Southwest markets.[112] In retrospect, the possibilities of national intervention to advance the Southeastern cotton interests in international markets during the Depression did indeed venture into the utopian, as did Vance's hopes for comprehensive land reform. But for the most part, Vance's thinking on regional planning was based on the premise of agency in human geography and was far more theoretically coherent and sound than Odum's.

Vance was also more willing to critique federal policy, without Odum's concern over reviving (or seeming to revive) Southern "sectional grievances." Vance recognized actors and interests and made grounded policy recommendations. He did not rely on conceptual neologisms like "technicways" to address the Southern situation frontally. Vance believed that the South was still trapped in the colonial economy, attempting to export low-cost agricultural products to buy expensive manufactured goods made elsewhere. To address this problem, he endorsed urbanization, industrialization, and a diversified agriculture beyond the single staple crop.

Like his mentor, Vance saw the potential for regional planning "as the quickest and most efficient route to a mature economy," but he also "characteristically pointed out that any such program would have to take into account the entrenched folkways of a people still under the sway of the plantation mentality."[113] In his restatement in 1935 of the regional planning dilemma of the South, which he recognized as in transition, if only temporarily, Vance concluded,

> A system of small owners producing all the variety of fruits, vegetables, and staple crops of which the South is capable, supplementing their live-at-home-agriculture with as much cash farming as the

markets at home and abroad will absorb—is not this the South's logical answer to threatened economic nationalism? Granted this is no release from the binding pressures of the colonial economy, the area has the prospect of attacking its submarginal land problem, of new uses for its pine forests, of the development of part time rural industries based on the wider use of hydroelectric power, along with a slowly increasing industrialism. Here, it seems, is the nobler task of regional planning. . . . Here in the South we have the beginnings of agricultural extension, cooperation, and the direction of production. For this structure we need a foundation. That foundation is farm ownership and the abandonment of mono-culture, the one crop system.[114]

REGIONAL PLANNING INSTITUTIONS

Odum was fundamentally an institutionalist. If his concepts for regional planning could be fuzzy, their institutional structure was clear. Historian George Simpson summarizes Odum's proposed regional planning institutional design as a tripartite administration resembling his organizational arrangements for his various interrelated University of North Carolina positions. At the highest level of the bureaucracy, Odum envisioned a nine-member federal planning agency with an extensive mandate and prerogatives, fully staffed by "research and planning experts" who could advise the board in its work to "carry on a continuous inventory of the Nation, to advise the President, Congress, and the Supreme Court, and to act as a buffer between the States and regions and the national government."[115] Each state would have a similar if smaller-scaled planning agency, also with nine members and a research staff, that would advise various state government agencies and act as a middleman between the regions and federal agency and smaller local offices.[116]

Finally, Odum proposed a regional planning agency comprising members from the state agencies as well as other regional groups, like the TVA, which would serve "as a buffer between States and the United States planning agency and the national government."[117] In collaboration, these three levels of bureaucratic administration would address three planning categories: "physical planning, economic planning, and social and cultural planning."[118] If not quite Ward's sociocracy, this agency would nevertheless be an appointed body, likely inspired by the President's Research Committee on Social Trends: a brain trust for social planning and engineering, above the fray of party politics.

Odum's IRSS colleague and coauthor Katharine Jocher posthumously praised him as a "practical theorist," a man who understood the close relationships between theory, research, and action: "He had a favorite saying: 'It won't work if it isn't sound theory.'"[119] In truth, he was an opportunist. Beardsley Ruml, director of the Laura Spelman Rockefeller Memorial fund, called him the "master manipulator" of the Northern philanthropic networks, to which he had entrée through his Columbia colleagues, as well as his friendship with Will Alexander and their relationship through the Commission on Interracial Cooperation.[120] Throughout his career, Odum would propose, initiate, and sometimes fail in his ambitions to create groups and organizations that could scaffold his boundless project ideas. Odum's favorite saying could easily have been rephrased: "It won't work unless it gets funded."

In May 1927, Ruml met with Odum in New York to reassess the work itinerary they'd initially agreed to in Charlotte back in 1924. By the end of the month, Odum understood that the IRSS needed to move in the direction of local and regional study so as to not miss out on the opportunity to be the central source for Southern sociology. If Odum's objectivist sociology colleagues failed to appreciate this turn, his benefactor did value it, and that set Odum on a new course to reframe the IRSS's work—already regional in focus—as officially and explicitly regional. Money followed. The Rosenwald Fund gave $50,000 to the University of North Carolina Press for a regional research scholarship fund, managed by a committee to be nominated by the SSRC.[121] In 1930, Odum convinced the SSRC to establish a satellite Southern Regional Committee, of which he served as the first chair. The following year, in December 1931, Jackson Davis of the General Election Board and Edmund Day of the Rockefeller Foundation agreed to fund a Southern regional study conducted by Odum and the Southern Regional Committee, with the funds to be administered by the SSRC. Odum increasingly "committed himself to regional research," obtaining the "money, the bureaucracy, the graduate students and colleagues to gather and process the information."[122] As mentioned earlier, one could argue that his entire "regional-sectional" theoretical distinction was based on interpersonal jealousies with Benjamin Kendrick over the Southern Regional Committee leadership.[123]

In January 1936, with the support of the Southern Regional Committee and IRSS researchers, the Southern regional study was published as Odum's *Southern Regions*. In June of that year, Odum hosted a ten-day conference at Chapel Hill, funded by the General Election Board, called the Institute on Southern Regional Development and Social Sciences. Its goal was to assess the findings published in *Southern Regions* and how best to implement them in plans. From this event, Odum developed the idea for a Council on Southern Regional Development, which he proposed in January 1938 at an Atlanta meeting of social science leaders. This council would be an independent organization with a twelve-year program and a $2 million budget to be raised from private individuals and foundations (much like the IRSS he ran at the University of North Carolina).[124] It would focus on four general themes: race relations, land tenure and farm relations, economics and labor relations, and public relations and administration—not coincidentally, the same themes on which Odum and his institute focused, thereby positioning him as the council's de facto leader.[125]

But Odum faced opposition from other Southern political groups insisting on a more ideologically rooted platform, as well as alternative proposals from like-minded groups concerning how and who best to lead such planning efforts, and this resistance ultimately scuttled his plans.[126] He privately complained about "so many diversified groups in the South, each one bent on doing the whole job in its own way."[127] That summer, President Roosevelt declared the South the nation's top economic problem, both problematizing and claiming the region as a national planning issue. Roosevelt's declaration essentially rendered the Southern planning leadership point moot, at least from Odum's perspective. Writing to Will Alexander again in 1940, Odum capitulated, committing to continue in his manifold efforts "cheerfully but stubbornly, using a punting game, and develop good teams and strategy."[128]

President Roosevelt launched his candidacy as a regionalist president at the University of Virginia round table, in which Odum had participated, in 1931. By 1938, his National Emergency Council's (NEC's) *Report on Economic Conditions of the South* had incorporated Southern regionalist discourse into its discussion of the region's economic woes. Historian Ira Katznelson observes two essential rhetorical lessons that New Dealers learned from Odum: The first was the value of "an equilibrium of silence" that elided "the sharpness of Jim Crow's racial dimension," thus analytically transforming the South into a "more ordinary, if poor, region that could be melded into a larger American sectional mosaic." The second was that, "through the use of modern social science, data could be classified by many other categories than race."[129] In Katznelson's view, both Odum and the Roosevelt administration, knowing that they needed the continued support of the Southern planter elite, hoped that these two strategies "would shift the dominant language from an explicit and often embarrassing justification of white supremacy to a concern for the South irrespective of race. Segregation would stay, but there would be no need to talk about it."[130] The NEC's report on the South evaded the central issues of racial segregation, emphasizing instead the overall indexes of poverty, "as if the race issue did not exist."¹³¹ By the time of its publication, however, the "willful amnesia and quiet accommodation of racism on the part of New Deal leaders were becoming untenable" for them and the Roosevelt administration, if not for Odum himself.¹³²

If the NEC report was a kind of comprehensive regional survey fashioned after Odum's *Southern Regions*, it—along with the furor that it and Roosevelt's "no. 1 economic problem" response to it prompted, especially in the South—also arguably marked the watershed moment at which Roosevelt's New Deal shifted to a more concerted approach to Southern economic restructuring. "It was not so much that the New Deal withered after 1938 as that it headed south," in what became not only a massive restructuring effort but also "the end of the administration's conciliation of southern interests."¹³³ New Deal programs attempted to address the kinds of restructuring for which Vance had advocated. Although not always completely successful, these efforts had sufficient effect to provoke pushback from the traditional Southern elitist sectors that had been appeased up to that point by policy deference, particularly through the Farm Security Administration's programs, the National Youth Administration, and the Fair Labor Standards Act of 1938.¹³⁴ As the TVA had co-opted popular grassroots sentiment, the New Deal co-opted regionalism and regional planning from the South and instrumentalized them toward national objectives.¹³⁵ Similar to many contemporaneous European movements, much of the Southern regionalist movement remained regionalist and did not return to a separatist, competing nationalism. Nevertheless, Odum's case for a regional-national planning in many respects concluded in 1938, particularly as America moved into World War II, which offered a regional identity that also (and perhaps mostly) "supplied the corresponding national identity [with] local roots."¹³⁶

As for Odum's ambitions for regional planning after 1938, historian George Tindall notes that the NPB and the PWA funded consultants for Southern state planning agencies in the 1930s, and by 1935, all Southern governors had established planning-standards boards. In 1940, seven Southern governors established the Southern Regional Planning Commission, but they neither achieved nor even aspired to Odum's broad cultural planning ambition: "The state boards had scarcely moved beyond general survey and research before the pressure for economic development in the late 1930's and 1940's caused their transformation or absorption into industry-hunting agencies."¹³⁷ Rather than planning for industrial development through regional research and balanced planning, Odum and the IRSS's ambitions for the South were reduced to the Sunbelt's crude courting of Northern industrial expansion though antilabor policies and slack environmental regulation.

Lafayette, Mississippi, July 9, 1938. "Land destroyed by gullies, but they still insist upon straight row cultivation." Howard Washington Odum Papers, Wilson Special Collections Library, UNC–Chapel Hill.

> One of the great paradoxes of social engineering is that it seems at odds with the experience of modernity generally. Trying to jell a social world, the most striking characteristic of which appears to be flux, seems rather like trying to manage a whirlwind.
> —JAMES C. SCOTT

CONCLUSION

STATELESS SOUTHERN PLANNING DOCTRINE

Southern regionalists, in their conceptualizations of section (past), region (future), folk, and planning, were at once ashamed by what they found in their social surveys of the South and proud of its forward-looking development "potentialities."[1] Howard W. Odum, particularly in his later years, was quick to criticize the developmental obstacles posed by "Southern leadership" and their multiple faults, launching a broad range of attacks on Old South institutions and problems. He was even quicker and sharper, however, in his defense of the South, defects and all, from Northern "outsider" criticism of his region.[2]

In contrast to the utopian, "revolutionary 'here and now'" of modern planning proposals for new urban and metropolitan forms—such as those of Le Corbusier, Frank Lloyd Wright, or Ebenezer Howard—Southern regionalists' utopian thinking (Odum's in particular) traversed time, backward and forward, historicist and ahistorical, both outside and above the fray of that same "now."[3] Ultimately, Rupert B. Vance's "frank acceptance" of utopianism in regional planning, with its regard for the dictum of Patrick Geddes and Victor Branford to "survey before plan," was more in line with Odum's resigned sense that due to Southern politics and folkways, regional planning and its promise for the South were realistic neither at that time nor for the foreseeable future. Geographer Claude Raffestin, discussing territoriality and the work of Henri Lefebvre, observes that "everyday life most often occurs in territorial morphologies that are not contemporaneous to the relations of which territoriality is woven."[4] In many ways, this statement speaks to the profound radical conservatism of US regionalism in the interwar period as a coordinated effort to preserve outdated regional-territorial morphologies and territoriality, particularly in the South.[5]

Swedish social scientist Gunnar Myrdal, a contemporary of Odum's, described Southern social scientists of the period—clearly referring to the reformist regionalists—as Southern liberals, a "unique species" and "definitely a political minority."[6] "For decades," he continued, "[they] have been acting as the trusted advisors and executors of the Northern philanthropists who wanted to do something for the region. During the thirties they received a much more potent trusteeship; namely, to bring the New Deal into effect in the South. The power and prestige of this function, and, even more, the entire series of recent changes in the Southern social scene, have given them a high political importance. . . . They are, indeed, the cultural façade of the South."[7]

When evaluating the "sources of New Deal reformism," Rexford Tugwell—certainly no Southern Agrarian, being a member of Franklin Delano Roosevelt's brain trust and a thought leader in his administration—came to a similar conclusion. Citing the importance of New Dealers like Henry A. Wallace, Mordecai Ezekiel, and Louis Bean (the forces behind the establishment of the Agricultural Adjustment Administration), FDR's Treasury secretary Henry Morgenthau Jr., and the many others who worked in the period to devise and promote "agricultural relief," particularly in the South, he wrote that while not all of these figures "were rich with city background . . . many of them were."[8] Tugwell considered Odum an essential part of this group, asserting that the Southern regionalists espoused the "only 'real' regional theory during the 1930s."[9]

Odum contained multitudes, and he tried to bridge contradictions. Historian Daniel Singal frames the Southern Jim Crow era as a move from Victorian to Modern thought, deciding ultimately that Odum was "an artist, not an activist; a teacher, not a planner; a Modernist, but by the skin of his teeth."[10] This argument is compelling, but, similar to Odum's work, it falls into the trap of an evolutionary history that coheres along developmental narratives. Odum's legacy seems closer to the interpretive complexity that philosopher Marshall Berman assigns to the great writer of the city Jane Jacobs, of whom he asserts, "Like so many modernists . . . [she] moves in the twilight zone where the line between the richest and most complex modernism and the rankest bad faith of modernist anti-modernism is very thin and elusive, if indeed there is a line at all."[11] Jacobs's nemesis Robert Moses was an urban planner educated in the culture of 1920s New York regional planning. Like Odum, he left a complicated legacy.[12] Moses sought to modernize New York into an industrial economy despite the high cost of the destruction wreaked on much of the city's social richness. Berman, recalling an interaction in 1967 with futurologist Herman Khan about Moses's modernization plans for the Bronx, asks, "Why did the futurologist's laughter make me want to cry?" before answering his own question: Because it ignored the "starkest fact of modern life: that the split in the minds and wound in the hearts of men and women on the move . . . were just as real and just as deep as the drives and dreams that made us go."[13]

These were the same ambivalent sentiments of the Depression, a period during which Odum's concern about the rapid pace of progress and technology, and even his highly specific cultural anxiety over Southern reform, resonated briefly throughout the United States. This was the regional-national frame Odum had imagined and hoped for, in which Southern preoccupations were not eschewed as backward but integrated into the national mosaic of respected regional autonomies joined in a national collaborative collective. Roosevelt's 1938 summer declaration of the South as the nation's "number one problem," and his administration's slow adjustment away from its willful Southern racial blindness as World War II approached, seemed to quash those hopes.[14]

Southern and national gains cut both ways. The Tennessee Valley Authority (TVA), proclaimed the greatest regional planning project of the period, was helped to fruition by the efforts of its social science team, which included Rupert Vance and Thomas Woofter Jr.—both of whom had worked at some point with Odum at his Institute for Research in Social Science (IRSS) at the University of North Carolina—along with former members of the Regional Planning Association of America (RPAA). To a great degree, however, the TVA—the project political scientist James C. Scott calls "the United States' high modernist experiment and the grandaddy of all regional development projects"— was simply the continuation of Southern extraction in the form of cheap energy administered through a centralized, nationally funded facility.[15] At the national level, the US Department of Agriculture adopted many of the Southern regionalists' planning policies and recommendations for the agricultural sector, which both Odum and Vance viewed and advocated as a way to revitalize the Southern economy without changing its social structure.[16] Moreover, the FDR administration included Southern representatives advocating for planters'-bloc interests, particularly concerning the traditional staples of cotton, rice, sugar, and tobacco, essentially making the Department of Agriculture "the *de facto* regional planning body for the South."[17]

If, as urban planning scholar Clyde Woods believes, the US South was the birthplace of regional planning following the Civil War, he also observed that the result of this outgrowth, from Reconstruction policies through the TVA, was that the "working class constituency was jettisoned while Northern corporate blocs and dominant blocs of regional capital reaped the primary benefits."[18] The history underscores the innocence, or political naïveté—willful or not—underlying the regionalists' imaginary, the "time-specific" cultural cohesiveness of which in fact represented "the power of certain groups to impose their norms on the majority," although such power relations also needed to be "constantly readjusted as the imposed norms changed."[19] More often than not, this regionalist imaginary also provided "corresponding national identity [with] local roots."[20] The international governing lessons of the TVA and the broader New Deal have since demonstrated that development projects, through regional planning, helped other countries consolidate and strengthen centralized state power over broader territories.[21]

In Odum's attempts to essentialize region as a Southern ontology, the transitional flux of the historical period—as well as other conceptual obstacles—prevented him from resolving the synoptic definition that he eternally sought. To be fair, the historical debates over revolution and continuity, such as the competition between the interests of the planter bloc and New South industrialists in the post-Reconstruction South, among many other Odumesque dichotomies, continued to occupy Southern historians well after Odum's death in 1954.[22] But for Odum, conceptually hedging his bets, playing both angles on issues, and his "old familiar fence-sitting" atop what he hoped to be the status quo also characterized his lifelong modus operandi.[23] As has been demonstrated repeatedly throughout this book, such was his neo-Hegelian strategy that never quite synthesized but always seemed to intrigue.

Plans for the South in the first half of the twentieth century occupied a continuum ranging from the staunchly conservative proposals of the most committed Southern Agrarians to the more radical plans of H. C. Nixon's Southern Policy Committee or Myles Horton's Highlander Folk School. Southern regionalists' moderate calls for "balance" sought to rhetorically console the entire political spectrum of allegiance.[24] In their planning mode, meanwhile, Southern regionalist proposals included large-scale relocation of communities away from the South's depleted soil regions, proposed entirely new cash-crop industries "carefully chosen to mesh with local markets and resources," and recommended an accelerated, planned northern migration of half of the Black Southern population to avoid potential social conflict between white "folks" and increasing Black demands for civil rights.[25] Similar to Odum's hyperbolic proposal in 1954, prompted by his contemplation of the South's imminent integration, for an eventual integration of *all* world nations, these regional proposals were radical in scope. As historian Daniel T. Rodgers observes, they resembled "Southern Rexford Tugwells, ready to rearrange the South's clumsily scattered pieces with sublime confidence."[26]

High modernism in the context of the state—dominant in the West from the tail end of the Industrial Revolution to the commencement of World War I and undoubtedly an influence on Odum and his institute—has been described by James Scott as providing a particularly "sweeping vision of how the benefits of technical and scientific progress might be applied—usually through the state—in every field of human activity."[27] The application of this vision and its accompanying "*prescriptions* for a new society" necessitated "simplified, utilitarian *descriptions*" by state officials who, "through the exercise of state power," could also "bring the facts into line with their representations."[28] Such a trajectory is particularly characteristic of Vance's work, in which he continually practiced the utilitarian statist's abstraction of "nature" into "natural resources" for regional differentiation.[29] The lack of an autonomous state, however, reduced the Southern social science descriptions into "plans for making plans."[30]

Among the many internal tensions of Southern regionalists, often even within their own arguments, statelessness remained the central insurmountable challenge. Without a Southern regional state, their regional planning was doctrine, not practice, a dilemma confirmed by FDR's famous problematizing of the South as the nation's "number one" issue.[31] Historically, the Confederacy had pushed Southern regional economic and political interests to a nationalist secession and civil war—a sectional specter that Southern regionalism tirelessly sought to explain away through its "nation first," futurist regionalism. In his own conceptualization, "Odum advocated a cultural regionalism that would withstand the onslaught of industrialism with its ruthless tendencies toward cultural leveling ... [of] territorially integrated regional societies."[32] His "regional-national social planning," however, was insistently debated within the multiple "landscapes of America."[33]

Writing in 1941, Marion D. Irish compared the approaches of the "Chapel Hill [regionalist] planners" and the "Nashville Agrarians," noting, "One suspects that Chapel Hill, which is really no less Southern than Nashville, might have preferred autonomy but realized that this is inherently impossible."[34] Odum knew that his regional planning proposals required outside resources in the form of "cooperative assistance in men and money and technics, from federal aid, from business enterprise, from endowed agencies" in order for the South to "transvaluate its deficiencies into adequacy."[35] For the IRSS and the University of North Carolina, as well as for other Southern land-grant universities and colleges and programs for public health, public works, social security, and agriculture, this "cooperative assistance" came largely from both federal sources and private philanthropic groups such as the Carnegie Corporation, the Rosenwald Fund, and the Rockefeller Foundation.[36]

Vanderbilt Agrarian Donald Davidson expressed uncertainty and concern about the place of Southern regionalists' proposals within the broader national frame, questioning whether "federal 'intervention' along such regional lines [would] actually incorporate regional considerations as a part of the democratic process, or ... merely increase the functioning power and efficiency of a Leviathan state."[37] Davidson was a reactionary and a proudly "unreconstructed" Southerner, but he knew enough to understand that the profoundly political implications of Southern regionalist proposals were not being addressed directly, whether he agreed with them or not. Nevertheless, although he was anxious that Southern regionalists like Odum were simply aiding and abetting the national Leviathan in the South, he also praised their work in providing precisely the state-like "descriptions" of the region needed to better inform national policy, noting, "The New Regionalists of social science, moving perhaps in line with forces and feelings that they themselves cannot chart, are beginning to perform some of the functions that a nation expects of its statesmen."[38] In expectedly qualified praise, Davidson argued that the ado about the Nashville–Chapel Hill battle had resolved via truce: "Without using political language they are showing us that social legislation on a national scale implies a better understanding of the actual structure of our society than humanitarian reformers of other days have troubled to obtain."[39]

But these roles were consultative. There was never a Southern nationalist challenge to the country, nor even recommendations for regional constitutional reform. As reflected in his participation on the President's Committee on Social Trends, Odum imagined his own role as part of an executive committee that would oversee regional clusters of the newly forming state planning boards, which provided the most approachable institutional platforms for his sociocratic dreams of telic policy recommendations.[40] For Odum, a Southern institutionalist, the failure of his attempt to organize a

Council on Southern Regional Development and FDR's declaration of the South as the nation's top economic problem—both in 1938—represented the ultimate defeats of his planning aspirations. The convictions underpinning his work, and the technicways proposals he developed in the 1940s, lacked the applied urgency of a government policy research program that he might otherwise be able to lead.

Perhaps Odum's final recompense for his years spent cautioning about the imposition of stateways ambitions and insisting on resilient folkways traditions was the lack of a state—national, regional, or local—to fully endorse his own policy recommendations.[41] Social engineering, social planning, and, ultimately, regional planning all required a state to fund, authorize, and lead public action; without those, Odum's work remained a predominantly circumscribed *folk* engineering. Historian Michael Milligan calls this hesitancy Odum's "contradictions of public service" and observes "two competing voices" in his planning proposals: "the public voice lauding technology as the primary ingredient for realizing a more affluent and efficient South, and the sociological voice implicating technology for all that was repugnant about modernization."[42]

Odum's advocacy for social action via planning was undercut by his concern for how that same action could move too rapidly and precipitate too much change in the Southern social structure. He emphasized "practical design" in addressing "the fundamental questions concerning the region ... only proportional to [a] realistic inventory of fact and of the actualities of what is to be done."[43] Odum's characteristic response regarding these actualities was "not much ... in the immediate future."[44] After receiving the feedback he had sought from colleagues on his concept of regionalism, he mused, "It is my belief that those who think that regionalism is sociology and good sociology have a certain feel for the thing. It is a sort of identification with land, people, institutions, folkways, etc."[45] What Odum asked for was a sympathetic understanding of his facts, his "new romantic realism," a "poetic sociology," essentially a *Southern* sociology, in the tradition of George Fitzhugh and Henry Hughes, aiming to provide the descriptive simplifications and legitimation of social and power structures to maintain the status quo through regionalized and local statecraft. But without a regional state, there was no autonomous regional plan.[46]

Rupert Vance's Southern regional planning was more specific if no less ambitious, proposing as a "minimal task ... the reconstruction of agriculture; the integrated development of industry; and the movement of the area out of the colonial economy."[47] Vance saw clearly that poverty was the region's greatest challenge and concluded, "As long as the region's indices of income remain the lowest in the nation, to speak of freedom and cultural autonomy for the common man of the South is sheerest irony."[48] Perhaps equally ironic, however, was that the breadth of those challenges was impossible to face without assistance from those very (federal, Northern) institutions on which Odum so often called.

Absent a constitutionally authorized, authoritative regional governing body, the Southern regionalists found a surrogate institution in the Southern university. In 1919, the University of North Carolina appointed as its president Harry Woodburn Chase, who had studied with Odum under G. Stanley Hall at Clark University. Hall, in the Wardian tradition, held the conviction that the university should serve as society's designer and leader of social change, and both Chase and Odum carried this institutional enthusiasm to North Carolina amid the wave of New South initiatives and a nascent industrial economy that required an educated workforce. Theirs was an institutionalist psychology exported to the South, along with Hall's behavioralist interest in adolescence, that would also influence Odum's understanding of education and social engineering.[49]

Odum was also inspired by Franklin Giddings, his mentor at Columbia University, and was able to leverage his connections among Giddings's alumni for entrée into post–World War I philanthropic society up north. Columbia was also a center of biological racist thought in academe, of which Giddings was an advocate. W. E. B. Du Bois noted that the "real frontal attack on Reconstruction . . . came from Columbia and Johns Hopkins," advanced in particular by "professors of political science and history."[50] Just as the Southern university and its research required Northern benefactors, Odum certainly had his Northern academic mentors in mind, along with the Southern "folk," when publishing his work on the "Negro problem" and Black Southern folklore. The notions, fears, and myths of race were central not only to the construction of the region that Odum and colleagues reflected and recycled, but also to the national network of academic institutions and social sciences in which they participated.

The political power relationships embedded within this network were, as Clyde Woods notes, intrinsically tied to the academics whose doctrines called for and helped design (and benefit from) US regional planning policies. As political scientist Cedric Robinson affirms, this network of "white intelligentsia—academician and otherwise" served "as idealogues for both the victorious northern industrial capital and a now chastened southern agrarian capital." Members of the network used the language and techniques of social science to "[reweave] social and historical legends" designed to reinforce "the exploitative projects of those ruling classes," and crush the dangers to those projects posed by "the political consciousness of Black labor, white labor, and immigrant labor."[51] Such were the postbellum academic circumstances and agreements that made the "whole United States... Southern!"[52]

The naturalization and mystification of these social practices and relationships, achieved by submerging them within an organic fusion of natural and social sciences, were central to the social engineering, folk engineering, and regional planning that dominated the first half of the twentieth century. In the South, as Myrdal also observed, such approaches meant that Southern regionalists sought to help Black Americans "get a fairer share of education, housing, employment and relief," no mean task at the height of the Jim Crow era, but certainly not to help them obtain any real "social equality."[53] Southern regionalists believed that their "broader focus on issues of economic, social, and education reforms of the South as a whole" would ultimately improve conditions "even for" Black people, creating a rising tide that would lift all boats without needing to disturb the social order through such inconveniences as affording Black Southerners power, equality, equal marriage rights, or the like.[54]

Within this academic environment, it is thus no surprise that, despite the University of North Carolina's reputation as the most liberal, progressive university in the South, truly critical cries for reform came neither from the state's flagship public university nor from Odum's IRSS. Noting the work of Margaret Hagood and Arthur Raper as exceptions, historian Allen Tullos views Odum's regionalism and its scholarship as "fatally compromised," both by his indebtedness to Northern philanthropy and his need to ingratiate himself with the powers that be in North Carolina.[55] In contrast with both Myles Horton's Highlander Folk School in Tennessee and Lewis Mumford's increasing criticism of state power and the ascension of the post–World War II military-industrial complex, Tullos observes that "under Odum's guidance the Institute for Research in Social Science conducted its few industrial studies with gingerly care for the sensibilities of mill owners and state's business and political leadership."[56] Odum's need for a "conflict-free theory of social change" was imposed partially by his concern "about Rockefeller grants or university patronage," whereas critics such as Mumford "spoke from a position of greater independence."[57]

Of the early era of US regional planning doctrine, John Friedmann and Clyde Weaver observe that planning was understood as "a method to improve the cultural as well as material circumstances of regional communities, indeed, the two goals were held to be inseparable, on structural as well as epistemological grounds."[58] In an earlier essay, published just a few years after Odum's death, Friedmann noted that "whether there was not, indeed, a conflict among these objectives is a question that was not apparently considered" in those first rounds.[59] Ultimately, however, "regional planning was an extraordinarily ambitious subject which hoped to achieve a unification of economics and geography, and, in addition, to introduce new sociological perspectives."[60] Friedmann and Weaver conclude that, following World War II, the cultural spatial systems approach, in line with Odum's general proposals, was soon "shunned" by sociology, economics, and political science. Scholars in these disciplines left it largely to geographers, more in line with Vance and Carl O. Sauer, and a few economists to continue "somewhat uneasily allied in their attempt to fashion a field of regional studies and planning."[61]

After his plans for the Council on Southern Regional Development were dashed, Odum channeled his energies back into the University of North Carolina. In 1946 he helped found the school's Department of City and Regional Planning—among the region's first—headed by John A. Parker.[62] After World War II, when the RPAA re-formed as the Regional Development Council of America, Clarence Stein invited Odum, Vance, and their North Carolina colleagues to form a Southeastern chapter of the council to expand its agenda beyond New York.[63] This institutional merger of various US first-round regional planning initiatives of the interwar period was appropriate at the twilight of that era, just as it had been when born of Frederick Jackson Turner's frontier theory, articulated at the closing of the US frontier. The Southern regionalists sought to fix their land through static, essentialized survey precisely at moments when modernization, urbanization, and out-migration disrupted any kind of public schemes for organic balance, or even the imaginations thereof. In time, Southern regional planning, along with the rest of the country, moved into functionalist modeling, transportation planning, and economic development, and the engineering field returned to its traditional constructive practices.[64]

After World War II, labor-intensive industries moved south, along with the continuation of natural resource extraction and processing industries.[65] In Vance's terms, these developments brought many more "colonial" economic relationships into the region, thereby further exacerbating the existing intraregional socioeconomic unevenness.[66] More importantly, though, the pretense of a cultural regional planning, perhaps always an ideological chimera, simply aided along those processes of national economic integration already underway. As Friedmann and Weaver assert, "Regional planning, then, could serve as midwife to a spatial pattern in the ordering of activities that would in any event occur; it could not change that pattern. Any dramatic departure from familiar forms would require a very different kind of politics."[67] The TVA, for example, inspired by Geddes's river basin regional planning and originally sold to the public as an improvement for territorial catchment, may have made grand cultural and infrastructural promises to begin with, but it also further displaced communities that were already being uprooted due to Depression hardships. The authority ultimately delivered predominantly extractive, functional results in the form of cheap electricity for a service area far beyond the initial vision.[68] If regional planning was part of the regionalist movement helping provide "corresponding national identity [with] local roots," in tandem in the South, it also further ordered and articulated racialized regional labor, resources, and markets into the national political economy.[69]

Nevertheless, the Southern regionalists' conflation of cultural and economic objectives as evolutionary processes with catalytic opportunities for telic policy and intervention deeply impacted what was to become the discourse and practice of "development" for the Global South.[70] As a cultural parallel, many have noted the deep influence of William Faulkner's writing on the post–World War II literary "boom" generation of Latin American writers, particularly through images of pastoral patriarchy, colonial gothic, and folk *costumbrismo* across a shared hemispheric mythistory.[71] John Friedmann's work in Chile with the Ford Foundation served as a key nexus for development work in Latin America by connecting his training under Tugwell at the University of Chicago, his doctoral research on regional planning and the TVA, and his knowledge of Southern regionalism in the service of regional and national planning policy recommendations, particularly emphasizing the rural-urban dynamic of what he idealized as "agropolitan development."[72] Friedmann's proposals also sought to develop and integrate regions and their resources into larger national and international economic networks. That Friedmann carried on Odum's legacy by theorizing development in terms of the rural and urban spheres, working across international networks composed of philanthropic foundations, academic institutions, social science, and regional planning, is, of course, absolutely appropriate.

The legacy of regional planning's cultural claims for regional governance has emerged in works ranging from Joel Garreau's *Nine Nations of North America* (1981) to more recent publications advocating for US "megaregions."[73] Such research generally advocates for functionalism centered on transportation planning and for variations of bioregionalist operationalized land-use coordination reform. Megaregions are geographic metropolitan clusters, similar to Jean Gottmann's megalopolitan proposal, re-formed from corridors into various "global" territorial polygons. They are at once subnational and extranational but are still, even at "mega" size, smaller than the six geographic regions Odum proposed. Echoing Odum, the functionalist approach of works advocating megaregions tends to elide issues of polity and power in these new regional formations, imagining instead that their management might assume technical/administrative functions that could avoid political turmoil. As Edward Soja has pointed out, such lacunae are inherent to "regional differentiation within and between locales," which "is in turn the setting for a contingent regionalism, an active consciousness and assertiveness of particular regions, vis-à-vis other regions, as territorial and social enclosures. As an expression of territoriality of locales, regionalism is grounded in the geography of power."[74] His clarity echoes Vance's colonial analysis of the North-South interregional political economy and the South's need to escape it. No technical vision, no endless listing of facts can wish away this enduring structural tension, irrespective of whether it surfaces through fiction, folk, social science, or regional planning.

NOTES

ACKNOWLEDGMENTS

1. Alexander von Humboldt is often cited as the "father of ecology," without the "modern" qualifier. See Wulf, *Invention of Nature*.
2. James Hataway, "Eugene Odum: The Father of Modern Ecology," *UGA Today Columns* (online), January 9, 2018, https://news.uga.edu/the-father-of-modern-ecology/.

INTRODUCTION

1. Tindall, "Significance of Howard W. Odum"; H. Odum, *Folk, Region, and Society*; Brazil, *Howard W. Odum*; O'Brien, *Idea of the American South*; King, *Southern Renaissance*; Reed, "Sociology"; Singal, *War Within*; Tullos, *Habits of Industry*; Tullos, "Politics of Regional Development"; Milligan, "Contradictions of Public Service"; S. Matthews, *Capturing the South*. See Goldfield, "New Regionalism" and *Region, Race, and Cities*, for an overview of Odum and urbanization.
2. Friedmann and Weaver, *Territory and Function*, 35.
3. Perloff, *Education for Planning*; Goodsell, *Administration of a Revolution*; Padilla, *Tugwell's Thoughts on Planning*, 9–15.
4. Sarbib, "University of Chicago," 77; Gorelik, *Ciudad Latinoamericana*.
5. Dorman, *Revolt of the Provinces*; Spann, "Franklin Delano Roosevelt."
6. Tullos, "Politics of Regional Development," 111; Bellin, "Certain Brand of Humanism."
7. Tullos, "Politics of Regional Development," 113.
8. H. Odum, "Patrick Geddes' Heritage," 280; Tullos, "Politics of Regional Development," 117–18.
9. Mumford, "Regions—to Live In," 151.
10. John A. Parker to Howard W. Odum, March 30, 1950, box 91, folder 3164, Howard Washington Odum Papers, 1908–1982 collection, Wilson Special Collections Library, University of North Carolina at Chapel Hill. Parker was head of the newly formed Department of City and Regional Planning at the University of North Carolina and invited Odum on Stein's behalf.
11. H. Odum, "Patrick Geddes' Heritage"; Novak, *Lewis Mumford and Patrick Geddes*.
12. Jordan, *Machine-Age Ideology*, 129.
13. Jordan, *Machine-Age Ideology*, 129.
14. Schwartz, "Robert Moses," 131.
15. Friedmann and Weaver, *Territory and Function*; Moravánszky and Kegler, *Re-Scaling the Environment*; Olsson, *Agrarian Crossings*; Gorelik, *Ciudad Latinoamericana*.

16. Fei, *China's Gentry*; Fisher, *City and Regional Planning*; A. Gilbert, "New Regional Geography"; Haney, *When Modern Was Green*; Moravánszky and Kegler, *Re-Scaling the Environment*; Patel, *New Deal*.

17. Botar and Wünsche, *Biocentrism and Modernism*.

18. Redfield, "Folk Society."

19. H. Odum, "Lynching, Fears, and Folkways."

20. Friedmann and Weaver, *Territory and Function*; Weaver, *Regional Development*; Soja, *Postmodern Geographies*.

21. Wilkerson, *Warmth of Other Suns*.

22. Friedmann, "Concept"; Friedmann and Alonso, *Regional Development and Planning*; Dorman, *Revolt of the Provinces*.

23. Tindall, "Significance of Howard W. Odum," 298.

24. Friedmann, *Spatial Structure of Economic Development*; Selznick, *TVA and the Grass Roots*; Scott, *Seeing Like a State*, 1–8; Woods, *Development Arrested*; J. Gilbert, *Planning Democracy*. Scott calls the TVA "the United States' high-modernist experiment and the granddaddy of all regional development projects." Scott, *Seeing Like a State*, 6.

25. Rodgers, *Atlantic Crossings*; S. Ward, "Re-Examining the International Diffusion"; Hein, "Exchange of Planning Ideas"; Orillard, "Transnational Building of Urban Design"; Silver, "Urban Planning"; Silver and Moeser, *Separate City*; Goldfield, *Region, Race, and Cities*; L. Larsen, *Urban South*; Olsson, *Agrarian Crossings*; Alex Sayf Cummings, "The Emergence of Urban Planning in the South, 1880–1930," *Tropics of Meta: Historiography for the Masses* (blog), March 26, 2018, https://tropicsofmeta.com/2018/03/26/the-emergence-of-urban-planning-in-the-south-1880-1930/.

26. Kwak, "Interdisciplinarity in Planning History"; Goulet and Birch, "Modeling Interdisciplinarity."

27. Sandercock, *Making the Invisible Visible*, 1–31.

28. Sandercock, *Making the Invisible Visible*, 4.

29. Sandercock, *Making the Invisible Visible*, 2–3n2.

30. Rodgers, *Atlantic Crossings*; Brazil, *Howard W. Odum*.

31. Coffey and Skipper, *Navigating Souths*; Olsson, *Agrarian Crossings*; Gorelik, *Ciudad Latinoamericana*.

32. Santayana, *Selected Critical Writings*, 155; Bramen, *Uses of Variety*, 17.

33. Bramen, *Uses of Variety*, 21.

34. Weaver, *Regional Development*, 45.

35. Hertzler, "American Regionalism."

36. Schlesinger, *Rise of the City*.

37. N. Smith, *Uneven Development*.

38. Brenner, *New State Spaces*, 119; Soja, *Postmodern Geographies*, 164–65.

39. Gramsci, *Southern Question*; Mayo, "Gramsci, the Southern Question"; Soja, *Postmodern Geographies*, 38–39.

40. Brenner, *New State Spaces*; Amin and Pearce, *Accumulation on a World Scale*; Raymond Williams, *Country and the City*; Arrighi, *Long Twentieth Century*; Wallerstein, *World-Systems Analysis*.

41. Soja, *Postmodern Geographies*, 117.

42. Soja, *Postmodern Geographies*, 151.

43. Markusen, *Regions*, 16–17.
44. Markusen, *Regions*, 16–17.
45. Weaver, *Regional Development*, 46; Soja, *Postmodern Geographies*, 165–67.
46. Benevolo, *Origins*; P. Hall, *Cities of Tomorrow*.
47. P. Hall, *Cities of Tomorrow*, 2–12.
48. Vigier, *Régions et régionalisme*; Weaver, *Regional Development*, 45.
49. Weaver, *Regional Development*, 42.
50. Weaver, *Regional Development*, 45.
51. Weaver, *Regional Development*, 47–49; P. Hall, *Cities of Tomorrow*.
52. Spann, *Designing Modern America*; Novak, *Lewis Mumford and Patrick Geddes*; Scott and Bromley, *Envisioning Sociology*.
53. Geddes, *Cities in Evolution*; Welter, *Biopolis*.
54. Weaver, *Regional Development*, 50; Geddes, *Cities in Evolution*.
55. Friedmann and Weaver, *Territory and Function*; Weaver, *Regional Development*; Welter, *Biopolis*; Moravánszky and Kegler, *Re-Scaling the Environment*; Gorelik, *Ciudad Latinoamericana*.
56. Boardman, *Worlds of Patrick Geddes*; Tullos, "Politics of Regional Development"; Welter, *Biopolis*.
57. O'Brien, *Idea of the American South*, xxv; Berman, *All That Is Solid*.
58. Bramen, *Uses of Variety*, 121; Howard, "Unraveling Regions"; Brodhead, *Cultures of Letters*; Sundquist, "Realism and Regionalism."
59. Storm, "Regionalism in History," 252.
60. Storm, "Regionalism in History," 259.
61. Storm, "Regionalism in History," 252.
62. Dorman, *Revolt of the Provinces*; J. Thomas, "Holding the Middle Ground," 47–49; Bramen, *Uses of Variety*.
63. Tullos, *Habits of Industry*, 291.
64. Tindall, *Emergence of the New South*, 589; Kazin, *On Native Grounds*, 485.
65. Woodward, *Burden of Southern History*, 15.
66. Vance, "Regional Concept as a Tool," 135; Reed and Singal, *Regionalism and the South*; Reed, *Surveying the South*; S. Matthews, *Capturing the South*.
67. Milligan, "Contradictions of Public Service," 200; D. Ross, *Origins*, 311–13, 347–67, 386–88.
68. Mumford, *Culture of Cities*; Friedmann, "Concept"; Tullos, "Politics of Regional Development"; Fishman, *American Planning Tradition*.
69. H. Odum, *Southern Regions*, 57; O'Brien, *Idea of the American South*, 64. See White and White, *Intellectual versus the City*; and Marx, *Machine in the Garden*.
70. Mayer, "Basquiat in History," 41.
71. D. Ross, *Origins*, 150. See also Popper, *Poverty of Historicism*.
72. D. Ross, *Origins*, 150–51; Seligman, "Economics and Social Progress," 55–57, 59–60; Seligman, *Principles of Economics*, 108.
73. Rodgers, "Regionalism," 4.
74. Fishman, *American Planning Tradition*.
75. Vance and Demerath, *Urban South*; Silver and Moeser, *Separate City*; Goldfield, *Region, Race, and Cities*.

76. H. Odum, "Case for Regional-National"; Odum and Moore, *American Regionalism*; Dorman, *Revolt of the Provinces*.

77. Pells, *Radical Visions*, 3; Dorman, *Revolt of the Provinces*, 7.

78. Raymond Williams, *Raymond Williams*; Raymond Williams, *Country and the City*; Brooks, "On Creating"; Trachtenberg, "Mumford in the Twenties."

79. Pells, *Radical Visions*, 33.

80. Crawford, *Building the Workingman's Paradise*, 46.

81. Zorbaugh, *Gold Coast and the Slum*, 254–58; Fairfield, *Mysteries of the Great City*, 159.

82. Hays, *Response to Industrialism*, 86; Crawford, *Building the Workingman's Paradise*, 46–47.

83. Crawford, *Building the Workingman's Paradise*, 47. See Gladden, *Applied Christianity*.

84. F. Taylor, *Principles of Scientific Management*.

85. Friedmann, "Two Centuries," 14.

86. Crawford, *Building the Workingman's Paradise*, 46.

87. United States Department of Labor Bureau of Labor Statistics, *Welfare Work for Employees*, 8; Crawford, *Building the Workingman's Paradise*, 48.

88. Ehsani, "Social Engineering," 362n3. See also Giddings, "Social Work and Societal Engineering." For Odum's early social welfare work, see Rotabi, "Ecological Theory."

89. Jordan, *Machine-Age Ideology*, 172.

90. Hermann Heller, "Political Science" in Seligman and Johnson, *Encyclopaedia of the Social Sciences*, 12:207; Jordan, *Machine-Age Ideology*, 172n38.

91. Friedmann, "Two Centuries," 14; D. Ross, *Origins*. See also discussion of Condorcet and the material and defense objectives of cultural unity in codes and standardization practices of social engineering in Scott, *Seeing Like a State*, 90–93, 183–91. Scott states, "A state that improved its population's skills, vigor, civic morals, and work habits would increase its tax base and field better armies." Scott, *Seeing Like a State*, 91.

92. Friedmann, "Two Centuries," 15.

93. Friedmann, "Two Centuries," 16; Hayek, *Counter-Revolution of Science*, 113.

94. Friedmann, "Two Centuries," 16; Veblen, *Place of Science*; Padilla, *Tugwell's Thoughts on Planning*, 9–15; Simon, *Administrative Behavior*.

95. Crawford, *Building the Workingman's Paradise*, 48.

96. Scott, *Seeing Like a State*, 100.

97. Scott, *Seeing Like a State*, 100; Adas and Chan, *Machines as the Measure*, 380; Wolin, *Politics and Vision*.

98. Hayek, *Counter-Revolution of Science*.

99. Soule, *Coming American Revolution*, 304; Soule, "Planning for Agriculture," 206; Soule, *Planned Society*; Jordan, *Machine-Age Ideology*, 210, 208–14.

100. Olmsted, *Cotton Kingdom*.

101. Marcuse, "Housing," 40–49; M. Simpson, "Meliorist 'versus' Insurgent Planners"; P. Hall, *Cities of Tomorrow*, chap. 2.

102. J. Hall, *Like a Family*.

103. Raper, *Preface to Peasantry*, 4–5, 149, 171; Singal, *War Within*, 334, chap. 2; Cobb, *Most Southern Place on Earth*; Woods, *Development Arrested*; Tyler, "Impact of the New Deal"; Coclanis, "Southern Economy."

104. Heath, *Constructive Liberalism*; Cobb, *Most Southern Place on Earth*; Tyler, "Impact of the New Deal."

105. Odum, "Social and Mental Traits"; Wundt, *Elemente der Völkerpsychologie*. On Wundt's folk-soul concept, see S. Matthews, *Capturing the South*, 30.

106. Giddings, "Social Work and Societal Engineering."

107. Milligan, "Contradictions of Public Service."

108. Friedmann, "Two Centuries," 24–26. Scott refers to the term *mētis*, derived from the classical Greek, meaning "knowledge that can only come from practical experience." Scott, *Seeing Like a State*, 6.

109. King, *Southern Renaissance*.

110. Dorman, *Revolt of the Provinces*, 138.

111. MacKaye, *New Exploration*, 33–35.

112. Dorman, *Revolt of the Provinces*, 138.

113. George Simpson in Odum, *Folk, Region, and Society*, 219.

114. Odum and Jocher, *In Search of Regional Balance*, 15.

115. H. Odum, "From Community Studies to Regionalism," 15–16; Vance, "Howard Odum's Technicways."

116. H. Odum, "From Community Studies to Regionalism," 15–16; Vance, "Howard Odum's Technicways."

117. H. Odum, "From Community Studies to Regionalism," 15–16; Vance, "Howard Odum's Technicways."

118. H. Odum, "From Community Studies to Regionalism," 15–16; Vance, "Howard Odum's Technicways."

119. H. Odum, "From Community Studies to Regionalism," 15–16; Vance, "Howard Odum's Technicways."

120. H. Odum, "From Community Studies to Regionalism," 15–16; Vance, "Howard Odum's Technicways."

121. George Simpson in H. Odum, *Folk, Region, and Society*, 220.

122. George Simpson in H. Odum, *Folk, Region, and Society*, 220.

123. George Simpson in H. Odum, *Folk, Region, and Society*, 221; H. Odum, "Folk Sociology as a Subject Field." See H. Odum, *Folk, Region, and Society*, 322.

124. Fairfield, *Mysteries of the Great City*, 158–63; Zorbaugh, *Gold Coast and the Slum*, 254–60.

125. Milligan, "Contradictions of Public Service," 215.

126. Friedmann and Weaver, *Territory and Function*, 3–4.

127. Bramen, *Uses of Variety*, 118–19.

128. Robinson, *Black Marxism*.

129. Singal, *War Within*, 29.

130. Singal, *War Within*, 25.

131. Woods, *Development Arrested*, 21.

132. Bauer, "Economic Progress and Living Conditions"; Tugwell, "Sources"; Friedmann, "Concept"; Friedmann and Alonso, *Regional Development and*

Planning; Friedmann and Weaver, *Territory and Function*; Welter, *Biopolis*; Cobb, *Most Southern Place on Earth*; Coclanis, "Southern Economy."

133. Friedmann and Alonso, *Regional Development and Planning*, 3–4; Soja, *Postmodern Geographies*; Ogburn, *Social Change*.

134. Bauer, "Economic Progress and Living Conditions"; Friedmann, "Concept."

135. N. Smith, *Uneven Development*; Weaver, *Regional Development*; Soja, *Postmodern Geographies*.

136. Reed, "Sociology"; Dorman, *Revolt of the Provinces*.

137. Mumford, "Regions—to Live In," 151; P. Hall, *Cities of Tomorrow*, 161.

138. A. Gilbert, "New Regional Geography."

139. A. Gilbert, "New Regional Geography," 210.

140. A. Gilbert, "New Regional Geography," 210–11; Entrikin, "Diffusion Research"; Solot, "Carl Sauer."

141. Grantham, "Regional Imagination"; Cobb, *Most Southern Place on Earth*; Tyler, "Impact of the New Deal," 251.

142. Johnson and Johnson, *Research in Service to Society*.

143. Vance, "Regional Concept as a Tool"; H. Odum, *Promise of Regionalism*.

144. Friedmann and Weaver, *Territory and Function*, 5.

145. Vance, "Concept of the Region"; Vance, *Human Geography*; H. Odum, *Southern Regions*; Odum and Moore, *American Regionalism*.

146. O'Brien, *Idea of the American South*, xxii.

147. Polk, *Southern Accent*, 219; Grantham, "Regional Imagination," 10.

148. Grantham, "Regional Imagination," 16.

149. Reed and Singal, *Regionalism and the South*, xiii; Grantham, "Regional Imagination," 17.

150. Rudel and Fu, "Requiem," 807.

151. Rudel and Fu, "Requiem," 807.

152. Rudel and Fu, "Requiem," 817; Weaver, *Regional Development*.

153. Rudel and Fu, "Requiem," 805–8.

154. Vance, "Sociological Implications," 46.

155. White and White, *Intellectual versus the City*; Marx, *Machine in the Garden*.

156. Locke, *Decade of Negro Self-Expression*; Mumford, *Culture of Cities*; Sauer, "Personality of Mexico"; Redfield, "Folk Society"; Collier, *John Collier Reader*; Dorman, *Revolt of the Provinces*; Bramen, *Uses of Variety*; Hurston, *"You Don't Know Us Negroes."*

157. Mumford, *Golden Day*; Bramen, *Uses of Variety*; Dorman, *Revolt of the Provinces*.

158. Soja, *Postmodern Geographies*, 121; Spirn, "Authority of Nature"; Wolschke-Bulmahn, *Nature and Ideology*.

159. Friedmann, "Concept," 4.

160. H. Odum, "Case for Regional-National."

161. Milligan, "Contradictions of Public Service," 310n41; H. Odum, *Southern Regions*, 1–11, 27, 187–91, 207–37, 255, 481–87.

162. Katznelson, *Fear Itself*, 168–72.

163. Woods, *Development Arrested*, 134.

164. Rodgers, "Regionalism," 3–4.

165. Myrdal, *American Dilemma*, 468–72; Kammen, *People of Paradox*; Krieger, *City on a Hill*. John Shelton Reed, a University of North Carolina sociologist of the generation after Odum, dismissed regional folk sociology as "an unfortunate development, an unstable and eclectic compound of neo-Hegelianism and conservative Social Darwinism." Reed, "Sociology," 172. See Hofstadter, *Social Darwinism*.

166. Martin Luther King Jr., "'The Rising Tide of Racial Consciousness,' Address at the Golden Anniversary Conference of the National Urban League," New York, September 6, 1960, transcript from the Martin Luther King, Jr., Research and Education Institute, Stanford University, https://kinginstitute.stanford.edu/king-papers/documents/rising-tide-racial-consciousness-address-golden-anniversary-conference; Carlton and Coclanis, "Another 'Great Migration'"; Myrdal, *American Dilemma*, 468–72.

167. Vance, "Regional Concept as a Tool," 85.

168. Lewis Mumford to Howard W. Odum, December 18, 1937, and March 3, 1938, box 24, folders 400–424, Howard Washington Odum Papers, 1908–1982 collection, Wilson Special Collections Library, University of North Carolina at Chapel Hill.

169. Wirth, "Limitations of Regionalism," 392.

170. Singal, *War Within*, 147–52; Sanders, *Howard W. Odum's Folklore Odyssey*; Rodgers, "Regionalism," 21; H. Odum, *Understanding Society*.

171. O'Brien, *Idea of the American South*, xxv.

172. Tullos, *Habits of Industry*, 298.

173. J. Thomas, "Holding the Middle Ground," 61.

174. Tindall, "Significance of Howard W. Odum," 307; Singal, *War Within*; 116.

175. See Scott, *Seeing Like a State*, 6.

CHAPTER 1

1. Weaver, *Regional Development*; P. Hall, *Cities of Tomorrow*.

2. Geddes, *Cities in Evolution*, xxvi, chaps. 15 and 16.

3. P. Hall, *Cities of Tomorrow*, 147–48.

4. Welter, *Biopolis*, 10; Teitz, "Regional Development Planning." See also Vance, *Human Factors*, 208, for Spencer's influence on regionalism.

5. R. Smith, "Botanical Survey," 387; Goldfield, *Region, Race, and Cities*; Welter, *Biopolis*. See also MacKaye, *New Exploration*, for the influence of MacKaye's forestry training.

6. Geddes, *Cities in Evolution*; P. Hall, *Cities of Tomorrow*.

7. Lubove, *Community Planning in the 1920s*; Friedmann and Weaver, *Territory and Function*; Spann, *Designing Modern America*.

8. Odum, *Man's Quest*, 505.

9. Mumford, *Sketches from Life*, 478.

10. Mumford, *My Works and Days*, 108.

11. K. Larsen, "From the RPAA to the RDCA."

12. Batty and Marshall, "Thinking Organic, Acting Civic," 2.

13. Mumford, *My Works and Days*, 107.

14. H. Odum, *American Epoch*, x; Singal, *War Within*, 133; Dorman, *Revolt of the Provinces*, 50.

15. Dorman, *Revolt of the Provinces*, 50.

16. Dorman, *Revolt of the Provinces*, 276.

17. Stuart Chase, "The Concept of Planning," July 11, 1931, transcript from the Round Table on Regionalism at the University of Virginia Institute of Public Affairs, box 62, folder 798, Howard Washington Odum Papers, 1908–1982 collection, Wilson Special Collections Library, University of North Carolina at Chapel Hill (hereafter Odum Papers). Charles Edward Clark is the Yale Law School dean to whom he refers. See also Pells, *Radical Visions*, 61–69.

18. Dorman, *Revolt of the Provinces*, 275. Wilson Gee was named the first director of the University of Virginia's rival Institute for Research in the Social Sciences in 1926. See Singal, *War Within*, 303.

19. Mumford, *Sketches from Life*, 478.

20. Tugwell, "Sources," 266.

21. Spann, "Franklin Delano Roosevelt," 192.

22. "Address by Governor Franklin Delano Roosevelt of New York on State Planning, July 6, 1931," transcript from the Round Table on Regionalism at the University of Virginia Institute of Public Affairs, box 62, folder 798, Odum Papers.

23. "Address by Governor Franklin Delano Roosevelt of New York on State Planning."

24. Mumford, *Sketches from Life*, 478.

25. Tindall, *Emergence of the New South*, 586–87.

26. Mumford, *My Works and Days*, 107.

27. Benton MacKaye, "Cultural Aspects of Regionalism," July 9, 1931, transcript from the Round Table on Regionalism at the University of Virginia Institute of Public Affairs, box 62, folder 798, Odum Papers.

28. D. Ross, *Origins*; Bannister, *Sociology and Scientism*.

29. MacKaye, "Cultural Aspects of Regionalism"; Vance, *Human Geography*, 483–84.

30. Weaver, *Regional Development*; Welter, *Biopolis*.

31. MacKenzie, Robert E. Park, and Ernest W. Burgess coauthored the 1925 book *The City*, a foundational text for what came to be known as the Chicago School of Human Ecology.

32. Roderick D. MacKenzie, "Sociological and Economic Aspects of Regionalism," July 10, 1931, transcript from the Round Table on Regionalism at the University of Virginia Institute of Public Affairs, box 62, folder 798, Odum Papers.

33. J. Thomas, "Holding the Middle Ground"; Fishman, "Metropolitan Tradition"; P. Hall, *Cities of Tomorrow*, 149–202.

34. Benevolo, *Origins*; Hahn, "Hunting, Fishing, and Foraging"; Daniel, *Breaking the Land*; Woods, *Development Arrested*; Coclanis, "Southern Economy."

35. Friedmann and Weaver, *Territory and Function*.

36. Howard W. Odum, "Sociological Aspects of Regionalism," July 10, 1931, transcript from the Round Table on Regionalism at the University of Virginia Institute of Public Affairs, box 62, folder 798, Odum Papers.

37. Odum, "Sociological Aspects of Regionalism."

38. Odum, "Sociological Aspects of Regionalism."
39. Odum and Moore, *American Regionalism*, 12.
40. Tindall, "Significance of Howard W. Odum," 298.
41. Odum, "Sociological Aspects of Regionalism."
42. Odum, "Sociological Aspects of Regionalism."
43. H. Odum, *Race and Rumors of Race*; Woods, *Development Arrested*, 134–36; Tyler, "Impact of the New Deal," 450.
44. Dainotto, "'All the Regions.'"
45. Transcript notes correctly attribute "place, work, folk" to Le Play and not Geddes.
46. John Gould Fletcher, "Cultural Aspects of Regionalism," July 9, 1931, transcript from the Round Table on Regionalism at the University of Virginia Institute of Public Affairs, box 62, folder 798, Odum Papers.
47. Harvey, "Southern Religion and Southern Culture," 436.
48. Fletcher, "Cultural Aspects of Regionalism."
49. Karanikas, *Tillers of a Myth*.
50. John Gould Fletcher to Allen Tate, December 19, 1930, in Dorman, *Revolt of the Provinces*, 232.
51. Stringfellow Barr, "Cultural Aspects of Regionalism," July 9, 1931, transcript from the Round Table on Regionalism at the University of Virginia Institute of Public Affairs, box 62, folder 798, Odum Papers. Barr opaquely attributed the "crisis of tradition" phrase to "a French writer," but Hannah Arendt later discussed the concept in her 1954 essay "The Crisis in Education."
52. Donald Davidson to John Donald Wade, March 3, 1934, box 21, folder 342, Odum Papers.
53. Frank, *Re-Discovery of America*, 205–8; Dorman, *Revolt of the Provinces*, 103.
54. Barr, "Cultural Aspects of Regionalism."
55. Friedmann and Alonso, *Regional Development and Planning*; Dorman, *Revolt of the Provinces*; Milligan, "Contradictions of Public Service."
56. Dorman, *Revolt of the Provinces*, 295–96; Selznick, *TVA and the Grass Roots*.
57. Dorman, *Revolt of the Provinces*, 296; Soja, *Postmodern Geographies*.
58. Dorman, *Revolt of the Provinces*, 296.
59. Selznick, *TVA and the Grass Roots*; Shapley, "TVA Today"; Friedmann and Weaver, *Territory and Function*, 5.
60. Hargrove, *Prisoners of Myth*.
61. Sosna, *In Search of the Silent South*, 149; S. Davis, "South"; Schulman, *From Cotton Belt to Sunbelt*, viii, 51; Carlton and Coclanis, *Confronting Southern Poverty*; Sullivan, *Days of Hope*; Tyler, "Impact of the New Deal," 450.
62. Katznelson, *Fear Itself*, 169–72.
63. H. Odum, "Case for Regional-National," 16.
64. Tindall, *Emergence of the New South*, 598.
65. Schulman, *From Cotton Belt to Sunbelt*, viii, 5; Tyler, "Impact of the New Deal," 450.
66. Tyler, "Impact of the New Deal"; Sitkoff, *New Deal for Blacks*; K. Davis, *FDR*.
67. Tindall, "Significance of Howard W. Odum," 299.

68. Myrdal, *American Dilemma*; Sosna, *In Search of the Silent South*.

69. O'Brien, *Idea of the American South*, 76; Tindall, "Significance of Howard W. Odum," 300n40. Quote from a letter from Howard W. Odum to Prentiss M. Terry, August 15, 1938, and a letter from Odum to Emily H. Clay, August 15, 1938. Clay was assistant to Will Alexander of the interracial committee. Rodgers, "Regionalism," 11n17.

70. O'Brien, *Idea of the American South*, 75.

71. Du Bois, *Souls of Black Folk*, 2.

72. Milligan, "Contradictions of Public Service," 223.

73. H. Odum, "Approach to Diagnosis," 16. See H. Odum, *Folk, Region, and Society*, 67–107.

74. Vance, *Human Geography*, 467–81; Kendrick, "Colonial Status"; Tindall, *Emergence of the New South*, 433–72; S. Davis, "South"; Rodgers, "Regionalism," 11n17; Coclanis, "Southern Economy."

75. Cobb, *Selling of the South*; Cobb and Namorato, *New Deal and the South*; Sosna, *In Search of the Silent South*, 147; Schulman, *From Cotton Belt to Sunbelt*, 51–55; Brenner, *New State Spaces*; Tyler, "Impact of the New Deal," 450.

76. Boisier, *Diseño de planes regionales*; Lo and Salih, *Growth Pole Strategy*; Friedmann and Weaver, *Territory and Function*; Escobar, *Encountering Development*; T. Mitchell, *Rule of Experts*; Brenner, *New State Spaces*; Gorelik, *Ciudad Latinoamericana*.

77. Friedmann and Weaver, *Territory and Function*, 108–9.

78. Martin, "New Economics"; Martin and Sunley, "Post-Keynesian State"; Brenner, *New State Spaces*, 114–71n1; Botar and Wünsche, *Biocentrism and Modernism*; Moravánszky and Kegler, *Re-Scaling the Environment*; Gorelik, *Ciudad Latinoamericana*.

79. Kendrick, "Southern Confederation of Learning"; Donald Davidson to John Donald Wade, March 3, 1934, box 21, folder 342, Odum Papers; Irish, "Proposed Roads to the New South"; Tindall, *Emergence of the New South*, 575–606; O'Brien, *Idea of the American South*, 16–19, 55–69.

80. Davidson, "Where Regionalism and Sectionalism Meet." See H. Odum, *Folk, Region, and Society*.

81. Donald Davidson to Howard W. Odum, March 21, 1934, box 21, folder 342, Odum Papers. See H. Odum, *Folk, Region, and Society*.

82. Rubin and Jacobs, *Southern Renascence*, 84–100; H. Odum, *Folk, Region, and Society*, 202–18.

83. Ohio was likely a reference to Sherwood Anderson, a kind of mentor to Faulkner.

84. Guy B. Johnson, introduction to H. Odum, *Folk, Region, and Society*, 3–5.

85. Johnson, introduction, 3–5.

86. Singal, *War Within*, 134; H. Odum, *American Epoch*; Reed, *Surveying the South*.

87. Du Bois, *Philadelphia Negro*; Du Bois, *Souls of Black Folk*; Du Bois, *Quest of the Silver Fleece*; Du Bois, *Dark Princess*; Hurston, *Mules and Men*; Hurston, *Their Eyes Were Watching God*; Hemenway, *Zora Neale Hurston*; Terry, "Fiction of W. E. B. Du Bois"; Hurston, *"You Don't Know Us Negroes."*

88. Watkins, "What Stand Did Faulkner Take?," 49; Dorman, *Revolt of the Provinces*, 34.

89. Dorman, *Revolt of the Provinces*, 100, 221. Dorman discusses Faulkner's perceived contradiction of resource opulence and fenced private property in *Absalom, Absalom!* See also Saikku, "Faulkner and the 'Doomed Wilderness'"; and Aiken, *William Faulkner and the Southern Landscape*.

90. Singal, *War Within*, 139. Singal uses an example from H. Odum's *American Epoch* celebrating the Southern plantation heritage he appreciates in the architecture of the White House.

91. McWilliams, *New Regionalism*, 7, 20, 23; Critser, "Political Rebellion of Carey McWilliams," 39; Dorman, *Revolt of the Provinces*.

92. Patrick Geddes to Victor Branford quoted in Boardman, *Worlds of Patrick Geddes*, 194.

93. D. Ross, *Origins*, 53–97; Friedmann and Weaver, *Territory and Function*; Weaver, *Regional Development*, chaps. 1–4.

94. Latour, "Impact of Science Studies."

CHAPTER 2

1. Friedmann and Weaver, *Territory and Function*, 25; Hofstadter, *Age of Reform*; D. Ross, *Origins*, chaps. 3, 5, 6.

2. Friedmann and Weaver, *Territory and Function*, 26; Dewey, *Liberalism and Social Action*; Dewey, *School and Society*; Dewey, *Democracy and Education*; D. Ross, *Origins*, 162–72. See also Fairfield, *Mysteries of the Great City*, 159–63.

3. Friedmann and Weaver, *Territory and Function*, 27–28; Veblen, *Place of Science*; D. Ross, *Origins*, 204–17.

4. Friedmann and Weaver, *Territory and Function*, 27–28; Gruchy, "Economics of the National Resources Committee"; Gruchy, "Concept of National Planning"; Jordan, *Machine-Age Ideology*, chap. 1.

5. Fosdick, *Story of the Rockefeller Foundation*.

6. "Why Cows?," Odum Institute for Research in Social Science, accessed March 1, 2024, https://odum.unc.edu/whycows/.

7. Foner, "If Lincoln Hadn't Died."

8. African American and white women would have to wait until the twentieth century for the legal enshrinement of these rights.

9. Foner, *Reconstruction*; Gates, *Stony the Road*.

10. For discussions of these myths, see Singal, *War Within*, 117; and Brazil, *Howard W. Odum*.

11. Tullos, *Habits of Industry*, 295.

12. S. Matthews, *Capturing the South*, 24.

13. Cobb, *Most Southern Place on Earth*; Woods, *Development Arrested*.

14. Dorman, *Revolt of the Provinces*, 51; Wiebe, *Search for Order*; D. Ross, *Origins*.

15. Milligan, "Contradictions of Public Service," 3; Fine, *Progressive Evolutionism*.

16. Woods, *Development Arrested*, 134; Singal, *War Within*, 33, 135–40.

17. Brazil, *Howard W. Odum*, 75.
18. Brazil, *Howard W. Odum*, 73–74.
19. S. Matthews, *Capturing the South*, 25; Brazil, *Howard W. Odum*, 75–76, 86–88, 104–7, 118; Bailey, *Race Orthodoxy*; Drake, "Moralizing the Folk."
20. Gaston, *New South Creed*; Brazil, *Howard W. Odum*.
21. Singal, *War Within*, 31.
22. Bailey, *Race Orthodoxy*. The original text does not capitalize the word "negro."
23. Woodward, *Origins of the New South*, 355.
24. Park, review of *Race Orthodoxy*, 449.
25. Park, review of *Race Orthodoxy*, 449.
26. W. Thomas, "Howard W. Odum's Social Theories"; Milligan, "Contradictions of Public Service," chap. 3.
27. Thomas Pearce Bailey to W. E. B. Du Bois, November 7, 1914, MS 312, W. E. B. Du Bois Papers, Special Collections and University Archives, University of Massachusetts Amherst Libraries.
28. Thomas Pearce Bailey to W. E. B. Du Bois, November 7, 1914.
29. Miller, "Race-ism and the City"; Morris, *Scholar Denied*.
30. Brazil, *Howard W. Odum*; S. Matthews, *Capturing the South*.
31. S. Matthews, *Capturing the South*, 30.
32. S. Matthews, *Capturing the South*, 30.
33. Rodgers, "Regionalism," 9; Morauta et al., "Indigenous Anthropology."
34. O'Brien, *Idea of the American South*, 34–37.
35. O'Brien, *Idea of the American South*, 34; S. Matthews, *Capturing the South*, 30.
36. Howard W. Odum, handwritten notes on the back of Image 3167 of Series 6, Photographs, Howard Washington Odum Papers, 1908–1982 collection, Wilson Special Collections Library, University of North Carolina at Chapel Hill.
37. Tullos, *Habits of Industry*, 296; D. Ross, *G. Stanley Hall*; Benjamin, *Brief History of Modern Psychology*, 63–68.
38. Tullos, "Politics of Regional Development," 116; H. Odum, "Editorial Notes," *Social Forces* 3, no. 1 (1924): 139, 144–45; H. Odum, "Patrick Geddes' Heritage."
39. O'Brien, *Idea of the American South*, 34–35.
40. D. Ross, *Origins*.
41. Rodgers, "Regionalism," 5.
42. D. Ross, *Origins*; Morris, *Scholar Denied*.
43. Fairfield, "Alienation of Social Control."
44. Odum and Moore, *American Regionalism*, 154.
45. H. Odum, *Southern Regions*; O'Brien, *Idea of the American South*.
46. S. Matthews, *Capturing the South*, 25.
47. Rodgers, "Regionalism," 8.
48. Rodgers, "Regionalism," 18.
49. Odum, *Southern Regions*; Odum and Moore, *American Regionalism*.
50. Brazil, *Howard W. Odum*; O'Brien, *Idea of the American South*; Woods, *Development Arrested*.
51. Green and Driver, "W. E. B. Du Bois," 319.

52. E. Wright, "W. E. B. Du Bois"; E. Wright, *Jim Crow Sociology*.
53. Kantor, "Howard W. Odum," 279.
54. Rodgers, *Atlantic Crossings*; Morris, *Scholar Denied*.
55. Tullos, *Habits of Industry*, 295.
56. O'Brien, *Idea of the American South*, 36–37; Tullos, *Habits of Industry*, 295.
57. Milligan, "Contradictions of Public Service," 3–4.
58. Grantham, "Regional Imagination," 8.
59. S. Matthews, *Capturing the South*, 41; Grantham, "Regional Imagination," 4; Brunner, *Growth of a Science*, 7–8; L. Wilson, *University of North Carolina*, 207–21.
60. Rodgers, *Atlantic Crossings*, 352–55.
61. Cobb, *Most Southern Place on Earth*, 185, 200; Tyler, "Impact of the New Deal," 451.
62. Singal, *War Within*, 119.
63. S. Matthews, *Capturing the South*, 41; Johnson and Johnson, *Research in Service to Society*, 14–26.
64. Singal, *War Within*, 119.
65. Cobb, *Selling of the South*.
66. Tullos, *Habits of Industry*, 287.
67. Tullos, *Habits of Industry*, 288.
68. Grantham, "Regional Imagination," 6–7.
69. D. Ross, *Origins*.
70. Grantham, "Regional Imagination," 4; Pierson, *Graduate Work*.
71. The University of North Carolina Press web page states, "Established in 1922, UNC Press was the first university press in the South and one of the first in the nation." See https://uncpress.org/about/.
72. Tullos, *Habits of Industry*, 290; Grantham, "Regional Imagination."
73. Singal, *War Within*, 120–25.
74. Singal, *War Within*, 120.
75. H. Odum, "More Articulate South," 732.
76. Stephen Ramos, interview by James C. Cobb, May 4, 2022.
77. Milligan, "Contradictions of Public Service," 43.
78. H. Odum, "Editorial Notes," *Social Forces* 1, no. 1 (1922): 57–58.
79. Brazil, "*Social Forces* and Sectional Self-Scrutiny," 76; Sosna, *In Search of the Silent South*, 45; Milligan, "Contradictions of Public Service," 55n52.
80. Jordan, *Machine-Age Ideology*, 153; H. Odum, *Folk, Region, and Society*; Johnson and Johnson, *Research in Service to Society*; Singal, *War Within*.
81. D. Ross, *Origins*.
82. H. Odum, "More Articulate South"; Milligan, "Contradictions of Public Service," 47–48.
83. D. Ross, *Origins*.
84. Milligan, "Contradictions of Public Service," 114; H. Odum, *Southern Regions*, 583; O'Brien, *Idea of the American South*, 13.
85. Jordan, *Machine-Age Ideology*, chap. 6; Fosdick, *Story of the Rockefeller Foundation*.
86. Fosdick, *Story of the Rockefeller Foundation*.
87. Fosdick, *Story of the Rockefeller Foundation*, 196.

88. Fosdick, *Story of the Rockefeller Foundation*, 196.

89. Fairfield, *Mysteries of the Great City*, 161-63.

90. Worcester and Sibley, *Social Science Research Council*, 18-19; H. Odum, *Folk, Region, and Society*, viii.

91. Bulmer and Bulmer, "Philanthropy and Social Science," 390.

92. Johnson and Johnson, *Research in Service to Society*, 19.

93. Bulmer and Bulmer, "Philanthropy and Social Science," 391; Milligan, "Contradictions of Public Service," 114-17.

94. Fosdick, *Story of the Rockefeller Foundation*, 207.

95. Fosdick, *Story of the Rockefeller Foundation*, 200.

96. Fosdick, *Story of the Rockefeller Foundation*, 201.

97. Fosdick, *Story of the Rockefeller Foundation*, 201.

98. O'Brien, *Idea of the American South*, 70-71; Fosdick, *Story of the Rockefeller Foundation*, 200-201.

99. Milligan, "Contradictions of Public Service," 125; Brazil, *Howard W. Odum*; O'Brien, *Idea of the American South*, 71; Seim, *Rockefeller Philanthropy*, 135.

100. Milligan, "Contradictions of Public Service," 115.

101. Beardsley Ruml to Howard W. Odum, December 10, 1929, box 9, folder 198 Howard Washington Odum Papers, 1908-1982 collection, Wilson Special Collections Library, University of North Carolina at Chapel Hill; O'Brien, *Idea of the American South*, 44-50, 70-80; Milligan, "Contradictions of Public Service," 39.

102. Milligan, "Contradictions of Public Service," chaps. 2 and 3.

103. Milligan, "Contradictions of Public Service," 116-17n47 for Odum correspondence; O'Brien, *Idea of the American South*, 46-47; Bulmer, "Support for Sociology," 186, 189, 190; Bannister, *Sociology and Scientism*, 180.

104. Milligan, "Contradictions of Public Service," 123.

105. Milligan, "Contradictions of Public Service," 127-30.

106. Milligan, "Contradictions of Public Service," 53.

107. Singal, *War Within*, 122.

108. Broschart, "Research in the Service of Society."

109. Herring, *Welfare Work in Mill Villages*. Odum later wrote the foreword to Herring's book *Southern Industry and Regional Development*; see H. Odum, *Folk, Region, and Society*, 137-42. Brazil, *Howard W. Odum*; Singal, *War Within*, 304; Tullos, *Habits of Industry*, 294, 298-99; J. Hall, *Like a Family*.

110. Singal, *War Within*, 126.

111. Harvey, "Southern Religion and Southern Culture," 440.

112. H. L. Mencken, "Mencken Finds Daytonians Full of Sickening Doubts about Value of Publicity," *Baltimore Evening Sun*, July 9, 1925.

113. H. Odum, "Duel to the Death"; Milligan, "Contradictions of Public Service," 52.

114. Singal, *War Within*, 127.

115. Barnes, "Recent Books," 343.

116. Bernard, "Psychoanalysis"; Singal, *War Within*, 126; Brazil, *Howard W. Odum*.

117. Gerald W. Johnson, "Chase of North Carolina," *American Mercury*, September 1926, 77-82; Singal, *War Within*, 126.

118. Howard W. Odum to Luther L. Bernard, March 7, 1925, box 4, folder 51, Howard Washington Odum Papers, 1908–1982 collection, Wilson Special Collections Library, University of North Carolina at Chapel Hill; Singal, *War Within*, 127.

119. Singal, *War Within*, 127.

120. Milligan, "Contradictions of Public Service," 56; O'Brien, *Rethinking the South*, 184–89.

121. Milligan, "Contradictions of Public Service," 120.

122. Milligan, "Contradictions of Public Service," 120–21.

123. Tullos, "Politics of Regional Development"; H. Odum, *Folk, Region, and Society*; Johnson and Johnson, *Research in Service to Society*; Broschart, "Research in the Service of Society."

124. Singal, *War Within*, 305; Ellis, "T. J. Woofter Jr."

125. Singal, *War Within*, 305.

126. Reed and Singal, *Regionalism and the South*, xiii.

127. Singal, *War Within*, 306.

128. Singal, *War Within*, 307.

129. G. B. Johnson, "Rupert Bayless Vance."

130. Singal, *War Within*, 309.

131. Reed and Singal, *Regionalism and the South*, xvi.

132. Singal, *War Within*, 311.

133. Singal, *War Within*, 315.

134. Singal, *War Within*, 320.

135. Singal, *War Within*, 319.

136. Singal, *War Within*, 319.

137. W. E. B. Du Bois to Anson Phelps Stokes, November 1, 1937, in Du Bois, *Correspondence*, 152–53. Du Bois notes this in his correspondence, and it was the reason for his initial protest to work with Johnson. See also Lewis, *W. E. B. Du Bois*, 442, 444; and Singal, *War Within*, 322.

138. G. B. Johnson, "Does the South Owe?"

139. Singal, *War Within*, 325.

140. Milligan, "Contradictions of Public Service," 304.

141. Ellis, "T. J. Woofter Jr.," 243.

142. Ellis, "T. J. Woofter Jr.," 243.

143. Ellis, "T. J. Woofter Jr.," 243.

144. Arthur Franklin Raper, "Negro Dependency in the Southern Community," folder 19, Arthur Franklin Raper Papers, 1910–1981 collection, Wilson Special Collections Library, University of North Carolina at Chapel Hill.

145. Singal, *War Within*, 330; Myrdal, *American Dilemma*.

146. Lewis, *W. E. B. Du Bois*, 477–78. Raper and Du Bois were colleagues who shared mutual admiration. See also Du Bois, *Correspondence*, 139, 153; and Singal, *War Within*, 330–35.

147. Davidson, *Attack on Leviathan*, 304, 286; Singal, *War Within*, 335nn60–62.

148. Singal, *War Within*, 337.

149. Singal, *War Within*, 125.

150. H. Odum, "Editorial Notes," *Social Forces* 2, no. 2 (1924): 282–86; Giddings, "Societal Variables."

CHAPTER 3

1. H. Odum, *American Epoch*, xi.
2. H. Odum, *American Epoch*, x.
3. Odum and Jocher, *Introduction to Social Research*, 83; Brazil, *Howard W. Odum*, 602; Milligan, "Contradictions of Public Service," 141–55.
4. H. Odum, *American Epoch*, x.
5. H. Odum, "Folk and Regional Conflict."
6. Rupert B. Vance quoted in Singal, *War Within*, 315. Vance used the adjective in his critique of Odum and Moore's *American Regionalism*, stating that he was "wanting a more hardboiled view of social change."
7. Sutherland, "Harry Estill Moore."
8. Odum and Moore, *American Regionalism*, 29; H. Odum, *Folk, Region, and Society*, 168–69.
9. H. Odum, "Notes on the Study," 168; Milligan, "Contradictions of Public Service," 247.
10. Spencer Howard, "Wonder Boy—Herbert Hoover as Secretary of Commerce," *Hoover Heads* (blog), Herbert Hoover Library and Museum at the National Archives, March 2, 2021, https://hoover.blogs.archives.gov/2021/03/03/wonder-boy-herbert-hoover-as-secretary-of-commerce/.
11. Herbert Hoover, foreword to *Recent Social Trends*, by W. Mitchell; Hoover, *Memoirs*, 312; Tobin, "Studying Society," 537.
12. Bernard, "Transition to an Objective Standard," 532, 534; Bulmer, "Methodology"; Jordan, *Machine-Age Ideology*, 89.
13. Natasha Porfirenko and Michael C. Conkin, "Register of the United States: President's Research Committee on Social Trends Records" (finding aid), Hoover Institution Library and Archives, Stanford University, Online Archive of California, https://oac.cdlib.org/findaid/ark:/13030/tf8b69n9bo/.
14. W. Mitchell, *Backward Art of Spending*, 71; Wesley C. Mitchell, "Economics and Social Engineering," quoted in Thornton, *Science and Social Change*, 313; M. Smith, "Mitchell, Wesley Clair"; Jordan, *Machine-Age Ideology*, 147n28.
15. Milligan, "Contradictions of Public Service," 66; Bulmer, "Methodology"; D. Ross, *Origins*, 156–57.
16. W. Mitchell, *Backward Art of Spending*, 49; Jordan, *Machine-Age Ideology*, 182.
17. Jordan, *Machine-Age Ideology*, 183.
18. Dykhuizen et al., *Life and Mind*, 9:235; Berle, "Trend of the Turn," 535.
19. Beard, "President's Committee's Recent Social Trends," 596; Jordan, *Machine-Age Ideology*, 183.
20. Vance, "Regional Concept as a Tool," 121.
21. Howard W. Odum, "Memorandum on Publicity Notes for Mr. Strother," September 21, 1929, box 9, folder 190; Odum to Edmund Day, September 2, 1929, and Odum to William Ogburn, October 25, 1929, box 14, folders 183–199, Howard Washington Odum Papers, 1908–1982 collection, Wilson Special Collections Library, University of North Carolina at Chapel Hill (hereafter Odum Papers); O'Brien, *Idea of the American South*, 48n46; Milligan, "Contradictions of Public Service," 165.

22. Angell, "*Recent Social Trends.*"
23. Milligan, "Contradictions of Public Service," 133–38.
24. Griffin, "Promise of a Sociology," 53.
25. H. Odum, *Folk, Region, and Society*, xi.
26. Bulmer, "Methodology." Odum was among the committee's executive staff of three, alongside Ogburn and Hoover's liaison, executive secretary E. E. Hunt.
27. W. Wilson, *City Beautiful Movement*; Woods, *Development Arrested*; Peterson, *Birth of City Planning*.
28. Chicago Fair Committee to George Burgess, August 21, 1928, quoted in Dawes, *Century of Progress*; Jordan, *Machine-Age Ideology*, 186.
29. Howard W. Odum to John Sewell, January 13, 1931, folder 11-213, in "City of Progress" papers, University of Illinois at Urbana–Champaign; Jordan, *Machine-Age Ideology*, 187n3.
30. Odum, *Man's Quest*, 102–3; Milligan, "Contradictions of Public Service," 89.
31. H. S. Person, "Engineering," quoted in Seligman and Johnson, *Encyclopaedia of the Social Sciences*, 5:546; Jordan, *Machine-Age Ideology*, 173.
32. Fosdick, *Story of the Rockefeller Foundation*, 197.
33. Howard W. Odum, "Notes on the Development of the Social Science Division of a Century of Progress," October 10, 1931, box 18, folders 247–263, Odum Papers; Jordan, *Machine-Age Ideology*, 188.
34. Jordan, *Machine-Age Ideology*, 188–91.
35. Jordan, *Machine-Age Ideology*, 151.
36. Milligan, "Contradictions of Public Service," 133.
37. D. Ross, *Origins*, xiii; Mills, *Sociological Imagination*, 12; Soja, *Postmodern Geographies*, 13.
38. H. Odum, *Southern Pioneers, American Masters*, and *Man's Quest*; Odum and Jocher, *Introduction to Social Research*; H. Odum, *Understanding Society, American Sociology*.
39. Tindall, "Significance of Howard W. Odum"; Reed, "Sociology"; S. Matthews, *Capturing the South*.
40. Brazil, *Howard W. Odum*, 241.
41. Johnson and Johnson, *Research in Service to Society*, 166.
42. H. Odum, *Social Forces* 1, no. 1 (1922): 56–57; Brazil, *Howard W. Odum*, 285–87, 325, 385; Milligan, "Contradictions of Public Service," 44.
43. Singal, *War Within*, 133; Nelson, "Regional Planning as Cultural Criticism."
44. Milligan, "Contradictions of Public Service," 155.
45. O'Brien, *Idea of the American South*, 3–4.
46. O'Brien, *Idea of the American South*, 4.
47. Herder, *J. G. Herder*; see O'Brien, *Idea of the American South*, 4n4, for full references.
48. Bannister, *Sociology and Scientism*; D. Ross, *Origins*.
49. D. Ross, *Origins*, 30.
50. D. Ross, *Origins*, 30; Calhoun, *Disquisition on Government*; Faust, *Sacred Circle*; E. Wright, "W. E. B. Du Bois."
51. Reed, *Surveying the South*, 7.

52. D. Ross, *Origins*, 32; Fitzhugh, *Sociology for the South*, 8, 70–71, 151–52, 176; Woods, *Development Arrested*.

53. Fitzhugh, *Sociology for the South*; Wish, *George Fitzhugh*; Frazier, "Sociological Theory," 265.

54. Hughes, *Treatise on Sociology*; Frazier, "Sociological Theory," 265.

55. Kaufman et al., *Capitalism, Slavery, and Republican Values*; Woodward, *Tom Watson: Agrarian Rebel*; D. Ross, *Origins*, 32; Hahn, *Roots of Southern Populism*. John Shelton Reed asserts provocatively that Odum's sociology resembled that of Hughes and Fitzhugh more than that of his own contemporaries at the Chicago School, Max Weber, or Emile Durkheim. See Reed, *Surveying the South*, 7.

56. Darwin, *Origin of Species*; Spencer, *Social Statics*.

57. Runkle, "Marxism and Charles Darwin."

58. Bannister, *Social Darwinism*, 15.

59. Hofstadter, *Social Darwinism*; Bannister, *Social Darwinism*.

60. Galton, *Inquiries into Human Faculty*, 24–25; López-Durán, *Eugenics in the Garden*.

61. Bannister, *Social Darwinism*, 16.

62. Gruber, *Darwin on Man*, xx; Bannister, *Social Darwinism*, 15.

63. Odum and Jocher, *Introduction to Social Research*, 411–15; Farrall, *Origins and Growth*; Welter, *Biopolis*, 187–89; Batty and Marshall, "Thinking Organic, Acting Civic." Along with Batty and Marshall, Welter draws distinctions between Geddes's neo-Lamarckian position on evolution and the neo-Darwinian position. Nevertheless, in the context of social planning as an advocated policy, this distinction is beside the point.

64. Osterweis, *Romanticism and Nationalism*, 24–40, 151–52; O'Brien, *Idea of the American South*, 4n5.

65. O'Brien, *Idea of the American South*, 5; Singal, *War Within*; Coclanis, "Southern Economy."

66. Harvey, "Southern Religion and Southern Culture," 436.

67. Tate, *Essays of Four Decades*; O'Brien, *Idea of the American South*, 27n72. See discussion of Agrarians and literary "Cantonism" as culture projects against modernization in King, *Southern Renaissance*, 51–57; B. Moore, *Social Origins of Dictatorship*, 491–96; Gaston, *New South Creed*.

68. Mumford, *Golden Day*; Dorman, *Revolt of the Provinces*, 2.

69. Walker, "Mr. Grote's 'Theory'"; Pearson, *Grammar of Science*; D. Ross, *Origins*, 59.

70. D. Ross, *Origins*, 60.

71. D. Ross, *Origins*, 85.

72. D. Ross, *Origins*, 87.

73. D. Ross, *Origins*, 88; Bannister, *Sociology and Scientism*; Milligan, "Contradictions of Public Service," 68–90.

74. Hofstadter, *Social Darwinism*, 12.

75. Barnes, "Two Representative Contributions," 151.

76. Milligan, "Contradictions of Public Service," 76; L. Ward, "Contributions to Social Philosophy," 802–8; Bierstedt, *American Sociological Theory*, 52–69, 83–84.

77. Dealey et al., "Lester Frank Ward."

78. Frazier, "Sociological Theory," 256.

79. Dealey et al., "Lester Frank Ward" quoted in H. Odum, *American Masters*, 81; Dealey, "Masters of Social Science."

80. D. Ross, *Origins*, 92.

81. L. F. Ward, "The Claims of Political Science" in Ward et al., *Glimpses of the Cosmos*, 3:334; L. Ward, *Dynamic Sociology*, 2:156, 249–52, 395; D. Ross, *Origins*, 92.

82. L. Ward, *"Theory of the Leisure Class."*

83. Barnes, "Two Representative Contributions," 153.

84. Barnes, "Two Representative Contributions," 155.

85. Barnes, "Two Representative Contributions," 162.

86. Barnes, "Two Representative Contributions," 164n3.

87. Barnes, "Two Representative Contributions," 164, paraphrasing from L. Ward, *Dynamic Sociology*, 2:245–50; L. Ward, *Pure Sociology*, 568–69; L. Ward, *Outlines of Sociology*, 187–89; L. Ward, *Psychic Factors*, 309–12.

88. D. Ross, *Origins*, 91; Frazier, "Sociological Theory," 266.

89. Gillette, "Critical Points."

90. H. Odum, "Regional Development"; H. Odum, *United States Planning Agency*; see also H. H. Odum, *Folk, Region, and Society*, 403–26.

91. Giddings, *Scientific Study*, chaps. 2–3; Milligan, "Contradictions of Public Service," 72.

92. D. Ross, *Origins*, 154.

93. D. Ross, *Origins*, 130, 146–47.

94. D. Ross, *Origins*, 128.

95. Woods, *Development Arrested*, 97.

96. Giddings, *Principles of Sociology*, 17; Frazier, "Sociological Theory," 266.

97. Myrdal, *American Dilemma*, 1132; Green and Driver, "W. E. B. Du Bois"; Morris, *Scholar Denied*.

98. Du Bois, "Study of the Negro Problems," 1; Green and Driver, "W. E. B. Du Bois," 311.

99. Giddings, *Studies in the Theory*, chap. 5; Odum and Jocher, *Introduction to Social Research*, 213.

100. Giddings, *Scientific Study*, 165–67; Giddings, "Social Work and Societal Engineering," 13–14; Jordan, *Machine-Age Ideology*, 131–32.

101. D. Ross, *Origins*, 220; Giddings, *Theory of Socialization*, 38–39; Giddings, *Inductive Sociology*, 6; Bannister; *Sociology and Scientism*, 79.

102. Known then as the American Sociological Society, the group officially changed its name to American Sociological Association in 1959; see Hill, "American Sociological Association."

103. Bannister; *Sociology and Scientism*, 106; Sumner, *Folkways*, chap. 1; H. Odum, *Understanding Society*, chap. 12.

104. Bannister; *Sociology and Scientism*, 106; Sumner, *Folkways*, chap. 1.

105. Sumner, *Folkways*, 76; Bannister; *Sociology and Scientism*, 98.

106. Sumner, *Folkways*, 74; Frazier, "Sociological Theory," 266.

107. Myrdal, *American Dilemma*, 2:1031–32; Frazier, "Sociological Theory," 266n9.

108. Small, "Points of Agreement," 63–64; D. Ross, *Origins*, 221.

109. Bannister, *Sociology and Scientism*, 108.

110. Bannister, *Sociology and Scientism*, 108.

111. Milligan, "Contradictions of Public Service," 103–6.

112. Ross, "American Social Science and the Idea of Progress" quoted in Haskell, *Authority of Experts*, 157–75; Milligan, "Contradictions of Public Service," 103–4.

113. Johnson and Johnson, *Research in Service to Society*.

114. Milligan, "Contradictions of Public Service," 116–17, 120.

115. Milligan, "Contradictions of Public Service," 114.

116. Jordan, *Machine-Age Ideology*, 132.

117. Odum and Jocher, *Introduction to Social Research*, 102–7; Milligan, "Contradictions of Public Service," 111.

118. Milligan, "Contradictions of Public Service," 159–60; Brazil, *Howard W. Odum*, 587–88.

119. Howard W. Odum to Charles Merriam, June 19 and October 7, 1925, and Odum to Beardsley Ruml, October 7, 1925, box 4, folders 56–82, Odum Papers; Brazil, *Howard W. Odum*, 456–59; Milligan, "Contradictions of Public Service," 136n86.

120. H. Odum, "Folk and Regional Conflict"; H. Odum, *American Epoch*.

121. Howard W. Odum to Ernest Burgess, May 21, 1930, and Odum to William Ogburn May 20, 1930, in box 17, folders 218–46, Odum Papers; Milligan, "Contradictions of Public Service," 163n139.

122. H. Odum, *American Epoch*, 59–61, 64–65, 83–84, 292–95; Singal, *War Within*, 129–35; Dorman, *Revolt of the Provinces*, 97, 136, 181; S. Matthews, *Capturing the South*; Milligan, "Contradictions of Public Service," 141.

123. Singal, *War Within*, 112.

124. Singal, *War Within*, 116.

125. Singal, *War Within*, 131–32.

126. Soja, *Postmodern Geographies*, 2.

127. O'Brien, *Idea of the American South*, 51–53.

128. H. Odum, *American Epoch*, 30–65, Milligan, "Contradictions of Public Service," 148.

129. H. Odum, *American Epoch*, 313, 329–30; Dorman, *Revolt of the Provinces*, 136 (my italics).

130. Myrdal, *American Dilemma*, 471.

131. Milligan, "Contradictions of Public Service," 149.

132. Milligan, "Contradictions of Public Service," 149; Howard W. Odum, "Sociological Aspects of Regionalism," July 10, 1931, transcript from the Round Table on Regionalism at the University of Virginia Institute of Public Affairs, box 62, folder 798, Odum Papers.

133. Milligan, "Contradictions of Public Service," 150.

134. H. Odum, *American Epoch*, ix–x, 17–29, 327–29, 338–39; Milligan, "Contradictions of Public Service," 152.

135. Bulmer, "Quantification and Chicago Social Science," 317–20, 327–28; Bannister, *Sociology and Scientism*, 174–75; Milligan, "Contradictions of Public Service," 164; F. Matthews, *Quest for an American Sociology*.

136. Blumer, "Science without Concepts," 515–33; Bannister, *Sociology and Scientism*, 176, 190–92, 209, 212, 217; Milligan, "Contradictions of Public Service," 165.

137. Entrikin, "Carl O. Sauer, Philosopher," 390.

138. Carl O. Sauer to Howard W. Odum, October 4, 1934, box 21, folders 337–61, Odum Papers; Milligan, "Contradictions of Public Service," 157.

139. Carl O. Sauer to Howard W. Odum, January 23, 1935, box 22, folders 362–85, Odum Papers.

140. Carl O. Sauer to Howard W. Odum, February 7, 1935, box 22, folders 362–85, Odum Papers.

141. Sauer, *Road to Cíbola*; Sauer, *Basin and Range Forms*; see also Sauer, "Personality of Mexico."

142. Gorelik, *Ciudad Latinoamericana*.

143. Redfield, "Folk Society."

144. Kaplan, "Nation, Region, and Empire," 252; Brodhead, *Cultures of Letters*; Bramen, *Uses of Variety*, 123.

145. Rudel and Fu, "Requiem."

146. Sauer to H. Odum, October 4, 1934. The word "our" is underlined in the letter.

147. Dorman, *Revolt in the Provinces*, xiii.

148. Mills, "Professional Ideology," 165–80; Soja, *Postmodern Geographies*, 12–15; Milligan, "Contradictions of Public Service," 79.

CHAPTER 4

1. H. Odum, *Folk, Region, and Society*, ix.
2. H. Odum, *Folk, Region, and Society*, v.
3. Berman, *All That Is Solid*, 236.
4. Singal, *War Within*, 17.
5. Bruner, *On Knowing*, 32, 35; Singal, *War Within*, 17.
6. Singal, *War Within*, 17; Coclanis, "Southern Economy."
7. Lynn, *Mark Twain*, 5; Singal, *War Within*, 17.
8. O'Brien, *Idea of the American South*, xxv.
9. Fine, *Progressive Evolutionism*; Milligan, "Contradictions of Public Service," 3.
10. O'Brien, *Idea of the American South*; Singal, *War Within*. "Go slow" refers to William Faulkner's quote in his "Letter to a Northern Editor" of March 5, 1956, that essentially admonishes the NAACP to slow down civil rights ambitions.
11. Rodgers, "Regionalism," 22.
12. Baldwin, "Faulkner and Desegregation," 569.
13. Baldwin, "Faulkner and Desegregation," 568.
14. Payne, "Whole United States."
15. Payne, "Whole United States," 85.
16. Payne, "Whole United States," 85.
17. Logan, *Negro in American Life*; Bruce, *Black American Writing*. See also Northern white Democrats' opposition of the 1934 Costigan-Wagner antilynching bill in Katznelson, *Fear Itself*, 166–68.

18. Cell, *Highest Stage of White Supremacy*, 2–5; Payne, "Whole United States," 86.

19. Cell, *Highest Stage of White Supremacy*, 2–5; Payne, "Whole United States," 86; Gaston, *New South Creed*.

20. Cell, *Highest Stage of White Supremacy*, 2–5; Payne, "Whole United States," 86.

21. David Brion Davis, "Free at Last: The Enduring Legacy of the South's Civil War Victory," *New York Times*, August 26, 2001, sec. 4, 1; Payne, "Whole United States," 87.

22. Cell, *Highest Stage of White Supremacy*, chap. 7, 182–83; Gaston, *New South Creed*, chap. 4; Payne, "Whole United States," 87.

23. C. Vann Woodward, "New South Fraud Is Papered by Old South Myth," *Washington Post*, July 9, 1961, E3; G. Wright, "Economic Revolution," 161; Cobb, "Making Sense."

24. Spann, *Designing Modern America*, 32; Ramos, "Regional Planning Association of America," 732.

25. Fairfield, "Alienation of Social Control"; Erickson and Highsmith, "Neighborhood Unit."

26. W. E. B. Du Bois to Alexander Bing, April 24, 1929, quoted in Allaback, *Marjorie Sewell Cautley*, 78; K. Larsen, "From the RPAA to the RDCA," 748n67.

27. "Summary of Discussions of Problems Connected with a Garden City, at a Series of Conferences of the Regional Planning Association of America at the Hudson Guild Farm, October 8 and 9, 1927" (unpublished minutes, October 8 and 9, 1927), 6, box 180, Lewis Mumford Papers, Special Collections, Van Pelt Library, University of Pennsylvania, Philadelphia; K. Larsen, "From the RPAA to the RDCA," 748n68.

28. Kaplan, "Nation, Region, and Empire," 252; Bramen, *Uses of Variety*, 123; Brodhead, *Cultures of Letters*.

29. Fairfield, "Alienation of Social Control."

30. Morris, *Scholar Denied*.

31. Park, "Urban Community as Spatial Pattern"; Fairfield, "Alienation of Social Control," 425. The presentation was originally titled "The Concept of Position in Sociology" and retitled in publication the following year.

32. Park, "Urban Community as Spatial Pattern," 3–18.

33. Park, "Urban Community as Spatial Pattern"; Fairfield, "Alienation of Social Control," 425.

34. Ralph H. Turner, introduction to *Robert E. Park* (Chicago: University of Chicago Press, 1967), xvii; Bracey, Meier, and Rudwick, eds., *Black Sociologists*, 6; Green and Driver, "W. E. B. Du Bois," 325.

35. Ring, "Nature of Reform," 360.

36. Ring, "Nature of Reform," 360.

37. Raper, *Tragedy of Lynching*; Singal, *War Within*, 330–36; Link, *Paradox of Southern Progressivism*.

38. Singal, *War Within*, 330n53; Dykeman and Stokely, *Seeds of Southern Change*, 140–41; Ring, "Nature of Reform," 387.

39. Link, *Paradox of Southern Progressivism*; Ring, "Nature of Reform," 387–90. See also Du Bois, "Lynching Industry."

40. H. Odum, "Lynching, Fears, and Folkways," 719–20; W. Thomas, "Conservative Currents," 121–25; Milligan, "Contradictions of Public Service," 307–13.

41. H. Odum, "Lynching, Fears, and Folkways," 39; Kneebone, *Southern Liberal Journalists*, 77–84.

42. King, *Southern Renaissance*, 41–42.

43. King, *Southern Renaissance*, 45–46; Lewis, *W. E. B. Du Bois*, 444.

44. King, *Southern Renaissance*, 41; Robbins, "Charles S. Johnson," 64, 73; Milligan, "Contradictions of Public Service," 309.

45. Guy B. Johnson, "Report to the Commission on Interracial Cooperation" quoted in H. Odum, *Southern Regions*, 487; King, *Southern Renaissance*, 45–46; Myrdal, *American Dilemma*, 471.

46. King, *Southern Renaissance*, 46; Dorman, *Revolt of the Provinces*, 187.

47. King, *Southern Renaissance*, 46.

48. King, *Southern Renaissance*, 46.

49. Woods, *Development Arrested*, 133–41.

50. Dorman, *Revolt of the Provinces*, 185; H. Odum, *Southern Regions*, 487; O'Brien, *Idea of the American South*, 70–79.

51. H. Odum, *Southern Regions*, 487.

52. Dorman, *Revolt of the Provinces*, 186.

53. Dorman, *Revolt of the Provinces*, 186.

54. Jordan, *Machine-Age Ideology*, 153.

55. Milligan, "Contradictions of Public Service," 310n41; H. Odum, *Southern Regions*, 1–11, 481–87.

56. Dorman, *Revolt of the Provinces*, 84–85.

57. Odum and Jocher, *In Search of Regional Balance*, 15; Dorman, *Revolt of the Provinces*, 9; H. Odum, "Religious Folk-Songs," 1–2; Sanders, "Effort toward Good Will," 49. See Morrison, *Playing in the Dark*, for traditions of racial surrogacy.

58. Milligan, "Contradictions of Public Service," 248–49.

59. Singal, *War Within*, 141; S. Matthews, *Capturing the South*.

60. Gallagher, *American Caste*, 178–79; Myrdal, *American Dilemma*, 96n35; Morris, *Scholar Denied*.

61. Odum and Johnson, *Negro Workaday Songs*, x; Odum and Johnson, *Negro and His Songs*, 8–13; Milligan, "Contradictions of Public Service," 130n73.

62. S. Matthews, *Capturing the South*, 22.

63. Sanders, "Effort toward Good Will," 49; H. Odum, *Race and Rumors of Race*.

64. H. Odum, *Southern Regions*, 487, 483, 481; O'Brien, *Idea of the American South*, 70–79; Dorman, *Revolt of the Provinces*, 187n47.

65. Kneebone, *Southern Liberal Journalists*, 87–88, Milligan, "Contradictions of Public Service," 300–301nn21–22.

66. Guy B. Johnson quoted in H. Odum, *Folk, Region, and Society*, 4; Du Bois, *Souls of Black Folk*, 10; Douglass, "Color Line."

67. James Baldwin, "Letter from a Region in My Mind," *New Yorker*, November 17, 1962, 143, www.newyorker.com/magazine/1962/11/17/letter-from-a-region-in-my-mind. Gerald W. Johnson also later recognized that the white South in fact had not dramatically changed its racial attitudes. See G. W. Johnson, "After Forty Years."

68. Rothstein, *Color of Law*.

69. Pettigrew, *Sociology of Race*, xxi–xxiii; Myrdal, *American Dilemma*, 1031–32, 1035–45, 1048–57; Frazier, "Sociological Theory," 266–71; Milligan, "Contradictions of Public Service," 300–302.

70. Morris, *Scholar Denied*, 195–223.

71. Myrdal, *American Dilemma*, 470; Van Sickle, *Planning for the South*, 38–39.

72. A. Gilbert, "New Regional Geography," 209–28, 217; Soja, *Postmodern Geographies*, 118–37, 92–93; Woods, *Development Arrested*, 26.

73. Katznelson, *Fear Itself*, 170; Dorman, *Revolt of the Provinces*, 169–74; Woods, *Development Arrested*; Coclanis, "Southern Economy."

74. Hofstadter, *Age of Reform*, 101.

75. Baldwin, "Faulkner and Desegregation," 572.

76. Milligan, "Contradictions of Public Service," 128n69; Johnson and Johnson, *Research in Service to Society*, 134; Tindall, *Emergence of the New South*, 310–12.

77. Tindall, *Emergence of the New South*, 310–12; Milligan, "Contradictions of Public Service," 128; Woods, *Development Arrested*; S. Matthews, *Capturing the South*.

78. Odum quoted in Locke, *Decade of Negro Self-Expression*, 4.

79. Staub, *Voices of Persuasion*, 79; Hemenway, *Zora Neale Hurston*, 89.

80. Hurston, *Mules and Men*, 2–3; S. Matthews, *Capturing the South*, 59.

81. Green, *Words and Ways*, 46; Staub, *Voices of Persuasion*, 79; Reed, *Surveying the South*, 3; S. Matthews, *Capturing the South*, 62nn84–85.

82. Brazil, *Howard W. Odum*, 488; Johnson and Johnson, *Research in Service to Society*, 23, 123; S. Matthews, *Capturing the South*, 45n58.

83. Kaplan, *Zora Neale Hurston*, 118–20, 126, 135, 151; S. Matthews, *Capturing the South*, 64n89.

84. S. Matthews, *Capturing the South*, 31; Woods, *Development Arrested*, 100–101. The interpreted influence on Odum is from studies with Hall and his reading of Wundt, *Elemente der Völkerpsychologie*.

85. S. Matthews, *Capturing the South*, 50–52.

86. Singal, *War Within*, 144.

87. D. L. Chambers to Howard W. Odum, October 26, 1931, box 18, folders 247–263, Howard Washington Odum Papers, 1908–1982 collection, Wilson Special Collections Library, University of North Carolina at Chapel Hill. Includes sales figures. See also Singal, *War Within*, 144n53.

88. See Kammen, *People of Paradox*, for similar oppositional framing.

89. Berlin, *Making of African America*, chap. 4.

90. Dorman, *Revolt of the Provinces*, 99.

91. Brooks, *America's Coming-of-Age*, 163; Brooks, "Literary Life," 219, 182–96; Dorman, *Revolt of the Provinces*, 22, 101. See also MacKaye, *New Exploration*.

92. Brooks, "On Creating"; Raymond Williams, *Raymond Williams*, chap. 3; Trachtenberg, "Mumford in the Twenties," 30.

93. Trachtenberg, "Mumford in the Twenties," 30; Cassidy, "On the Subject."

94. Cassidy, "On the Subject"; Storm, "Regionalism in History"; Storm, *Culture of Regionalism*; Moravánszky and Kegler, *Re-Scaling the Environment*.

95. See Robinson, *Black Marxism*, 291–93.

96. Giddings, *Principles of Sociology*, 329; Woods, *Development Arrested*, 97.

97. Trachtenberg, "Mumford in the Twenties," 30; T. Mitchell, *Rule of Experts*, chap. 7.

98. Soja, *Postmodern Geographies*, 165; Rodgers, *Atlantic Crossings*, 320.

99. Bramen, *Uses of Variety*, 118.

100. Bramen, *Uses of Variety*, 118.

101. Singal, *War Within*, 139.

102. Shapiro, "Place of Culture," 119; Storm, "Regionalism in History"; Storm, *Culture of Regionalism*.

103. Brinton, *American Hero-Myths*, 35; Du Bois, "Conservation of Races," 8; Shapiro, "Place of Culture," 121n8; Miller, "Race-ism and the City," 98n12.

104. Shapiro, "Place of Culture," 119–25; Brinton, "Races and Peoples," *American Race, Religions of Primitive Peoples*.

105. Robert Frost, "The Gift Outright," lines 1–3, in Lathem, *Poetry of Robert Frost*. See also Kammen, *People of Paradox*, 287–88.

106. Shapiro, "Place of Culture," 119–25.

107. Stanton, *Leopard's Spots*; Shapiro, "Place of Culture"; Stocking, "Persistence of Polygenist Thought in Post-Darwinian Anthropology," in *Race, Culture, and Evolution*, 44–68; Shapiro, "Place of Culture," 122n11. Shapiro uses "*locus in quem*."

108. Turner, "Significance of the Frontier," 197–200.

109. Shapiro, "Place of Culture," 127–28.

110. Turner, *Frontier in American History*, 4.

111. Shapiro, "Place of Culture," 129.

112. Botkin, *Folk-Say*, 15; Dorman, *Revolt of the Provinces*, 83.

113. Dorman, *Revolt of the Provinces*, 84.

114. Leopold, "Wilderness"; MacKaye, *New Exploration*, 202–3.

115. Dorman, *Revolt of the Provinces*, 84.

116. Dorman, *Revolt of the Provinces*, 84.

117. Mumford, *Golden Day*, 20; Mumford, introduction to MacKaye, *New Exploration*, xv.

118. H. Odum, *American Epoch*, 19; H. Odum, *Southern Regions*, 227. Singal discusses Ulrich B. Philips's hesitancy to use the word "frontier" because of its crude connotations. See Singal, *War Within*, 140.

119. H. Odum, *Understanding Society*, 291, chap. 15.

120. Vance, "Concept of the Region"; Vance, *Human Geography*.

121. Vance, "Concept of the Region," 213–14; Brunhes et al., *Human Geography*, 36–41, 48–52; Le Play quoted in Sorokin, *Contemporary Sociological Theories*, 66–73.

122. Vance, *Human Geography*, 69; Dorman, *Revolt of the Provinces*, 87.

123. Kirby, "Bioregionalism: Landscape and Culture," 19–43.

124. Vance, "Is Agrarianism for Farmers?," in Reed and Singal, *Regionalism and the South*, 70; Dorman, *Revolt of the Provinces*, 184.

125. King, *Southern Renaissance*, 44.

126. U. Phillips, *Life and Labor*; Aiken, *Cotton Plantation*; W. Taylor, *Cavalier and Yankee*, 301–2; Singal, "Ulrich B. Phillips." The "civilizing" plantation theme is best personified in the Thomas Sutpen character arc in William Faulkner's *Absalom, Absalom!* Sutpen drives slave labor and a European architect to essentially pull his plantation out of a swamp.

127. Spillman, "Agricultural Ladder"; H. Odum, *Southern Regions*, 23, 55; Dorman, *Revolt of the Provinces*, 183; Tullos, "Geography and Justice"; Morris, *Scholar Denied*, 8–9.

128. Vance, *Regional Reconstruction*, 3; U. Phillips, *Life and Labor*.

129. Twelve Southerners, *I'll Take My Stand*; Woods, *Development Arrested*, 132–36.

130. H. Odum, *American Epoch*, 34–38; Singal, *War Within*, 138.

131. H. Odum, *American Epoch*, 342; Singal, *War Within*, 139.

132. Vance, "Concept of the Region"; Vance, *Human Geography*.

133. Vance, *Human Geography*, 61.

134. Vance, *Human Geography*, chap. 4, 72. Vance cites Olmsted, *Journey through Texas*, 62.

135. Raper, *Tragedy of Lynching*, i, 166–71, 193–96, 439–40; Singal, *War Within*, 333.

136. Singal, *War Within*, 335–36; Raper and Reid, *Sharecroppers All*, v; King, *Southern Renaissance*, 49.

137. Raper and Reid, *Sharecroppers All*, 215; Singal, *War Within*, 337.

138. Heath, *Constructive Liberalism*, chap. 10.

139. Woods, *Development Arrested*, 131.

140. Singal, *War Within*, 16.

141. Coclanis, "Southern Economy," 465.

142. Coclanis, "Southern Economy," 467–68.

143. Woods, *Development Arrested*, 132; Dorman, *Revolt of the Provinces*, xiv.

144. Tullos, "Geography and Justice," 140.

145. Berlin, *Making of African America*, chap. 4.

146. Coclanis, "Southern Economy," 482; Vance, *All These People*, 131.

147. H. Odum, *Southern Regions*, 484.

148. Quoted in Meier, *Negro Thought*, 274; Bramen, *Uses of Variety*, 16.

149. Schlesinger, *Rise of the City*; Vance and Demerath, *Urban South*; Goldfield, *Region, Race, and Cities*.

150. Bramen, *Uses of Variety*, 116, discussing the work of Horace Kallen (*Culture and Democracy*) and W. E. B. Du Bois.

151. Bramen, *Uses of Variety*, 119.

152. Shapiro, "Place of Culture"; Miller, "Race-ism and the City"; Dorman, *Revolt of the Provinces*, xiii.

153. Bramen, *Uses of Variety*, 119.

154. Du Bois, *Souls of Black Folk*, chap. 1.

155. Morris, *Scholar Denied*, chap. 2.

156. Greg Johnson, "The Times and Life of W. E. B. Du Bois at Penn," PennToday, University of Pennsylvania, February 22, 2019, https://penntoday.upenn.edu/news/times-and-life-web-du-bois-penn.

157. Morris, *Scholar Denied*, 47–49.

158. Morris, *Scholar Denied*, 47.

159. Miller, "Race-ism and the City"; Du Bois, *Philadelphia Negro*.

160. Du Bois, "Negroes of Farmville"; Morris, *Scholar Denied*, 49n127, 67.

161. Miller, "Race-ism and the City," 98.

162. Morris, *Scholar Denied*, 49.
163. Hunter, "Bridge," 14.
164. Bramen, *Uses of Variety*, 149, 151.
165. Green and Driver, "W. E. B. Du Bois," 320.
166. Du Bois, *Souls of Black Folk*, 57.
167. E. Ross, "Sectionalism and Its Avoidance," 484–87.
168. Egerton, *Americanization of Dixie*; Payne, "Whole United States."
169. W. E. B. Du Bois to Howard W. Odum, June 23, 1942, box 29, folders 513–530, Howard Washington Odum Papers, 1908–1982 collection, Wilson Special Collections Library, University of North Carolina at Chapel Hill.
170. MacKaye, "Appalachian Trail"; Mumford, introduction to MacKaye, *New Exploration*, xiv–xv.
171. J. Thomas, "Holding the Middle Ground," 39.
172. J. Thomas, "Holding the Middle Ground," 41.
173. J. Thomas, "Holding the Middle Ground," 42.
174. MacKaye, *New Exploration*, 195; J. Thomas, "Holding the Middle Ground," 42–43.
175. Benton MacKaye to Lewis Mumford, December 3, 1926, MacKaye Papers, Baker-Berry Library, Dartmouth College, Hanover, NH; MacKaye, *New Exploration*, 195. See J. Thomas, "Holding the Middle Ground," 42–43nn8–9.
176. MacKaye, *New Exploration*, 200.
177. MacKaye, *New Exploration*, 198.
178. MacKaye, *New Exploration*, 200.
179. Spann, *Designing Modern America*, 40.
180. H. Odum, "Approach to Diagnosis," 10.
181. H. Odum, "Approach to Diagnosis," 11.
182. Milligan, "Contradictions of Public Service," 323.
183. H. Odum, "Approach to Diagnosis," 29.
184. H. Odum, "Approach to Diagnosis," 29.
185. H. Odum, "Approach to Diagnosis," 16.
186. H. Odum, "Approach to Diagnosis," 37.
187. Tullos, *Habits of Industry*, 298.
188. James Baldwin, "Letter from a Region in My Mind," *New Yorker*, November 17, 1962, www.newyorker.com/magazine/1962/11/17/letter-from-a-region-in-my-mind.
189. Vance and Demerath, *Urban South*, viii; Vance, "Regional Concept as a Tool."
190. Vance and Demerath, *Urban South*, vii.
191. Vance and Demerath, *Urban South*, ix.
192. Reed and Singal, introduction to *Regionalism and the South*, xv–xx.
193. Key, *Southern Politics*, 673; Cobb, "Urbanization and the Changing South"; Lassiter and Kruse, "Bulldozer Revolution," 691. Goldfield, *Region, Race, and Cities*, 38 quotes Key as saying "urbanization contained the seeds of political revolution in the South."
194. H. Odum, "Approach to Diagnosis," 70.
195. Nicholls, "Southern Tradition," 189.

196. Bramen, *Uses of Variety*, 116.

197. Bramen, *Uses of Variety*, 116. She refers to William James's concept of "each-form" in James, *Pluralistic Universe*.

198. Dorman, *Revolt of the Provinces*, 9.

199. Dorman, *Revolt of the Provinces*, 10, 9.

200. Bramen, *Uses of Variety*, chap. 3.

201. Pells, *Radical Visions*, 33.

202. Davidson, *Attack on Leviathan*, 12–20; Dorman, *Revolt of the Provinces*, 17.

203. Berman, *All That Is Solid*, 111.

204. Lippman, *Preface to Morals*, 19–20; Dorman, *Revolt of the Provinces*, 24.

205. Berman, *All That Is Solid*, 125.

206. Milligan, "Contradictions of Public Service," 131–38.

207. O'Brien, *Idea of the American South*, 18.

CHAPTER 5

1. O'Brien, *Idea of the American South*, 63–69.

2. O'Brien, *Idea of the American South*, 80.

3. O'Brien, *Idea of the American South*, 80.

4. E. Wright, "W. E. B. Du Bois," 462.

5. E. Wright, "W. E. B. Du Bois," 462.

6. Howard W. Odum to Ellsworth Faris, July 27, 1942, box 5, folder 518, Howard Washington Odum Papers, 1908–1982 collection, Wilson Special Collections Library, University of North Carolina at Chapel Hill (hereafter Odum Papers); O'Brien, *Idea of the American South*, 85.

7. F. Stuart Chapin to Howard W. Odum, June 18, 1942, box 29, folders 513–530, Odum Papers.

8. Read Bain to Howard W. Odum, June 15, 1942, box 24, folder 518. Odum Papers. Emphasis in the original.

9. Tullos, "Politics of Regional Development," 115.

10. W. E. B. Du Bois to Howard W. Odum, June 25, 1942, boxes 29–30, folders 513–530, Odum Papers; Ogburn, *Social Change*; E. Wright, "W. E. B. Du Bois," 462.

11. Maurice Davie to Howard W. Odum, June 24, 1942, box 24, folder 519, and C. Arnold Anderson to Howard W. Odum, August 3, 1942, box 29, folder 523, Odum Papers; O'Brien, *Idea of the American South*, 86n42.

12. Rupert B. Vance, memorandum, "Manuscript on *American Regionalism*," January 21, 1938, box 25, folders 425–450, Odum Papers; Singal, *War Within*, 315.

13. Friedmann and Weaver, *Territory and Function*; Weaver, *Regional Development*; Fishman, "Metropolitan Tradition."

14. Jensen, *Regionalism in America*, xii. Jensen's book was published two years after the conference with a foreword written by Felix Frankfurter, the Supreme Court justice nominated by Roosevelt. See Hirsch, *Enigma of Felix Frankfurter*. Conference papers were published in the book.

15. Friedmann and Weaver, *Territory and Function*; Weaver, *Regional Development*; Welter, *Biopolis*.

16. Mood, "Origin, Evolution, and Application"; Carstensen, "Development and Application."

17. O'Brien, *Idea of the American South*, 40. The University of Wisconsin state model inspired Odum, as well as Eugene Branson's work at the University of Georgia. See Brazil, *Howard W. Odum*; and Ward and Radomski, *Proud Traditions and Future Challenges*.

18. Vance, "Sociological Implications."

19. Wirth, "Limitations of Regionalism"; H. Odum, *Promise of Regionalism*; O'Brien, *Idea of the American South*, 70–93.

20. Friedmann, "Concept," 5. Friedmann refers to Southern regionalists as "the Southern School of regionalists."

21. Vance, "Regional Concept as a Tool," 124. See Parsons, *Essays in Sociological Theory*, chaps. 1 and 2.

22. Vance "Regional Concept as a Tool," 124–25.

23. Vance "Regional Concept as a Tool," 125.

24. Vance "Regional Concept as a Tool," 125.

25. H. Odum, "From Community Studies to Regionalism," 257.

26. Vance "Regional Concept as a Tool," 119–26; H. Odum, *Promise of Regionalism*.

27. Odum and Moore, *American Regionalism*, 15–16.

28. Odum and Moore, *American Regionalism*, 17. See O'Brien, *Idea of the American South*, 83–84, for discussion of gestalt.

29. Vance, "Implications of the Concepts," 85.

30. Lewis Mumford to Howard W. Odum, December 18, 1937, and March 3, 1938, boxes 25–26, folders 425–450, Odum Papers. See also Milligan, "Contradictions of Public Service," 278.

31. Wirth, "Limitations of Regionalism," 392.

32. Tugwell, "Sources"; Pells, *Radical Visions*, 23–27; D. Ross, *Origins*, 311–13, 347, 367, 386–88; Milligan, "Contradictions of Public Service," 200n78; Rodgers, *Atlantic Crossings*.

33. Park and Burgess, *City*; F. Matthews, *Quest for an American Sociology*; Fairfield, "Alienation of Social Control."

34. Milligan, "Contradictions of Public Service," 200.

35. Tönnies, *Community and Society*.

36. Vance, *Regional Reconstruction*; Kendrick, "Colonial Status"; Tindall, *Emergence of the New South*, chap. 13.

37. Vance, *Human Geography*, 467–68; Woodward, *Origins of the New South*, 291–320; Aiken, *Cotton Plantation*.

38. Vance, *Regional Reconstruction*, 13–14.

39. H. Odum, *Southern Regions*, 353, Tindall, *Emergence of the New South*, 594.

40. Cobb, *Selling of the South*; Weaver, *Regional Development*; Soja, *Postmodern Geographies*; Brenner, *New State Spaces*.

41. H. Odum, "Case for Regional-National"; Tugwell, "Sources."

42. Brazil, *Howard W. Odum*; Milligan, "Contradictions of Public Service."

43. O'Brien, *Idea of the American South*, 46.

44. H. Odum, *Folk, Region, and Society*, xii; Vance quoted in H. Odum, *Folk, Region, and Society*, 110.

45. Johnson and Johnson, *Research in Service to Society*.

46. Tullos, *Habits of Industry*, 302; Tindall, *Emergence of the New South*.

47. Friedmann and Bloch, "American Exceptionalism," 577. See discussion comparing US Southern poverty with that in rural Mexico in Olsson, *Agrarian Crossings*.

48. O'Brien, *Idea of the American South*, 40; Challen, *Sociological Analysis of Southern Regionalism*, 19.

49. Tullos, "Politics of Regional Development," 117.

50. Tullos, "Politics of Regional Development," 117n30. Quoted from a letter from Mumford to Tullos, February 17, 1977.

51. Odum and Jocher, *Introduction to Social Research*, 247.

52. Scott and Bromley, *Envisioning Sociology*.

53. Tullos, "Politics of Regional Development."

54. Sarkis, "Le Corbusier's 'Geo-Architecture.'" Hashim Sarkis makes the point that Le Corbusier's concept of "geo-architecture" addressed territorial planning and aesthetics at the regional scale.

55. H. Odum, "Folk and Regional Conflict."

56. H. Odum, "Case for Regional-National," 15. Most of Odum's writings on region emphatically stress that region "serves nation first."

57. Vance, *Human Geography*, 19.

58. Milligan, "Contradictions of Public Service," 268.

59. Vance, "Implications of the Concepts," 85; Vance, "Concept of the Region," 208–16; Milligan, "Contradictions of Public Service."

60. Vance, "Concept of the Region," 208.

61. Vance, "Concept of the Region," 209.

62. Vance, "Concept of the Region," 211–12.

63. Paul Vidal de la Blanche quoted in Mukerjee, *Regional Sociology*, 237; Vance, "Concept of the Region," 213n21.

64. Vance, "Concept of the Region," 213n19. For Odum's *Southern Regions*, institute researchers drew widely from these kinds of sources to generate the quantitative data.

65. Le Play quoted in Sorokin, *Contemporary Sociological Theories*, 63–98; Vance, "Concept of the Region," 213n23.

66. Brunhes et al., *Human Geography*, 36–41, 48–52; Vance, "Concept of the Region," 213–14.

67. Vance, "Concept of the Region," 214.

68. Tullos, "Politics of Regional Development," 115–20.

69. Vance, "Concept of the Region," 217–18.

70. Vance, "Concept of the Region," 217.

71. Robert W. Buere quoted in Vance, "Concept of the Region," 217; Brenner, *New State Spaces*, 119; Cater, *Regenerating Dixie*.

72. Vance, "Concept of the Region," 217.

73. Vance, "Concept of the Region," 218.

74. Vance, *Human Geography*, 484.

75. Vance, *Human Geography*, 485.
76. Vance, *Human Geography*, 486.
77. Vance, *Human Geography*, 489.
78. Vance, *Human Geography*, 489.
79. Vance, *Human Geography*, 489–90.
80. Vance, *Human Geography*, 491.
81. Vance, *Human Geography*, 491.
82. Vance, *Human Geography*, 491.
83. Vance, *Human Geography*, 491.
84. Vance, *Human Geography*, 491.
85. Vance, *Human Geography*, 508.
86. Vance, *Human Geography*, 509.
87. Kropotkin, *Fields, Factories, and Workshops*; Weaver, *Regional Development*, 42; P. Hall, *Cities of Tomorrow*, chap. 5; Reclus, *Anarchy, Geography, Modernity*.
88. Vance, *Human Geography*, 509.
89. Vance, *Human Geography*, 509–10.
90. Vance, *Human Geography*, 511.
91. Wirth, "Limitations of Regionalism," 393.
92. Vance, *Human Geography*, 5–6.
93. Tindall, "Significance of Howard W. Odum," 293.
94. Tindall, "Significance of Howard W. Odum," 293.
95. Tindall, "Significance of Howard W. Odum," 298.
96. Dorman, *Revolt of the Provinces*, 51.
97. Vance and Jocher, "Howard W. Odum," 207; Lebrun, "Near Encyclopedia."
98. Tindall, "Significance of Howard W. Odum," 298.
99. Simpson quoted in H. Odum, *Folk, Region, and Society*, 219.
100. H. Odum, "Folk and Regional Conflict."
101. H. Odum, *Folk, Region, and Society*, 247n27.
102. Milligan, "Contradictions of Public Service," 243.
103. Odum and Jocher, *Introduction to Social Research*, 244–45; P. Hall, *Cities of Tomorrow*, chap. 2; Peterson, *Birth of City Planning*, chap. 2.
104. Odum and Jocher, *Introduction to Social Research*, 245.
105. Odum and Jocher, *Introduction to Social Research*, 245; Giddings, *Scientific Study*, 183; Jordan, *Machine-Age Ideology*, 84–90.
106. Odum and Jocher, *Introduction to Social Research*, 250; Giddings, *Scientific Study*, 187.
107. Odum and Jocher, *Introduction to Social Research*, 255.
108. Odum and Jocher, *Introduction to Social Research*, 255.
109. Odum and Jocher, *Introduction to Social Research*, 409; Milligan, "Contradictions of Public Service," 250–52.
110. Odum and Jocher, *Introduction to Social Research*, 409.
111. Odum and Jocher, *Introduction to Social Research*, 411.
112. Milligan, "Contradictions of Public Service," 304–10.
113. H. Odum, "Folk and Regional Conflict"; H. Odum, *Southern Regions*, 87–99.
114. H. Odum, *Folk, Region, and Society*, 250.
115. H. Odum, *Folk, Region, and Society*, 242.

116. H. Odum, *Folk, Region, and Society*, 242n16. Odum cites Robert E. Park's discussion of Sumner's concepts in Rice, *Methods in Social Science*, 157–58.

117. H. Odum, *Folk, Region, and Society*, 244–45n22; Giddings, "Intensive Sociology," 10–11.

118. Milligan, "Contradictions of Public Service," 246n24; H. Odum, "Folk and Regional Conflict"; H. Odum, "Notes on the Study," 164–70.

119. Wissler, "Culture-Area Concept," 882; Odum and Moore, *American Regionalism*, 1–34n10.

120. H. Odum, *Folk, Region, and Society*, 254.

121. H. Odum, "Folk and Regional Conflict," 15–17.

122. Odum and Jocher, *In Search of Regional Balance of America*, 15–16; Vance, "Howard Odum's Technicways"; Kantor, "Howard W. Odum."

123. Tullos, "Politics of Regional Development." Beardsley Ruml of the Rockefeller Foundation called Odum the "master manipulator" in securing grants for the institute. See Milligan, "Contradictions of Public Service," 3; and S. Matthews, *Capturing the South*, chap. 1.

124. Turner, *Significance of Sections*; Odum and Moore, *American Regionalism*, 16, 35–51; Kantor, "Howard W. Odum," 283–87.

125. Tullos, *Habits of Industry*, 294; Turner, *Significance of Sections*.

126. King, *Southern Renaissance*.

127. On race, Ross observed, "[As Black Americans] drift north, more northerners are able to get the southern white man's point of view on the race question." E. Ross, "Sectionalism and Its Avoidance," 484.

128. H. Odum, "Regionalism vs. Sectionalism."

129. Odum and Moore, *American Regionalism*, 35.

130. Odum and Moore, *American Regionalism*, 14.

131. O'Brien, *Idea of the American South*, 55–69; Kendrick, "Southern Confederation of Learning"; Donald Davidson to John Donald Wade, March 3, 1934, box 21, folder 342, Odum Papers.

132. O'Brien, *Idea of the American South*, 60.

133. H. Odum, *Southern Regions*, chap. 10.

134. O'Brien, *Idea of the American South*, 60.

135. O'Brien, *Idea of the American South*, 61.

136. O'Brien, *Idea of the American South*, 61n28, O'Brien interview by Rupert B. Vance; Gerald Johnson to Howard W. Odum, May 10, 1938, box 20, folder 438, Odum Papers; H. Odum, *Southern Regions*, 9; Johnson and Johnson, *Research in Service to Society*, 178–80.

137. O'Brien, *Idea of the American South*, 85–93n43; Riemer, "Theoretical Aspects of Regionalism," 279.

138. Odum and Moore, *American Regionalism*, 1–3.

139. Odum and Moore, *American Regionalism*, 14.

140. Odum and Moore, *American Regionalism*, 15.

141. Odum and Moore, *American Regionalism*, 15.

142. Odum and Moore, *American Regionalism*, 15.

143. Odum and Moore, *American Regionalism*, 11; H. Moore, *What Is Regionalism?*; Johnson and Johnson, *Research in Service to Society*, 179.

144. Odum and Moore, *American Regionalism*, 1–34; Grantham, "Regional Imagination," 16–17; O'Brien, *Idea of the American South*, 83–85; Milligan, "Contradictions of Public Service," 270.

145. Vance, "Regional Concept as a Tool," 132.

146. O'Brien, *Idea of the American South*, 86.

147. O'Brien, *Idea of the American South*, 62.

148. George T. Renner to Howard W. Odum, March 13, 1942, box 24, folder 515. Odum Papers.

149. H. Odum, *Southern Regions*, 623.

150. Renner to Odum, March 13, 1942.

151. Howard W. Odum to George T. Renner, March 24, 1942, box 24, folder 515, Odum Papers.

152. Hagood, "Statistical Methods"; Vance, "Regional Concept as a Tool," 131–32.

153. Vance, "Regional Concept as a Tool," 132.

154. H. Odum, "Sociological Approach," 279; O'Brien, *Idea of the American South*, 85.

155. O'Brien, *Idea of the American South*, 63.

156. O'Brien, *Idea of the American South*, 63.

157. O'Brien, *Idea of the American South*, 67.

158. Mumford, *Culture of Cities*, 330; Dorman, *Revolt of the Provinces*, 1–18; C. Wilson, *New Regionalism*, 13–14; H. Odum, *Southern Regions*, 587; O'Brien, *Idea of the American South*, 67.

159. W. T. Couch to Virginius Dabney, March 13, 1935, University of North Carolina Press Records #40073, University Archives, Wilson Special Collections Library, University of North Carolina at Chapel Hill; Dorman, *Revolt of the Provinces*, 291n21.

160. Jordan, *Machine-Age Ideology*, 13, 142; D. Ross, *Origins*.

161. Davidson, "Where Regionalism and Sectionalism Meet," 25.

162. Davidson to Wade, March 3, 1934.

163. Davidson to Wade, March 3, 1934.

164. O'Brien, *Idea of the American South*, 59.

165. Selznick, *TVA and the Grass Roots*; Downs, *Transforming the South*.

166. Howard W. Odum to University of North Carolina president Harry Woodburn Chase, February 1926, box 6, folders 84–120, Odum Papers; Dorman, *Revolt of the Provinces*, 262.

167. H. Odum, *Southern Regions*, 579–80, 534; Dorman, *Revolt of the Provinces*, 264.

168. Milligan, "Contradictions of Public Service," 267n69; O'Brien, *Idea of the American South*, 80–89.

169. Dorman, *Revolt of the Provinces*, 262.

CHAPTER 6

1. Merriam, "National Resources Planning Board," 1075.

2. Tindall, *Emergence of the New South*, 587.

3. National Planning Board, Federal Emergency Administration of Public Works, *Final Report—1933-34*.

4. Friedmann and Weaver, *Territory and Function*, 67. See 81–82n19 for the National Resources Committee Technical Committee's list of special studies. National Resources Committee Technical Committee on Regional Planning, *Regional Factors in National Planning*, v–vi. See also Woofter, "Southern Population"; and Ellis, "T. J. Woofter, Jr."

5. Friedmann and Weaver, *Territory and Function*, 67.

6. National Resources Committee Technical Committee on Regional Planning, *Regional Factors in National Planning*, 20; Friedmann and Weaver, *Territory and Function*, 67.

7. National Resources Committee Technical Committee on Regional Planning, *Regional Factors in National Planning*, 143; Friedmann and Weaver, *Territory and Function*, 67.

8. Friedmann and Weaver, *Territory and Function*, 68.

9. Friedmann and Weaver, *Territory and Function*, 68–69.

10. Friedmann and Weaver, *Territory and Function*, 69.

11. Friedmann and Weaver, *Territory and Function*, 69.

12. P. Hall, *Cities of Tomorrow*, chap. 5; Rowe, *Making a Middle Landscape*, chaps. 1–2; Fishman, "Death and Life"; Fishman, *American Planning Tradition*; Fishman, "Century of Regionalisms."

13. Weaver, *Regional Development*, 29; Benevolo, *Origins*; P. Hall, *Cities of Tomorrow*.

14. Katharine Jocher in H. Odum, *Folk, Region, and Society*, 355–57.

15. Friedmann and Weaver, *Territory and Function*; Weaver, *Regional Development*; Soja, *Postmodern Geographies*; Rowe, *Making a Middle Landscape*; Fishman, *American Planning Tradition*; Wakeman, *Practicing Utopia*.

16. Kantor, "Howard W. Odum," 287.

17. H. Odum, "Folk Sociology as a Subject Field," 208; Lorwin, "Social Aspects."

18. H. Odum, "Folk Sociology as a Subject Field"; see H. Odum, *Folk, Region, and Society*, 324.

19. Bauer, "Economic Progress and Living Conditions," 303–5; Friedmann, "Concept."

20. Echoing some of the observations about the *Recent Social Trends* report, *Plan for Planning* was also the name for the final report of the National Resource Planning Board. See Jordan, *Machine-Age Ideology*, 235–43. For "Plan for Planning" coined by Charles E. Merriam, see Jones, "Plan for Planning."

21. Kantor, "Howard W. Odum," 283.

22. Later published in *Social Forces*. See H. Odum, "Case for Regional-National."

23. H. Odum, "Case for Regional-National," 6.

24. H. Odum, "Case for Regional-National," 6.

25. H. Odum, "Case for Regional-National," 7.

26. H. Odum, "Case for Regional-National," 8.

27. H. Odum, "Case for Regional-National," 9.

28. H. Odum, "Case for Regional-National," 9.

29. Woofter, "Subregions of the Southeast"; H. Odum, *Southern Regions*, chap. 10. See also Vance, "What of Submarginal Areas?"

30. H. Odum, "Case for Regional-National," 19.

31. H. Odum, "Case for Regional-National," 18.

32. H. Odum, "Case for Regional-National," 7. See also Simpson, "Howard W. Odum," 105.

33. Katharine Jocher in H. Odum, *Folk, Region, and Society*, 356.

34. King, *Southern Renaissance*, 47–48; Tindall, *Emergence of the New South*, 594.

35. King, *Southern Renaissance*, 47.

36. King, *Southern Renaissance*, 47.

37. Milligan, "Contradictions of Public Service," 215.

38. Tindall, *Emergence of the New South*, 584; Odum and Moore, *American Regionalism*, viii; King, *Southern Renaissance*, 47.

39. Dorman, *Revolt of the Provinces*, 133–34; MacKaye, *New Exploration*.

40. H. Odum, *Man's Quest*, 503.

41. H. Odum, *Man's Quest*, 503.

42. H. Odum, *Man's Quest*, 503; Dealey et al., "Lester Frank Ward."

43. Krieger, *City on a Hill*.

44. Milligan, "Contradictions of Public Service," 76–77.

45. H. Odum, *Man's Quest*, 504.

46. H. Odum, *Man's Quest*, 503.

47. H. Odum, *Man's Quest*, 503–20; H. Odum, *American Sociology*, 81–82; Brazil, *Howard W. Odum*, 556–58; Milligan, "Contradictions of Public Service," 76–77.

48. H. Odum, *Man's Quest*, 504.

49. H. Odum, *Man's Quest*, 515.

50. H. Odum, *Man's Quest*, 515.

51. H. Odum, *Man's Quest*, 516.

52. H. Odum, *Man's Quest*, 519; Mukerjee, *Regional Sociology*; H. Odum, "Sociology in the Contemporary World," 340–41; Milligan, "Contradictions of Public Service," 159. See Neilson, *Roads to Knowledge*, for Radhakamal Mukerjee's influence.

53. H. Odum, *Man's Quest*, 519.

54. E. Burgess, "Social Planning and the Mores."

55. E. Burgess, "Social Planning and the Mores," 1.

56. E. Burgess, "Social Planning and the Mores," 1.

57. E. Burgess, "Social Planning and the Mores," 1.

58. E. Burgess, "Social Planning and the Mores," 2.

59. Pareto, *Sociological Writings*; E. Burgess, "Social Planning and the Mores," 2–3.

60. George L. Simpson in H. Odum, *Folk, Region, and Society*, 220.

61. Sumner, *Folkways*, iv; E. Burgess, "Social Planning and the Mores," 2.

62. Sumner, *Folkways*, iii; E. Burgess, "Social Planning and the Mores," 3.

63. Sumner, *Folkways*, iii–iv; E. Burgess, "Social Planning and the Mores," 3.

64. Sumner, *Folkways*, iii–iv; Odum and Jocher, *Introduction to Social Research*, 240–60; E. Burgess, "Social Planning and the Mores," 4.

65. E. Burgess, "Social Planning and the Mores," 4.
66. E. Burgess, "Social Planning and the Mores," 10.
67. E. Burgess, "Social Planning and the Mores," 10.
68. E. Burgess, "Social Planning and the Mores," 11.
69. Harold L. Ickes quoting Soule, *Planned Society*; E. Burgess, "Social Planning and the Mores," 12; Jordan, *Machine-Age Ideology*, 210.
70. E. Burgess, "Social Planning and the Mores," 12.
71. E. Burgess, "Social Planning and the Mores," 12.
72. E. Burgess, "Social Planning and the Mores," 18.
73. Pells, *Radical Visions*, 33.
74. E. Burgess, "Social Planning and the Mores," 16; Zinn, *New Deal Thought*.
75. Rosalind Williams, "Lewis Mumford," 56n61; Geddes, "Fourth Talk: The Valley in the Town," in *Talks from the Outlook Tower*, 346.
76. Rosalind Williams, "Lewis Mumford," 56n61; Geddes, "Fourth Talk: The Valley in the Town," in *Talks from the Outlook Tower*, 346.
77. Geddes, *Cities in Evolution*, 62–64; Rosalind Williams, "Lewis Mumford," 57.
78. Mumford, *Culture of Cities*, 326.
79. H. Odum, "On a Closer Cooperation between the Physical Sciences and the Social Sciences," *Harvard Alumni Bulletin*, July 7, 1939, 1124-28. See H. Odum, *Folk, Region, and Society*, 369–70.
80. H. Odum, *Understanding Society*, chap. 12. See H. Odum, *Folk, Region, and Society*, 260.
81. H. Odum, "On a Closer Cooperation between the Physical Sciences and the Social Sciences," *Harvard Alumni Bulletin*, July 7, 1939, 1124-28. See H. Odum, *Folk, Region, and Society*, 365–71.
82. Vance, "Howard Odum's Technicways," 457; Vance, "Odum, Howard W.," in Sills, Merton, and Wallerstein, *International Encyclopedia*, 270–71.
83. H. Odum, *Southern Regions*, 428.
84. H. Odum, "Patrick Geddes' Heritage," 279.
85. H. Odum, "Patrick Geddes' Heritage," 279–81; H. Odum, "Sociology in the Contemporary World"; Eldridge, "Implications of Regionalism."
86. Vance, "Howard Odum's Technicways," 457.
87. Vance, "Howard Odum's Technicways," 458; Veblen, *Theory of the Leisure Class*.
88. Vance, "Howard Odum's Technicways," 459.
89. Vance, "Howard Odum's Technicways," 459.
90. Odum and Jocher, *In Search of Regional Balance*, 15–16; Vance, "Howard Odum's Technicways"; Kantor, "Howard W. Odum," 288.
91. Odum and Jocher, *In Search of Regional Balance*, 15–16; Vance, "Howard Odum's Technicways"; Kantor, "Howard W. Odum," 288.
92. H. Odum, "Folk Sociology as a Subject Field." See H. Odum, *Folk, Region, and Society*, 322.
93. Ogburn, *Social Change*.
94. H. Odum, "Folk Sociology as a Subject Field." See H. Odum, *Folk, Region, and Society*, 322.
95. Vance, *Human Geography*, 482.

96. Vance, *Human Geography*, 482.

97. Vance, *Human Geography*, 482.

98. Vance, *Human Geography*, 483. Vance compares regional planning with science, quoting Isaiah Bowman: "Science is like the pioneer in making things happen instead of waiting for them to happen. . . . Every scientific truth goes pioneering." Bowman, *Pioneer Fringe*, 76.

99. Vance, *Human Geography*, 483.

100. Vance, *Human Geography*, 483.

101. Vance, *Human Geography*, 483.

102. Vance, *Human Geography*, 483.

103. Vance, *Human Geography*, 483.

104. Vance, *Human Geography*, 484.

105. Vance, *Regional Reconstruction*, 2.

106. Vance, *Human Geography*, 493–96.

107. Vance, *Regional Reconstruction*, 14–21.

108. Vance, *Regional Reconstruction*, 16–17.

109. Vance, *Regional Reconstruction*, 17.

110. Vance, *Regional Reconstruction*, 17.

111. See Tugwell, "Sources"; Mertz, *New Deal Policy*; Woods, *Development Arrested*; Tyler, "Impact of the New Deal"; S. Phillips, *This Land, This Nation*; J. Gilbert, *Planning Democracy*; and Olsson, *Agrarian Crossings*, for the impact of the New Deal on Southern agricultural discussions.

112. H. Odum, "Case for Regional-National," 17–23; Vance, *Human Geography*, 493–96.

113. Reed and Singal, *Regionalism and the South*, xvii.

114. Vance, *Regional Reconstruction*, 25, 31.

115. Simpson, "Howard W. Odum," 105.

116. Simpson, "Howard W. Odum," 105.

117. Simpson, "Howard W. Odum," 105.

118. Simpson, "Howard W. Odum," 105.

119. Jocher in H. Odum, *Folk, Region, and Society*, 355.

120. Beardsley Ruml to Howard W. Odum, December 10, 1929, box 9, folder 198, Howard Washington Odum Papers, 1908–1982 collection, Wilson Special Collections Library, University of North Carolina at Chapel Hill; O'Brien, *Idea of the American South*, 44–50, 70–80.

121. O'Brien, *Idea of the American South*, 48.

122. O'Brien, *Idea of the American South*, 49–50.

123. O'Brien, *Idea of the American South*, 55–69.

124. Tindall, *Emergence of the New South*, 583–86.

125. Tindall, "Significance of Howard W. Odum," 299.

126. Myrdal, *American Dilemma*, 468–69; O'Brien, *Idea of the American South*, 70–80.

127. Howard W. Odum to Prentiss M. Terry, August 15, 1938, box 19, folder 425, Howard Washington Odum Papers, 1908–1982 collection, Wilson Special Collections Library, University of North Carolina at Chapel Hill; Tindall, *Emergence of the New South*, 586n43.

128. Howard W. Odum to Will W. Alexander, February 17, 1940, box 21, folder 473, Howard Washington Odum Papers, 1908-1982 collection, Wilson Special Collections Library, University of North Carolina at Chapel Hill; Tindall, *Emergence of the New South*, 586n43.

129. Katznelson, *Fear Itself*, 168-72.

130. Katznelson, *Fear Itself*, 169; Carlton and Coclanis, *Confronting Southern Poverty*, 32-37n58; Carlton and Coclanis, "Another 'Great Migration'"; Carter, "Editor Says"; Ransom and Sutch, *One Kind of Freedom*, 176-86.

131. Katznelson, *Fear Itself*, 172.

132. Katznelson, *Fear Itself*, 172.

133. Schulman, *From Cotton Belt to Sunbelt*, viii, 51; Tyler, "Impact of the New Deal," 449-50.

134. Schulman, *From Cotton Belt to Sunbelt*, 50-58; Tyler, "Impact of the New Deal," 449-50; Sosna, "More Important Than the Civil War?," 148-50.

135. Selznick, *TVA and the Grass Roots*; Storm, "Regionalism in History."

136. Storm, "Regionalism in History," 252.

137. Tindall, *Emergence of the New South*, 587-88; Lepawsky, *State Planning and Economic Development*, 8-33; Lepawsky, "Government Planning in the South"; Cobb, *Selling of the South*.

CONCLUSION

1. Dorman, *Revolt of the Provinces*, 50-53.
2. Milligan, "Contradictions of Public Service," 151-52.
3. Fishman, *Urban Utopias*, 6; Wakeman, *Practicing Utopia*.
4. Raffestin, "Space, Territory, and Territoriality," 129; Lefebvre, *Everyday Life*; Lefebvre, *Production of Space*.
5. Pells, *Radical Visions*, 3; Dorman, *Revolt of the Provinces*, 7.
6. Myrdal, *American Dilemma*, 467, 470.
7. Myrdal, *American Dilemma*, 466-67.
8. Tugwell, "Sources," 273-74; Beard, "Historical Approach to the New Deal"; J. Gilbert, *Planning Democracy*.
9. Friedmann and Weaver, *Territory and Function*, 35n15; Zinn, *New Deal Thought*, 77-103; Padilla, *Tugwell's Thoughts on Planning*.
10. Singal, *War Within*, 152.
11. Berman, *All That Is Solid*, 324.
12. Caro, *Power Broker*, 515, 519, 547, 548, 568, 614, 654, 659, 665-67, 897, 913, 916-17, 943; Ballon and Jackson, *Robert Moses and the Modern City*.
13. Berman, *All That Is Solid*, 328; see also Fishman, "Death and Life."
14. Katznelson, *Fear Itself*, 172, 186-87.
15. Scott, *Seeing Like a State*, 6; Hargrove, *Prisoners of Myth*.
16. Kunze, "Purnell Act."
17. Woods, *Development Arrested*, 21-22; Tugwell, "Sources"; Tyler, "Impact of the New Deal."
18. Woods, *Development Arrested*, 21; Du Bois, *Freedmen's Bureau*; Bentley, *History of the Freedmen's Bureau*.

19. A. Gilbert, "New Regional Geography," 217; Martin and Nonn, "La notion d'intégration régionale'"; Woods, *Development Arrested*, 26.

20. Storm, "Regionalism in History," 252.

21. Fei, *China's Gentry*; Fisher, *City and Regional Planning*; Weaver, *Regional Development*; Brenner, *New State Spaces*; Schivelbusch, *Three New Deals*; Moravánszky and Kegler, *Re-Scaling the Environment*; Olsson, *Agrarian Crossings*; Dostalík, "Organicists."

22. G. Wright, *Old South, New South*; Cobb, "Beyond Planters and Industrialists."

23. Milligan, "Contradictions of Public Service," 215; Tullos, *Habits of Industry*, 295.

24. Rodgers, "Regionalism," 13n21; Couch, "Agrarian Programme"; Nixon, *Forty Acres and Steel Mules*; Preskill, *Education in Black and White*; Tullos, *Habits of Industry*, 297–98. Rodgers notes that Odum was cited by both Donald Davidson ("Howard Odum and the Sociological Proteus") *and* Arthur Raper and Ira De Augustine Reid in *Sharecroppers All*.

25. Rodgers, "Regionalism," 13–14n22; Vance, *Human Geography*, chap. 8; Vance, "Economic Future"; Vance, "How Can the Southern Population?"; H. Odum, *Southern Regions*, chaps. 6–7; H. Odum, "Regional Quality and Balance," 283.

26. H. Odum, "Approach to Diagnosis"; Rodgers, "Regionalism," 14.

27. Scott, *Seeing Like a State*, 90n11.

28. Scott, *Seeing Like a State*, 90.

29. N. Smith, *Uneven Development*; Scott, *Seeing Like a State*, 13.

30. W. Mitchell, *Backward Art of Spending*, 49; Jordan, *Machine-Age Ideology*, 182.

31. Friedmann and Weaver, *Territory and Function*, 1–7.

32. Friedmann and Weaver, *Territory and Function*, 5.

33. Friedmann and Weaver, *Territory and Function*, 5.

34. Irish, "Proposed Roads to the New South," 21.

35. H. Odum, *Southern Regions*, 582; Irish, "Proposed Roads to the New South," 21.

36. Irish, "Proposed Roads to the New South," 21.

37. Davidson, *Attack on Leviathan*, 64; Tullos, "Politics of Regional Development," 114–15.

38. Davidson, *Attack on Leviathan*, 64.

39. Davidson, *Attack on Leviathan*, 64.

40. H. Odum, "Regional Development"; Simpson, "Howard W. Odum," 105.

41. Purcell, "For Democracy." See also Fesler, *Area and Administration*, for a discussion of government functions and administrative areas inspired by Odum and the regionalists.

42. Milligan, "Contradictions of Public Service," 177n26; H. Odum, *Southern Regions*, 2–3, 21–22, 27, 53, 231, 237, 331–39, 371, 505.

43. H. Odum, *Southern Regions*, ix, 577; Irish, "Proposed Roads to the New South," 19.

44. H. Odum, "Case for Regional-National," 7.

45. Howard W. Odum to Ellsworth Faris, July 27, 1942, box 24, folder 522, Howard Washington Odum Papers, 1908–1982 collection, Wilson Special Collections Library, University of North Carolina at Chapel Hill.

46. H. Odum, *American Epoch*, x; Singal, *War Within*, 133–34; Reed, *Surveying the South*, 7.

47. Vance, "Regional Planning," 62.

48. Vance, "Regional Planning," 62.

49. D. Ross, *G. Stanley Hall*; O'Brien, *Idea of the American South*, 33–35.

50. Du Bois, *Black Reconstruction in America*, 718–20; Robinson, *Black Marxism*, 188; J. Burgess, *Reconstruction and the Constitution*; Dunning, *Reconstruction, Political and Economic*.

51. Robinson, *Black Marxism*, 188.

52. Payne, "Whole United States."

53. Myrdal, *American Dilemma*, 472.

54. Myrdal, *American Dilemma*, 472; Vance, *Regional Reconstruction*, 3–7, 24–25.

55. Tullos, "Politics of Regional Development," 115; Hagood, *Mothers of the South*; Raper, *Preface to Peasantry*; Raper and Reid, *Sharecroppers All*.

56. Tullos, "Politics of Regional Development," 115, 113n6. For Mumford's increasing criticism of the political use of technology, see Mumford, *Myth of the Machine*.

57. Tullos, "Politics of Regional Development," 115–16; Myrdal, *American Dilemma*, 472.

58. Friedmann and Weaver, *Territory and Function*, 41.

59. Friedmann, "Planning Region," 3.

60. Friedmann and Weaver, *Territory and Function*, 124.

61. Friedmann and Weaver, *Territory and Function*, 124–25; Perloff et al., *Regions, Resources, and Economic Growth*; Duncan et al., *Metropolis and Region*; Siebert, *Regional Economic Growth*; Richardson, *Regional Growth Theory*; Richardson, *Regional and Urban Economics*.

62. Johnson and Johnson, *Research in Service to Society*, 293; Huggins, "Evolution of City and Regional Planning"; Silver, "Urban Planning"; Kaiser et al., "ACSP Distinguished Educator."

63. John A. Parker extended the honorary invitation to Odum on Clarence Stein's behalf. John A. Parker to Howard W. Odum, March 30, 1950, box 91, folder 3164, Howard Washington Odum Papers, 1908–1982 collection, Wilson Special Collections Library, University of North Carolina at Chapel Hill. See also Mumford, "Regional Planning Association."

64. Perloff, *Education for Planning*; Perloff et al., *Regions, Resources, and Economic Growth*; Friedmann and Weaver, *Territory and Function*; McMath, *Engineering the New South*.

65. McLaughlin and Robock, *Why Industry Moves South*; Cobb, *Selling of the South*.

66. Mandel, *Capitalism and Regional Disparities*; N. Smith, *Uneven Development*; Soja, "Regions in Context."

67. Friedmann and Weaver, *Territory and Function*, 172.

68. Perloff and Wingo, *Natural Resource Endowment*; Friedmann and Weaver, *Territory and Function*, 187n4; Downs, *Transforming the South*.

69. Storm, "Regionalism in History," 252; Friedmann and Alonso, *Regional Development and Planning*, 3–5; Robinson, *Black Marxism*; Brenner, *New State Spaces*.

70. Escobar, *Encountering Development*.

71. McNeil, *Mythistory and Other Essays*; Márquez, "Faulkner in Latin America"; Olsson, *Agrarian Crossings*.

72. Friedmann, *Regional Development Policy*; Friedmann, "Planning as Innovation"; Friedmann and Stöhr, "Uses of Regional Science"; Friedmann, "General Theory of Polarized Development"; Sanyal, "Planners' Planner." Friedmann also made regional planning development policy for Bangladesh; see Friedmann and Douglass, "Agropolitan Development." Gorelik, *Ciudad Latinoamericana*.

73. Garreau, *Nine Nations*; C. Ross, *Megaregions: Planning for Global Competitiveness*; Harrison and Hoyler, *Megaregions*; Ibañez et al., *Third Coast Atlas*; Barnett, *Designing the Megaregion*; Yaro et al., *Megaregions and America's Future*.

74. Soja, *Postmodern Geographies*, 150–51.

BIBLIOGRAPHY

Adas, Michael, and Martha A. Chan. *Machines as the Measure of Men: Science, Technology, and Ideologies of Western Dominance*. 2nd ed. Ithaca, NY: Cornell University Press, 2015.
Aiken, Charles S. *The Cotton Plantation South since the Civil War*. Baltimore: Johns Hopkins University Press, 1998.
———. *William Faulkner and the Southern Landscape*. Athens: University of Georgia Press, 2009.
Allaback, Sarah. *Marjorie Sewell Cautley: Landscape Architect for the Motor Age*. Athens, GA: Library of American Landscape History, 2022.
Amin, Samir. *Accumulation on a World Scale: A Critique of the Theory of Underdevelopment*. Translated by Brian Pearce. New York: Monthly Review Press, 1974.
Angell, Robert Cooley. "*Recent Social Trends in the United States*: Report of the President's Research Committee; I. Summary and Comment." *Michigan Law Review* 31, no. 5 (March 1933): 638–58. https://doi.org/10.2307/1281547.
Arrighi, Giovanni. *The Long Twentieth Century: Money, Power, and the Origins of Our Times*. London: Verso, 1994.
Bailey, Thomas Pearce. *Race Orthodoxy in the South, and Other Aspects of the Negro Question*. New York: Neale, 1914.
Baldwin, James. "Faulkner and Desegregation." *Partisan Review* 23, no. 4 (Fall 1956): 568–73.
Ballon, Hilary, and Kenneth T. Jackson. *Robert Moses and the Modern City: The Transformation of New York*. New York: W. W. Norton, 2007.
Bannister, Robert C. *Social Darwinism: Science and Myth in Anglo-American Social Thought*. Philadelphia: Temple University Press, 1979.
———. *Sociology and Scientism: The American Quest for Objectivity, 1880–1940*. Chapel Hill: University of North Carolina Press, 1987.
Barnes, Harry Elmer. "Recent Books Bearing on the History of Thought and Culture." *Social Forces* 4, no. 2 (1925): 418–22. https://doi.org/10.1093/sf/4.2.418.
———. "Two Representative Contributions of Sociology to Political Theory: The Doctrines of William Graham Sumner and Lester Frank Ward." *American Journal of Sociology* 25, no. 1 (1919): 1–23.
Barnett, Jonathan. *Designing the Megaregion: Meeting Urban Challenges at a New Scale*. Washington, DC: Island, 2020.
Batty, Michael, and Stephen Marshall. "Thinking Organic, Acting Civic: The Paradox of Planning for Cities in Evolution." *Landscape and Urban Planning* 166 (2017): 4–14. https://doi.org/10.1016/j.landurbplan.2016.06.002.
Bauer, Catherine. "Economic Progress and Living Conditions: An Argument for Regional Planning and Urban Dispersal in Developing Countries with Limited Resources." *Town Planning Review* 24, no. 4 (1954): 296–311.

Beard, Charles A. "The Historical Approach to the New Deal." *American Political Science Review* 28, no. 1 (1934): 11–15.

———. "The President's Committee's Recent Social Trends in the United States." Review of *Recent Social Trends in the United States: Report of the President's Research Committee on Social Trends*, by Wesley Clair Mitchell. *Yale Review*, no. 22 (1933): 595–96.

Bellin, Eric. "A Certain Brand of Humanism: Lewis Mumford, Matthew Nowicki, and the Architectural Pedagogy of North Carolina State College, 1948–1952." In *Change, Architecture, Education, Practices: Proceedings of the Association of Collegiate Schools of Architecture Conference, Barcelona*, edited by Martha Thorne and Xavier Costa, 331–37. Washington, DC: Association of Collegiate Schools of Architecture, 2012.

Benevolo, Leonardo. *The Origins of Modern Town Planning*. Cambridge, MA: MIT Press, 1971.

Benjamin, Ludy T. *A Brief History of Modern Psychology*. 2nd ed. Hoboken, NJ: Wiley, 2014.

Bentley, George R. *A History of the Freedmen's Bureau*. Philadelphia: University of Pennsylvania Press, 1955.

Berle, A. A. "The Trend of the Turn." Review of *Recent Social Trends in the United States: Report of the President's Research Committee on Social Trends*, by Wesley Clair Mitchell. *Saturday Review of Literature* 9 (1933): 533–35.

Berlin, Ira. *The Making of African America: The Four Great Migrations*. New York: Viking, 2010.

Berman, Marshall. *All That Is Solid Melts into Air: The Experience of Modernity*. New York: Simon and Schuster, 1982.

Bernard, Luther Lee. "Psychoanalysis: Three Wise Men Travel West from Vienna." *Social Forces* 4, no. 2 (1925): 426–29. https://doi.org/10.1093/sf/4.2.426.

———. "The Transition to an Objective Standard of Social Control." *American Journal of Sociology* 16, no. 4 (1911): 519–37.

Bierstedt, R. *American Sociological Theory: A Critical History*. Cambridge, MA: Academic, 1981.

Blumer, Herbert. "Science without Concepts." *American Journal of Sociology* 36, no. 4 (1931): 515–33. https://doi.org/10.1086/215473.

Boardman, Philip. *The Worlds of Patrick Geddes: Biologist, Town Planner, Re-Educator, Peace-Warrior*. London: Routledge, 1978.

Boardman, Philip, and Lewis Mumford. *Patrick Geddes, Maker of the Future*. Chapel Hill: University of North Carolina Press, 1944.

Boisier, Sergio. *Diseño de planes regionales: Métodos y técnicas de planificación regional*. Madrid: Colegio Oficial de Ingenieros de Caminos, Canales y Puertos, Centro de Perfeccionamiento, 1976.

Boles, John B., ed. *A Companion to the American South*. Malden, MA: Blackwell, 2002.

Botar, Oliver A. I., and Isabel Wünsche, eds. *Biocentrism and Modernism*. Farnham, UK: Ashgate, 2011.

Botkin, Benjamin Albert, ed. *Folk-Say: A Regional Miscellany*. Norman: University of Oklahoma Press, 1929.

Bowman, Isaiah. *The Pioneer Fringe*. New York: American Geographical Society of New York, 1931.

Bracey, John H., Jr., August Meier, and Elliott Rudwick, eds. *The Black Sociologists: The First Half Century*. Belmont, CA: Wadsworth, 1971.

Bramen, Carrie Tirado. *The Uses of Variety: Modern Americanism and the Quest for National Distinctiveness*. Cambridge, MA: Harvard University Press, 2000.

Brazil, Wayne. *Howard W. Odum: The Building Years, 1884–1930*. New York: Garland, 1988.

———. "*Social Forces* and Sectional Self-Scrutiny." In *Perspectives on the American South: An Annual Review of Society, Politics, and Culture*, edited by Merle Black and John Shelton Reed, 2:73–104. London: Gordon and Breach Science, 1984.

Brenner, Neil. *New State Spaces: Urban Governance and the Rescaling of Statehood*. Oxford: Oxford University Press, 2004.

Brinton, Daniel Garrison. *American Hero-Myths: A Study in the Native Religions of the Western Continent*. Philadelphia: H. C. Watts, 1882. Reprint, New York: Johnson Reprint, 1970.

———. *The American Race: A Linguistic Classification and Ethnographic Description of the Native Tribes of North and South America*. Philadelphia: D. McKay, 1901.

———. "Races and Peoples: Lectures on the Science of Ethnography." *Nature* 44, no. 1128 (1891): 124. https://doi.org/10.1038/044124a0.

———. *Religions of Primitive Peoples*. New York: Negro Universities Press, 1969.

Brodhead, Richard H. *Cultures of Letters: Scenes of Reading and Writing in Nineteenth-Century America*. New York: G. P. Putnam's Sons, 1897. Reprint, Chicago: University of Chicago Press, 1993.

Brooks, Van Wyck. *America's Coming-of-Age*. New York: B. W. Huebsch, 1915. Reprint, Garden City, NY: Doubleday, 1958.

———. "The Literary Life." In *Civilization in the United States: An Inquiry by Thirty Americans*, edited by Harold E. Stearns, 179–98. New York: Harcourt Brace, 1922.

———. "On Creating a Usable Past." *Dial* 64, no. 11 (1918): 337–41.

Broschart, Kay Richards. "Research in the Service of Society: Women at the Institute for Research in Social Science." *American Sociologist* 33, no. 3 (2002): 92–106.

Bruce, Dickson D. *Black American Writing from the Nadir: The Evolution of a Literary Tradition, 1877–1915*. Baton Rouge: Louisiana State University Press, 1989.

Brundage, W. Fitzhugh, Laura F. Edwards, and Jon F. Sensbach, eds. *A New History of the American South*. Chapel Hill: University of North Carolina Press, 2023.

Bruner, Jerome Seymour. *On Knowing: Essays for the Left Hand*. Cambridge, MA: Belknap Press of Harvard University Press, 1962.

Brunhes, Jean, Isaiah Bowman, Richard Elwood Dodge, and Irville C. LeCompte. *Human Geography: An Attempt at a Positive Classification, Principles and Examples*. Chicago: Rand, McNally, 1920.

Brunner, Edmund de Schweinitz. *The Growth of a Science: A Half-Century of Rural Sociological Research in the United States*. New York: Harper, 1957.

Brustein, William. *The Social Origins of Political Regionalism: France, 1849-1981*. Berkeley: University of California Press, 1988.

Bulmer, Martin. "The Methodology of Early Social Indicator Research: William Fielding Ogburn and 'Recent Social Trends,' 1933." *Social Indicators Research* 13, no. 2 (1983): 109-30.

———. "Quantification and Chicago Social Science in the 1920s: A Neglected Tradition." *Journal of the History of the Behavioral Sciences* 17, no. 3 (1981): 312-31. https://doi.org/10.1002/1520-6696(198107)17:3.

———. "Support for Sociology in the 1920s: The Laura Spelman Rockefeller Memorial and the Beginnings of Modern, Large-Scale, Sociological Research in the University." *American Sociologist* 17, no. 4 (1982): 185-92.

Bulmer, Martin, and Joan Bulmer. "Philanthropy and Social Science in the 1920s: Beardsley Ruml and the Laura Spelman Rockefeller Memorial, 1922-29." *Minerva* 19, no. 3 (1981): 347-407.

Burgess, Ernest W. "Social Planning and the Mores." In *Human Side of Social Planning, Selected Papers from the Proceedings of the American Sociological Society*, edited by Ernest W. Burgess and Herbert Blumer, 1-18. Chicago: American Sociological Society, 1935.

Burgess, Ernest W., and Herbert Blumer, eds. *Human Side of Social Planning: Selected Papers from the Proceedings of the American Sociological Society*. Chicago: American Sociological Society, 1935.

Burgess, John William. *Reconstruction and the Constitution, 1866-1876*. New York: C. Scribner's Sons, 1902.

Calhoun, John C. *A Disquisition on Government*. Charleston, SC: Walker and James, 1851. Reprint edited by H. Lee Cheek Jr. South Bend, IN: St. Augustine's, 2007.

Carlton, David L., and Peter A. Coclanis. "Another 'Great Migration': From Region to Race in Southern Liberalism, 1938-1945." *Southern Cultures* 3, no. 4 (1997): 37-62.

———. *Confronting Southern Poverty in the Great Depression: The Report on Economic Conditions of the South with Related Documents*. Boston: Bedford / St. Martin's, 1996.

———. *The South, the Nation, and the World: Perspectives on Southern Economic Development*. Charlottesville: University of Virginia Press, 2003.

Caro, Robert A. *The Power Broker: Robert Moses and the Fall of New York*. New York: Alfred A. Knopf, 1974.

Carstensen, Vernon. "The Development and Application of Regional-Sectional Concepts, 1900-1950." In Jensen, *Regionalism in America*, 99-118.

Carter, Elmer A. "The Editor Says: America's Number 1 Problem." *Opportunity: Journal of Negro Life* 16 (August 1938): 228-29.

Cash, Wilbur J. *The Mind of the South*. New York: A. A. Knopf, 1941.

Cassidy, Donna M. "'On the Subject of Nativeness': Marsden Hartley and New England Regionalism." *Winterthur Portfolio* 29, no. 4 (Winter 1994): 227-45.

Cater, Casey P. *Regenerating Dixie: Electric Energy and the Modern South*. Pittsburgh: University of Pittsburgh Press, 2019.

Cell, John Whitson. *The Highest Stage of White Supremacy: The Origins of Segregation in South Africa and the American South*. Cambridge: Cambridge University Press, 1982.

Challen, Paul. *A Sociological Analysis of Southern Regionalism: The Contributions of Howard W. Odum*. Lewiston, NY: Edwin Mellen, 1992.

Chapin, F. Stuart. "Social Theory and Social Action." *American Sociological Review* 1, no. 1 (1936): 1–11. https://doi.org/10.2307/2083858.

Clawson, Marion. *New Deal Planning: The National Resources Planning Board*. Baltimore: Published for Resources for the Future by Johns Hopkins University Press, 1981.

Cobb, James C. "Beyond Planters and Industrialists: A New Perspective on the New South." *Journal of Southern History* 54, no. 1 (1988): 45–68. https://doi.org/10.2307/2208520.

———. "Making Sense of Southern Economic History." *Georgia Historical Quarterly* 71, no. 1 (1987): 53–74.

———. *The Most Southern Place on Earth: The Mississippi Delta and the Roots of Regional Identity*. New York: Oxford University Press, 1992.

———. *Redefining Southern Culture: Mind and Identity in the Modern South*. Athens: University of Georgia Press, 1999.

———. *The Selling of the South: The Southern Crusade for Industrial Development, 1936-1980*. Baton Rouge: Louisiana State University Press, 1982.

———. "Urbanization and the Changing South: A Review of the Literature." *South Atlantic Urban Studies* 1 (1977): 253–66.

Cobb, James C., and Michael V. Namorato, eds. *The New Deal and the South: Essays*. Jackson: University Press of Mississippi, 1984.

Coclanis, Peter A. "The Southern Economy in the Long Twentieth Century." In Brundage, Edwards, and Sensbach, *New History of the American South*, 464–96.

Coffey, Michele Grigsby, and Jodi Skipper. *Navigating Souths: Transdisciplinary Explorations of a U.S. Region*. Athens: University of Georgia Press, 2017.

Collier, John. *The John Collier Reader*. New York: Alfred A. Knopf, 1972.

Conybeare, Frederick Cornwallis. *Myth, Magic, and Morals: A Study of Christian Origins*. London: Watts, 1909.

Couch, W. T. "An Agrarian Programme for the South." *American Review* 3 (1934): 313–26.

Crawford, Margaret. *Building the Workingman's Paradise: The Design of American Company Towns*. London: Verso, 1995.

Critser, Greg. "The Political Rebellion of Carey McWilliams." *UCLA Historical Journal* 4 (1983): 34–65.

Cronon, William. *Nature's Metropolis: Chicago and the Great West*. New York: W. W. Norton, 1991.

———. *Uncommon Ground: Toward Reinventing Nature*. New York: W. W. Norton, 1995.

Dainotto, Roberto Maria. "'All the Regions Do Smilingly Revolt': The Literature of Place and Region." *Critical Inquiry* 22, no. 3 (1996): 486–505.

Daniel, Pete. *Breaking the Land: The Transformation of Cotton, Tobacco, and Rice Cultures since 1880*. Urbana-Champaign: University of Illinois Press, 1985.

Darwin, Charles. *On the Origin of Species and the Voyage of the Beagle.* 1859. Reprint, Berkeley: Graphic Arts Books, 2012.

Davidson, Donald. *The Attack on Leviathan: Regionalism and Nationalism in the United States.* Chapel Hill: University of North Carolina Press, 1938.

———. "Howard Odum and the Sociological Proteus." *American Review* 8 (February 1937): 285–417.

———. "Where Regionalism and Sectionalism Meet." *Social Forces* 13, no. 1 (1934): 23–31. https://doi.org/10.2307/2570213.

Davis, Kenneth S. *FDR: The New Deal Years, 1933–1937; A History.* New York: Random House, 1986.

Davis, Steve. "The South as 'the Nation's No. 1 Economic Problem': The NEC Report of 1938." *Georgia Historical Quarterly* 62, no. 2 (1978): 119–32.

Dawes, Rufus C. *A Century of Progress: Report of the President to the Board of Trustees, March 14, 1936.* Chicago: Century of Progress International Exposition, 1936.

Dealey, James Quayle. "Masters of Social Science: Lester Frank Ward." *Social Forces* 4, no. 2 (1925): 257–72. https://doi.org/10.1093/sf/4.2.257.

Dealey, James Quayle, Edward Alsworth Ross, Franklin H. Giddings, et al. "Lester Frank Ward." *American Journal of Sociology* 19, no. 1 (1913): 61–78.

Derrida, Jacques. *Margins of Philosophy.* Translated with additional notes by Alan Bass. Chicago: University of Chicago Press, 1982.

Dewey, John. *Democracy and Education.* Mineola, NY: Dover, 2004.

———. *Liberalism and Social Action.* Amherst, NY: Prometheus Books, 2000.

———. *The Public and Its Problems.* Chicago: Swallow, 1954.

———. *The School and Society.* Chicago: University of Chicago Press, 1943.

Dorman, Robert L. *Revolt of the Provinces: The Regionalist Movement in America, 1920–1945.* Chapel Hill: University of North Carolina Press, 1993.

Dostalík, Jan. "The Organicists: Planners, Planning, and the Environment in Czechoslovakia (1914–1949)." *Planning Perspectives* 32, no. 2 (2017): 147–73. https://doi.org/10.1080/02665433.2016.1261731.

Douglass, Frederick. "The Color Line." *North American Review* 132, no. 295 (1881): 567–77.

Downs, Matthew L. *Transforming the South: Federal Development in the Tennessee Valley, 1915–1960.* Baton Rouge: Louisiana State University Press, 2014.

Drake, Jamil W. "Moralizing the Folk: The Negro Problem, Racial Heredity, and Religion in the Progressive Era." In *To Know the Soul of a People: Religion, Race, and the Making of Southern Folk,* edited by Jamil W. Drake, 14–45. Oxford: Oxford University Press, 2022. https://doi.org/10.1093/oso/9780190082680.003.0002.

Du Bois, W. E. B. *Black Reconstruction in America.* New York: Harcourt, Brace and Howe, 1935. Republished with an introduction by David Levering Lewis. New York: Atheneum, 1992.

———. "The Conservation of Races." In *The Problem of the Color Line at the Turn of the Century: The Essential Early Essays,* edited by Nahum Dimitri Chandler, 51–66. New York: Fordham University Press, 2014.

———. *The Correspondence of W. E. B. Du Bois*. Edited by Herbert Aptheker. Amherst: University of Massachusetts Press, 1973.

———. *Dark Princess: A Romance*. Jackson, MS: Banner Books, 1995.

———. *The Freedmen's Bureau*. Boston: Atlantic Monthly Company, 1901.

———. "The Lynching Industry." *Crisis*, February 1915, 196–98.

———. "The Negroes of Farmville, Virginia: A Social Study." *Bulletin of the Department of Labor* 14 (January 1898): 1–38.

———. *The Philadelphia Negro: A Social Study*. Philadelphia: University of Pennsylvania, 1899. Reprint edited with an introduction by E. Digby Baltzell. New York: Schocken Books, 1967.

———. *The Quest of the Silver Fleece*. Chicago: A. C. McClurg, 1911. Reprint, New York: Arno, 1969.

———. *The Souls of Black Folk*. Chicago: A. C. McClurg, 1903. Republished with an introduction by John Edgar Wideman. New York: Vintage Books / Library of America, 1990.

———. "The Study of the Negro Problems." *Annals of the American Academy of Political and Social Science* 11 (January 1898): 1–23.

Duncan, Otis Dudley, William Richard Scott, Stanley Lieberson, Beverly Davis Duncan, and Hal H. Winsborough. *Metropolis and Region*. Baltimore: Published for Resources for the Future by Johns Hopkins Press, 1960.

Dunning, William Archibald. *Reconstruction, Political and Economic, 1865–1877*. New York: Harper and Brothers, 1907.

Dykeman, Wilma, and James Stokely. *Seeds of Southern Change: The Life of Will Alexander*. Chicago: University of Chicago Press, 1962.

Dykhuizen, George, Jo Ann Boydston, and Harold Taylor. *The Life and Mind of John Dewey*. Carbondale: Southern Illinois University Press, 1973.

Egerton, John. *The Americanization of Dixie: The Southernization of America*. New York: Harper's Magazine Press, 1974.

Ehsani, Kaveh. "Social Engineering and the Contradictions of Modernization in Khuzestan's Company Towns: A Look at Abadan and Masjed-Soleyman." *International Review of Social History* 48, no. 3 (2003): 361–99. https://doi.org/10.1017/S0020859003001123.

Eldridge, Hope Tisdale. "The Implications of Regionalism to Folk Sociology with Illustrations from the Southern Regions." *Social Forces* 22, no. 1 (October 1943): 41–43.

Elliott, Emory, Cathy N. Davidson, Patrick O'Donnell, Valerie Smith, and Christopher P. Wilson, eds. *The Columbia History of the American Novel*. New York: Columbia University Press, 1991.

Ellis, Mark. "T. J. Woofter Jr. and Government Social Science Research during the New Deal, World War II, and the Cold War." *Journal of Policy History* 32, no. 3 (2020): 241–72. https://doi.org/10.1017/S0898030620000081.

Entrikin, J. Nicholas. "Carl O. Sauer, Philosopher in Spite of Himself." *Geographical Review* 74, no. 4 (October 1984): 387–408. https://doi.org/10.2307/215023.

———. "Diffusion Research in the Context of the Naturalism Debate in Twentieth Century Geographic Thought." In *The Transfer and Transformation of Ideas and*

Material Culture, edited by Peter J. Hugill and D. Bruce Dickson, 165–78. College Station: Texas A&M University Press, 1988.

Erickson, Ansley T., and Andrew R. Highsmith. "The Neighborhood Unit: Schools, Segregation, and the Shaping of the Modern Metropolitan Landscape." *Teachers College Record* 120, no. 3 (2018): 1–36.

Escobar, Arturo. *Encountering Development: The Making and Unmaking of the Third World*. Princeton, NJ: Princeton University Press, 1995.

Fairfield, John D. "Alienation of Social Control: The Chicago Sociologists and the Origins of Urban Planning." *Planning Perspectives* 7, no. 4 (1992): 418–34. https://doi.org/10.1080/02665439208725758.

———. *The Mysteries of the Great City: The Politics of Urban Design, 1877–1937*. Columbus: Ohio State University, 1993.

Farrall, Lyndsay Andrew. *The Origins and Growth of the English Eugenics Movement, 1865–1925*. New York: Garland, 1985.

Faulkner, William. *Absalom, Absalom!* New York: Random House, 1936.

Faust, Drew Gilpin. *A Sacred Circle: The Dilemma of the Intellectual in the Old South, 1840–1860*. Baltimore: Johns Hopkins University Press, 1977.

Fei, Xiaotong. *China's Gentry: Essays on Rural-Urban Relations*. Chicago: University of Chicago Press, 1953.

Fesler, James W. *Area and Administration*. Tuscaloosa: University of Alabama Press, 1949.

Fine, William F. *Progressive Evolutionism and American Sociology, 1890–1920*. Ann Arbor: UMI Research Press, 1979.

Fisher, Jack C. *City and Regional Planning in Poland*. Ithaca, NY: Cornell University Press, 1966.

Fishman, Robert, ed. *The American Planning Tradition: Culture and Policy*. Washington, DC: Woodrow Wilson Center Press, 2000.

———. "A Century of Regionalisms: The Regional Plan Association of New York and the Regional Planning Association of America in Comparative Perspective." *Planning Perspectives* 38, no. 4 (2023): 779–97. doi:10.1080/02665433.2023.2224993. https://doi.org/10.1080/02665433.2023.2224993.

———. "The Death and Life of American Regional Planning." In *Reflections on Regionalism*, edited by Bruce Katz, 107–26. Washington, DC: Brookings Institution Press, 2001.

———. "The Metropolitan Tradition in American Planning." In Fishman, *American Planning Tradition*, 65–86.

———. *Urban Utopias in the Twentieth Century: Ebenezer Howard, Frank Lloyd Wright, and Le Corbusier*. New York: Basic Books, 1977.

Fitzhugh, George. *Sociology for the South; or, The Failure of Free Society*. New York: B. Franklin, 1965.

Foner, Eric. "If Lincoln Hadn't Died . . . Would the Disastrous Reconstruction Era Have Taken a Different Course?" *American Heritage* 58, no. 6 (Winter 2009): 47–48.

———. *Reconstruction: America's Unfinished Revolution, 1863–1877*. New York: Harper and Row, 1989.

———. *Who Owns History? Rethinking the Past in a Changing World.* New York: Hill and Wang, 2002.
Fosdick, Raymond Blaine. *The Story of the Rockefeller Foundation.* New York: Harper and Brothers, 1952.
Frank, Waldo David. *The Re-Discovery of America: An Introduction to a Philosophy of American Life.* New York: Charles Scribner's Sons, 1929.
Frazier, E. Franklin. "Sociological Theory and Race Relations." *American Sociological Review* 12, no. 3 (1947): 265–71. https://doi.org10.2307/2086515.
Frederickson, Kari. "The South and the State in the Twentieth Century." In Brundage, Edwards, and Sensbach, *New History of the American South*, 392–431.
Friedmann, John. "The Concept of a Planning Region." *Land Economics* 32, no. 1 (1956): 1–13. https://doi.org/10.2307/3159570.
———. "A General Theory of Polarized Development." Working paper INT-2296. The Ford Foundation Urban and Regional Advisory Program in Chile, December 1967.
———. *The Good Society: A Personal Account of its Struggle with the World of Social Planning and a Dialectical Inquiry into the Roots of Radical Practice.* Cambridge, MA: MIT Press, 1979.
———. "Planning as Innovation: The Chilean Case." *Journal of the American Institute of Planners* 32, no. 4 (1966): 194–204. https://doi.org/10.1080/01944366608978495.
———. *Regional Development Policy: A Case Study of Venezuela.* Cambridge, MA: MIT Press, 1966.
———. *The Spatial Structure of Economic Development in the Tennessee Valley: A Study in Regional Planning.* Chicago: University of Chicago Press, 1955.
———. "Two Centuries of Planning Theory: An Overview." In *Explorations in Planning Theory*, edited by Luigi Mazza, 10–29. New York: Routledge, 2017.
Friedmann, John, and William Alonso. *Regional Development and Planning: A Reader.* Cambridge, MA: MIT Press, 1964.
Friedmann, John, and Robin Bloch. "American Exceptionalism in Regional Planning, 1933–2001." *International Journal of Urban and Regional Research* 14, no. 4 (1990): 576–601. https://doi.org/10.1111/j.1468-2427.1990.tb00158.x.
Friedmann, John, and Mike Douglass. "Agropolitan Development: Towards a New Strategy for Regional Planning in Asia." In Lo and Salih, *Growth Pole Strategy and Regional Development Policy*, 163–92.
Friedmann, John, and Walter Stöhr. "The Uses of Regional Science: Policy Planning in Chile." *Papers in Regional Science* 18, no. 1 (1967): 207–22. https://doi.org10.1111/j.1435-5597.1967.tb01366.x.
Friedmann, John, and Clyde Weaver. *Territory and Function: The Evolution of Regional Planning.* Berkeley: University of California Press, 1979.
Gallagher, Buell Gordon. *American Caste and the Negro College.* New York: Columbia University Press, 1938.
Galton, Francis. *Inquiries into Human Faculty and Its Development.* 2nd ed. London: J. M. Dent, 1907.
Garreau, Joel. *The Nine Nations of North America.* Boston: Houghton Mifflin, 1981.

Gaston, Paul M. *The New South Creed: A Study in Southern Mythmaking*. New York: Alfred A. Knopf, 1970.
Gates, Henry Louis, Jr. *Stony the Road: Reconstruction, White Supremacy, and the Rise of Jim Crow*. New York: Penguin, 2019.
Geddes, Patrick. *Cities in Evolution*. London: Williams & Norgate, 1915.
———. *Talks from the Outlook Tower*. 1925. In *Patrick Geddes: Spokesman for Man and the Environment: A Selection*, edited by Marshall Stalley, sec. 3. New Brunswick, NJ: Rutgers University Press, 1972.
Giddings, Franklin Henry. *Inductive Sociology: A Syllabus of Methods, Analyses and Classifications, and Provisionally Formulated Laws*. New York: Macmillan, 1901.
———. "An Intensive Sociology: A Project." *American Journal of Sociology* 36, no. 1 (1930): 1–14.
———. *The Principles of Sociology: An Analysis of the Phenomena of Association and of Social Organization*. New York: Macmillan, 1896.
———. *The Scientific Study of Human Society*. Chapel Hill: University of North Carolina Press, 1924.
———. "Social Work and Societal Engineering." *Journal of Social Forces* 3, no. 1 (1924): 7–15. https://doi.org/10.2307/3005457.
———. "Societal Variables." *Social Forces* 1, no. 4 (1923): 345–50. https://doi.org/10.2307/3004936.
———. *Studies in the Theory of Human Society*. New York: Macmillan, 1922.
———. *The Theory of Socialization: A Syllabus of Sociological Principles*. New York: Macmillan, 1897.
Gilbert, Anne. "The New Regional Geography in English and French-Speaking Countries." *Progress in Human Geography* 12, no. 2 (1988): 208–28. https://doi.org/10.1177/030913258801200203.
Gilbert, Jess Carr. *Planning Democracy: Agrarian Intellectuals and the Intended New Deal*. New Haven, CT: Yale University Press, 2015.
Gillette, John M. "Critical Points in Ward's 'Pure Sociology.'" *American Journal of Sociology* 20, no. 1 (1914): 31–67.
Gladden, Washington. *Applied Christianity: Moral Aspects of Social Questions*. Boston: Houghton, Mifflin, 1866.
Goist, Park Dixon. "Lewis Mumford and 'Anti-Urbanism.'" *Journal of the American Institute of Planners* 35, no. 5 (1969): 340–47. https://doi.org/10.1080/01944366908977246.
Goldfield, David R. "The New Regionalism." *Journal of Urban History* 10, no. 2 (1984): 171–86.
———. *Region, Race, and Cities: Interpreting the Urban South*. Baton Rouge: Louisiana State University Press, 1997.
———. "The Rise of the Sunbelt." In Boles, *Companion to the American South*, 474–93.
Gooch, Robert Kent. *Regionalism in France*. New York: Century Company for the Institute for Research in the Social Sciences, University of Virginia, 1931.
Goodsell, Charles T. *Administration of a Revolution; Executive Reform in Puerto Rico under Governor Tugwell, 1941–1946*. Cambridge, MA: Harvard University Press, 1965.

Gorelik, Adrián. *La ciudad Latinoamericana: Una figura de la imaginación social del siglo XX*. Vol. 38. Buenos Aires: Siglo XXI Editores, 2022.
Gottmann, Jean. *Megalopolis: The Urbanized Northeastern Seaboard of the United States*. New York: MIT Press with Twentieth Century Fund, 1962.
Goulet, Andrea, and Eugenie L. Birch. "Modeling Interdisciplinarity: Spaces of Modern Paris through Literature and Design." In *Teaching Space, Place, and Literature*, edited by Robert Tally Jr., 99–110. London: Routledge, 2017.
Gramsci, Antonio. *The Southern Question*. Translated by Pasquale Verdicchio. Toronto: Guernica Editions, 2005.
Grantham, Dewey W. "The Regional Imagination: Social Scientists and the American South." *Journal of Southern History* 34, no. 1 (1968): 3–32. https://doi.org/10.2307/2205472.
———. *Southern Progressivism: The Reconciliation of Progress and Tradition*. Knoxville: University of Tennessee Press, 1983.
Gras, Christian, and Georges Livet. *Régions et régionalisme en France du XVIIIe siècle à nos jours*. Paris: Presses Universitaires de France Paris, 1977.
Green, Dan S., and Edwin D. Driver. "W. E. B. Du Bois: A Case in the Sociology of Sociological Negation." *Phylon* 37, no. 4 (1976): 308–33. https://doi.org/10.2307/274496.
Green, Paul. *Words and Ways: Stories and Incidents from My Cape Fear Valley Folklore Collection*. Raleigh: North Carolina Folklore Society, 1968.
Griffin, Larry J. "The Promise of a Sociology of the South." *Southern Cultures* 7, no. 1 (Spring 2001): 50–75.
Gruber, Howard E. *Darwin on Man: A Psychological Study of Scientific Creativity*. 2nd ed. Chicago: University of Chicago Press, 1981.
Gruchy, Allan G. "The Concept of National Planning in Institutional Economics." *Southern Economic Journal* 6, no. 2 (October 1939): 121–44.
———. "The Economics of the National Resources Committee." *American Economic Review* 29, no. 1 (March 1939): 60–73.
Haar, Charles M. "Regionalism and Realism in Land-Use Planning." *University of Pennsylvania Law Review* 105, no. 4 (1957): 515–37.
Hagood, Margaret Jarman. *Mothers of the South: Portraiture of the White Tenant Farm Woman*. Chapel Hill: University of North Carolina Press, 1939.
———. "Statistical Methods for Delineation of Regions Applied to Data on Agriculture and Population." *Social Forces* 21, no. 3 (1943): 287–97. https://doi.org/10.2307/2570665.
Hahn, Steven. "Hunting, Fishing, and Foraging: Common Rights and Class Relations in the Postbellum South." *Radical History Review* 1982, no. 26 (1982): 37–64. https://doi.org/10.1215/01636545-1982-26-37.
———. *The Roots of Southern Populism: Yeoman Farmers and the Transformation of the Georgia Upcountry, 1850–1890*. Oxford: Oxford University Press, 2006.
Hall, G. Stanley. *Adolescence: Its Psychology and Its Relations to Physiology, Anthropology, Sociology, Sex, Crime, Religion and Education*. New York: Appleton, 1904.
Hall, Jacquelyn Dowd. *Like a Family: The Making of a Southern Cotton Mill World*. Chapel Hill: University of North Carolina Press, 2000.

Hall, Peter. *Cities of Tomorrow: An Intellectual History of Urban Planning and Design in the Twentieth Century*. Oxford, UK: Blackwell, 1988.

———. *The Theory and Practice of Regional Planning*. London: Pemberton, 1970.

Haney, David H. *When Modern Was Green: Life and Work of Landscape Architect Leberecht Migge*. New York: Routledge, 2010.

Hargrove, Erwin C. *Prisoners of Myth: The Leadership of the Tennessee Valley Authority, 1933–1990*. Princeton, NJ: Princeton University Press, 1994.

Harrison, John, and Michael Hoyler, eds. *Megaregions: Globalization's New Urban Form?* Cheltenham, UK: Edward Elgar, 2015.

Harvey, Paul. "Southern Religion and Southern Culture in the Twentieth Century." In Brundage, Edwards, and Sensback, *New History of the American South*, 432–63.

Haskell, Thomas L. *The Authority of Experts: Studies in History and Theory*. Bloomington: Indiana University Press, 1984.

Hays, Samuel P. *The Response to Industrialism, 1885–1914*. Chicago: University of Chicago Press, 1957.

Heath, Milton Sydney. *Constructive Liberalism: The Role of the State in Economic Development in Georgia to 1860*. Cambridge, MA: Harvard University Press, 1954.

Hein, Carola. "The Exchange of Planning Ideas from Europe to the USA after the Second World War: Introductory Thoughts and a Call for Further Research." *Planning Perspectives* 29, no. 2 (2014): 143–51. https://doi.org/10.1080/02665433.2014.886522.

Hemenway, Robert E. *Zora Neale Hurston: A Literary Biography*. Urbana-Champaign: University of Illinois Press, 1977.

Herder, Johann Gottfried. *J. G. Herder on Social and Political Culture*. Translated and edited by Frederick M. Barnard. London: Cambridge University Press, 1969.

Herring, Harriet Laura. *Southern Industry and Regional Development*. Chapel Hill: University of North Carolina Press, 1940.

———. *Welfare Work in Mill Villages: The Story of Extra-Mill Activities in North Carolina*. Chapel Hill: University of North Carolina Press, 1929.

Hertzler, J. O. "American Regionalism and the Regional Sociological Society." *American Sociological Review* 3, no. 5 (1938): 738–48. https://doi.org/10.2307/2084693.

Hill, Michael R. "American Sociological Association." *The Blackwell Encyclopedia of Sociology*. Vol. 1, edited by George Ritzer. Malden, MA: Blackwell Publishing, 2007. https://doi.org/10.1002/9781405165518.wbeosa047.

Hirsch, H. N. *The Enigma of Felix Frankfurter*. New York: Basic Books, 1981.

Hofstadter, Richard. *The Age of Reform: From Bryan to F. D. R.* New York: Vintage Books, 1955.

———. *Social Darwinism in American Thought*. Boston: Beacon, 1992.

Hoover, Herbert. *The Memoirs of Herbert Hoover*. 3 vols. New York: Macmillan, 1951.

Howard, June. "Unraveling Regions, Unsettling Periods: Sarah Orne Jewett and American Literary History." *American Literature* 68, no. 2 (1996): 365–84.

Huggins, Koleen Alice Haire. "The Evolution of City and Regional Planning in North Carolina, 1900–1950." PhD diss., Duke University, 1967.

Hughes, Henry. *Treatise on Sociology, Theoretical and Practical*. New York: Negro Universities Press, 1968.

Hughes, Thomas Parke, and Agatha C. Hughes. *Lewis Mumford: Public Intellectual*. New York: Oxford University Press, 1990.

Hugill, Peter J., and D. Bruce Dickson. *The Transfer and Transformation of Ideas and Material Culture*. College Station: Texas A&M University Press, 1988.

Hunter, Marcus Anthony. "A Bridge over Troubled Urban Waters: W. E. B. Du Bois's *The Philadelphia Negro* and the Ecological Conundrum." *Du Bois Review: Social Science Research on Race* 10, no. 1 (2013): 7–27. https://doi.org/10.1017/S1742058X13000015.

Hurston, Zora Neale. *Mules and Men*. Philadelphia: J. B. Lippincott, 1935. Republished with a preface by Franz Boas and foreword by Arnold Rampersad. New York: HarperPerennial, 1990.

———. *Their Eyes Were Watching God*. Philadelphia: J. B. Lippincott, 1937. Republished with a foreword by Edwidge Danticat. New York: HarperCollins, 2000.

———. *"You Don't Know Us Negroes" and Other Essays*. Edited by Henry Louis Gates Jr. and Genevieve West. New York: Amistad, 2022.

———. *Zora Neale Hurston: A Life in Letters*. Edited by Carla Kaplan. New York: Doubleday, 2002.

Ibañez, Daniel, Clare Lyster, Charles Waldheim, and Mason White. *Third Coast Atlas: Prelude to a Plan*. New York: Actar, 2017.

Irish, Marion D. "Proposed Roads to the New South, 1941: Chapel Hill Planners vs. Nashville Agrarians." *Sewanee Review* 49, no. 1 (1941): 1–27.

James, William. *A Pluralistic Universe*. Cambridge, MA: Harvard University Press, 1977.

Jensen, Merrill, ed. *Regionalism in America*. Foreword by Felix Frankfurter. Madison: University of Wisconsin Press, 1951.

Johnson, Gerald W. "After Forty Years—Dixi [sic]." *Virginia Quarterly Review* 41, no. 2 (1965): 192–201.

———. *The Wasted Land*. Chapel Hill: University of North Carolina Press, 1937.

Johnson, Guy Benton. "Does the South Owe the Negro a New Deal?" *Social Forces* 13, no. 1 (1934): 100–103. https://doi.org/10.2307/2570224.

———. *Folk Culture on St. Helena Island, South Carolina*. Chapel Hill: University of North Carolina Press, 1930.

———. "Rupert Bayless Vance, 1899–1975." *Social Forces* 54, no. 2 (1975): 467–69.

Johnson, Guy Benton, and Guion Griffis Johnson. *Research in Service to Society: The First Fifty Years of the Institute for Research in Social Science at the University of North Carolina*. Chapel Hill: University of North Carolina Press, 1980.

Jones, Byrd L. "A Plan for Planning in the New Deal." *Social Science Quarterly* 50, no. 3 (1969): 525–34.

Jordan, John M. *Machine-Age Ideology: Social Engineering and American Liberalism, 1911–1939*. Chapel Hill: University of North Carolina Press, 1994.

Kaiser, Edward J., Raymond J. Burby, and David R. Godschalk. "ACSP Distinguished Educator, 1994: John A. Parker." *Journal of Planning Education and Research* 38, no. 2 (2018): 233–35. https://doi.org/10.1177/0739456X18759176.

Kallen, Horace Meyer. *Culture and Democracy in the United States.* New York: Boni and Liveright, 1924.

Kammen, Michael G. *People of Paradox: An Inquiry Concerning the Origins of American Civilization.* Ithaca, NY: Cornell University Press, 1990.

Kantor, Harvey A. "Howard W. Odum: The Implications of Folk, Planning, and Regionalism." *American Journal of Sociology* 79, no. 2 (1973): 278–95.

Kaplan, Amy. "Nation, Region, and Empire." In Elliott et al., *Columbia History of the American Novel*, 240–66.

Karanikas, Alexander. *Tillers of a Myth: Southern Agrarians as Social and Literary Critics.* Madison: University of Wisconsin Press, 1966.

Katznelson, Ira. *Fear Itself: The New Deal and the Origins of Our Time.* New York: Liveright, 2013.

Kaufman, Allen, Elizabeth Fox-Genovese, and Eugene D. Genovese. *Capitalism, Slavery, and Republican Values: Antebellum Political Economists, 1819–1848.* Austin: University of Texas Press, 1982.

Kazin, Alfred. *On Native Grounds: An Interpretation of Modern American Prose Literature.* New York: Reynal and Hitchcock, 1942.

Kendrick, Benjamin B. "The Colonial Status of the South." *Journal of Southern History* 8, no. 1 (1942): 3–22.

———. "A Southern Confederation of Learning: Higher Education and the New Regionalism in the South." *Southwest Review* 19, no. 2 (1934): 182–95.

Key, V. O. *Southern Politics in State and Nation.* New York: A. A. Knopf, 1949.

King, Richard H. *A Southern Renaissance: The Cultural Awakening of the American South, 1930–1955.* New York: Oxford University Press, 1980.

Kirby, Jack Temple. "Bioregionalism: Landscape and Culture in the South Atlantic." In Wilson, *New Regionalism*, 19–43.

Kneebone, John T. *Southern Liberal Journalists and the Issue of Race, 1920–1944.* Chapel Hill: University of North Carolina Press, 1985.

Kousser, J. Morgan, and James M. McPherson, eds. *Region, Race, and Reconstruction: Essays in Honor of C. Vann Woodward.* New York: Oxford University Press, 1982.

Krieger, Alex. *City on a Hill: Urban Idealism in America from the Puritans to the Present.* Cambridge, MA: Belknap Press of Harvard University Press, 2019.

Kropotkin, Petr Alekseevich. *Fields, Factories and Workshops Tomorrow.* London: Houghton Mifflin Harcourt, 1899.

Kunze, Joel P. "The Purnell Act and Agricultural Economics." *Agricultural History* 62, no. 2 (1988): 131–49.

Kwak, Nancy. "Interdisciplinarity in Planning History." In *The Routledge Handbook of Planning History*, edited by Carola Hein, 25–34. Abingdon, UK: Routledge, 2017.

Larsen, Kristin. "From the RPAA to the RDCA—Communitarian Regionalism as a Consistent Theme." *Planning Perspectives* 38, no. 4 (2023): 741–57. https://doi.org/10.1080/02665433.2023.2215732.

Larsen, Lawrence H. *The Urban South: A History*. Lexington: University Press of Kentucky, 1990.

Lassiter, Matthew D., and Kevin M. Kruse. "The Bulldozer Revolution: Suburbs and Southern History since World War II." *Journal of Southern History* 75, no. 3 (2009): 691–706.

Lathem, Edward Connery, ed. *The Poetry of Robert Frost*. New York: Henry Holt, 1969.

Latour, Bruno. "The Impact of Science Studies on Political Philosophy." *Science, Technology, and Human Values* 16, no. 1 (1991): 3–19.

Lebrun, Harvey. "A Near Encyclopedia of Social Planning." *Social Forces* 16, no. 2 (1937): 278–85. https://doi.org/10.2307/2570533.

Lee, Roger, and Jane Wills. *Geographies of Economies*. London: Arnold, 1997.

Lefebvre, Henri. *Everyday Life in the Modern World*. Milton: Taylor and Francis Group, 2023.

———. *The Production of Space*. Translated by Donald Nicholson-Smith. Oxford, UK: Blackwell, 1991.

Leopold, Aldo. "Wilderness as a Form of Land Use." *Journal of Land and Public Utility Economics* 1, no. 4 (1925): 398–404. https://doi.org/10.2307/3138647.

Lepawsky, Albert. "Government Planning in the South." *Journal of Politics* 10, no. 3 (1948): 536–67. https://doi.org/10.2307/2126178.

———. *State Planning and Economic Development in the South*. Washington, DC: Committee of the South, National Planning Association, 1949.

Lewis, David Levering. *W. E. B. Du Bois*. New York: H. Holt, 1993.

Link, William A. *The Paradox of Southern Progressivism, 1880–1930*. Chapel Hill: University of North Carolina Press, 1992.

Lippmann, Walter. *A Preface to Morals*. New York: Macmillan, 1929.

Lo, Fu-Chen, and Kamal Salih. *Growth Pole Strategy and Regional Development Policy: Asian Experience and Alternative Approaches*. Oxford, UK: Published for the United Nations Centre for Regional Development by Pergamon Press, 1978.

Locke, Alain LeRoy, ed. *A Decade of Negro Self-Expression*. With a foreword by Howard W. Odum. Charlottesville, VA: Michie, 1928. Reprint, Sacramento: Creative Media Partners, 2018.

Logan, Rayford Whittingham. *The Negro in American Life and Thought: The Nadir, 1877–1901*. New York: Dial, 1954.

López-Durán, Fabiola. *Eugenics in the Garden: Transatlantic Architecture and the Crafting of Modernity*. Austin: University of Texas Press, 2018.

Lorwin, Lewis L. "Social Aspects of the Planning State." *American Political Science Review* 28, no. 1 (1934): 16–22.

Lubove, Roy. *Community Planning in the 1920s: The Contribution of the Regional Planning Association of America*. Pittsburgh: University of Pittsburgh Press, 1964.

Luigia La Penta, Barbara, and Giorgio Ciucci. *The American City: From the Civil War to the New Deal*. Cambridge, MA: MIT Press, 1979.

Lynn, Kenneth Schuyler. *Mark Twain and Southwestern Humor*. Boston: Little, Brown, 1960.

MacKaye, Benton. "An Appalachian Trail: A Project in Regional Planning." *Journal of the American Institute of Architects* 9 (October 1921): 323–30.

———. *The New Exploration: A Philosophy of Regional Planning.* Edited with an introduction by Lewis Mumford. Urbana-Champaign: University of Illinois Press, 1962.

Mandel, Ernest. *Capitalism and Regional Disparities.* Toronto: New Hogtown, 1973.

Manganiello, Christopher J. *Southern Water, Southern Power: How the Politics of Cheap Energy and Water Scarcity Shaped a Region.* Chapel Hill: University of North Carolina Press, 2015.

Marcuse, Peter. "Housing in Early City Planning." *Journal of Urban History* 6, no. 2 (1980): 153–76. https://doi.org/10.1177/009614428000600203.

Markusen, Ann R. *Regions: The Economics and Politics of Territory.* Totowa, NJ: Rowman and Littlefield, 1987.

———. *The Rise of the Gunbelt: The Military Remapping of Industrial America.* New York: Oxford University Press, 1991.

Márquez, Antonio C. "Faulkner in Latin America." *Faulkner Journal* 11, no. 1 (1995): 83–100.

Martin, Jean-Paul, and Henri Nonn. "La notion d'"intégration régionale.'" *Travaux De L'Institut De Géographie De Reims* 41, no. 1 (1980): 33–46.

Martin, Ron. "The New Economics and Politics of Regional Restructuring: The British Experience." In *Regional Policy at the Crossroads*, edited by Erik Swyngedouw, Louis Albrechts, Frank Moulaert, and Peter Roberts, 27–51. London: Jessica Kingsley, 1989.

Martin, Ron, and Peter Sunley. "The Post-Keynesian State and the Space Economy." In *Economy: Critical Essays in Human Geography*, edited by Ron Martin, 459–73. London: Routledge, 2017.

Marx, Karl, and Friedrich Engels. *The Communist Manifesto.* 1848. Reprint edited by Jeffrey C. Isaac. New Haven, CT: Yale University Press, 2012.

Marx, Leo. *The Machine in the Garden: Technology and the Pastoral Ideal in America.* New York: Oxford University Press, 2000.

Matthews, Fred H. *Quest for an American Sociology: Robert E. Park and the Chicago School.* Montreal: McGill-Queen's University Press, 1977.

Matthews, Scott L. *Capturing the South: Imagining America's Most Documented Region.* Chapel Hill: University of North Carolina Press, 2018.

Mayer, Marc. "Basquiat in History." In *Basquiat*, edited by Marc Daniel Mayer and Fred Hoffman, 41–57. London: Merrell, 2005.

Mayo, Peter. "Gramsci, the Southern Question and the Mediterranean." In Sultana and Buhagiar, *Educational Scholarship across the Mediterranean*, 86–102.

McLaughlin, Glenn Everett, and Stefan Hyman Robock. *Why Industry Moves South: A Study of Factors Influencing the Recent Location of Manufacturing Plants in the South.* Washington, DC: Committee of the South, National Planning Association, 1949.

McMath, Robert C. *Engineering the New South: Georgia Tech, 1885–1985.* Athens: University of Georgia Press, 1985.

McNeill, William Hardy. *Mythistory and Other Essays*. Chicago: University of Chicago Press, 1986.

McWilliams, Carey. *The New Regionalism in American Literature*. Seattle: University of Washington Book Store, 1930.

Meier, August. *Negro Thought in America, 1880-1915: Racial Ideologies in the Age of Booker T. Washington*. Ann Arbor: University of Michigan Press, 1966.

Mencken, Henry L. "The Sahara of the Bozart." *New York Evening Mail* 13 (1917): 69–82.

Merriam, Charles E. "The National Resources Planning Board; A Chapter in American Planning Experience." *American Political Science Review* 38, no. 6 (1944): 1075–88. https://doi.org/10.2307/1949845.

Mertz, Paul E. *New Deal Policy and Southern Rural Poverty*. Baton Rouge: Louisiana State University Press, 1978.

Miller, Zane L. "Race-ism and the City: The Young Du Bois and the Role of Place in Social Theory, 1893–1901." *American Studies* 30, no. 2 (1989): 89–102.

Milligan, Michael James. "The Contradictions of Public Service: A Study of Howard Odum's Intellectual Odyssey." PhD diss., University of Virginia, 1994. https://doi.org/10.18130/V3-4804-XW51.

Mills, C. Wright. "The Professional Ideology of Social Pathologists." *American Journal of Sociology* 49, no. 2 (September 1943): 165–80.

———. *The Sociological Imagination*. New York: Oxford University Press, 1959.

Mitchell, Timothy. *Rule of Experts: Egypt, Techno-Politics, Modernity*. Berkeley: University of California Press, 2002.

Mitchell, Wesley Clair. *The Backward Art of Spending Money, and Other Essays*. New York: McGraw-Hill, 1937.

———. *Recent Social Trends in the United States: Report of the President's Research Committee on Social Trends*. New York: McGraw-Hill, 1934.

Mood, Fulmer. "The Origin, Evolution, and Application of the Sectional Concept, 1750–1900." In Jensen, *Regionalism in America*, 5–97.

Moore, Barrington. *Social Origins of Dictatorship and Democracy: Lord and Peasant in the Making of the Modern World*. Boston: Beacon, 1966.

Moore, Harry Estill. *What Is Regionalism?* Chapel Hill: University of North Carolina Press, 1937.

Morauta, Louise, Ann Chowning, Current Issues Collective (B. Kaspou and others), et al. "Indigenous Anthropology in Papua New Guinea [and Comments and Reply]." *Current Anthropology* 20, no. 3 (1979): 561–76. https://doi.org/10.1086/202325.

Moravánszky, Ákos, and Karl R. Kegler. *Re-Scaling the Environment: New Landscapes of Design, 1960–1980*. Vol. 2 of *East West Central: Re-Building Europe, 1950–1990*, edited by Ákos Moravánszky. Basel, Switzerland: Birkhäuser, 2017.

Morris, Aldon D. *The Scholar Denied: W. E. B. Du Bois and the Birth of Modern Sociology*. Oakland: University of California Press, 2015.

Morrison, Toni. *Playing in the Dark: Whiteness and the Literary Imagination*. Cambridge, MA: Harvard University Press, 1992.

Mukerjee, Radhakamal. *Regional Sociology*. New York: Century, 1926.

Mumford, Lewis. *The Culture of Cities*. New York: Harcourt Brace, 1938.
———. *The Golden Day: A Study in American Experience and Culture*. Boston: Beacon, 1957.
———. *The Myth of the Machine: The Pentagon of Power*. New York: Harcourt Brace, 1970.
———. *My Works and Days: A Personal Chronicle*. New York: Harcourt Brace Jovanovich, 1979.
———. "The Regional Planning Association of America: Past and Future." *Planning Perspectives* 38, no. 4 (2023): 737–39. Essay dated September 21, 1948; published posthumously. https://doi.org/10.1080/02665433.2023.2216489.
———. "Regions—to Live In." *Survey Graphic* 54, no. 3 (1925): 151–52.
———. *Sketches from Life: The Autobiography of Lewis Mumford; The Early Years*. New York: Dial, 1982.
———. *Technics and Civilization*. New York: Harcourt Brace, 1934.
Mumford, Lewis, and Patrick Geddes. *Lewis Mumford and Patrick Geddes: The Correspondence*. Edited by Frank G. Novak. London: Routledge, 1995.
Murphy, Paul V. *The Rebuke of History: The Southern Agrarians and American Conservative Thought*. Chapel Hill: University of North Carolina Press, 2001.
Myrdal, Gunnar. *An American Dilemma: The Negro Problem and Modern Democracy*. New York: Harper and Brothers, 1944. Reprint, New York: Harper and Row, 1962.
National Planning Board, Federal Emergency Administration of Public Works. *Final Report—1933-34*. Washington, DC: US Government Printing Office, 1934.
National Resources Committee Technical Committee on Regional Planning. *Regional Factors in National Planning and Development*. Washington, DC: US Government Printing Office, 1935.
Neilson, William Allan. *Roads to Knowledge*. New York: W. W. Norton, 1932.
Nelson, Garrett Dash. "Regional Planning as Cultural Criticism: Reclaiming the Radical Wholes of Interwar Regional Thinkers." *Regional Studies* 55, no. 1 (2021): 127–37. https://doi.org/10.1080/00343404.2020.1737664.
Nicholls, William H. "Southern Tradition and Regional Economic Progress." *Southern Economic Journal* 26, no. 3 (1960): 187–98. https://doi.org/10.2307/1054951.
Nixon, Herman Clarence. *Forty Acres and Steel Mules*. Chapel Hill: University of North Carolina Press, 1938.
Norton, Frederick O. *The Rise of Christianity: A Historical Study of the Origin of the Christian Religion*. Chicago: University of Chicago Press, 1924.
O'Brien, Michael. *The Idea of the American South, 1920-1941*. Baltimore: Johns Hopkins University Press, 1990.
———. *Rethinking the South: Essays in Intellectual History*. Baltimore: Johns Hopkins University Press, 1988.
O'Connor, William Thomas. *Naturalism and the Pioneers of American Sociology*. Washington, DC: Catholic University of America Press, 1942.
Odum, Eugene P. *Fundamentals of Ecology*. Philadelphia: W. B. Saunders, 1953.
Odum, Howard W. *An American Epoch: Southern Portraiture in the National Picture*. New York: H. Holt, 1930.

———. *American Masters of Social Science: An Approach to the Study of the Social Sciences through a Neglected Field of Biography*. New York: H. Holt, 1927.

———. *American Sociology: The Story of Sociology in the United States through 1950*. New York: Longmans, Green, 1951.

———. "An Approach to Diagnosis and Direction of the Problem of Negro Segregation in the Public Schools of the South: A Symposium." *Journal of Public Law* 3, no. 1 (1954): 8–37.

———. "The Case for Regional-National Social Planning." *Social Forces* 13, no. 1 (October 1934a): 6–23. https://doi.org10.2307/2570212.

———. *Cold Blue Moon, Black Ulysses Afar Off*. Indianapolis: Bobbs-Merrill, 1931. Reprint, New York: Kraus, 1972.

———. "The Duel to the Death." *Social Forces* 4, no. 1 (1925): 189–94. https://doi.org/10.1093/sf/4.1.189.

———. "Editorial Notes." *Social Forces* 1, no. 1 (1922): 56–61.

———. "Editorial Notes." *Social Forces* 2, no. 2 (1924): 282–86. https://doi.org/10.1093/sf/2.2.282.

———. "Editorial Notes." *Social Forces* 3, no. 1 (1924): 139–46. https://doi.org/10.1093/sf/3.1.139.

———. "Folk and Regional Conflict as a Field of Sociological Study." *Publications of the Sociological Society of America* 35 (1931): 17.

———. *Folk, Region, and Society: Selected Papers of Howard W. Odum*. Edited by Katharine Jocher, Guy B. Johnson, George C. Simpson, and Rupert B. Vance. Chapel Hill: University of North Carolina Press, 1964.

———. "Folk Sociology as a Subject Field for the Historical Study of Total Human Society and the Empirical Study of Group Behavior." *Social Forces* 31, no. 3 (1953): 193–223.

———. "From Community Studies to Regionalism." *Social Forces* 23, no. 3 (1945): 245–58. https://doi.org/10.2307/2572290.

———. "Lynching, Fears, and Folkways." *Nation*, December 30, 1931.

———. *Man's Quest for Social Guidance: The Study of Social Problems*. New York: H. Holt, 1927.

———. "A More Articulate South—Editorial Notes." *Social Forces* 2, no. 5 (1924): 730–35.

———. "Notes on the Study of Regional and Folk Society." *Social Forces* 10, no. 2 (1931): 164–75.

———. "On a Closer Cooperation between the Physical Sciences and the Social Sciences." *Harvard Alumni Bulletin*, July 7, 1939.

———. "Orderly Transitional Democracy." *Annals of the American Academy of Political and Social Science* 180, no. 1 (1935): 31–39.

———. "Patrick Geddes' Heritage to 'the Making of the Future.'" *Social Forces* 22, no. 3 (1944): 275–81. https://doi.org/10.2307/2571970.

———. *The Promise of Regionalism*. Madison: University of Wisconsin Press, 1951.

———. *Race and Rumors of Race: Challenge to American Crisis*. Chapel Hill: University of North Carolina Press, 1943.

———. *Rainbow Round My Shoulder: The Blue Trail of Black Ulysses*. Indianapolis: Bobbs-Merrill, 1928. Reprint, New York: Kraus, 1972.

———. "Regional Development and Governmental Policy." *Annals of the American Academy of Political and Social Science* 206 (1939): 133–41.

———. "Regionalism vs. Sectionalism in the South's Place in the National Economy." *Social Forces* 12, no. 3 (1934): 338–54. https://doi.org/10.2307/2569923.

———. "The Regional Quality and Balance of America." *Social Forces* 23, no. 3 (1945): 269–85. https://doi.org/10.2307/2572292.

———. "Religious Folk-Songs of Southern Negroes." *American Journal of Religious Psychology and Education* 3 (July 1909): 265–365.

———. "Social and Mental Traits of the Negro." PhD diss., Columbia University, 1910.

———. "A Sociological Approach to the Study and Practice of American Regionalism: A Factorial Syllabus." *Social Forces* 20, no. 4 (1942): 425–36. https://doi.org/10.2307/2570875.

———. "Sociology in the Contemporary World of Today and Tomorrow." *Social Forces* 21 (1943): 390–96.

———. *Southern Pioneers in Social Interpretation*. Chapel Hill: University of North Carolina Press, 1925.

———. *Southern Regions of the United States*. Chapel Hill: University of North Carolina Press, 1936.

———. *Understanding Society: The Principles of Dynamic Sociology*. New York: Macmillan, 1947.

———. *The United States Planning Agency*. Chapel Hill: Institute for Research in Social Science, University of North Carolina, 1943.

———. *Wings on My Feet: Black Ulysses at the Wars*. Indianapolis: Bobbs-Merrill, 1929.

Odum, Howard W., and Katharine Jocher, eds. *In Search of the Regional Balance of America*. Chapel Hill: University of North Carolina Press, 1945.

Odum, Howard W., and Katharine Jocher. *An Introduction to Social Research*. New York: H. Holt, 1929.

Odum, Howard W., and Guy B. Johnson. *The Negro and His Songs: A Study of Typical Negro Songs in the South*. Chapel Hill: University of North Carolina Press, 1925.

———. *Negro Workaday Songs*. Chapel Hill: University of North Carolina Press, 1926.

Odum, Howard W., and Harry E. Moore. *American Regionalism: A Cultural-Historical Approach to National Integration*. New York: H. Holt, 1938.

Ogburn, William F. *Social Change with Respect to Culture and Original Nature*. New York: Viking, 1937.

Olmsted, Frederick Law. *The Cotton Kingdom: A Traveller's Observations on Cotton and Slavery in the American Slave States; Based upon Three Former Volumes of Journeys and Investigations*. New York: Mason Brothers, 1861.

———. *A Journey through Texas; or, A Saddle-Trip on the Southwestern Frontier: With a Statistical Appendix*. New York: Dix, Edwards, 1857.

Olsson, Tore C. *Agrarian Crossings: Reformers and the Remaking of the US and Mexican Countryside*. Princeton, NJ: Princeton University Press, 2017.

Orillard, Clément. "The Transnational Building of Urban Design: Interplay between Genres of Discourse in the Anglophone World." *Planning Perspectives* 29, no. 2 (2014): 209–29.

Osterweis, Rollin G. *Romanticism and Nationalism in the Old South*. New Haven, CT: Yale University Press, 1949.

Padilla, Salvador M, ed. *Tugwell's Thoughts on Planning*. Rio Pedras: University of Puerto Rico Press, 1975.

Pareto, Vilfredo. *Sociological Writings*. Edited by Samuel E. Finer. Translated by Derick Mirfin. New York: Frederick A. Praeger, 1966.

Park, R. E. Review of *Race Orthodoxy in the South and Other Aspects of the Negro Problem*, by Thomas Pearce Bailey. *Journal of Negro History* 1, no. 4 (1916): 447–49. https://doi.org/10.2307/3035619.

———. *Robert E. Park on Social Control and Collective Behavior: Selected Papers*. Edited by R. H. Turner. Chicago: University of Chicago Press, 1967.

———. "The Urban Community as a Spatial Pattern and a Moral Order." *Publications of the American Sociological Society* 20 (1925): 1–14.

Park, Robert Ezra, and E. W. Burgess. *The City*. Chicago: University of Chicago Press, 1925.

Parsons, Talcott. *Essays in Sociological Theory*. Glencoe, IL: Free Press, 1954.

Patel, Kiran Klaus. *The New Deal: A Global History*. Princeton, NJ: Princeton University Press, 2016.

Payne, Charles M. "'The Whole United States Is Southern!': *Brown v. Board* and the Mystification of Race." *Journal of American History* 91, no. 1 (2004): 83–91. https://doi.org/10.2307/3659615.

Pearson, Karl. *The Grammar of Science*. London: Walter Scott, 1892.

Pells, Richard H. *Radical Visions and American Dreams: Culture and Social Thought in the Depression Years*. Middletown, CT: Wesleyan University Press, 1984.

Perloff, Harvey S. *Education for Planning: City, State and Region; Essays*. Baltimore: Published for Resources for the Future by Johns Hopkins Press, 1957.

Perloff, Harvey S., Edgar S. Dunn Jr., Eric E. Lampard, and Richard F. Muth. *Regions, Resources, and Economic Growth*. Baltimore: Published for Resources for the Future by the Johns Hopkins Press, 1960.

Perloff, Harvey S., and Lowdon Wingo. *Natural Resource Endowment and Regional Economic Growth*. Washington, DC: Resources for the Future, 1960.

Perry, Imani. *South to America: A Journey below the Mason-Dixon to Understand the Soul of a Nation*. New York: ECCO, 2022.

Peterson, Jon A. *The Birth of City Planning in the United States, 1840–1917*. Baltimore: Johns Hopkins University Press, 2003.

Pettigrew, Thomas F. *The Sociology of Race Relations: Reflection and Reform*. New York: Free Press, 1980.

Phillips, Sarah T. *This Land, This Nation: Conservation, Rural America, and the New Deal*. New York: Cambridge University Press, 2007.

Phillips, Ulrich Bonnell. *Life and Labor in the Old South*. Boston: Little, Brown, 1963.

Pierson, Mary Bynum Holmes. *Graduate Work in the South*. Chapel Hill: University of North Carolina Press, 1947.

Polk, William Tannahill. *Southern Accent: From Uncle Remus to Oak Ridge*. New York: Morrow, 1953.

Popper, Karl R. *The Poverty of Historicism*. London: Routledge and Kegan Paul, 1957.

Preskill, Stephen. *Education in Black and White: Myles Horton and the Highlander Center's Vision for Social Justice*. Oakland: University of California Press, 2021.

Purcell, Mark. "For Democracy: Planning and Publics without the State." *Planning Theory* 15, no. 4 (2016): 386–401. https://doi.org/10.1177/1473095215620827.

Raffestin, Claude. "Space, Territory, and Territoriality." *Environment and Planning D: Society and Space* 30, no. 1 (2012): 121–41.

Ramos, Stephen J. "The Regional Planning Association of America at 100: A New Exploration." *Planning Perspectives* 38, no. 4 (2023): 731–35. https://doi.org/10.1080/02665433.2023.2222027.

———. "Southern Regionalism: Social Science and Regional-National Planning in the Interwar U.S. South." *Planning Perspectives* 38, no. 4 (2023): 799–817. https://doi.org/10.1080/02665433.2023.2215731.

Ransom, Roger L., and Richard Sutch. *One Kind of Freedom: The Economic Consequences of Emancipation*. Cambridge: Cambridge University Press, 1977.

Raper, Arthur Franklin. *Preface to Peasantry: A Tale of Two Black Belt Counties*. Chapel Hill: University of North Carolina Press, 1936.

———. *The Tragedy of Lynching*. Chapel Hill: University of North Carolina Press, 1933.

Raper, Arthur Franklin, and Ira De Augustine Reid. *Sharecroppers All*. Chapel Hill: University of North Carolina Press, 1941.

Reclus, Elisée. *Anarchy, Geography, Modernity: The Radical Social Thought of Elisée Reclus*. Edited and translated by John P. Clark and Camille Martin. Lanham, MD: Lexington Books, 2004.

Redfield, Robert. "The Folk Society." *American Journal of Sociology* 52, no. 4 (1947): 293–308.

———. *Tepoztlán, a Mexican Village: A Study of Folk Life*. Chicago: University of Chicago Press, 1930.

Redfield, Robert, and Alfonso Villa Rojas. *Chan Kom: A Maya Village*. Washington, DC: Carnegie Institution of Washington, 1934.

Reed, John Shelton. "Sociology and the Study of American Regions." *Appalachian Journal* 7, no. 3 (1980): 171–79.

———. *Surveying the South: Studies in Regional Sociology*. Columbia: University of Missouri Press, 1993.

Reed, John Shelton, and Daniel Joseph Singal, eds. *Regionalism and the South: Selected Papers of Rupert Vance*. Chapel Hill: University of North Carolina Press, 1982.

Rice, Stuart Arthur, ed. *Methods in Social Science: A Case Book Compiled under the Direction of the Committee on Scientific Method in the Social Sciences of the Social Science Research Council*. Chicago: University of Chicago Press, 1931.

Richardson, Harry Ward. *Regional and Urban Economics*. Harmondsworth, UK: Penguin, 1978.

———. *Regional Growth Theory*. London: Macmillan, 1973.

Riemer, Svend. "Theoretical Aspects of Regionalism." *Social Forces* 21, no. 3 (March 1943): 275–80.

Ring, Natalie J. "The Nature of Reform in the Early Twentieth-Century South." In Brundage, Edwards, and Sensbach, *New History of the American South*, 359–91.

Robbins, Richard. "Charles S. Johnson." In *Black Sociologists: Historical and Contemporary Perspectives*, edited by James E. Blackwell and Morris Janowitz, 56–84. Chicago: University of Chicago Press, 1974.

Robinson, Cedric J. *Black Marxism: The Making of the Black Radical Tradition*. Chapel Hill: University of North Carolina Press, 2000.

Rodgers, Daniel T. *Atlantic Crossings: Social Politics in a Progressive Age*. Cambridge, MA: Belknap Press of Harvard University Press, 1998.

———. "Regionalism and the Burdens of Progress." In *Region, Race, and Reconstruction: Essays in Honor of C. Vann Woodward*, edited by J. Morgan Kousser and James M. McPherson, 3–26. Oxford: Oxford University Press, 1982.

Rose, Willie Lee. *Rehearsal for Reconstruction: The Port Royal Experiment*. With an introduction by C. Vann Woodward. Indianapolis: Bobbs-Merrill, 1964.

Ross, Catherine Laverne. *Megaregions: Planning for Global Competitiveness*. Washington, DC: Island, 2009.

Ross, Dorothy. *G. Stanley Hall: The Psychologist as Prophet*. Chicago: University of Chicago Press, 1972.

———. *The Origins of American Social Science*. Cambridge: Cambridge University Press, 1991.

Ross, Edward Alsworth. "Sectionalism and Its Avoidance." *Journal of Social Forces* 2, no. 4 (1924): 484–87. https://doi.org/10.2307/3005211.

Rotabi, Karen Smith. "Ecological Theory Origin from Natural to Social Science or Vice Versa? A Brief Conceptual History for Social Work." *Advances in Social Work* 8, no. 1 (2007): 113–29.

Rothstein, Richard. *The Color of Law: A Forgotten History of How Our Government Segregated America*. New York: Liveright, 2017.

Rowe, Peter G. *Making a Middle Landscape*. Cambridge, MA: MIT Press, 1991.

Rubin, Louis D., Jr., and Robert D. Jacobs, eds. *Southern Renascence: The Literature of the Modern South*. Baltimore: Johns Hopkins Press, 1953.

Rudel, Tom, and Chun Fu. "A Requiem for the Southern Regionalists: Reforestation in the South and the Uses of Regional Social Science." *Social Science Quarterly* 77, no. 4 (1996): 804–20.

Runkle, Gerald. "Marxism and Charles Darwin." *Journal of Politics* 23, no. 1 (1961): 108–26. https://doi.org/10.2307/2127074.

Saikku, Mikko. "Faulkner and the 'Doomed Wilderness' of the Yazoo-Mississippi Delta." *Mississippi Quarterly* 58, no. 3 (2005): 529–57.

Sandercock, Leonie. *Making the Invisible Visible: A Multicultural Planning History*. Berkeley: University of California Press, 1998.

Sanders, Lynn Moss. "'An Effort toward Good Will and Good Wishes': Folk Studies and Howard Odum's Changing View of Race." *Southern Cultures* 3, no. 2 (1997): 47–66.

———. *Howard W. Odum's Folklore Odyssey: Transformation to Tolerance through African American Folk Studies*. Athens: University of Georgia Press, 2003.

Santayana, George. *Selected Critical Writings of George Santayana*. Edited by Norman Henfrey. London: Cambridge University Press, 1968.

Sanyal, Bish. "A Planners' Planner: John Friedmann's Quest for a General Theory of Planning." *Journal of the American Planning Association* 84, no. 2 (2018): 179–91. https://doi.org/10.1080/01944363.2018.1427616.

Sanyal, Bishwapriya, Lawrence J. Vale, and Christina D. Rosan, eds. *Planning Ideas That Matter: Livability, Territoriality, Governance, and Reflective Practice*. Cambridge, MA: MIT Press, 2012.

Sarbib, Jean-Louis. "The University of Chicago Program in Planning: A Retrospective Look." *Journal of Planning Education and Research* 2, no. 2 (1983): 77–81.

Sarkis, Hashim. "Le Corbusier's 'Geo-Architecture' and the Emergence of Territorial Aesthetics." In Moravánszky and Kegler, *Re-Scaling the Environment*, 115–34.

Sauer, Carl Ortwin. *Basin and Range Forms in the Chiricahua Area*. Berkeley: University of California Press, 1930.

———. *The Morphology of Landscape*. Berkeley: University of California Press, 1925.

———. *The Road to Cíbola*. New York: AMS, 1980.

Sauer, Carl O. "The Personality of Mexico." *Geographical Review* 31, no. 3 (1941): 353–64. https://doi.org/10.2307/210171.

Schivelbusch, Wolfgang. *Three New Deals: Reflections on Roosevelt's America, Mussolini's Italy, and Hitler's Germany, 1933–1939*. New York: Metropolitan Books, 2006.

Schlesinger, Arthur Meier, Sr. *The Rise of the City, 1878–1898*. Columbus: Ohio State University Press, 1999.

Schulman, Bruce J. *From Cotton Belt to Sunbelt: Federal Policy, Economic Development, and the Transformation of the South, 1938–1980*. New York: Oxford University Press, 1991.

Schwartz, Joel. "Robert Moses and City Planning." In Ballon and Jackson, *Robert Moses and the Modern City*, 130–33.

Scott, James C. *Seeing Like a State: How Certain Schemes to Improve the Human Condition Have Failed*. New Haven, CT: Yale University Press, 1998.

Scott, John, and Ray Bromley. *Envisioning Sociology: Victor Branford, Patrick Geddes, and the Quest for Social Reconstruction*. Albany: State University of New York Press, 2013.

Seim, David L. *Rockefeller Philanthropy and Modern Social Science*. London: Routledge, 2015.

Seligman, Edwin R. A. "Economics and Social Progress." *Publications of the American Economic Association* 3 (August 1903): 52–70.

———. *Principles of Economics, with Special Reference to American Conditions*. 10th ed. New York: Longmans, Green, 1923.

Seligman, Edwin R. A., and Alvin Johnson, eds. *Encyclopaedia of the Social Sciences*. Vols. 5 and 6. New York: Macmillan, 1931.

Selznick, Philip. *TVA and the Grass Roots: A Study of Politics and Organization*. Berkeley: University of California Press, 1984.

Shapiro, Henry D. "The Place of Culture and the Problem of Identity." In *Appalachia and America: Autonomy and Regional Dependence*, edited by Allen Batteau, 111–41. Lexington: University Press of Kentucky, 1983.

Shapley, Deborah. "TVA Today: Former Reformers in an Era of Expensive Electricity." *Science* 194, no. 4267 (1976): 814–18.

Siebert, Horst. *Regional Economic Growth: Theory and Policy*. Scranton, PA: International Textbooks, 1969.

Sills, David L., Robert King Merton, and Immanuel Maurice Wallerstein, eds. *International Encyclopedia of the Social Sciences*. New York: Macmillan, 1968.

Silver, Christopher. "Urban Planning in the New South." *Journal of Planning Literature* 2, no. 4 (1987): 371–83. https://doi.org/10.1177/088541228700200401.

Silver, Christopher, and John V. Moeser. *The Separate City: Black Communities in the Urban South, 1940–1968*. Lexington: University Press of Kentucky, 1995.

Simon, Herbert Alexander. *Administrative Behavior: A Study of Decision-Making Processes in Administrative Organizations*. New York: Free Press, 1997.

Simpson, George L., Jr. "Howard W. Odum and American Regionalism." *Social Forces* 34 (1955): 101–6.

Simpson, Michael. "Meliorist 'versus' Insurgent Planners and the Problems of New York, 1921–1941." *Journal of American Studies* 16, no. 2 (1982): 207–28.

Singal, Daniel Joseph. "Ulrich B. Phillips: The Old South as the New." *Journal of American History* 63, no. 4 (1977): 871–91. https://doi.org/10.2307/1893614.

———. *The War Within: From Victorian to Modernist Thought in the South, 1919–1945*. Chapel Hill: University of North Carolina Press, 1982.

Sitkoff, Harvard. *A New Deal for Blacks: The Emergence of Civil Rights as a National Issue*. New York: Oxford University Press, 1978.

Small, Albion W. "Points of Agreement among Sociologists." *American Journal of Sociology* 12, no. 5 (1907): 633–55.

Smith, Mark C. "Mitchell, Wesley Clair (1874–1948), Economist." In *American National Biography*. Oxford: Oxford University Press for the American Council of Learned Societies, 2000. https://doi.org/10.1093/anb/9780198606697.article.1400415.

Smith, Neil. *American Empire: Roosevelt's Geographer and the Prelude to Globalization*. Berkeley: University of California Press, 2003.

———. *Uneven Development: Nature, Capital, and the Production of Space*. New York: Blackwell, 1984.

Smith, Robert. "Botanical Survey of Scotland I: Edinburgh District." *Scottish Geographical Magazine* 16 (1900): 385–446.

Sociological Review. Unsigned review of *The Encyclopaedia of the Social Sciences*, edited by E. R. A. Seligman and Alvin Johnson. a22, no. 3 (July 1930): 186–94. https://doi.org/10.1111/j.1467-954X.1930.tb01759.x.

Soja, Edward W. *Postmodern Geographies: The Reassertion of Space in Critical Social Theory*. London: Verso, 1989.

———. "Regions in Context: Spatiality, Periodicity, and the Historical Geography of the Regional Question." *Environment and Planning D: Society and Space* 3, no. 2 (1985): 175–90. https://doi.org/10.1068/d030175.

Solot, Michael. "Carl Sauer and Cultural Evolution." *Annals of the Association of American Geographers* 76, no. 4 (1986): 508–20.

Sorokin, Pitirim Aleksandrovich. *Contemporary Sociological Theories*. New York: Harper and Row, 1928.

Sosna, Morton. *In Search of the Silent South: Southern Liberals and the Race Issue*. New York: Columbia University Press, 1977.

———. "More Important Than the Civil War? The Impact of World War II on the South." In *Perspectives on the American South: An Annual Review of Society, Politics, and Culture*, edited by James C. Cobb and Charles R. Wilson, 4:145–61. New York: Gordon and Breach Science, 1987.

Soule, George Henry. *The Coming American Revolution*. New York: Macmillan, 1934.

———. *A Planned Society*. New York: Macmillan, 1935.

———. "Planning for Agriculture." *New Republic* 69 (October 1931): 204–6.

Spann, Edward K. *Designing Modern America: The Regional Planning Association of America and Its Members*. Columbus: Ohio State University Press, 1996.

———. "Franklin Delano Roosevelt and the Regional Planning Association of America, 1931–1936." *New York History* 74, no. 2 (1993): 185–200.

Spencer, Herbert. *Social Statics: Man versus the State*. Vol. 7. New York: D. Appleton, 1892.

Spillman, William J. "The Agricultural Ladder." *American Economic Review* 9, no. 1 (1919): 170–79.

Spirn, Anne Whiston. "The Authority of Nature: Conflict and Confusion in Landscape Architecture." In Wolschke-Bulmahn, *Nature and Ideology*, 249–61.

Stanton, William Ragan. *The Leopard's Spots: Scientific Attitudes toward Race in America, 1815–59*. Chicago: University of Chicago Press, 1960.

Staub, Michael E. *Voices of Persuasion: Politics of Representation in 1930s America*. Cambridge: Cambridge University Press, 1994.

Stewart, Mart A. "Southern Environmental History." In Boles, *Companion to the American South*, 405–23.

Stocking, George W., Jr. *Race, Culture, and Evolution; Essays in the History of Anthropology*. New York: Free Press, 1968.

Storm, Eric. *The Culture of Regionalism: Art, Architecture and International Exhibitions in France, Germany and Spain, 1890–1939*. Manchester, UK: Manchester University Press, 2010.

———. "Regionalism in History, 1890–1945: The Cultural Approach." *European History Quarterly* 33, no. 2 (2003): 251–65. https://doi.org/10.1177/02656914030332005.

Sullivan, Patricia. *Days of Hope: Race and Democracy in the New Deal Era*. Chapel Hill: University of North Carolina Press, 1996.

Sultana, Ronald G., and Michael A. Buhagiar, eds. *Educational Scholarship across the Mediterranean: A Celebratory Retrospective*. Comparative Education and the Mediterranean Region, vol. 3. Leiden, The Netherlands: Brill, 2021.

Sumner, William Graham. *Folkways: A Study of Sociological Importance of Usages, Manners, Customs, Mores, and Morals.* Boston: Ginn, 1913.

Sundquist, Eric. "Realism and Regionalism." In *Columbia Literary History of the United States*, edited by Emory Elliott, Martha Banta, Terence Martin, David Minter, Marjorie Peloff, and Daniel B. Shea, 501–24. New York: Columbia University Press, 1988.

Sussman, Carl. *Planning the Fourth Migration: The Neglected Vision of the Regional Planning Association of America.* Cambridge, MA: MIT Press, 1976.

Sutherland, Robert L. "Harry Estill Moore, 1897–1966." *American Sociologist* 2, no. 1 (1967): 29–30.

Swyngedouw, Eric, Louis Albrechts, Frank Moulaert, and Peter Roberts, eds. *Regional Policy at the Crossroads: European Perspectives.* London: J. Kingsley, 1989.

Tate, Allen. *Essays of Four Decades.* Chicago: Swallow, 1968.

Tate, Gayle T., and Lewis A. Randolph. *The Black Urban Community: From Dusk till Dawn.* New York: Palgrave Macmillan, 2006.

Taylor, Frederick Winslow. *The Principles of Scientific Management.* New York: Harper, 1942.

Taylor, William Robert. *Cavalier and Yankee: The Old South and American National Character.* New York: Oxford University Press, 1993.

Teitz, Michael B. "Regional Development Planning." In Sanyal, Vale, and Rosan, *Planning Ideas That Matter*, 127–52.

Terry, Jennifer. "The Fiction of W. E. B. Du Bois." In *The Cambridge Companion to W. E. B. Du Bois*, edited by Shamoon Zamir, 48–63. Cambridge: Cambridge University Press, 2008.

Thomas, John L. "Holding the Middle Ground." In Fishman, *American Planning Tradition*, 33–64.

Thomas, William B. "Conservative Currents in Howard Washington Odum's Agenda for Social Reform in Southern Race Relations, 1930–1936." *Phylon* 45, no. 2 (1984): 121–34. https://doi.org/10.2307/274474.

———. "Howard W. Odum's Social Theories in Transition: 1910–1930." *American Sociologist* 16, no. 1 (1981): 25–34.

Thornton, Jesse. *Science and Social Change.* Washington, DC: Brookings Institution, 1939.

Tindall, George B. *The Emergence of the New South, 1913–1945.* Baton Rouge: Louisiana State University Press, 1967.

———. "The Significance of Howard W. Odum to Southern History: A Preliminary Estimate." *Journal of Southern History* 24, no. 3 (1958): 285–307. https://doi.org/10.2307/2954985.

Tobin, William A. "Studying Society: The Making of 'Recent Social Trends in the United States, 1929–1933.'" *Theory and Society* 24, no. 4 (1995): 537–65.

Tönnies, Ferdinand. *Community and Society.* Translated and edited by Charles Price Loomis. East Lansing: Michigan State University Press, 1957. Reprint, New York: Harper and Row, 1963.

Trachtenberg, Alan. "Mumford in the Twenties: The Historian as Artist." *Salmagundi*, no. 49 (1980): 29–42.

Tugwell, R. G. "The Sources of New Deal Reformism." *Ethics* 64, no. 4 (1954): 249–76. https://doi.org/10.1086/290956.

Tullos, Allen. "Geography and Justice in the Black Belt: Regionalism Comes with the Territory." In Wilson, *New Regionalism*, 135–47.

———. *Habits of Industry: White Culture and the Transformation of the Carolina Piedmont*. Chapel Hill: University of North Carolina Press, 1989.

———. "The Politics of Regional Development: Lewis Mumford and Howard W. Odum." In Hughes and Hughes, *Lewis Mumford: Public Intellectual*, 110–20.

Turner, Frederick Jackson. *The Frontier in American History*. New York: H. Holt, 1920.

———. *The Significance of Sections in American History*. With an introduction by Max Farrand. New York: H. Holt, 1932.

———. "The Significance of the Frontier in American History." In *Annual Report of the American Historical Association*, edited by the Smithsonian Institution, 197–227. Washington, DC: US Government Printing Office, 1894.

Turner, Jonathan H., and Peter R. Turner. *The Structure of Sociological Theory*. 6th ed. Belmont, CA: Wadsworth, 1998.

Twelve Southerners [Donald Davidson, John Gould Fletcher, Henry Blue Kline, et al.]. *I'll Take My Stand: The South and the Agrarian Tradition*. New York: Harper, 1930.

Tyler, Pamela. "The Impact of the New Deal and World War II on the South." In Boles, *Companion to the American South*, 444–60.

United States Department of Labor Bureau of Labor Statistics. *Welfare Work for Employees in Industrial Establishments in the United States*. Bulletin of the United States Bureau of Labor Statistics, no. 250. Washington, DC: US Government Printing Office, 1919.

Vance, Rupert B. *All These People: The Nation's Human Resources in the South*. In collaboration with Nadia Danilevsky. Chapel Hill: University of North Carolina Press, 1945.

———. "The Concept of the Region." *Social Forces* 8, no. 2 (1929): 208–18. https://doi.org/10.2307/2569581.

———. "The Economic Future of the Old Cotton Belt." *Southern Workman* 65, no. 3 (March 1936): 85–92.

———. "Howard Odum's Technicways: A Neglected Lead in American Sociology." *Social Forces* 50, no. 4 (1972): 456–61. https://doi.org/10.2307/2576788.

———. "How Can the Southern Population Find Gainful Employment?" *Journal of Farm Economics* 22, no. 1 (1940): 198–205. https://doi.org/10.2307/1232044.

———. *Human Factors in Cotton Culture: A Study in the Social Geography of the American South*. Chapel Hill: University of North Carolina Press, 1929.

———. *Human Geography of the South: A Study in Regional Resources and Human Adequacy*. Chapel Hill: University of North Carolina Press, 1932.

———. "Implications of the Concepts 'Region' and 'Regional Planning.'" *Publications of the American Sociological Society* 29 (August 1935): 85–93.

———. "Is Agrarianism for Farmers?" In Reed and Singal, *Regionalism and the South*.

———. "Planning the Southern Economy." *Southwest Review* 20, no. 2 (1935): 111–23.
———. "The Regional Concept as a Tool for Social Research." 1951. In Reed and Singal, *Regionalism and the South*, 155–75.
———. "Regional Planning with Reference to the Southeast." *Southern Economic Journal* 3, no. 1 (1936): 55–65.
———. *Regional Reconstruction: A Way Out for the South*. Chapel Hill: University of North Carolina Press, 1935.
———. "The Sociological Implications of Southern Regionalism." *Journal of Southern History* 26, no. 1 (February 1960): 44–56.
———. "What of Submarginal Areas in Regional Planning?" *Social Forces* 12, no. 3 (1934): 315–29. https://doi.org/10.2307/2569921.
Vance, Rupert B., and Nicholas J. Demerath, eds. *The Urban South*. Chapel Hill: University of North Carolina Press, 1954.
Vance, Rupert B., and Katharine Jocher. "Howard W. Odum." *Social Forces* 33, no. 3 (1955): 203–17. https://doi.org/10.1093/sf/33.3.203.
Van Sickle, John V. *Planning for the South: An Inquiry into the Economics of Regionalism*. Nashville: Vanderbilt University Press, 1943.
Veblen, Thorstein. *The Place of Science in Modern Civilisation and Other Essays*. New York: B. W. Huebsch, 1919.
———. *The Theory of the Leisure Class*. Auckland, New Zealand: Floating Press, 1918.
Vidal de La Blache, Paul. *Principles of Human Geography*. Edited by Emmanuel de Martonne. Translated by Millicent Todd. New York: Henry Holt, 1926.
Vigier, Philippe. *Régions et régionalisme en France au XIXe siècle*. Paris: Presses Universitaires de France, 1977.
von Hayek, Friedrich August. *The Counter-Revolution of Science: Studies on the Abuse of Reason*. Glencoe, IL: Free Press, 1952.
Wakeman, Rosemary. *Practicing Utopia: An Intellectual History of the New Town Movement*. Chicago: University of Chicago Press, 2016.
Walker, Francis A. "Mr. Grote's Theory of Democracy." *Bibliotheca sacra* 25 (October 1868): 687–90.
Wallerstein, Immanuel Maurice. *World-Systems Analysis: An Introduction*. Durham, NC: Duke University Press, 2004.
Ward, David, and Noel Radomski. *Proud Traditions and Future Challenges: The University of Wisconsin–Madison Celebrates 150 Years*. Madison: Published for the Office of the Chancellor by the Office of University Publications, University of Wisconsin–Madison, 1999.
Ward, Lester Frank. "Contributions to Social Philosophy: XII. Collective Telesis." *American Journal of Sociology* 2, no. 6 (1897): 801–22.
———. *Dynamic Sociology, or Applied Social Science, as Based upon Statical Sociology and the Less Complex Sciences*. 2 vols. New York: D. Appleton, 1920.
———. *Outlines of Sociology*. New York: Macmillan, 1923.
———. *The Psychic Factors of Civilization*. Boston: Ginn, 1901.
———. *Pure Sociology: A Treatise on the Origin and Spontaneous Development of Society*. New York: Macmillan, 1903.

———. "*The Theory of the Leisure Class*: Thorstein Veblen." *American Journal of Sociology* 5, no. 6 (1900): 829–37. https://doi.org/10.1086/210938.
Ward, Lester Frank, Emily Palmer Cape, and Sarah Emma Simons. *Glimpses of the Cosmos*. 4 vols. New York: G. P. Putnam's Sons, 1913.
Ward, Stephen V. "Re-Examining the International Diffusion of Planning." In *Urban Planning in a Changing World: The Twentieth Century Experience*, edited by Robert Freestone, 40–60. London: Routledge, 2000.
Watkins, Floyd C. "What Stand Did Faulkner Take?" In *Faulkner and the Southern Renaissance: Faulkner and Yoknapatawpha*, edited by Doreen Fowler and Ann J. Abadie, 40–62. Jackson: University Press of Mississippi, 1981.
Weaver, Clyde. *Regional Development and the Local Community: Planning, Politics, and Social Context*. Chichester, UK: Wiley, 1984.
Welter, Volker. *Biopolis: Patrick Geddes and the City of Life*. Cambridge, MA: MIT Press, 2002.
White, Morton, and Lucia White. *The Intellectual versus the City: From Thomas Jefferson to Frank Lloyd Wright*. Cambridge, MA: Harvard University Press, 1962.
White, Richard. *The Organic Machine*. New York: Hill and Wang, 1995.
Whitman, Walt. *Leaves of Grass*. 1855. Reprint, New York: Vintage Books / Library of America, 1991.
Wiebe, Robert H. *The Search for Order, 1877–1920*. New York: Hill and Wang, 1967.
Wilkerson, Isabel. *The Warmth of Other Suns: The Epic Story of America's Great Migration*. New York: Random House, 2010.
Williams, Raymond. *The Country and the City*. New York: Oxford University Press, 1975.
———. *Raymond Williams on Culture and Society: Essential Writings*. Edited by Jim McGuigan. Los Angeles: Sage, 2014.
Williams, Rosalind. "Lewis Mumford as a Historian of Technology in Technics and Civilization." In Hughes and Hughes, *Lewis Mumford: Public Intellectual*, 43–65.
Wilson, Charles Reagan, ed. *The New Regionalism: Essays and Commentaries*. Jackson: University Press of Mississippi, 1998.
Wilson, Francille Rusan. *The Segregated Scholars: Black Social Scientists and the Creation of Black Labor Studies, 1890–1950*. Charlottesville: University of Virginia Press, 2006.
Wilson, Louis Round. *The University of North Carolina, 1900–1930: The Making of a Modern University*. Chapel Hill: University of North Carolina Press, 1957.
Wilson, William Henry. *The City Beautiful Movement*. Baltimore: Johns Hopkins University Press, 1989.
Wirth, Louis. "The Limitations of Regionalism." In Jensen, *Regionalism in America*, 381–93.
Wish, Harvey. *George Fitzhugh: Propagandist of the Old South*. Baton Rouge: Louisiana State University Press, 1943.
Wissler, Clark. "The Culture-Area Concept in Social Anthropology." *American Journal of Sociology* 32, no. 6 (1927): 881–91.
Wolin, Sheldon S. *Politics and Vision: Continuity and Innovation in Western Political Thought*. Princeton, NJ: Princeton University Press, 2004.

Wolschke-Bulmahn, Joachim, ed. *Nature and Ideology: Natural Garden Design in the Twentieth Century*. Washington, DC: Dumbarton Oaks, 1997.

Woods, Clyde Adrian. *Development Arrested: The Blues and Plantation Power in the Mississippi Delta*. London: Verso, 1998.

Woodward, C. Vann. *The Burden of Southern History*. Baton Rouge: Louisiana State University Press, 1960. Reprinted with a new foreword by William E. Leuchtenburg. Baton Rouge: Louisiana State University Press, 1993.

———. *Origins of the New South, 1877–1913*. Baton Rouge: Louisiana State University Press, 1951.

———. *Tom Watson: Agrarian Rebel*. New York: Macmillan, 1938.

Woofter, T. J., Jr. "Southern Population and Social Planning." *Social Forces* 14, no. 1 (1935): 16–22. https://doi.org/10.2307/2569977.

———. "The Subregions of the Southeast." *Social Forces* 13, no. 1 (1934): 43–50. https://doi.org/10.2307/2570216.

Worcester, Kent, and Elbridge Sibley. *Social Science Research Council, 1923–1998*. New York: Social Science Research Council, 2001.

Wright, Earl, II. *Jim Crow Sociology: The Black and Southern Roots of American Sociology*. Cincinnati, OH: University of Cincinnati Press, 2020.

———. "W. E. B. Du Bois, Howard W. Odum and the Sociological Ghetto." *Sociological Spectrum* 34, no. 5 (2014): 453–68. https://doi.org/10.1080/02732173.2014.923797.

Wright, Frank Lloyd. *The Living City*. New York: Bramhall House, 1958.

Wright, Gavin. "The Economic Revolution in the American South." *Journal of Economic Perspectives* 1, no. 1 (1987): 161–78. https://doi.org/10.1257/jep.1.1.161.

———. *Old South, New South: Revolutions in the Southern Economy since the Civil War*. Baton Rouge: Louisiana State University Press, 1996.

Wright, Julian. *The Regionalist Movement in France, 1890–1914: Jean Charles-Brun and French Political Thought*. Oxford: Clarendon, 2003.

Wulf, Andrea. *The Invention of Nature: Alexander von Humboldt's New World*. New York: Knopf, 2015.

Wundt, Wilhelm Max. *Elemente der Völkerpsychologie: Grundlinien Einer Psychologischen Entwicklungsgeschichte der Menschheit*. 2nd ed. Leipzig: Kröner, 1913.

Yaro, Robert D., Ming Zhang, and Frederick R. Steiner. *Megaregions and America's Future*. Cambridge, MA: Lincoln Institute of Land Policy, 2022.

Zinn, Howard. *New Deal Thought*. Indianapolis: Bobbs-Merrill, 1966.

Zorbaugh, Harvey Warren. *The Gold Coast and the Slum: A Sociological Study of Chicago's Near North Side*. Chicago: University of Chicago Press, 1930.

INDEX

Italic page numbers refer to illustrations.

American Epoch, An (Odum), 110, 134, 142, 162; and Thomas Pierce Bailey's influence, 52; Herbert Blumer on, 92; and Howard Odum's presentation of Southern sectionalism, 92; and portraiture method, 72, 73, 88, 91. *See also* Odum, Howard; portraiture technique

American Regionalism (Odum and Moore), 6, 73, 127, 153; critical reception of, 27, 129, 130, 151; and incoherent criteria defining regions, 150; reviewed by IRSS researchers, 152. *See also* Moore, Harry; Odum, Howard

American Sociological Association. *See* American Sociological Society

American Sociological Society, 84, 213n102, 129; and Earnest Burgess, 168; Howard Odum's 1930 Presidential Address to, 16, 73, 136, 142, 144, 145; Howard Odum's appointment as president of, 76, 152; and Robert Park, 101; and Lester Frank Ward, 83

Appalachian Trail proposal, 24, 35, 135, 159; and interregionalism of W. E. B. Du Bois, 27, 119, 121, 122, 123. *See also* MacKaye, Benton

Bailey, Thomas Pearce: and W. E. B. Du Bois, 52; and G. Stanley Hall, 50; and Howard Odum, 25, 50, 51, 52, 71, 78; and *Race Orthodoxy in the South, and Other Aspects of the Negro Problem*, 51, 52; white Southern racial ideology of, 51, 52

Baldwin, James, 124; on "color line," 105, 106; and William Faulkner's gradualism on race, 99, 100

Barr, Stringfellow, 33, 39, 40

Blumer, Herbert, 92, 93, 168

Boas, Frank, 112; and G. Stanley Hall, 53, *53*; and Zora Neale Hurston, 107; and methods of Howard Odum, 108, 126, 144

Branford, Victor, 135; and Patrick Geddes, 33, 135, 138, 175, 184; and regional planning's aspired poeticism, 19, 33; and Rupert Vance, 138, 175, 184

Branson, Eugene Cunningham, 58; and Howard Odum, 56, 60, 223n17

Burgess, Ernest, 173; and American Sociological Society, 168, 169, 170, 171, 172; and human ecology, 93, 202n31; and William Graham Sumner's folkways concepts, 169, 170; on Tennessee Valley Authority, 169, 170

Chase, Harry Woodburn: and Howard Odum, 57, 59, 60, 61, 190; as University of North Carolina president, 58, 59, 190

Chase, Stuart, 32, 33, 34

Civil War: and Confederacy, 80, 100; and Howard Odum, 72; and plantation system, 116; and white South's perception of Northern colonial rule, 106, 134

Columbia University: and biological racist thought, 190; and Frank Boas, 107, 126, 144; and early sociology, 83; and Zora Neale Hurston, 107; IRSS replication at, 66; meliorist social science at, 15; and Wesley Mitchell, 75; and Howard Odum's network, 63, 65, 87, 179, 190; and Howard Odum's PhD work, 54, 55, 60, 71, 92, 126, 144; and Rupert Vance, 67, and Thomas Woofter Jr., 69

conferences, 163, 168; and Institute on Southern Regional Development and Social Sciences (1936), 179, 180; on international psychology at Clark University (1909), 53, *53*; on regionalism at University of Wisconsin–Madison (1949), 130–32, 222n14; and University of Virginia Round Table on Regionalism (1931), 2, 25, 28, 31–45, 58, 203n51. *See also* American Sociological Society

Darwin, Charles: and intellectual history of social sciences in United States, 35, 64, 112; Herbert Spencer's misinterpretation of, 26, 80

Darwinism, social: and conservative stance against social progress, 81, 103, 167, 201n165; and Franklin Giddings, 84; and Herbert Spencer, 26, 80; and William Sumner, 81

Davidson, Donald: and John Gould Fletcher, 38, 39; and mistrust of major infrastructure projects, 27, 28, 48, 154, 155, 188; and Howard Odum, 40, 43, 44, 147, 153, 154, 155; racism of, 153; and Arthur Raper, 70; and Southern regionalists' veneer of apoliticism, 154; on Frederick Jackson Turner's frontier concept, 125. *See also* Southern Agrarians

Dewey, John, 75; and intellectual traditions of social planning, 13, 47, 48, 84, 155, 159

Du Bois, W. E. B., 209n146; on African American historical claims for redress, 117; on African American migration to northern United States, 118; on ambiguity of Southern regionalism, 84; and Thomas Pearce Bailey, 52; and Black interregional experience, 27, 120, 121, 126; early life and education of, 54, 55, 119; and Gunnar Myrdal, 106; and national scope of regionalism and planning thought, 24, 42, 58; and Howard Odum, 55, 105, 129, 130; and *Philadelphia Negro*, 27, 52, 55, 120, 121, 126; on racism at elite Northern universities, 190; and social scientists' equivocation on racial discrimination, 101, 105, 117; and *Souls of Black Folk*, 42, 52, 121, 126; and Thomas Woofter Jr., 69

engineering, social, 86; and Harry Woodburn Chase, 58; and Chicago School, 17, 101; and early twentieth-century US social sciences, 13, 191; and Franklin Giddings, 84; and G. Stanley Hall, 52; and New Deal ideology, 14, 74; of new immigrant South workforce, 14; and Howard Odum, 11, 71, 76, 77, 110, 145, 155, 164, 190; and James C. Scott, 198n91; and Thorstein Veblen, 12, 13, 48; and Lester Frank Ward, 82, 83

Faulkner, William, 9, 219n126; and James Baldwin, 99, 100, 215n10;

and Howard Odum, 43, 44, 204n83, 205n89; and post–World War II Latin America, 193

Fitzhugh, George, 189; and intellectual history of social sciences in United States, 26, 79, 212n55; and Southern social structure, 79, 80, 189

Fletcher, John Gould, 34, 38, 39, 40

folklore, 134; and conservative cultural aims of interwar US regional planning, 5; and Johann Gottfried Herder, 79; imagined within evolutionary change, 15, 22, 48, 91, 92, 118; and indigenism, 109, 110, 112, 113, 118, 125; and Guy Johnson, 68, 69; and migration from the South, 118; and Howard Odum, 54, 91, 92. *See also* folklore, Black

folklore, Black: and Black Ulysses trilogy, 108, 109, *109*, 110, 118, 142; and W. E. B. Du Bois, 105; and Zora Neale Hurston, 107; and Guy Johnson, 68, 126, 142; and Howard Odum, 50, 68, 97, 88, 104, 105, 107, 141; and scholarly predominance of white researchers, 27, 107; and scholar's challenge of authenticity, 107. *See also* folklore

Friedmann, John, 159; on history of social sciences, 13; and Howard Odum's legacy and work, 1, 15, 193; at University of Chicago, 1, 2; on US regional planning doctrine, 191, 192

frontier, 11, 20, 219n118. *See also* Turner, Frederick Jackson

Geddes, Patrick: and Darwinian social planning, 80, 212n63; and emergence of US regional planning, 8, 31, 32, 33, 39, 135, 171; and G. Stanley Hall, 54; and Benton MacKaye, 122; and Lewis Mumford, 8, 172; Howard Odum's ode to, 173; and Outlook Tower, 24, 31, 32, 44, 45, 135; and river basin development ideas, 158, 192; and "survey before plan" dictum, 160, 184; and technicways, 171, 172, 173; and Rupert Vance, 28, 138, 175

Giddings, Franklin: and inaugural *Social Forces* article, 60; and consciousness of kind, 6, 26, 54, 84, 85; and descriptive social science, 63, 73, 86; as mentor to Howard Odum, 6, 54, 77, 151, 190; Howard Odum's work influenced by, 25, 26, 71, 84, 110, 143, 145, 172; racist views of, 110, 190; and William Graham Sumner and Lester Frank Ward, 83, 84, 85, 142, 172

Hagood, Margaret Jarman, 19, 66, 191, 152

Hall, G. Stanley: and Thomas Pearce Bailey, 50, 52; and Clark University Psychology Conference Group, 53, *53*; as Howard Odum's mentor, 4, 25, 52; and Howard Odum's reformist institutionalism, 54, 57, 59, 190; on universities as engineers of societal change, 54, 190

Hoover, Herbert, 48, 69, 74, 75. *See also* President's Research Committee on Social Trends

Hughes, Henry: defense of slavery, 79; and history of social sciences in United States, 26, 79; and Howard Odum, 189, 212n55

Hurston, Zora Neal: literary achievement of, 44; on white academic perspectives on race and Black folklore, 27, 107, 108

Indigenous peoples: and 1833 Treaty of Chicago, 76; Maya, 95; mythologized by regionalists, 112, 113, 118, 137; and Carl Sauer, 95. *See also* folklore: and indigenism

INDEX

271

Institute for Research in Social Science (IRSS), 57, 156; and agenda of reformist regional social science, 19, 61, 71, 93, 95, 141, 159, 167; and agenda of Southern "area studies" research, 132, 134, 179; and conservative Southern interests, 64, 65, 66, 73, 88, 191; and empirical descriptive methods, 93, 127, 136, 144; first five years of, 19, 60, 63–66, 88, 134, 179; legacy of, 45, 96; and New Deal development in the South, 29, 41, 181; and Howard Odum's academic networks, 4, 24, 25, 87, 146; and Howard Odum's philanthropic networks, 4, 23, 63, 87, 134, 146, 188; and quantitative methods, 26, 88, 137, 148; and racial violence, 55, 103, 105, 106, 107, 136, 144; replication of, 66; repudiation of New South by, 66–70; and Rockefeller Memorial, 61, 62, 66, 86, 87; and Carl Sauer, 93, 94, 95; and *Southern Regions of the United States*, 26, 143, 148, 149, 179; and University of Virginia Round Table on Regionalism, 2, 32, 36; and visionary researchers, 66–71; withholding critical calls for reform, 191. *See also* Hagood, Margaret Jarman; Jocher, Katherine; Johnson, Guy; Odum, Howard; Raper, Arthur; Vance, Rupert; Woofter, Thomas, Jr.

IRSS. *See* Institute for Research in Social Science

Jim Crow South: framing of between Victorian and Modern thought, 184; migration out of, 17, 83; Howard Odum's upbringing and education in, 49, 50, 72; against social planning, 16; and *Souls of Black Folk* (Du Bois), 121; and Southern regionalist equivocation on racism, 3, 5, 103, 104, 105, 108, 123, 174, 180, 191; and white brutality and supremacy, 99, 100, 102, 116, 174

Jocher, Katherine, 174; and IRSS, 19, 66; and *Introduction to Social Research*, 88, 142, 143, 144, 151; on Howard Odum, 179

Johnson, Guy: and Black folk songs, 107, 108, 126, 142; and collaboration with Howard Odum, 98, 103, 105, 107, 108, 126, 142; and *Folk Culture on St. Helena Island*, 10, 68, 138; and IRSS, 10, 19, 66; on Howard Odum, 78, 149; research and gradualist views on race of, 68, 69, 104; on tension between folkways and progress, 44

Kendrick, Benjamin, 147, 162, 179

MacKaye, Benton, 201n5; and evolutionary balance, 113; and intellectual history of social planning, 15, 16; and metropolitan cultural expansion, 159, 166; at University of Virginia Round Table on Regionalism, 32, 34, 35, 138. *See also* Appalachian Trail proposal

Merriam, Charles, 61, 63, 75, 77, 88, 157

migration: international, 3, 36, 83, 95, 111, 119; and Southern regionalists' equilibrium concept, 3, 192; US rural-to-urban, 36, 83, 70, 83, 118, 162; US South-to-North, 36, 83, 109, 118, 151; white, 118. *See also* migration, African American

migration, African American, 17, 70, 109, 118, 120, 121; and W. E. B. Du Bois, 120, 121; and planning schemes, 187; and Arthur Raper, 70; and Edward Ross, 121, and Thomas Woofter Jr., 69. *See also* migration

Mississippi, 44, 50, 51, 54, 68, 71, 78, 177, 182

Mitchell, Wesley, 63, 75, 77, 157

Moore, Harry: and definition of regionalism, 23, 132, 133; and Howard Odum, 6, 23, 73, 127, 129, 132, 133

Mumford, Lewis, 24, 81; on culture and modernity, 10, 22, 101, 110, 114, 150, 172, 191, 234n56; and definitions

of regionalism, 2, 10, 16, 23, 133;
and Patrick Geddes, 8, 32, 172; and
Howard Odum, 2, 96, 135, 136, 150,
153, 167, 172; on Southern Agrarians,
33, 39; and *Survey Graphic* 1925
issue, 2, 32, 135, 136, 167; and
University of Virginia Round Table
on Regionalism, 32, 33, 34, 35, 36, 39
Myrdal, Gunnar, 106, 184, 191

National Emergency Council (NEC), 28, 41, 42, 43, 180, 181
National Resources Committee (NRC), 151; and cultural-scientific imperative of regionalism, 158; and functional turn of regional planning, 159; as National Planning Board, 157, 158, 162, 181; and *Regional Factors in National Planning and Development*, 158
New Deal, 70, 186; and Howard Odum, 28, 29, 160, 162, 165, 180, 181, 184; question of South's position within, 25, 40, 41, 42, 104, 117, 124, 181; and race and racial oppression, 5, 180, 181, 193; and social engineering, 14, 170; and sociologists, 168; Southern regionalism's influence on, 3, 4, 5, 22, 159, 180, 184; and stateways-folkways tension, 170, 171. *See also* Tennessee Valley Authority
New South, 67, 81, 133, 146, 190; versus Old South, 3, 43, 99, 114, 186; and racial segregation, 51, 100; and reformist social science, 22, 59, 70, 80, 99

Odum, Howard, *46, 57, 156*; ambivalent positions taken by, 78, 186, 191; and accommodation of Southern white ideology and racism, 22, 23, 52, 103, 180, 181, 190; and American Sociological Society, 16, 73, 136, 142, 144, 145; and artistic realism, 72, 110, 111; biological racial difference argued by, 55, 144; and Black folk song research, 104, 105, 106, 107, 108, 118, 126; and Century of Progress International Exposition, 76, 77; and criteria defining regions, 148, *148*, 149, *149*, 150, 151, 152, 153; and criticism from conservative Southern interests, 64, 88; and criticism from Donald Davidson, 153, 154, 155; critique of Jim Crow by, 123; death of, 17, 23, 106, 186, 191; early life of, 49, 50, 70; and elitism of folkways concept, 165, 166; and evolutionary view of folk society, 15, 16, 91, 145; and evolutionary view of regions and sections, 147, 153, 154, 160, 162, 173; and William Faulkner, 43, 44, 204n83, 205n89; gradualist views on race relations of, 105, 107, 108, 118, 121, 123, 124; and graduate studies, 50, 51, 52, 53, 54, 55, 56; importance of letters to, 48, 49; and Benjamin Kendrick, 147, 162, 179; legacy of, 6, 26, 185, 186, 189, 193; and moderate critiques concerning race, 60, 108; and movement toward environmental racial definitions, 126; and 1949 conference at University of Wisconsin–Madison, 130–32; on plantation society, 14, 115; and President's Research Committee on Social Trends, 75–78, 162, 188; and proposed Council on Southern Regional Development, 28, 41, 180, 189, 192; and proposed regional planning institutions, 178–81; and regional-national social planning, 160, 162, 163, 164, 165; and prioritization of regional progress over issues of race, 22, 38, 102, 104, 111, 125; and Carl Sauer's human geography, 92–96; as segregationist, 3; as network operator, 26, 48, 70, 154, 179; and social engineering, 11, 71, 76, 77, 110, 145, 155, 164, 190; and southern regionalists' research on race, 27, 42, 103, 106, 107, 180; starting at University of North

Odum, Howard (*continued*)
    Carolina at Chapel Hill, 57; and technicways as counterweight to stateways, 16, 17, 155; and technicways in social engineering and planning, 76, 92, 145, 171–175, 189; and folkways and stateways, 16, 78, 103, 159, 171, 175, 189; and regional autonomy and federal framework, 3, 42, 173, 174; and Southern white folk culture and science, 64, 65, 71, 92, 142, 155, 183; and Frederick Jackson Turner's concepts, 27, 114, 115, 134, 146, 147, 154; at University of Georgia, 56; at University of Virginia Round Table on Regionalism, 32, 33, 36, 37, 38. *See also* folklore, Black; Institute for Research in Social Science; New Deal; Odum, Howard, authored and coauthored works by; Odum, Howard, intellectual and philanthropic networks of; Odum, Howard and Rupert Vance, divergences between; planning, regional-national social; portraiture technique; regionalism, Southern; Rockefeller Foundation; Rockefeller Memorial; Vance, Rupert
Odum, Howard, authored and co-authored works by: "The Case for National-Regional Social Planning," 163–65, 168; *Cold Blue Moon, Black Ulysses Afar Off*, 108; *Introduction to Social Research*, 88, 142, 143, 144, 145, 151; *Man's Quest for Social Guidance*, 76, 96, 135, 142, 166, 167, 168; *Negro and His Songs*, 108; *Negro Workaday Songs*, 108; *Rainbow Round My Shoulder*, 108, *109*; *Wings on My Feet*, 108. See also *American Epoch*; *American Regionalism*; folklore, Black: and Black Ulysses trilogy; *Southern Regions of the United States*
Odum, Howard, intellectual and philanthropic networks of, 4, 6, 15, 24, 25, 59, 190; criticism by, 26, 73, 88, 129, 130, 151, 152; and intellectual autonomy from Rockefeller agencies, 62, 63, 87, 94, 191. *See also* Bailey, Thomas Pearce; Branson, Eugene Cunningham; Columbia University; Davidson, Donald; Du Bois, W. E. B.; Geddes, Patrick; Giddings, Franklin; Hall, G. Stanley; Institute for Research in Social Science; Johnson, Guy; Moore, Harry; Park, Robert; Rockefeller Foundation; Rockefeller Memorial; Ruml, Beardsley; Social Science Research Council; Ward, Lester Frank
Odum, Howard, and Rupert Vance, divergences between: over agrarian-metropolitan tension in regional planning, 124, 189; over definitions of regions and regionalism, 23, 136, 149; over folkways and human geography, 20, 28, 138, 140, 141, 146, 174–78; over reverence for the South, 27, 67, 155; over social change, 130, 132; and sociological rigor, 27, 174

Park, Robert: and American Sociological Society, 101; on Thomas Pearce Bailey, 51; and human ecology, 10, 92, 93, 202n31; and Guy Johnson, 68; moderative views on race of, 102; and Howard Odum, 102, 226n116; at University of Chicago, 51, 101
planning, regional, *156*; emergence of, 1, 2, 18, 31, 32, 47, 159; evolutionary framework of, 3, 18, 26, 162, 170, 175; and interregionalism, 118–23; Howard Odum's formulation of, 158, 167, 168; and poets and poeticism, 19, 27, 33, 35, 38, 44, 45, 189; scholarship of, 1, 2, 5; Southern regionalism's connection to, 1–6, 17, 20, 24; after World War II, 2, 17, 21, 22, 124, 159, 191, 192. *See also* Geddes, Patrick; New Deal; Odum, Howard; planning, regional-national social; planning, social; regionalism, Southern;

Regional Planning Association of America; Tennessee Valley Authority; University of Virginia Round Table on Regionalism; Vance, Rupert

planning, regional-national social: and *Man's Quest for Social Guidance*, 166, 167; and Howard Odum's 1934 sabbatical travel, 162, 163; in Howard Odum's "Case for Regional-National Social Planning" speech, 163–65, 168; proposed institutions of, 178–81; and technicways, 171–74; between telesis and folkways, 165–71; and utopian ideas, 174–78, 183, 184. *See also* planning, regional; planning, social; regionalism, Southern

planning, social: and John Dewey, 47, 48, 155, 159; early twentieth-century roots of, 12, 13, 14; and equilibrium between folkways, stateways, and science, 16, 17, 23, 24, 28, 173, 174. *See also* planning, regional-national social; planning, regional; regionalism, Southern

plantation system: brutality of, 14, 106, 108, 116, 133; ties to frontier, 116; and New Deal, 180, 186; and Northern industrial colonialism, 106, 133, 177; within regionalists' evolutionary image of South, 114, 115, 116, 117, 118, 153; Southern Agrarians on, 125; and Southern myths, critiques of, 27, 70, 116

portraiture technique, 44; and ambivalence toward Southern status quo, 72, 73, 88, 91; and *American Regionalism*, 73, 74; as balance between folk culture and science, 73, 72, 73, 88, *89, 90,* 91; and character types, 91, 92; and William Faulkner, 44; as fusion of autobiography and sociology, 50, 52, 72; rebuked by Northern objectivists, 26, 74, 86, 87, 88, 91, 92, 129, 134, 152; romanticizing the plantation, 115, 116; and *Southern Regions of the United States,* 127, 148, *148*. See also *American Epoch*

President's Research Committee on Social Trends, 74–78, 141, 157, 162, 178, 188; and Wesley Mitchell, 75, 157; and Howard Odum, 75, 141, 159; and *Recent Social Trends,* 75, 157, 159; and Rockefeller Foundation, 75; and Social Science Research Council, 75; and Thomas Woofter Jr., 69

Progressive Era: and planning ideology, 40; and professionalization of social sciences and social work, 50, 58; and scientific management, 12, 47, 75; and social reform ideology, 12, 15, 51, 60, 74; and sociology, 82, 78; and Frederick Jackson Turner's frontier concept, 113

race: and artistic realism, 110, 111; and Black folklore studies, 27, 104–9; and Black migration, 17; and Franklin Giddings' consciousness of kind, 84; and interregionalism, 119–23; and proposed regional planning institutions, 180; relationship to place of, 3, 26, 111, 119, 124, 126; and social Darwinism and Spencerian social science, 80, 81; and Lester Frank Ward, 82, 83; Thomas Woofter Jr. on, 69. *See also* Du Bois, W. E. B.; Johnson, Guy; Vance, Rupert: on class and racial divisions

racism: and Black civil rights, 124, 187, 215n10; and Commission on Interracial Cooperation, 69, 103, 179; and complexity of Southern regionalism, 29, 134; and Donald Davidson, 153; and Franklin Giddings, 110, 190; and NAACP, 52, 215n10; and New Deal, 5, 180, 181; and pointed criticism of South, 70; Southern regionalists' equivocation toward, 16, 103, 104; and William Graham Sumner's mores, 85. *See also* Bailey, Thomas Pearce; Du Bois, W. E. B.; Institute

racism (*continued*)
for Research in Social Science; and racial violence; Jim Crow South; plantation system; Raper, Arthur; segregation, racial; slavery and enslaved people

Raper, Arthur, 209n146; and Commission on Interracial Cooperation, 69, 70; and IRSS researchers, 10, 19, 66, 73; and Howard Odum, 73; on plantation society, 14, 117; and *Sharecroppers All*, 10, 27, 70, 116, 117; on sharecropping and race, 27, 66, 70, 103, 104, 116; and *The Tragedy of Lynching*, 27, 70, 103, 116, 117

regionalism, Southern: and agrarian-metropolitan tension, 10, 11, *30*, 109, 111, 160, 186, 192; and flawed arrangement of states, 148–53; and folkways-stateways tension, 16, 26, 103, 109, 170, 174, 189; and empirical methods, 23, 93, 126, 135, 144, 150; genealogy and scholarship of, 1, 2, 5, 6–12, 78–86, 132–35, 159, 191, 192; and human geography, 92–96; and international development after World War II, 3, 4, 6, 193; and national intellectual and philanthropic networks, 6, 24, 25, 71, 134; and objectivists, 75, 77, 78, 86–92, 95, 105, 129, 152, 179; overview of Southern planning's connection to, 1–6, 17, 20, 24; and quantitative methods, 26, 54, 127, 137, 148, 150, 153, 224n64; and Southern Agrarians, 27, 125, 139, 147, 153–55; and tension between folkways and science, 4, 22, 28, 109; utopian, 16, 174–78, 183, 184. *See also* Institute for Research in Social Science; Jim Crow South; New Deal; Odum, Howard; Odum, Howard and Rupert Vance, divergences between; planning, social; portraiture technique; race and racial oppression; segregation, racial; Tennessee Valley Authority; Turner, Frederick Jackson; University of Virginia Round Table on Regionalism; Vance, Rupert

Regional Planning Association of America (RPAA), 8, 146, 192; on Appalachian Trail proposal, 122; and culture and human agency, 15, 138, 146, 158; establishment of, 1, 32, 123; and metropolitanism, 10, 11, 36; within national-regional thought network, 24; and New Deal, 29, 158, 159; and 1925 *Survey Graphic* issue, 32, 135; for racial segregation, 101; and Tennessee Valley Authority, 41, 185; and Frederick Jackson Turner's frontier concept, 17; and University of Virginia Round Table on Regionalism, 2, 32, 33, 34, 39, 41

Reid, Ira De Augustine: and *Sharecroppers All*, 10, 27, 70, 116, 117

Rexford, Tugwell, 2, 13, 34, 184, 187, 193

Rockefeller Foundation, 62, 179; and early post–World War I planning, 61; and 1949 conference at University of Wisconsin–Madison, 131; and Howard Odum, 63, 95, 104, 126, 134, 164, 179, 188; and President's Research Committee on Social Trends, 75. *See also* Odum, Howard, intellectual and philanthropic networks of

Rockefeller Memorial: and IRSS, 61, 62, 66, 86, 87; and Howard Odum, 63, 66, 69, 134, 164, 179; and Laura Spelman, 69, 179. *See also* Odum, Howard, intellectual and philanthropic networks of

Roosevelt, Franklin D., 168; early career in regionalism of, 157, 158; and National Emergency Council's *Report on Economic Conditions of the South*, 28, 41, 42, 180, 181, 185; and New Deal, 3, 5, 25, 28, 48, 180, 181, 184; at University of Virginia Round Table on Regionalism, 2, 34, 35, 36, 58

Ross, Edward, 121, 147, 226n127

RPAA. *See* Regional Planning Association of America
Ruml, Beardsley: appointment at Laura Spelman Rockefeller Memorial, 61; and Howard Odum, 61, 62, 63, 134, 179, 226n23; at Social Science Research Council, 61, 63

Sauer, Carl, 24, 192; endorsing Southern regionalists' work, 26, 93, 94, 95, 96; and human geography, 74, 93, 95, 96
segregation, racial, 66; and James Baldwin on William Faulkner's gradualism, 99, 100; and *Brown v. Board of Education*, 49, 99, 106, 124; and complexity of Jim Crow Southern reforms, 102; and New Deal, 180; and Howard Odum, 3, 23, 121, 123, 124, 126, 130; and *Plessy v. Ferguson*, 100, 101, 103, 105; in US planning practices, 101, 105
sharecropping, 118; and myth of civilizing plantation, 115; and plantation violence, 14; Rupert Vance on, 176, 177. *See also* Raper, Arthur
slavery and enslaved people, 14, 26, 49, 79, 100, 106; W. E. B. Du Bois on, 120; Howard Odum on, 115; Arthur Raper on, 116; Rupert Vance on, 115
Social Forces (Vance): and ameliorative social science, 60, 71; and Donald Davidson, 43, 147; establishment of, 19, 25, 59; and groups-of-states region definitions, 152; and Guy Johnson, 68; and Lewis Mumford, 136, 167; and Howard Odum's regionalist and social planning agenda, 129, 141, 159, 171; on racial issues, 68, 104, 121; and regional planning as social science, 136, 167; religious criticism of, 65; and Edward Ross, 121, 147; on sectionalism, 121, 147; and technicways, 172, 173; and Rupert Vance, 67, 136
Social Science Research Council (SSRC), 61, 75, 147, 162; and objectivist debates with IRSS and Howard Odum, 63, 73, 76, 88, 92, 152; and Howard Odum's network, 63, 68, 87, 179; portraiture method criticized by, 74, 134
Southern Agrarians, 27, 186, 187, 188; celebration of antebellum South by, 39, 115, 125, 147; and *I'll Take My Stand*, 9, 33, 38, 147; and Benjamin Kendrick, 147, 162; Lewis Mumford on, 33; Howard Odum on, 147; and University of Virginia Round Table on Regionalism, 34, 38, 39, 43; Rupert Vance on, 139. *See also* Davidson, Donald
Southern Regions of the United States, 15, 164; and diverse modes of sociological analysis, 26, 41, *89, 90*, 127, 143, 153, 224n64; groupings and statistical presentations in, 148–53, *148, 149,* 164; mixed reception of, 127, 129, 149, 150, 151, 152, 153; and proposed regional planning institutions, 179, 180, 181; and race, 104, 180, 181. *See also* Odum, Howard
Spencer, Herbert, 26, 32; and W. E. B. Du Bois, 84; and Franklin Giddings, 84; and Howard Odum, 106, 126; and roots of sociology, 80, 81, 82, 85; and Rupert Vance, 137, 201n4
SSRC. *See* Social Science Research Council
Sumner, William Graham: and Ernest Burgess, 169, 170; dissimilarities with Lester Frank Ward, 81, 82, 84, 155; and Franklin Giddings, 84; laissez-faire sociology of, 81; and Howard Odum, 26, 85, 103, 105, 135, 142, 144, 155, 169, 172; placing science within mores, 85, 155

technicways, 177, 189; and Patrick Geddes, 171, 172, 173; tension between state society and folk culture, 16, 17, 23, 76, 77, 92, 145, 155, 171–75

Tennessee Valley Authority (TVA), 3, 21, 131, *156*, 181; Ernest Burgess on, 169, 170; Donald Davidson on, 28, 154; and false promise of dynamic equilibrium, 41, 192, 193; international lessons of, 186; as outgrowth of Southern regional-national planning ideology, 5, 41, 138, 154, 174, 178, 185, 186; James C. Scott on, 185, 196n24; and South's relationship to New Deal, 25; and Thomas Woofter Jr., 69

Turner, Frederick Jackson, 131, 192; Donald Davidson on, 125; and frontier and plantation imagery, 115, 116; frontier theory of, 27, 112, 113, 119; regionalists' engagement with, 17, 113, 118; response to sectionalism of, 27, 134, 146, 147; and Edward Ross, 147. *See also* Odum, Howard: and Frederick Jackson Turner's concepts; Vance, Rupert: engaging with Frederick Jackson Turner

TVA. *See* Tennessee Valley Authority

University of Chicago, 62, 77; and Thomas Pearce Bailey, 51; and Herbert Blumer, 92, 168; as center for human ecology and sociology, 10, 24, 36, 83, 93, 101, 133, 202n31, 212n55; and John Friedmann, 2, 193; and Guy Johnson, 68; and Charles Merriam, 75; and Howard Odum, 87, 92; and Robert Park, 51, 101; and Beardsley Ruml, 61; and Carl Sauer, 93; and Rex Tugwell, 2, 193

University of Mississippi, 50, 51, 108

University of North Carolina at Chapel Hill, *57, 156*; arrival of Howard Odum at, 1, 56, 135, 195n10; as center of sociological and regional scholarship, 2, 19, 20, 59, 76, 190; moderate progressivism of, 191; and post–World War II regional planning, 192; and University of North Carolina Press, 27, 70, 76, 103, 179, 207n71; versus Southern Agrarians, 43. *See also* Chase, Harry Woodburn; Institute for Research in Social Science

University of Virginia: 25, 59, 66, 202n18. *See also* University of Virginia Round Table on Regionalism

University of Virginia Round Table on Regionalism, 2, 25; and common ground over folk sociology, 43, 44; divergences between Agrarians and Southern regionalists, 28, 33–43; and Roderick MacKenzie, 36; and Howard Odum, 32, 33, 36, 37, 38; and regional planning as art, 33, 34, 35, 38, 43, 44, 45; and regional planning background, 31–33; and Tennessee Valley Authority's dynamic equilibrium, 41. *See also* Barr, Stringfellow; Chase, Stuart; Fletcher, John Gould; Institute for Research in Social Science; MacKaye, Benton; Mumford, Lewis; Regional Planning Association of America; Roosevelt, Franklin D.

Vance, Rupert, *128*, 152; and Victor Branford, 138, 175, 184; on class and racial divisions, 140, 141, 176, 177; critiquing plantation culture, 115, 116; defining a region as amorphous, 132; defining regionalism as multifaceted, 136–41; early life and education of, 67; emphasizing human agency in regionalism, 95, 130, 141, 138, 146, 175, 176, 177; engaging with Frederick Jackson Turner, 114, 115, 116, 134, 137, 138; and Patrick Geddes, 28, 138, 175, 184; and *Human Geography of the South*, 10, 67, 95, 136, 138, 175, 176, 140, 141; and IRSS's regionalist agenda, 134, 135; and New Deal incorporation of Southern regionalist discourse, 184, 185; and 1949 conference at University of Wisconsin–Madison, 131, 132; on President's Research Committee on

Social Trends report, 75; research on southern cotton and land tenancy, 10, 66, 67, 68, 116, 136, 177; and *Social Forces*, 67, 136, 167; on Southern Agrarians, 139; on Southern colonial dependency, 133, 177, 178, 189, 194; and Southern regionalists' acceptance of utopianism, 174–78, 184, 187; and Herbert Spencer, 137, 201n4; on technicways, 173; on urbanization as locus for progress, 119, 124, 125. *See also* Odum, Howard, and Rupert Vance, divergences between

Veblen, Thorstein, 12, 13, 47, 48, 82, 170, 173

Ward, Lester Frank: and American Sociological Society, 83, 84; dissimilarities with William Graham Sumner, 81, 82, 85; education and early career of, 81; and Franklin Giddings, 83, 84, 85, 142; Howard Odum's engagement with, 83, 110, 142, 144, 155, 159, 166, 168; and telesis, 26, 81, 82, 83, 85, 155, 159, 166, 167; view of New Deal elitism raised by, 171

Weaver, Clyde, 1, 159, 191, 192

Whitaker, Charles, 101, 121, 123, 135

Woofter, Thomas, Jr., 19, 56, 66, 68, 69, 158, 185

www.ingramcontent.com/pod-product-compliance
Lightning Source LLC
Chambersburg PA
CBHW021851230426
43671CB00006B/346